# FRENCH FOREIGN LEGION
# COMMANDO

# FRENCH FOREIGN LEGION
# COMMANDO

HARRY A. DOBSON

# CONTENTS

# GLOSSARY OF TERMS

**12.7** – Machine gun chambered in 12.7mm or '.50 calibre'

**Anglophone** – English speaker

**Archtung** – 'Attention in German

**Bananier** – A person often in trouble

**Binôme** – Partner. Often refers to combat

**Blyat** – Versatile Russian swear word

**Cache** – A hole dug flush into the ground

**Chef d'équipe** – The man in command of a small team

**Chef de Groupe** – The man in command of a group of men

**Commando Spécialisé** – Specialised commando course

**Compagnie du combat** – Combat company

**Corvée** – Cleaning

**Elève caporal** – Caporal in training

**Engagé volontaire** – Volunteer to the French foreign legion

**FAMAS** – Rifle chambered in 5.56mm

**FOB** – Forward operations base

**Francophone** – French speaker

**Galon** – Patch of rank

**Gazelle** – Small helicopter, usually for a sniper

**Genie** – Engineer

**Ghillie suit** – Camouflage suit

**Glock** – Pistol chambered in 9mm

**Groupement Commando Montagne** – Mountain Commando Group

**Groupement Commando Parachutiste** – Parachute Commando Group
**HK 416** – Rifle chambered in 5.56mm
**HK 417** – Rifle chambered in 7.62mm
**Honneur et fidélité** – Honnour and loyalty, the Legions official motto
**J'ai pleine les couilles** – My balls are full
**Je m'en branle** – I don't care
**Kurwa** – Versatile Polish swear word
**Legio Patria Nostra** – The Legion is our fatherland, in Latin
**Matricule** – A unique number given to every Legionnaire
**Militaires du rang** – Regular soldiers
**Minimi** – Light machine gun chambered in 5.56mm/7.62mm
**Mission sentinelle** – Patrol missions in public places within France
**NH90** – Transport helicopter
**Nul a chier** – Shit
**Opex** – Tours of duty to a combat zone
**Ordinaire** – Mess hall
**Place d'arme** – parade ground
**Plate carrier** – body armour
**Plongeurs de Combat Genie** – Combat divers
**Pompe** – pressups
**Puma** – Transport helicopter
**Rassemblement** – Assembly
**Réveille** – Wake up
**Sieste** – siesta
**Sketch** – Doing things just for the sake of it or that are a waste of time
**Sous-officiers** – Non-commissioned officers
**Stagiaires** – Soldiers on a training course
**Tigre** – Attack helicopter
**VAB** – Armoured transport vehicle

# RANKS OF THE FRENCH FOREIGN LEGION

## Militaires du rang :

Légionnaire
Légionnaire de la première classe
Caporal
Caporal-Chef

## Sous-officiers :

Sergent
Sergent-Chef
Adjudant
Adjudant-Chef
Major

## Officiers :

Aspirant
Sous-Lieutenant
Lieutenant
Capitaine
Commandant
Lieutenant-Colonel
Colonel
Générale De Brigade
Générale De Division

A big thanks to my parents, my cousin Laura and my good friend Christian for helping me with this book.

I couldn't have done it without you.

The names of the people in the book have been changed or abbreviated to protect their identities. This is with the exception of the fallen. Their real names I have given, as they should be remembered.

# CHAPTER 1

It was hot and dark. All I could hear was the sound of the helicopter blades beating in the air and the engine roaring as I sat in the belly below. The floor was hard and I had my legs stretched out, leaning on my pack. I was crammed in with eleven of my comrades but all I could see of them was a dark outline, illuminated every now and again by a dull green LED flashing on the roof. Black shapes helmeted, armoured and armed to the teeth. There were three other helicopters just like ours, full of soldiers just like us, all flying abreast under the North African moon.

I flipped my night vision goggles down over my eyes and turned them on. My world became green and black and I could see my brothers clearer. David, the big Hungarian, sat across from me chewing some gum and he extended a gloved hand clutching the packet. I took a stick and chewed it, giving him the thumbs up. My rifle sat between my legs and I felt its familiar weight resting on me. I gripped the handle and placed a finger over the safety as I had a thousand times before, ready to flip it to 'fire' at a moment's notice.

I checked for the tenth time that my sidearm was secured in its holster and licked my dry lips. It was always hot here, even a kilometre above ground. The gunner held up a hand with all his fingers spread, holding it high and making sure we had all seen it. That meant five minutes until we landed. Outside, I could already hear the dull thud of the guns on the two attack helicopters that were circling the hot zone ahead. I gripped my rifle a little tighter. We were flying into a fight.

Serge, sitting beside me, was drumming his fingers on the stock of his rifle and nodding his head to a tune he was imagining. Santo was so still he looked as though he might be sleeping but then he adjusted and checked his watch. Sipp was flicking at the strap of his rifle. We had done this countless times. It was nothing new. Once on the ground, everything would become clear. We knew what we had to do.

Even so, I had the usual tension build in my gut. I would be lying if I said I wasn't afraid. But it was fear mingled with excitement too; I felt alive! As the noise of the helicopter's blades pounded in my ears, I thought back to all those years ago. The chain of events that had led me here, to become a commando in the French Foreign Legion. I thought of the trials I had already faced and overcome and the people I had met. It had been a long journey and I wondered exactly where it had begun…

My name is Harry. I grew up in the town of Halifax. It's one of those old industrial towns that you tend to see a lot of in West Yorkshire: grey stone buildings, bleak countryside and rainy skies. It wasn't a bad place to grow up. We lived at the end of a row of tightly packed terraced houses, in a big, detached house all on its own and the other kids in the neighbourhood thought we were rich. Not rich, but the Dobson family had always been very comfortably middle class. I was a spoilt kid for sure.

We lived there most of my childhood; my mother, father, brother and I. My father had worked hard creating his own business from scratch and had been steadily growing it since 1994. My mother at the time worked in recruitment and so both parents brought in a steady income, providing a stable environment in which my brother and I could live happily. More or less happily. My brother, Alfie, is 16 months older than me and was always much bigger.

Granted, most siblings fight, but my brother and I always took it a step too far; we would try to kill each other semi-regularly. It was a nightmare for our parents having to break us apart, or shout at us to bugger off outside as one of us hurtled after the other up and down the stairs. I'm not ashamed to admit that my brother kicked my arse for the vast majority of these scuffles, and I was usually left snivelling in a corner. There were times when Alfie could be particularly vindictive and seemed to torment me simply for the pleasure of it. I don't know why, and I don't think he does either, kids are just mean.

It wasn't all bad however, behind our house in Halifax there was an old mill pond in the back garden, around an acre of water which was fantastic to play in. When it was hot, we would push a canoe out onto the surface of the water and paddle around, and when it was cold it froze over, and we would try to break the ice by throwing stones at it. One winter the temperature dropped to ten below, freezing the ice so thick, my brother and I played a game of football on it until great cracking noises rumbled beneath our feet and we scampered to safety, shrieking in panicked excitement.

One summer, our father bought an old tractor tyre inner tube and built a square, wooden platform around it and floated the makeshift raft on the water for my brother and I to play on. On hot days, we would push it out into the middle of the lake and have 'raft wars,' each trying to wrestle the other into the water. Neither of us stayed dry for long.

In the corner of the garden there was an enormous beech tree under which my dad would organise 'Ray Mears nights.' These consisted of building a campfire and cooking a salmon on a latticework of sticks suspended above the flames. We had plenty of fun out there, and my parents being outdoor lovers themselves encouraged us to get outside as much as possible. Inevitably, we learn a lot from our fathers. As for my own father, he is the cleverest and wisest man I have ever known. Of course, I took him for granted. Who knows where he found the patience to put up with my brother and I. But whenever either of us needed entertaining, help with homework or for someone to break us apart, he was there. It's only now that I realise how lucky I was. I know, I really was a spoilt kid!

He is also the reason I love the outdoors, despite a few nerve-racking situations we found ourselves in from time to time. Once, he took me caving in the Yorkshire Dales where we waded through ankle deep water in naturally formed tunnels under the green hills, our head torches illuminating the stalagmites and stalactites. After wolfing down a tin of Heinz tomato soup heated in a more cavernous part of the cave system, we made for the exit. But to get out my father and I would have to crawl upwards on our stomachs and squeeze between two boulders.

Dad went first and after a bit of grunting and pushing, managed to wriggle his way outside, his form silhouetted against the sky I could now see above. But when it was my turn to climb up, I somehow managed to get stuck between the boulders, and once I had realised that I couldn't move, panic set in.

'Dad!, Dad I'm stuck!' I cried, breathing fast and thrashing around, only serving to anchor me further. Then, I began to imagine the clawed fingers of some ghoul my mind had conjured curling around my ankle and pulling me down into the darkness below. My boyish mind became terrified that I'd be stuck there forever.

'Daaaad!'

He jumped back down to me and lay flat on his stomach to look me in the eye.

'Harry, it's alright! Look at me, hey! Look at me! Calm down. Breathe.'

I tried to do as he said, taking long, shaky breaths and resting my limbs on the damp rock.

'Good, now give me your hands.'

I stretched my palms towards him as he stood and taking hold of both of my wrists, he yanked me out with one swift motion and then I was outside, shielding my eyes from the sunlight. He chuckled down at me and I gave him a weak smile, suddenly embarrassed about how distraught I had become over what he had shown me was nothing.

We were a very active family. At a young age Dad got me involved with his favourite sport at the time, squash. There is something satisfying about hearing the 'thwack' as you smash the rubber ball into the wall. It's much better than tennis if you ask me. And it had the added benefit of a great workout, as you would have to run to each corner and back to hit the ball before it bounced twice. Well maybe not so much for my dad who seemed never to move from the middle of the court and sent me running to-and-fro when we'd play.

But it was not until I took up Muay Thai that I finally found a sport that I knew I needed to be good at. I think what drove me to start was being sick of taking beating after beating from my older brother and wanting to give back as good as I got.

At fourteen, I had found a gym called 'Calder Thai' at the bottom of Halifax town on the 2nd floor of an old mill building. The head coach ran a rigorous two-hour class that whipped me into shape and toughened me up. But I remember hating it at first! Who enjoys getting punched in the face?

It took me some months before I began to appreciate the frustration and bruises I would receive as a reward for being knocked down during the sparring sessions. It was humbling to know that there was always someone better than me in that gym, let alone the rest of the combat sporting world. I would compete in the 'inter-club' competitions every now and again and fight an opponent from a different club in front of a sometimes-sizeable crowd.

As anyone who has trained combat sports will know, the first year of training will likely not be pleasant. You will have to take a lot of punches. The fun begins when you start to get the hang of the techniques and a bit of experience under your belt. Watching two seasoned Muay Thai fighters spar is like watching a synchronized dance. Great fun.

It was in this gym, as a young lad, that I learned one of my most valuable life lessons through sweat and blood: to stand my ground and take a punch. It was not enjoyable at first, my head was constantly rocked back as I was struck, my thighs were covered in purple bruises for failing to block roundhouse kicks and at the end of each session I would ask, why am I putting myself through this, wouldn't it be much easier to be at home?

But perhaps that was exactly the reason I ought to continue, the fact that it was a hardship to find the motivation to don my sports gear after school so I could go and get my arse kicked again was exactly the kind of thing that was going to toughen me up. I began to understand that I had to cultivate the discipline to be able to climb into the ring knowing the most talented guy in the club was going to wipe the floor with me. It would take me years of practice to build up the skill to be able to take a flurry of punches and kicks on my gloves and then riposte with my own combination, to see my strikes hit home and daze my opponent. Although I did not know it at the time, the same discipline would serve me well for matters other than boxing.

This is all really important by the way. To me, I mean. The reason I'm mentioning joining a boxing club in Halifax at all was because this was the beginning of my fighting career. Here is the birth of Harry A. Dobson the fledgling scrapper, one day to become Harry A. Dobson the Foreign Legion Commando! Don't worry, I'm not getting full of myself. Whenever I feel as though I'm becoming cocky, I always think back to the time I stepped on the head of a shovel and the handle whipped up and whacked me in the face, breaking my nose. Just like a cartoon!

Maybe because my brother and I fought all the time at home, I thought that was the way kids were supposed to interact with each other, so I was probably a little more aggressive at school than is normal. I was not a popular kid, I would always be getting myself into arguments or fights. I was combative and seemed to have to disagree with or mock everything anyone said just to goad them to anger, putting me at odds with many of them. I wasn't easy to get along with then, I still hadn't learned to properly socialise yet.

There was one incident at school during which I am guilty of taking things a little too far. I can remember quite clearly that we were stood with our classmates in the corridor waiting for an hour of history to start. Simon was showing everyone his art book with some sketches he had done as I stood with my back to the wall. I could see them all nodding in appreciation.

'That's good Simon,' they said, and he beamed in a content kind of way. Seeing him so happy pissed me off.

'Hey Simon, let's have a look.' I said.

Even before this incident we were not particularly fond of each other, so he scoffed in derision, turning his back to me to show his sketch book to someone else in the corridor. For some reason, that made something inside me snap. I don't think I was having a worse day than normal, it just struck me as incredibly rude.

I walked up behind him and tapped him on the shoulder. He turned around; eyebrows raised. Without missing a beat, I grabbed him by the lapels of his blazer and head-butted him with all the force I could muster.

A shocked kind of silence fell, broken only by Simon's horrified whimpers as he fruitlessly attempted to stem the stream of blood pouring from his broken nose. The other kids in the corridor looked at me open mouthed, backing away. I immediately knew I had gone too far. Have you ever had that feeling in the pit of your stomach when it feels like your about to shit yourself when you know you've majorly fucked up? I had that then. I tried to help Simon up, but he understandably shook me off and ran to the bathroom. I followed him in, ignoring the whispers of the other kids as they probably asked one another if I had gone completely insane.

In the bathroom, I watched him sob tears and blood into the sink not quite knowing what to do with myself. A few moments later, our history teacher burst in, saw the state Simon was in, looked at me and asked, 'what on earth happened?'

Knowing that there had been at least a dozen witnesses in the corridor and reckoning that the truth was my only option at this point I said simply, 'I head-butted him sir.'

'You head-butted him?' The look of incredulity on his face would have been comical under other circumstances. Not knowing how to reply I simply shrugged and nodded in confirmation.

Both of my parents were called a few hours later and opened the door of the headmaster's office to find me sitting anxiously with my hands between my knees. I'll never forget the looks of both worry and disappointment on their faces as the headmaster explained what had happened. If only the poor bastard had shown me his art book.

If I'm honest, I didn't even know I had it in me. But now I knew whatever that was, was there. It was like a boiling anger locked deep inside my head. In subsequent years I would have the chance to explore this darker side of myself and in doing so better understand it. But that hadn't happened yet. When I was young I had a short temper and was prone to lashing out. I hadn't learned to control my emotions, and this was the result.

I realise I may not be painting the most likeable picture of the person I am. Perhaps I don't give myself enough credit, I don't know. I have always been my own worst critic. But then perhaps that is exactly as it should be? Either way, I still had a long way to go and much to learn.

So, to wrap up my schooling years: the school I attended was a boarding school, I never displayed any particular academic prowess, I didn't have many friends/people didn't like me and I hated it.

I think it was the adherence to a strict set of rules and a programme even after school hours that I struggled with. For example, lights out was 22:00 and anyone caught talking after lights out would be sent to bed an hour early the next night! A dire punishment indeed for any 11-year-old. (Adult me would love to be tucked in an hour early each night).

We had dormitories too, in which the boys and girls were separated, and you had to learn to share a room with your peers, even if you didn't particularly like them. Looking back, it all seems if I was unknowingly training myself for the military life, even if the notion hadn't even crossed my mind at that point. What I wanted to be when I grew up seemed to change with the seasons. Before I knew it I was sixteen. I realised that sometime soon I would have to decide what to do with my future. A big decision needed to be made. But what? I had no idea. Should I go to university and study for three years to get a degree? It sounded fun, all that partying. It seemed to be what everyone else from school was doing anyway.

Doing a little research, I found that around 40% of 18-year-olds choose to go to university; it's just the done thing. But would it really be worth it for me? To come out £52,000 in debt? Now I know the government is very good about letting you pay it back (or not) over a long period of time. I just didn't like the idea of owing so much money. And the thought of sitting another bloody exam! The horror.

But hey, I'm a practical guy. Surely I should be out there doing stuff, going on an adventure or something.

As for work, there was my father's business. I could have worked for my dad in his educational electronics company and learn the ins and outs for a few years until the old man eventually decided to retire when, with any luck, he'd trust me enough to take over. I could certainly earn good money in time, plenty to support myself and maybe one day a family. But I didn't want that either, it was his company. I felt I had to find my own way.

So I had to think. I had to think about what I wanted, what was I going to do with my life? Perhaps I needed a plan of action. Instead of stumbling along blindly and being carried by life's current wherever it wanted to take me, maybe I ought to have a goal. Yes that's it! A goal, an objective! I'd have a direction. Apparently, I was also starting to sound like one of those tooth-whitened life coaches. But hey, you have to start somewhere, right?

I took a long, hard look at the person I was and found that I wasn't the biggest fan. I was weak in so many ways- mentally, physically. I hated it. I wanted to be strong and fearless, I wanted to be the hero of my own story and I never wanted to have to rely on anyone or anything to get by in life.

I wanted to make it my mission to be less useless and to show the world what I was capable of! Now I knew I needed to carve my own path and arrived at the conclusion that this had to begin with carefully selecting the environment in which I would work and live. As an individual seeking to better himself (as I always make an effort to be, with mixed results) I ought to choose an environment with room for personal growth that would challenge me. I needed to leave my cosy comfort zone of West Yorkshire behind and experience something else; I was ready to sink my teeth into a challenge.

Far from having a career path in mind, I had figured out that I wanted to be better. I still had to make a decision and choose a road that would lead me to this, an adventure of sorts. Yes! That was it, an adventure! But to where? And doing what? I would mull it over, and ultimately it would be my imagination that would decide for me. I'll explain…

I have always been a history lover, so it seemed only natural to choose it as one of my subjects for A-level. There are so many incredible stories to discover! When I read of the deeds of the first crusaders, or the struggle of Alfred the Great, it would send shivers down my spine and make my hair stand on end. I was engrossed in the epic tales and adventures of people long since dead.

I love to read historical fiction, authors that could bring legendary characters to life like Harald Hardrada who served in the infamous Varangian guard in Constantinople, or King Richard the Lionhearted who fought the fierce and cunning Salah al Din in the holy land and Hannibal Barca who, in an epic display of daring and recklessness, forced his army and one hundred elephants over the freezing Alps in winter to surprise the unsuspecting Romans on the plains of northern Italy below.

How could anyone find that boring? But my favourite hero of all was Alexander of Macedon, the man that led an army to the edge of the world, over mountains and deserts, faced innumerable hosts of Persians and hostile tribesmen, the most charismatic of leaders who loved his men. Alexander conquered most of the known world in a journey that became a legendary saga, eventually costing him his life.

What an incredible story. If by 33 (his age at the time of his death) I have achieved even a tiny fraction of what Alexander had, I will die a happy man. It makes you wonder what kind of a man he must have been, to have his soldiers follow him to alien lands such a long way from home. He was bold in his actions, calculating in his strategy and incredibly charismatic in his leadership. The most influential Greek ever to have lived, he is argued to be by some the greatest general of all history. It is not hard to see why.

This was exactly the kind of thing that inspired me as a young man. War and battle, conquest and campaigning, audacious cavalry charges and hopeless defences, reckless and courageous deeds that burned the names of great warriors into the pages of history.

Why should I not want the same, to try to be worthy to ride amongst the ranks of Alexander's companion cavalry, or to stand in the shield wall with Alfred's men at the battle of Edington against the heathen invaders! Maybe I was born a few hundred years too late, maybe I would have been right at home wielding an English longbow at the battle of Agincourt. Knowing my luck however I would probably have died at the age of eleven from some horrific disease. Or sold as a slave to a barbaric Irish warlord. Or, worst of all, I would have been born French!

I was young and foolish and idealistic. I understand far better now that the days when heroes would face off in glorious single combat or storm a fortress to rescue a captured lover are far behind us. War is unglamorous. I'm sure it always has been, but when I read about the accomplishments of these fascinating characters, I couldn't help but feel they had achieved the most noble and courageous things I had ever heard of. I wanted a piece of that glory for myself! I wanted to be remembered as Alexander is, immortalized, the man whose ambitions could never be satisfied.

Years later I see war quite differently now. At the time of writing this book, I have since seen men who dared to be bold and challenge the powerful and were blown to pieces or shot to bits as a result, their bodies mutilated by the terrifyingly effective instruments of modern warfare. And I have seen others left to rot into the vast sands of Africa, never knowing their names, and leaving them to be forgotten forever. The world is a harsh place, and reality does not care for my story or my ambitions. I have learnt that in war, luck is a far more desirable attribute. Be lucky, dear reader.

So, after absorbing all these stories like a sponge, it seemed that the next logical thing for me to do would be to join the army, right? I mean, where else does one find the kind of adventures that Bilbo Baggins found himself tangled up with in 'The Hobbit'? It was the beginnings of a plan that started to form in the back of my mind - my ticket to see the rest of the world! Unfortunately, however, there were a couple of little things I had to tie up first. Like my A-levels. What a bloody buzzkill.

And yet, going to college was good for me, I had left the small bubble of private school to join Huddersfield's largest college for general education. There were two thousand odd students, all coming from different backgrounds and walking down the hallways on campus you could get lost among the groups of young people laughing and joking, heading to their next class or to the canteen or the smoking area.

Unlike school, everyone wore their own clothes here, and I was intrigued at the way the other kids expressed themselves: fishnets, dyed bright pink hair and numerous piercings in questionable places. I, on the other hand, had no clue how to dress myself, and it didn't help either that I was more than a little self-conscious. I was an introverted lad and had one group of good mates, and generally went to my classes and kept my head down. I didn't even go out much with the few friends that I had, preferring instead to stay in the comfort of my home and play video games, at least for the first year or so. So although I liked the idea of adventure, socialising wasn't at the top of my list.

As for my social life in college, I began feeling left out when my friends, as soon as they had turned eighteen, (or before if they had fake ID's) began to swap out our board game Friday evenings for going out into town to explore the nightlife. This annoyed me, too. For some reason I had this strange aversion to doing anything particularly social despite being invited many times. Then one day when we met up on campus as usual, I asked them if they were coming over this Friday. They looked awkwardly down at their feet and mentioned something about an event at a club in Huddersfield town.

I was sick of being at home on my own and decided to see what the fuss was all about. Marcus and Evan, my close friends at the time, were excited to take me to my first rave and while waiting outside in the line Marcus pressed something into my palm, grinned and said, 'Take this'.

I knew what it was. Shrugging I put the pill in my mouth thinking I might as well give the night a proper go and washed it down with some bottled water that Marcus had to hand. Loud electronic music blasted my eardrums as we went inside to get drinks. The place was packed, bodies were pressed together dancing to the rapid boom of the speakers and I could feel the heat in the air. After a while, I had a sudden feeling of nausea and tapping Marcus and Evan on the shoulder I yelled into their ears that I needed to go outside to vomit and saw them exchange a knowing glance.

They followed me out into the smoking area where I sat on a bench for a moment, my head spinning. I leaned over the bench, ready to puke onto the concrete, cursing myself for having agreed to all this in the first place. God, what the fuck had they done to me?

And then, it hit me, the most incredible feeling of sheer euphoria washed over my entire body. Every nerve ending tingled and I was infused with a glorious, wondrous energy.

'YEEEEEEES!' I cried, laughing like a maniac, and Marcus and Evan whooped behind me in delight. Jumping up and down in an ecstatic frenzy, I clapped them both on the shoulder and yelled, 'thanks boys! I feel amazing!'

Then I heard the music differently, my body seeming to feel the sound waves more acutely, absorb them and send them flowing through the blood in my veins. I felt the music calling me and knew I needed to dance.

'Let's go back inside'. We danced our socks off until we were sweaty and chafed, and it wasn't until 6am that we stumbled out into the dawn bleary eyed and physically drained. What great carefree fun that was. Now I understood what all the fuss was about. I decided that from then on I needed to be more outgoing. What else was I missing out on?

I was an average student. I studied Maths, English and History and as an optional extended project I wrote a twenty-thousand-word historical fiction novella of the roman invasion of Britain. I had my hands full and despite knuckling down with a valiant effort in my second and final year, I received one grade less than I was hoping for in each subject. That was annoying because I have a cousin that went to Oxford University and two aunties that are professors in their subjects, but God damnit where I'm concerned the apple seems to have fallen very far from the family tree and then rolled down the bloody hill!

Exam season came and went, and when I got the results the thought of repeating the process by going to university for three years made me frown irritably. So I didn't go. The idea of the army was still there. Now it was a little more real, I had finished college and could sign up as soon as I felt I was ready.

It did seem to suit me more than anything else - I loved the outdoors, I was now adept at sports and craved adventure. In my head, if I joined the army I would be running around the woods with camouflage paint on my face and camped out with a bunch of friends. Sounds great! The more I thought about it, the more it sounded like a good idea. But as I would learn, the application process took months and I wanted to see a bit of the world in the meantime.

During my final months of college, I spotted an advert on the notice board in college of a 'Tanzanian gappers' scheme, one of those working holidays where they send young people to Africa for a month to help build a school. It sounded like a fantastic idea to me, and I decided to seize the opportunity, not because I felt any particular obligation to help some children in the developing world who were far less fortunate than I, but because it seemed like a great way to explore a bit more of the world (and myself). I supposed that helping someone in need was a bonus.

I was eighteen and showed up to Manchester airport where all the gappers would get on the flight to Kenya and then a connecting one to Tanzania. I met the rest of the bunch. There were around thirty or so, and one of the girls decided to do an icebreaker game where you all stand in a circle and say your name, try to remember the names of everyone who had spoken previously and something interesting about yourself. Fuck. I hate icebreaker games with a passion. Something interesting about myself? How about, 'this game is making me want to launch myself into the Boeing 747 engine taxiing on the runway outside'.

Well, I didn't say that, probably mumbling something along the lines of having an impressive homemade knife collection. There I go again, making friends.

Anyway, the important thing to take away from this was that it was my first solo trip and my first time in Africa, a continent I was destined to return to in later years. It was certainly interesting to see and experience a culture that starkly contrasted my own. In the area of Tanzania I happened to visit, people lived in houses made of mud, and carried wicker baskets on their heads and rode their donkeys laden with empty containers to the river to refill them for their daily water needs. The children ran bare footed over the baked earth and I had to wince as I imagined my own soft feet doing the same. The adults might scrape a living together farming or crafting objects from recycled rubber that washed up on the seashore. It was a far cry indeed from the wealthy metropolises of the United Kingdom. And yet the people seemed happy despite this, perhaps more so than back home. That was interesting. Perhaps it had something to do with the good weather.

One the second day of the trip I broke my foot playing football (I kicked the ground instead of the ball). Easy to do as a football is relatively small in comparison to the ground so the probability of you hitting the ground by mistake is actually pretty high. And I'm shit at football. I spent the rest of the month hopping around in an incredibly poorly made plaster cast that a local doctor charged me £30 for and resigned myself to a small building in the village to use my basic carpentry skills to make chairs for the school. It was my first little solo adventure, and despite the foot, very educational. It was time well spent.

Another place I would travel to in my eighteenth year that was a real eye opener for me, was Thailand. All this time I had been attending my Muay Thai classes at my local club and was beginning to get the hang of it. I had the brilliant idea of taking advantage of my free time to go and train at one of the famous Muay Thai schools on the island of Phuket. It was enormous fun, I met plenty of people, many of whom were also traveling from Europe, and tried to find a sustainable balance between drinking and training. I still remember it as one of the best months of my life.

The training was tough! Thai boxing is the number one sport in Thailand, and the instructors at the gym often had hundreds of fights under their belts before the age of twenty-five. To put this into perspective, Mike Tyson had fifty-eight professional bouts at the end of a long boxing career. They would make you suffer during the two and a half hour long sessions (one in the morning and one in the evening) and would hit you with the pads when you tried to catch your breath. There were some fantastic fighters there, and not all of them were Thai. Fighters from all over the world would come to train at the legendary Thai gyms that would often sponsor rising stars for the privilege of having their name next to the combatants on the advertising posters.

But there wasn't just the Muay Thai, Thailand is a whole lot of fun for any tourist. Between training sessions, and if I had the energy, I was free to explore the island. I loved the way the streets seemed to repeat themselves, you'd see a little restaurant next to a 7/11, next to a laundrette, next to a massage parlour, next to another little restaurant and so on.

I made a few friends from the gym, all of us coming from different countries to train, and together we explored some of the night life during our days off. It was great to blow off a little steam; dance, meet a few of the local girls and have a laugh. You had to be careful though, Thailand was full of ladyboys, something I hadn't encountered until then, and they were dangerously hard to tell apart from girls. It was always a good idea to befriend a local who could point them out to you with a trained eye before you took them back to your hotel room only to find a nasty surprise!

Upon my return from Thailand, I got a job as a labourer whilst I began the long application process to the British army. My dad advised me in all his paternal wisdom to join the army as an officer because it made more sense 'in the long run.' Young men seldom worry about the 'long run' but understanding that he probably knew what was best for me, I agreed.

The British army had foolishly left the responsibility of recruitment in the hands of a private company and so, understandably, back in 2015 the whole process was slow. So, I occupied my time with labouring and training whilst I waited to hear about an interview.

I ran a lot back then; I lost weight and became lean. You need to do a 2km run in under eleven minutes and fifteen seconds as a minimum requirement, but to qualify for the parachute regiment you had to do the same run in under eight minutes and fifteen seconds. I wanted to be in the elite of course so I pushed myself hard.

It was difficult at first, I had never properly ran before, and could hardly go thirty minutes without stopping. My body quickly adapted however, and I was soon capable of running the 8km from Halifax to Hebden Bridge along the canal and back at a decent pace. I had something to work toward, a clear goal, and it motivated me to push myself harder in the training.

I eventually had a letter in the post for an interview date and went out to buy myself a suit for it. I had applied to be either infantry or paras (if I was going to be in the army, I wanted to be a fighting man, not stuck in an office somewhere) and the Yorkshire infantry regiment had offered to see me.

The recruitment centre was a fancy old building opposite Clifford's tower in York city centre, and on the morning of the interview I nervously rang the bell and was ushered inside by a secretary. An older officer with grey hair trimmed short and neat, a shaven face and a crisp dress uniform showed me into the 'waiting room' which was more like a formal dining room, the centre of which was dominated by an enormous mahogany table surrounded by ornate chairs. On the table were trays of neat little sandwiches of various types - tuna, ham, salmon etc., miniature sausage rolls, crisps and tea - which the officer suggested I take a seat and help myself to. So I sat down and helped myself, perplexed at how bloody fancy it was.

There was another interviewee wearing a suit at the table and clearly my arrival had interrupted his conversation with the enlisted man as they continued where they had apparently left off. Listening, I learned that the other lad had gone to a school that the officer had recognised and, upon quizzing him further, the officer had been duly impressed that the lad had been captain of the rugby team. I swallowed. I had never been captain of anything.

I listened to them talk back and forth in their similar upper-class drawls until the officer decided it was time he saw me in his office.

The interview was standard enough, and I was asked all the questions you might expect to hear, 'How have you prepared physically for the army? Why do you think you would be good officer material? What is a good example of your leadership qualities? Do you have any serious health problems that we ought to know about?' I answered as best I could, conscious of the fact that ninety percent of applicants were over the age of twenty-two and had university degrees to boot.

The officer looked down at the notes he had been making and then sighed deeply and looked up at me with a somewhat pitiful expression. 'You're just not the sort of person we're looking for, Mister Dobson. You just don't have the experience. Perhaps if you went to university and came back after a few years...' I sat and nodded politely trying to mask the feeling of bitter disappointment welling within.

Damn, I had been hoping that I would be part of that special ten percent of applicants who were accepted without a degree. But who was I kidding? There was nothing special about me.

'I tell you what, I'll review your application and you'll receive a letter in a few days in the post with the final verdict alright?' We shook hands and that was that.

The letter, when it came, said much of the same, 'Dear Mister Dobson, we regret to inform you that your application to the Yorkshire regiment has been unsuccessful at this time, please follow the advice that your interviewer provided and know that you are welcome to try again in the future...'

It was hardly unfair though; I would have refused my application had the roles been reversed. But it didn't stop me from scrunching the letter up into a ball and throwing it to the corner of the living room.

I sighed. Fuck it, I'll just join as a private then. By this point my heart was already set on the army, I wouldn't quit now. In a way it was a kind of relief, the thought of being a baby-faced officer having to command veterans of Afghanistan was daunting. At least as a private I would be in the same boat as everyone else. I consoled myself with the fact that I wouldn't need a degree to join the parachute regiment as a regular soldier and went back to my daily routine of work and training.

Unfortunately there was a catch. To enlist as a soldier, I would have to effectively restart the application process. Filling out the online forms the computer told me that this could be in excess of a year! Well, that was hardly ideal. My brother had left home for university to start his new life some months prior, leaving me alone with my parents. My friends Marcus and Evan had local jobs and we all hung out regularly, but it was different now. They still smoked a lot of weed and went to a lot of raves to which I couldn't go, I had to work and train hard.

I was eighteen and restless and I felt as though life was passing me by and I was afraid I was beginning to stagnate. I needed to act, to do something with my bloody life, or I felt I never would. Looking back, I can see that I was impatient. At eighteen I was still so young, I had time to figure things out and make a few mistakes. But that's not how I felt at the time.

I would have 6 months before I could get into the army, another long stretch of time to kill. Isn't it a pain in the arse when life doesn't go to plan? It seems to happen far too often for my liking. I reluctantly forced myself to come to terms with it, busying myself with everyday life. Little did I know that it would not be for long. This is where things start to get interesting…

For a bit of a diversion, my father had heard of a project in France at a place called Guédelon and suggested we attend. They were building an entire medieval castle from scratch and it was the world's largest experimental archaeological project. You could pay to work there for a week and my father, knowing that this would appeal to me and that I could use a distraction, booked us a couple of places a few months prior.

One day we had been discussing the upcoming trip and what I would have to do after for my army application. I had been complaining about the lengthy process and seemingly disorganised system when my dad said jokingly, 'you could always join the French Foreign Legion after Guédelon. I can just drop you off in Paris and leave you there!'

I had frowned at him. 'What is the French Foreign legion?' I had asked him.

'Oh you've never heard of it? It's a special branch of the French military where people from any country in the world can join, and they're famous for taking criminals on the run too. Apparently it's super tough and quite romanticised.' He looked up and smiled wistfully. 'I often wish I'd given it a go as a young man.'

The French Foreign Legion, tough, mysterious and sure to be quite the adventure.

'Huh' I said, intrigued. I quizzed him for more information, but he didn't have the answers. Upon seeing that I was taking his suggestion seriously my dad became quite excited and laughed, 'I think you should do it! I'll leave you in Paris and think of an excuse to tell your mother.'

Now, most people would find the idea of joining an organisation like the French Foreign Legion a bit nuts. I'd have to uproot my life in the UK, move to France for 5 years and survive one of the toughest fighting forces in the world. Well, that's exactly the reason I wanted to do it. I would go where other men wouldn't dare, to discover lands unseen (at least by me) and meet people from every corner of the world! Before the end of the day I was daydreaming about Harry A. Dobson, the fearless Legionnaire, striking out with his trusted companions to hostile lands and fighting some unknown enemy. There was danger, excitement, action and glory! Surely, this is what Alexander of Macedon would have done, an adventure worthy of some of my favourite characters. Excellent!

I have a big grin on my face as I'm writing this because, of course, things never turn out the way I imagine them to. It was a nice fantasy nonetheless. In hindsight, I would find more adventure than I had bargained for…

I had a look online to try to find out more, but none of the information was as revealing as I would have liked. Of course, I found one of those French Foreign Legion promotional videos in which camouflaged soldiers seemed to do a myriad of exciting activities including obstacle courses, shooting rifles, swimming and climbing in an endless show reel. On the official website there was scarcely any more information to glean, save perhaps the different Legion regiments which meant nothing to me at the time, and a list of things to bring with you when you joined, which was comically small: a passport for identification, a set of civilian clothes, a toothbrush and a pair of flipflops.

I wondered what it would be like to serve with ex-convicts and ruffians from every corner of the planet. It began to sound like a fantastic idea back then, and I had been sure that I would love every second of it. I would go where only a small number of men had gone before, do the most difficult and challenging thing I could find to do. Perhaps this was a step up from the British army, even more dangerous and adventurous, surely that would make the prize of glory all the sweeter when I had done it!

My dad, though he was keen for me to go, had warned me that I wouldn't be the same man afterward. That it would likely change me forever. Brilliant! I had thought, let's go! And so, in an absurdly short amount of time, I was decided, full of inexhaustible optimism. I now had a purpose, a mission! Even when I learned that the bare minimum contract for any man hoping to join was five years and that this was non-negotiable, I still would not be deterred. Five short years, I had thought, five short years and it will all be over. I reasoned that it would be like doing secondary school again; that was five years was it not? And I had survived that. What's the problem?

The Guédelon trip finally came around and, hardly believing myself that I would not be returning home, I set out with a rucksack of the modest collection of items the website had said I would need. My mother certainly didn't believe my father and on the day of our departure to France we stood on the threshold as Dad pointed at me and said proudly to his wife, 'he's joining the Legion.'

Grinning stupidly at her I nodded in confirmation. She stood in the doorway of our home, hands on her hips, pursing her lips and frowning in disapproval at this not-very-funny joke. I told her I'd see her soon (I wouldn't see her again for the best part of a year) and off we went.

I had had my friends Marcus and Evan over several days previously to break the news to them but was met with a similar incredulous expression. 'Oh, okay.' They had nodded politely in the way people do when you tell them you're about to break the record for the words fastest marathon, but they haven't the heart to shoot you down. We said our goodbyes and shared a last smile as I turned away and prepared to leave the country and not return for a long time.

My dad and I arrived at the building site at Guédelon, dressed up as peasants to preserve the medieval authenticity and were soon put to work sawing wood and hacking away at stone before an audience of tourists. It truly is a fantastic project, the organisers wanted to keep everything as true to history as possible, and so only medieval building techniques were allowed, not a power tool in sight! The vast amount of stone required for the walls was sourced only a hundred metres from the castle itself for practicality and there was always a team of masons hacking away at the bedrock in the quarry. The clay for the roof and floor tiles was collected from a dried-up river bed nearby, and the nails and tools were made in the blacksmiths workshop. The wood was cut from trees in the forest and transported on site by a horse and cart.

Cutting the trees was a gargantuan task in itself mind you; my father and I had had a go at it, using one of those large two-man saws with enormous teeth and standing either side of a felled trunk it took us at least twenty minutes of work to cut through only once.

People back then were not stupid; they had some ingenious ways of doing things. Once the towers were built to a certain height, two gigantic wooden 'hamster wheels' were placed on the top and two men would walk in them. The wheels were connected to a beefy lever arm which held a thick rope that was wound upwards by the motion of the wheels. In this way great blocks of limestone could be lifted into the air on a kind of wooden platform attached to the rope.

During the week at Guédelon it dawned on me that I was in France. But not only was I in France, people spoke French here! I was planning on making France my home for the next five years, not only that but I would be serving in the French army. And I barely spoke a bloody word.

I hopelessly began trying to learn a bit of French. I had studied a little French at school and had of course thought it a complete waste of time. I hadn't applied myself in the slightest which resulted with a 'D' at GCSE to which I had never given a second thought. Shit, I thought, why didn't I just listen?

As it was, I could count to about ten, knew the days of the week, could say 'hello' and 'goodbye' and 'I would like.' That was about it. I would hate to have seen the look on my French teachers face if she had found out that after botching her subject, I went to join the French army. Hopefully the other new recruits would be in the same boat.

As we came towards the end of the week a kind of anxious tension built up in my gut. Anxiety mixed with excitement however, and I can't remember having many second thoughts. Sure, the voice of reason in my head might have said something along the lines of, 'are you sure this is a good idea? You can't even speak French for heaven's sake, I'm not sure you've really thought this through'. But the reckless voice cried louder, 'Fuck it! It'll be a laugh, what have you got to lose?'

Finally, the day came when we drove up to Paris toward the Foreign Legion recruitment centre there at Fort De Nogent. The hired car rolled to a stop and my father parked up and we got out to stare at the imposing pale stone walls and archways of the renaissance era fort. Above the entrance were the words, 'Légion Étrangère'. Foreign Legion. There was a soldier standing guard in combat fatigues holding the FAMAS, the French army's standard battle rifle. I took my rucksack out of the boot, which was all I had to my name, and shouldered it with a deep breath feeling the butterflies in my stomach. I turned to my dad who was wearing a half proud half, 'oh shit he is actually going through with it' kind of expression. I reckon there was a part of him then that thought, what have I done?

So this was it, the big decision, maybe the biggest decision. Things would not be the same after I was sure. And it would be tough. I could go back, it wasn't too late, I could be home in Halifax the very next day enjoying my mother's home-made cooking. I could sign up for university and be there by September studying history. But as soon as I had thought it, I dismissed it with disgust. How could

I be so weak? The thought of returning home with my tail between my legs having failed made me sick. No, I would go on, for better or worse, I would do it.

I looked up at my dad and said, 'Okay, I'm ready.'

We shook hands and he said, 'good luck boy.' I took a deep breath, turned away and headed towards the entrance. Before I had gone ten paces, he called out to me and I turned around. He snapped a picture of me on his phone. He likes that picture, I'm stood under the archway with, 'Légion Étrangère' written on the stone above my head, wearing a grim expression, skinny as you like, but determined. I gave him a last reassuring smile that I didn't at all feel and he waved. Another deep breath. I turned back to the fort and looked up at my future.

The next five years of my life would test me in every way imaginable, they would provide me with not at all the kind of challenge I was expecting, and they would change me forever. My adventure would take me from the freezing peaks of the Alpine mountains, to the ocean like deserts of the Sahara. I would meet all kinds of men, great men, despicable men, lost souls and inspiring heroes whose stories I will tell, worthy of the ancient sagas I love so much. I would make friends and lose them, I would fight plenty, with fists and firearms. A skinny, middle class boy from the north of England would enter those gates, and five years later a much more formidable man would exit them. Imperfect aye, but capable, and tough.

This is how I was made.

# CHAPTER 2

I was ushered into some dingy room built into the walls of the old fort by the guard. My eyes adjusted to see artificial yellow light illuminating a burly Sergeant in the middle of the room, and a little fella who I later found had come from Spain, sat at one of several desks, the rest of which were empty. The Spaniard looked just as apprehensive as I felt.

The Sergeant was emptying the belongings from a suitcase, which I assumed was the Spanish bloke's, and dumping them out on an empty table. He stopped what he has doing and turned to me, looking me up and down and grunted, gesturing for me to give him the old rucksack still on my shoulder. I gave it to him and stood back in silence. The other lad caught my eye and gave me a weak smile which I returned, and I was grateful to have someone else who was evidently another potential recruit.

The Sergeant finished with the other bag, and started on mine, throwing out the few pairs of socks and underwear, shorts and t-shirts I had with me. Eventually he found the book I had been reading and, taking an interest to it and apparently understanding English, paused to read the blurb. It was 'Dissolution,' one of the Shardlake series by C. J. Sansom, an enthralling murder mystery set in Tudor England in which the protagonist, hunchback lawyer Matthew Shardlake, is hired to unravel a mysterious series of deaths in what turns out to be a plot linked to the political turmoil caused by Henry VIII's controversial decision to dismantle the monastic system in England at the time.

I stood, not knowing exactly what to do with myself as the Sergeant looked at the cover of the book, up at me, then back to the book again. Eyeing me suspiciously one last time he finally gave a, 'hmph!' and dropped the book unceremoniously back on the table.

'Attendez ici!' Then repeated in accented English, 'wait here.' And left the room. I attempted to chat to the other guy but found it difficult to communicate because he spoke little English and neither of us spoke French. After an hour or so the Sergeant came back, and we were ushered through into the main courtyard of the fort, and then into one of the large, three storey buildings that dominated the space. There were offices there, and through open doorways I could see men in camouflage fatigues talking on the phone or typing away at computers.

Our details were taken, names, dates of birth, emergency contact details etc. and put into some database somewhere. After a bit more waiting, we were given a well-worn and ill-fitting standard French issue sports tracksuit to wear and told to leave our bags in one of the large bunk rooms on the top floor. Clearly, we were expected to wear the tracksuits and, under the watchful eye of the Caporal Chef who had taken out details, we changed quickly and jogged behind him as he strode back outside gesturing for us to follow. No words were exchanged and we followed in an anxious silence.

In Fort De Nogent, the recruits have their own 'room' in the walls of the fort (there are always many rooms built into the walls of old forts of this type) which was long and narrow and windowless in which everyone was expected to report to at 5:30am and stay inside until 22:00, when it was time to return to the sleeping quarters of the barracks for lights out. You were only allowed to leave the room and the small space outside the room in the courtyard where there were a few chairs, if they wanted you to do some kind of work, (often this would be scrubbing floors or toilets), to use the toilet yourself, or for meals. The only form of entertainment in the room was a single old table football table which was always occupied since there were around fifty of us at any one time crammed into the room.

Upon entering, I stood in the doorway with my new Spanish friend and scanned the room, taking in all the surroundings. In the dim room there were around forty men all wearing the same blue tracksuit, standing and chatting in groups, some sat joking together, others were alone. I felt completely out of place and imagined that I stuck out for some reason, that any minute now the room would fall silent and everyone would turn to me with an incredulous look on their faces as if to say, what on earth are you doing here? But they didn't.

Instead, we quickly found ourselves a couple of empty chairs against one wall. No one really paid much interest to us at all because as I would learn, people would come and go all the time. I would also learn that I shouldn't have felt out of place. The Legion is a haven for misfits like me, there is every shade of strange, every background you can think of and a thousand interesting stories waiting to be told. The Legion wasn't looking for the perfect soldier, they took any willing and able bodies and cared not a bit where you had come from or why or what you had done, so long as you met the entry requirements.

I should clarify now that the French Foreign Legion is strictly male only and has always been so. Among its ranks there is not a single woman, save for those brought in from French regular regiments to aide with administration. The result was that some aspects of life in the Legion felt prison-like, especially at Fort de Nogent. There was a 'yard' in which we were allowed to take air, three square meals a day at set times and everyone had to neatly make their beds in the morning or suffer the consequences.

Another thing that struck me was the bizarre collection of men that I could see before me once my eyes had properly adjusted. The men there were between the ages of seventeen and thirty-four, some looked old and worn, as if they had lived one life already and some were young and fresh, as if life was only just beginning. Some met my gaze and gave me a hard stare, tattooed and muscular they looked as though they had experienced some of the worst of life already. Others were as wide eyed as I, and some were fat and out of shape. What a strange mix of people.

As for ethnicity, there were all sorts, western Europeans, Eastern Europeans, Russians, Kazaks, Mongolians, Chinese, Koreans, Africans, north Americans, south Americans. You name a continent, hell, name a country, we had it all. Already you could see the separation of this cultural melting pot into groups, which we called, 'mafias' in the Legion.

Everyone had a mafia according to language and culture. For example, the 'mafia Russe' or Russian mafia, comprised of Russians, Ukrainians, Belarusians, Latvians, Estonians and Lithuanians but could also include Moldovans and Romanians as they sometimes spoke Russian too. All the old countries of the USSR tend to have some similarities in their culture, at least to my eyes, as well as a shared language, (I know some of them would cringe if they heard me say that. I mean, comparatively of course, similar in the way an Englishman and an Australian would have more in common with each other than with someone from Japan. The mafia Russe was also the strongest mafia as eastern Europeans are the most numerous group in the Legion. We often said if you speak French or Russian, you're doing okay. The waiting room was no different, there were plenty of tall, well-built eastern looking guys speaking in Russian.

Another large group would be the mafia espagnole, this would include countries like Spain of course, Argentina, Peru, Colombia, Venezuela, Mexico etc. There were already a group of them chatting in one corner of the room and, after a few minutes, my new friend plucked up the courage to join them and they were all soon babbling away in Spanish.

There were Africans too, usually from the ex-French colonies, who tended to band together because being black in the Legion could be isolating in of itself. The vast majority of men in the legion are from countries less tolerant of diversity. I have seen more than one swastika tattoo in my time. It felt in some ways as if I had just been dropped into a prison yard.

I got up and walked outside to enjoy the sun a bit and to avoid piercing stares when I heard English being spoken. Two Americans were speaking against a railing outside. Both were tall, one was well built and older, perhaps mid-thirties with dark hair, the other was slim and blonde and looked as young as I did. The younger one was called Steinrod and we would endure basic training together and become good friends.

I went over and introduced myself and we started to chat. Talking to the other guys over the next few weeks was about the only thing to do as all phones and electronic devices of any kind were banned. As it turned out, the other American claimed he had done several military contracting jobs for Blackwater, somewhere sandy, and returned home to rack up a huge gambling debt. Hoping that he might escape his debts in the Legion, he had then blown another several thousand euros at a casino in Paris before arriving at Fort De Nogent. Unfortunately for him, his application was refused in the end on medical grounds. The moment the regimental doctor had given the verdict, he was sent on his way and I never saw him again.

In contrast, Steinrod happened to be in a similar situation to myself. He came from a decent family and, not feeling that he was ready to spend the next three years studying, he had ventured abroad to France in search of adventure. I asked him about his name, and he laughed and said, 'yea, it's weird isn't it? That's my Legion name, the one they gave me.'

Because wanted criminals joined the ranks of the Legion, a totally new identity was given to everyone for around the first year of their service, and one could opt to keep their new name if they were on the run. Generally, however, it was more desirable to reclaim your old identity, as keeping the new one would have penalties such as you not being able to leave the country without explicit permission. I wondered if I would get one too.

Over the next two weeks people would come and go, a south African guy came, and after two days had left, having said to me something along the lines of, 'this is fucking bullshit, I didn't come all the way to France just to sit in a room. You know what? I think I'll go home, maybe I can get a better job there, at least I won't be sitting around all day.'

I suppose it was a kind of its own test in a way. All this sitting doing nothing gave guys time to think and mull things over. Guys left for a hundred different reasons of course, but sometimes the waiting would be enough to persuade those who were having second thoughts about this new life that there must be a better option.

Every now and again, a Sergeant would come and take a few of us to clean, I was selected once and we were ordered to march in single file to the guard house at the front gate where the Sergeant pointed at me and said something in French. I hadn't a bloody clue what he was saying, of course, and began to panic when he became angrier and angrier at my inaction, shouting and prodding me in the chest. It wasn't until he threw a mop and bucket at me that I understood what he was asking me to do. I hastily got to work mopping the floors, all too aware of the sniggering Caporals behind me who had been enjoying the little spectacle.

A couple of days later, Bailey arrived. He was very tall and spoke with a strong Australian accent, having heard of the fabled French Foreign Legion and came from half the world away to join. He was a great guy, one of those people who is always smiling and joking and is very difficult not to like, and we became fast friends. A day after that, a Norwegian bloke arrived who spoke flawless English (as the Nordics often do) whom we poked fun at because his shaved head had caught the sun which had burned him horribly and caused his already large forehead to swell up, giving him an uncanny likeness to a dolphin. Thus, we nicknamed him 'Dolphin boy', doubly apt because he seemed to chatter endlessly in a similar pitch a dolphin might.

And so, before I knew it, we had our own little mafia going. The English-speaking mafia is usually called the Anglophones, (English speakers) and is always a minority. During the couple of weeks at Fort de Nogent, we would debate what would happen next and worry as to whether we would be chosen to go to Aubagne, the mother base of the Legion, for the next stage in the selection. Every week there was a bus that would take fifteen to twenty of us away, places that would soon be replenished by the steady trickle of newcomers arriving daily.

There were only one or two tests we had to do in Paris. A Caporal Chef came into the room one day calling out names from a list on his clipboard and we were taken to a sports area to take the 'beep test', a running test in which you had to run from one end of a tennis court to the other in-between beeps in increments that became gradually shorter. How well you did would have an impact on your application.

Out of around thirty, Dolphin boy and I were the last men standing and failed the same beep. A handful of men were eliminated and would be escorted from the fort that very same day. Then they took us indoors to do a pull up test. If you fail to reach the required number, they show you to the door, your application being automatically rejected, hence why these tests were slightly nerve wracking, more so for some than others. Imagine you have spent the last of your savings on a one-way plane ticket to take you half the world away to France, pinning your last hopes on winning yourself a new life in the legion and how many pull ups you can do might decide your future. For me however, it was not a problem because I managed twenty-four pull ups, well over the minimum requirement. At least for that I was prepared.

There was also a basic cognitive test that we had to take in groups of five as the computers were required for them. The rest of us waited in a little room in the administrative building where there was a TV on the wall that played the same promotional video of the Legion on repeat. We watched the same camouflaged guys jump out of a helicopter into a river and then run the same obstacle course over and over while evocative music played.

Later on that day, Bailey and I received our new identities, and when we were ushered back to our regular windowless room we exchanged details excitedly. 'What did they give you?' I had asked him. He made a face and said, 'Eric Bailey.' clearly thinking there were better names to have.

'What did you get?'

Grinning, I said, 'William Dempsey!'

Bailey laughed, 'Oh not bad! Makes you sound like a movie star or something!' It could certainly have been worse, I thought. Apparently, the Caporal Chefs who chose them often used the names of characters in the latest book they were reading. There were some creative ones for sure. The only rule seemed to be, the first letter of your new surname had to be the same as the first letter of your old surname. In any case, Harry Dobson would officially cease to exist on paper for the next year and I took up the new mantle of William Dempsey. I hope I'm never investigated by MI5, it could look very suspicious...

After much anticipation, the day came when the Caporal Chef would call out the names of those who were to get the bus to the train station, and then the train on to Aubagne, a town near to the southern coast of France. It was the next phase in the selection process. There we would learn if we were to become Legionnaires or be sent away. Everyone assembled in the courtyard visibly fidgeting and impatient. Mine, Steinrod, Bailey and Dolphin boys' names were called along with my Spanish friend and ten or so others. We'd got past the first stage and would be leaving the next morning! Sure, we hadn't actually done anything yet but it was a great boost for morale.

The atmosphere in the bunkhouse before bed excitable; one guy had found an electric shaver and was shaving the heads of anyone who would let him as he said, 'you'll have to do it anyway' in decent English. There were all sorts of rumours were flying around about what would happen. A Moldovan guy was telling anyone who would listen in broken English that a friend had told him that they take you into a back room where you are beaten by three or four Sergeants before you can pass the selection. I wasn't so sure about this, but everyone agreed that there would be more tests.

Before leaving the next morning, we were all summoned to the administrative building where, standing in single file, we waited to sign an enormous document presented to us. I suspected it was our five-year contract. This was the first and only time I was ever to lay eyes on that document.

A Caporal Chef was screaming at everyone in French, and I assumed that, by the way all the French speakers were rushing, it was to hurry up. When it was my turn the Caporal Chef shouted, handing me a pen and pointing to a box on the very last page of my contract. I scribbled a signature, William Dempsey, as fast as I could and took my place with the others outside, never having read a word of my contract. It was written in French anyway.

We changed into civilian clothing, collected our bags and off we went, accompanied by a surly pair of Caporal Chefs who would escort us to Aubagne. Our train tickets were bought for us and before boarding the Caporal Chefs made us understand via any means they could, if we wanted to be in the Legion, we must get off the train at Marseille where another bus would be waiting to pick us up, and that it made not the slightest bit of difference to them if we failed to show up. No one would come looking, they would leave us behind. After that, we were left to our own devices.

Bailey and I headed straight for the bar in one of the last carriages and got ourselves a beer, revelling in this sudden freedom. Free from the brusque orders of the Caporal Chefs and Sergeants of Fort De Nogent that had become commonplace over the last week. It wouldn't last long however, we only had three hours of sipping our beer watching the beautiful French countryside zoom past the window before we had arrived and were being shouted at again.

After an hour on the coach we were at the gates of Aubagne. We stepped off into the sun. It was hot. Being directed to march single file in silence through the gates and up the road towards of the recruitment centre, we could see the 'place d'arme' or the regimental assembly point. It a vast expanse of tarmac dominated by the famous marble globe sculpture flanked by four nine-foot-tall stone legionnaires in traditional uniforms. The place d'arme was bordered by very immaculately kept roses and other flowers, and beyond that was the 'Musée de la Légion Étrangère,' the museum of the French Foreign Legion, open to tourists on certain days with the words, 'Legio Patria Nostra' written along the face.

But there was no time to gawp, two Sergeants had met the Caporal Chefs on the road and having exchanged a quick hello, began chivvying us along with quick hand gestures shouting, 'allez allez allez!' In Aubagne there is an entire section of the base fenced off and dedicated to the recruitment process, we would soon discover, as we entered through one gate and headed into a basement room of a large building. The Sergeants yelled and pushed until everyone was inside, lining the walls of the concrete basement. We exchanged bewildered glances as the Sergeants shouted orders in French. Fortunately, there were some Francophones (French speakers) amongst us who quickly began arranging their things on the floor in front of them. And then they began to strip. I gulped nervously.

'All your clothes, in your bag now!' A Sergeant shouted in English, and then repeated the same order in Russian. Soon enough, we were all as naked as the day we were born, and the Sergeants were collecting everything we owned and locking it away in a cage full of other bags. The only thing we were allowed to keep were our trainers and a watch. Before too long, and to my great relief as being completely naked in a room full of total strangers can make you feel quite vulnerable, the Sergeants came back with a 'uniform' for everyone. The uniform consisted of a pair of white socks, a pair of small blue shorts, a white tee-shirt, and an old cap to protect our heads from the sun. Then we collected an ancient little rucksack that looked like it had served through at least one world war containing a few toiletries and bedsheets on our way upstairs.

Upstairs and outside, the recruitment centre had its own little place d'arme with white lines making a grid, clearly to help the newcomers align themselves in formation. When the Sergeants had shouted us into a formation that satisfied them, a large Adjutant stepped out of the entrance of the building and spoke to us in slow French. I understood only a fraction but got the gist that here they would decide if they would send us to Castelnaudary, the 4ème Regiment Étrangère, for basic training, or if they would send us home.

Behind the recruitment centre and along the outskirts of the 1er Regiment Éntrangère, there was an area where the recruits would wait, much like we had done at Paris. Again, I was struck by the strange array of men that waited there too. In the sun, I could see clearly the diversity of the other hopefuls. They were white, black, brown or anything in between. But not only was it their appearance that separated them, it was their background, experience, age, language and culture. Rarely did they mix, no one quite seemed sure of the others and generally stuck with one of their own countrymen. If they were the only ones of their kind, they were forced to interact with others or would be alone.

From tattooed ex-convicts from eastern Europe that dominated the pull ups bars to accountants all the way from India to car thieves from south Africa, the yard at Aubagne had it all. How fantastic it was that we were all so different! And yet, there was something that linked all these men together. It seemed to a certain degree that we were all outcasts, searching for a new life or a second chance. That was why we were here after all, because we didn't fit in where we had come from. Why else would we have left? There, we waited.

This time there were a few differences, however. Out of the hundred or so potentials, some of them had already been given combat fatigues and a red band which they wore over their right arms and were called, 'rouge.' They were the lucky ones who had already been chosen to go to Castelnaudary. 'Castel' as we called it for short. The rest of us would watch them curiously as Caporal Chefs sometimes took them for parade or marching drills. Or to learn the Légionnaire code d'honneur, a seven-article code that served as a behavioural benchmark for young legionnaires to adhere to and that everyone must learn in French by heart.

Not only that, but this time there was an alarm that someone in the office would sound when our presence was required and everyone without exception had to report to the place d'arme at a sprint; the last man having to do push ups in front of everyone else as punishment for lateness. They might have us do 'corvée' (cleaning) or water the plants around the regimental place d'arme. Perhaps an interview as well, as that was all part of the process.

And here there were yet more tests. They had us run around a track, do more pull ups, this time with sit ups and push ups to boot. There were cognitive theory tests to pass too, basic mathematics, memory tests and abstract reasoning tests involving shapes and patterns. Many failed, and it soon became apparent why only one in every eight candidates was accepted. I was constantly anxious that someone would call my name after the siren had sounded and summon me to an office where they would tell me I had failed, just as they had to so many others.

I remember my first official interview: a Caporal Chef who spoke good English sat me down in front of him with a notepad and asked me why I wanted to join the legion in a monotonous tone that suggested it was the hundredth time he'd asked the same question that day. I said it was for the adventure and to challenge myself despite knowing how silly it probably sounded. He narrowed his eyes and asked me if I was in trouble with the police or ever had been in trouble with the police. I said no.

'Are you sure? I will find out and if you're lying that's it, you're done.' I shook my head again.

'Don't shake your head at me boy, here we say, 'no Caporal Chef!' How about drugs, have you ever done drugs?'

I gulped. 'No.' I lied.

He raised his eyebrows in disbelief, 'Never?'

'Never.'

'Hmphf! Off you go then.'

There was another one to one interview that we all had to do. It was called the 'Gestapo interview', during which you were shouted at a lot and told that you wouldn't last a day and had your bank cards cut up before your eyes to symbolise the death of your old identity.

At night, when the alarm sounded at 22:30, we assembled and ran upstairs to choose a bunk, brush our teeth and were in bed in minutes. For in the morning we would be woken at 05:00, would have to shave, remove the sheets from our beds and roll them into neat cylinders and put them into our bags, leave our little packs in an orderly group in the basement, all the while being harassed to hurry up by someone or other so that we could report to the yard where there was nothing to do but wait.

We passed the time chatting and speculating again, watching the steady stream of new and interesting faces come and go and looking on in envy as the reds were sent off to Castel. This meant they would choose a new batch within the next few days and we all hoped our names would be called.

Sure enough, the claxon wailed the next morning and everyone ran to the place d'arme, perhaps a little faster than usual. Names were called off a list, my own included, and the Adjutant divided us roughly into two groups around the same size so that one half of us were on one side of the place d'arme, and the other half were on the opposite side. I was so nervous I wouldn't be chosen, I hated the thought of returning home after failing at the first hurdle, defeated. I swore to myself right then and there that if I was chosen, no matter how hard the trials to come, I would never quit of my own accord.

The damn Adjutant seemed to pause for effect and there was a deathly silence. He raised a hand and pointed at my group and said,

'Vous êtes rouges!' Yes! I almost jumped up and down with elation, and I could feel the excitement of the others next to me too. From here on, the only reason I would be returning home was if I were to quit, and I had no intention of doing that.

Turning his gaze to the other group, he spoke in French once more. 'The Legion has no need for you. Go home.'

It felt fantastic to be going to the next phase, and I felt a boundless sense of optimism that made me smile. Later in my legion career, I would come to understand that passing this part was well within the realm of possibility for most. If you have two arms, two legs, a mouth full of teeth and are not a violent criminal, the chances are you'll be okay. Nevertheless, it was a victory.

We were issued camouflaged fatigues, a red arm band and boots and suddenly I felt a little bit more like a soldier. I was also starting to understand more French, or at least the Legion's own brand of French. With most people arriving like me and speaking next to no French, everyone had to learn it, and some picked it up faster than others. This all meant, however, that the general standard was very basic. Good for understanding orders but pretty poor for transitioning to the civilian world where one had to contend with the regular French accent, the rapid pace at which everyone seemed to speak and the comparatively complex structure of words.

Now however, instead of sitting around like the others, we were the ones doing marching drills and learning the code d'honneur. They gave us a piece of paper with the code printed on it, each of which was soon creased, torn and dirty from use. The code is as follows:

Article 1: Légionnaire, tu es un volontaire servant la France avec honneur et fidélité.

Article 2: Chaque légionnaire est ton frère d'arme, quelle que soit sa nationalité, sa race, sa religion. Tu lui manifestes toujours la solidarité étroite qui doit unir les membres d'une même famille.

Article 3: Respectueux des traditions, attaché à tes chefs, la discipline et la camaraderie sont ta force, le courage et la loyauté tes vertus.

Article 4: Fier de ton état de légionnaire, tu le montres dans ta tenue toujours élégante, ton comportement toujours digne mais modeste, ton casernement toujours net.

Article 5: Soldat d'élite, tu t'entraînes avec rigueur, tu entretiens ton arme comme ton bien le plus précieux, tu as le souci constant de ta forme physique.

Article 6: La mission est sacrée, tu l'exécutes jusqu'au bout et, s'il le faut, en opérations, au péril de ta vie.

Article 7: Au combat tu agis sans passion et sans haine, tu respectes les ennemis vaincus, tu n'abandonnes jamais ni tes morts, ni tes blessés, ni tes armes.

And translates to:

Article 1: Legionnaire, you are a volunteer serving France with honour and loyalty.

Article 2: Each legionary is your brother in arms, whatever his nationality, his race, his religion. You always show him the close solidarity which must unite the members of the same family.

Article 3: Respectful of traditions, attached to your leaders, discipline and camaraderie are your strength, courage and loyalty your virtues.

Article 4: Proud of your legionary status, you show it in your always elegant outfit, your always dignified but modest demeanour, your always clean barracks.

Article 5: Elite soldier, you train with rigor, you maintain your weapon as your most precious asset, you have constant concern for your physical form.

Article 6: The mission is sacred, you carry it out to the end and, if necessary, in operations, at the risk of your life.

Article 7: In combat you act without passion and without hatred, you respect the vanquished enemies, you never abandon your dead, your wounded, or your weapons.

The article I think best sums up the Legion is perhaps article six. 'You will follow those damn orders, even if it kills you!'

One of the other Anglophones had found a French-English dictionary and we all sat in the shade one day to translate it as there was not much else for us to do anyway. I had found it ironic that the motto of the French Foreign Legion was 'honneur et fidélité' and that the code d'honneur demanded that we be respectful, obedient and dignified even if these were some of the things that many of the men in the Legion were most lacking. I suppose that's why it had to be made and why the discipline had to be so high: to break men down and reform them in the way the Legion saw fit.

As Steinrod had left us to go to Castel a few days earlier, Bailey and I had a few days to kill together. Bailey was a funny character; he had worked in the mines back in Australia, and hunted kangaroo in his spare time or cruised around in Australian muscle cars called 'yutes'.

He was so tall he towered a foot above most men, and had a slightly ungainly walk due to his long limbs. He'd kind of swing his arms by his sides as he moved, often wearing a pleasantly endearing grin on his face as though he'd just finished laughing at a joke. It was hard to communicate with some of the other guys we spoke to. Not all of them could speak English, and even fewer spoke French, but whenever anyone tried to speak to Bailey - whether he understood or not- he'd just chuckle, nod his head and slap them good-naturedly on the shoulder. He was not the sort of guy that took life too seriously, and rarely took offence at anything. Instead, Bailey was always quite happy to go along with the flow and enjoy himself. He was a great guy to have around and did wonders to boost our morale.

He would also come out with these fantastic expressions like, 'he's a few kangaroos loose in the top paddock'. Which I took to mean someone was a little bit crazy, or 'he's a few stubbies short of a sixpack'. Which he used to refer to someone not blessed with intelligence.

And when I asked him about life in Australia he told me how he had worked in the mines; a relatively well paying job that allowed him to live comfortably with his long term girlfriend. Yet he told me that, 'there was just something missing, I needed to go out and see some stuff, you know?' I did, it was all too easy to relate to. Bailey, Steinrod and I were bound by a common goal: adventure. We had wanted to experience a little more of what the world had to offer and so far, we were not disappointed.

There were a few pull up bars and dips bars that I used, too, that were regularly occupied by a group of tattooed Hungarian ex-cons; one of whom was Horvath. He had done five and a half years for armed robbery and was someone I would not only do basic training with, but also share a room with later on.

The days were hot and time went slow until finally the reds were called into Aubagne's store rooms. We were issued with an enormous amount of kit in three separate, full bags that we then had to carry over to a coach one hot morning that was waiting to take us to Castel. No one had told us this of course, so the first we learned was when we were loading our bags into the storage space between the wheel arches and a Caporal Chef told us to, 'move your asses or you'll miss your last meal in the canteen!'

Our last meal? We exchanged apprehensive glances. No one knew for sure what would happen to us next or what kind of challenges we were about to face.

We ate quickly and, not even having the chance to bid farewell to some of the guys we had met and whose shoes we had filled a week previously, we were away. The gates of Aubagne closed behind us. We were about to find out what basic training in the French Foreign Legion would entail...

Castelnaudary is northeast of the Pyrenees mountains that divide the south of France and Spain. The scenery is beautiful in that part of the world and surely a fantastic place for tourists to visit. Legionnaires, however, hate it with a passion. Castel, the 4ème Regiment Éntrangère, is the place where the soldiers of the legion will do many of their standard training courses. Basic training, or 'instruction,' is around four months and Caporal training is two months; meaning almost everyone who finishes their five-year contract will have spent at least half a year there. Then there are the specialities courses - transmissions, medics and mechanics - that are all another four months, along with various other, shorter courses like driving or bureaucracy.

In short, Legionnaires are familiar with, and none too fond of, Castel. This is because there is no shortage of bullshit to wade through, or 'sketch' as we called it. Just inside the front gate there is a sign that reads, 'Ici, ç'est comme ça.' Meaning, 'here, that's just the way it is'. It might be difficult for me to describe just how well that sign sums up the general attitude at Castel. If you didn't like it, you could fuck off, and that is exactly what they would tell us every day.

The French Foreign Legion has always had a problem with desertion. In theory, after your five years' service you may acquire a French nationality which has been, along with the relatively decent western European wage, one of the most attractive elements for new recruits. Patriotism, a love for the French nation, will be for most, at the very bottom of their list of reasons to join.

Imagine you come from the poorest parts of Romania and have been looking for a way to leave your country in search of a better life and a western European passport. For anyone with an interest in the military, the Legion is going to be a sound option. You will not however, have any particular loyalty to France, these are not your people and this strange culture is not your own. Why would you feel that you had to stay if a better option were to present itself? Moreover, why would you risk your life in a potential war that might not be your own to defend values you do not wholeheartedly agree with?

Understandably, a lot of men leave before their contact is up and I have never blamed any of them for it. Out of the fifty or so that I did basic training with, probably just over half of us completed the minimum five-year stretch. Life in the Legion, especially the first few years, can be restrictive enough.

Sometimes all anyone is looking for is an excuse to not come back after the weekend. There was a Scottish lad who had been beaten by his Sergeant Chef after being late back to base one weekend, leaving his face a bit of a mess. Not a bad reason not to come back in my opinion. I had another friend, an American, who simply missed the last train back from Paris on a Sunday evening. That was enough for him to say 'fuck it', head straight for the airport and get the first plane back to the USA. Even my good friend Bailey would desert about halfway through his contract because his long-term girlfriend back in

Australia had given birth to twin boys. Not only was Bailey missing raising his children, but he wasn't earning enough money to support his quickly growing family with the Australian living costs.

One of the fantastic things about the Legion is that it functions, for most, as a tool that gives you a chance to carve out a better life for yourself. If a man thinks he can do better elsewhere why shouldn't he go?

I came close to deserting once myself, so I understood perfectly well why someone might. All the none commissioned officers or 'sous-officiers', knew and understood, too. However, being 'sous-officiers' they were all likely to have at least five years' service and therefore far less likely to desert as, after that point in your career, the quality of life generally improves, and roots have been put down. Many of them had brought their families over, for example.

You would have thought that having come up through the ranks would make them all more empathetic to our situations. It wasn't always the case unfortunately. For years after we complete basic training we are told the same thing, 'la portail est la bas!' The gates are over there. If you don't like it, leave. This did nothing to help the lamentably weak sense of fraternity present in much of the Legion and many would take this advice quite seriously.

Castel was, of course, the worst for this. Their aim was to weed out anyone not fully committed, and the first volunteer would present himself the day after we arrived.

The base at Castel is mostly built around the enormous place d'arme where regimental gatherings take place. We were put in the '1ère compagnie d'engage volunteers' as we couldn't call ourselves legionnaires until we had completed the kepi march. This had been one of the first lessons the newly acquainted forty-eight of us had received in the classrooms on the ground floor of the barracks. Along with the fact that in a week or so we would be sent out to the 'farm' to do our first and most intensive month of training.

The lesson was taken by our new 'chef de section'; a young lieutenant in command of the fifty or so of us, or a 'section', for the next four months. In the French army a 'groupe' is a combat group of around 10, a 'section' consists of several groups and a 'compagnie' is several sections.

He would also rattle off a great list of things we were not allowed to do and then introduced us to the men that would make our life hell for the duration of basic training. There was the second in command, Chef Raynaud - a somewhat rare Frenchman - a couple of Sergeants that would come and go, and the Caporals: Merino, Liquitay and Goldberg, along with a couple of others that would show up after a month or so.

Merino was by far the worst. He came from Spain and was small, slim, dark haired, and seemed to take a particular kind of pleasure from making us suffer. On the first day he had us running up and down the stairs from the barracks to the assembly point outside until we were sweating and sucking in air because none of us had met his incredibly fast standard the first time.

Once Merino had gotten bored for the moment, we were finally able to unpack a few of our things and have a chance to meet everyone else. Apart from Steinrod and Bailey, I didn't know anyone. But I quickly found out who could speak English well enough to converse with. It turned out there was another Englishman named Hughes, whom I shared a room with. We got talking and I learned that Hughes had supposedly been in the Royal marines back in the UK. After leaving the army life he had moved in with his girlfriend and had set up numerous dark web servers in their attic to earn some extra cash. Unfortunately for him, the police had cottoned on to this and raided his house much to the surprise of his girlfriend. Luckily, Hughes had been out at the time and upon hearing the news had booked himself the first flight to Paris to join the Legion.

Hughes also happened to be the fattest guy in the section. If he ever had been in the Royal Marines, he had certainly let himself go. This would make his life far more complicated than it needed to be. Overweight men in the Legion do not enjoy themselves, especially during basic training. If I had to give one piece of advice to someone looking to join, it would be to get yourself into the best physical shape first.

Halfway through our conversation we heard a commotion outside. Guys were crowding round the doorway to the room opposite to look in. I got up to look too and saw a kid who couldn't have been any older than myself sat on his bed and was hugging his knees, apparently crying. The guys watching him were sniggering and someone said, 'look, he misses mummy!' They all laughed. The kid hid his head with his hands and sobbed. I shook my head and left them to their entertainment. A few moments later Merino had mounted the stairs and shouted for the crowd to disperse, investigating its cause. He saw the kid and grinned.

'Come with me.' The kid picked himself up and, wiping his eyes, followed Merino back down the corridor.

It certainly was a culture shock. Up to then I had been free and privileged, treated like a human being, something I had clearly taken for granted. But now I had been plunged into a world in which I was constantly shouted and screamed at; had to endure the presence of guys I didn't like in the slightest who would use intimidation and the threat of violence to get what they wanted. I didn't have any free time as the time between scheduled activities would be filled with pointless bullshit like scrubbing the floor for the fifteenth time that day and I was told that I was completely welcome to throw in the towel at any moment. But you couldn't show weakness like that or you'd become the prey of not only the Caporals but the other guys too.

Then someone shouted, 'rassemblement!' which we quickly learned meant 'assembly'. Once shouted, we would have to sprint downstairs to the assembly point if we didn't want to do push ups for the next half an hour. Sometimes we did push ups for half an hour anyway.

Merino was waiting and once we were all present, he said, 'nul à chier.' That was shit. Merino then proceeded to lecture us about how we were the most useless section he had ever seen and that none of us would ever become legionnaires.

'Qui veut civil?' Who wants to become a civilian? Merino looked around expectantly at the kid who had been crying that he seemed to have purposely placed before the rest of us. The kid raised a trembling hand. Merino gave an evil little smile and cackled.

'Come forward.' he said gesturing, and the kid shuffled before the rest of the section, his eyes on the ground whilst everyone else's were on him, watching silently.

'Good, good,' Merino purred, patting him on the shoulder and making him quiver a little. 'Come with me, you can go home now.

There is no place for you here' And led him away. I think that the Caporals must have had a wager on how many guys would quit before the end of training. Merino seemed to take great pleasure in it anyway, and that was it for the kid, in an hour his bags were gone and so was he, the only thing that remained was an empty bunk.

Our section was housed on the first floor of a three-storey building in the 1ere compagnie, with other sections in the same building at various points in their instruction. The barracks were basic and around forty years old. Plain, square brown tiles made up the floor and the walls had once been painted a cream colour which seemed to have faded to a dull yellow over time. The toilets were plain and were void of toilet seats so as to be easier to clean and the showers were half cubicles with no doors. There was no privacy.

Metal wardrobes, bunk beds, a table and a stool were the only furniture in the rooms. Most rooms also housed one of the Caporals taking us for instruction so they could keep an eye on us. The rooms were cramped, and the metal wardrobes had to be shared which led to rising tempers if both men sharing had to access it at the same time. Also, the Caporals did regular checks of our wardrobes, which had to be kept open for inspection. The t-shirts had to be folded with a sheet of paper in the crease and so that the words 'Legion Éntrangère' printed on the back faced outwards, the socks folded together immaculately and everything cleanly ironed to perfection.

We were also issued with a formal dress uniform and were introduced to ironing shirts Legion style as Merino gave a demonstration on how to do it. On the summer shirts, there were three pleats on either breast that had to be 3.5cm apart, two pleats on either sleeve that had to be 5.3cm apart and three more pleats on the back that also had to be 5.3cm apart. Hughes and I worked as a pair, one would hold the shirt on the board and the other would iron in the pleats. We had to be careful though, if a Caporal came in and we were caught speaking English and not French, we would surely be scrubbing the toilets for the foreseeable future.

Everything was done in French now with no exceptions. If you didn't understand you had to ask one of the Francophones. We had a Frenchman in our section and a couple of Madagascans who had their work cut out for them explaining as best they could to everyone what the orders had been. We were given dictionaries that translated our first language to French to use for revision in what little spare time we might have. I made good use of it, figuring it was in my best interests to do so.

I think we had about four or five official French lessons in the entire four-month training period. It became clear that if you wanted to learn, you had to teach it to yourself. Some guys never learned. Chinese, Japanese and Koreans, for example, found it particularly difficult to pick it up - French being the polar opposite to their mother tongue and with an alien alphabet.

Other than ironing, revising and cleaning, we had to complete the standard fitness tests that were marked down and would be compared to our scores at the end. We had to do an eight-kilometre run with a 10kg bag, climb up a thick 3m rope twice, do a hundred metres in the pool and an obstacle course along with a few other tests. I have always been a good all-rounder and did decent in everything, which suited me perfectly because it kept me off the radar of the Caporals and Sergeants. Others, with Hughes at the forefront, were not so lucky. Those who did badly on the fitness tests were constantly harassed and were the favourites to scrub the toilets. Merino soon had a little group of 'favourites' that he liked to torture. A week in and we were already beginning to understand how the next four months would be. All this and we hadn't even touched a rifle, let alone shot one!

But that would soon come as our departure for the farm was imminent. We had to load all the equipment we would need into the JBC's (the French army's standard truck that hadn't changed since the 60's). Leaving our rooms completely bare, fifty of us were crammed into the back of two JBC's and our backsides were soon bruised by the cold steel benches. It almost felt good to be getting on with what was supposed to be the worst part of instruction after a hectic week at Castel.

I had managed to secure myself a spot next to Hughes near the end and we began to chat away in English, now that the Caporals were out of earshot up in the cabin.

'Hey, you, Dempsey! You can't speak French or what? Why do you speak English all the time?'

I turned to look who had spoken. A short and broad Romanian, I knew was called Mattei, was glaring at me two places down. I looked around and could hear at least five other languages being spoken as the other guys babbled away around us.

'Hey, everyone else here is speaking a different language, why did you single me out?'

'Because you always speak English, you're gonna get us in trouble with the Caporals!'

'Listen, I never speak English when the Caporals are around, okay? I'm not that stupid. And I heard you speaking Romanian only this morning!'

It was true, I had heard it myself. What made him think he could deny me speaking my mother tongue yet speak his own?

'Yea but that's because I can actually speak French, you can't, you're an idiot!' He sneered at me, baring his yellow teeth.

'Yea, well, you can go and fuck yourself.' I said and turned away.

'You watch your back!' He growled at the back of my head. I ignored him. It wasn't a good start.

The JBC's trundled along country roads in hilly terrain for the best part of an hour until they turned down a lane marked with the iconic symbol of the Legion's flaming grenade. As the JBC's came to a halt, I saw that the Farm was just that: a large old farmhouse with bare stone walls and a concrete floor. There was a bunk room, a classroom, a kitchen, an armoury and a few rooms for the instructors. Surrounding the farm was woodland through which we would soon be marching, running and crawling at all hours of the day. We didn't have much time to take all this in, however, before we were being shouted at to unload all the equipment. We were assigned a bunk between two and I shared with a Georgian bloke and again having only one wardrobe between the two of us.

The next month was a blur. We almost never had a free moment as so many activities were packed into each day, some of them clearly designed to keep us busy so we were not sat around. Any free time between activities Hughes, Bailey, Steinrod and I tended to gravitate together to talk quietly in English, and looking around, every other mafia was doing the same thing. Often however, we were too tired to even do that, and simply found somewhere to sit and close our eyes until Merino would run over and order us into formation again.

The daily routine was as follows, reveille before the sun was up, shave and have breakfast which consisted of a single piece of bread and a little plastic pot of jam. Then we would do sport, almost always running followed by bodyweight exercises conducted in sessions of broken down groups based on fitness capability. Chef Rinpoche took the fittest group and I struggled to keep pace with him, my lungs fit to burst.

After sport, we would shower and change into camouflage fatigues and practice dry firing shooting drills with the FAMAS, or march and sing in formation until lunch. Lunch was basic and never sufficient. Not only that but we never had the time to finish the small portions we got before a Sergeant shouted, 'stand!' and we were on our feet once more. Anyone caught eating stood up would be doing laps of the farm with his rifle above his head.

Post lunch activities would usually involve more physical activity, like running the various obstacle courses in the woods around the farm or marching. Dinner was much the same as lunch, save for the fact we were more tired and hungrier than we were several hours ago. In the evening, we would have lessons in the classroom. We had to learn a firearms code to be able to use them safely, the names of the different parts, how to take it apart, clean it and put it back together as well as the basics of combat theory. They taught us the ranking system, our rights as legionnaires, the different regiments that existed within the Legion and scratched at the surface of the Legions history. It was common for us to then do some manner of night-time activity, even if it was just guarding the farm in shifts from an unknown enemy.

During these shifts it was commonplace for the relieving pair to find their predecessors sleeping against a tree. It was a risky game we all played because if the Caporals decided to do a night-time check of the guard, there would be hell to pay. But it was worth it, we were all struggling to function properly on just several hours of sleep per night.

I remember feeling that it was the hardest thing I had ever done. Physically, I was always tired and we ran and marched for many kilometres every day, but that was only a fraction of the challenge. It was all a mental game. I had to learn to obey each command and unlearn how to think for myself. If the Caporals didn't ask me to do something, I wouldn't do it. I wasn't my own man anymore, I had to be where I was ordered and had no free time to be able to step back and breathe. The Caporals were fond of reminding me that I was worthless, a useless member of the worst section they had ever had to train. It was miserable, and I knew I wasn't the only one who felt that way.

Perhaps the hardest thing to adjust to was working together and accepting that we were going to get caught out for things and punished as a unit for the mistakes of one person. The attitude in the section towards someone could change overnight. One of the Caporals might check that the guards were patrolling the farm at 2am, for example, only to find that one of them was nowhere to be found and had failed to get out of bed. This would result in a double guard shift for everyone the next night, meaning we would have an extra couple of hours of guard and broken sleep. Or the section might have to do a timed march behind the notoriously fast Chef Raynaud and the inevitable stragglers would hold up the column causing the Chef to become furious and make us run a half marathon the next morning just for the hell of it.

I tried to keep my head down myself, which was straightforward enough. If you didn't fuck up and put effort into the sport and physical activities you'd likely be fine as there were always one or two 'bananiers', as we called them, who couldn't help but get everything wrong and were soon added to Merino's shit list. Not a nice place to be.

Once, before the sun had fully set, we were told to put on our combat gear, take our packs and were sent into a field in front of the farm where we were aligned into two neat rows. Looking around bewildered, we looked to the Sergeant for further instruction.

'You stay EXACTLY where you are.' He said. 'Bonne nuit.' And he left us. Being totally suspicious of their games and knowing they were trying to catch us out, we all took the instruction literally and rolled out our sleeping bags on the grass and climbed inside. It was soon silent as nobody wanted to pass up the opportunity to get some sleep in, but we all knew something was going to happen. I lay in my sleeping bag, realising after around thirty minutes that I had been tensing my muscles and grinding my teeth. There was a reason we weren't in the farmhouse, I was sure. The instructors were planning something and I hated not knowing what. But the fatigue eventually caught up with me and I managed to drift off into a fitful sleep.

'BANG!' Fuck. 'BANG BANG BANG! The training grenades exploded around us at 1am, jolting everyone awake and into a panic. I sat up in my sleeping bag trying to make sense of the situation. In the darkness, there was a hive of activity as my comrades scrambled all around me and the voices of men shouting filled my ears. What the hell was going on? My eyes were wide open and a sense of panic was building in my chest. What do I do? Next to me, I could just about make out the shape of another guy hurriedly pulling his boots on and decided that that was a good place to start. When gunshots cracked in the air it only pushed me to dress faster, not bothering to finish tying my laces before packing my sleeping gear into my bag.

All the instructors were screaming at the top of their lungs, firing blanks at us from their rifles and the air was full of noise. We packed the last of our things away, lightning fast, and were soon being pushed and shoved towards the stream some two hundred metres down the hill. The only thing illuminating the darkness was the weak light of the half moon and the flashes from the instructor's barrels as the blank cartridges fired. The fifty or so engagé volunteers were herded like frightened buffalo into the stream, and began splashing about, falling over one another in desperation, wanting to be as far away as possible from the instructors. I tripped on my unfastened laces falling flat on my face in the water, soaking my fatigues and I had to gasp as the cold knocked the wind out of me for a second. I tried to get up but was knocked back down again with an 'oof!' as someone else had barrelled into me from behind.

I scrambled to my feet and realised in horror that my rifle was no longer slung around my neck. I crouched in the water fumbling blindly around trying to feel for my FAMAS as a Caporal smacked me around the back of my head, demanding to know what I was doing. I found it! Pulling the firearm from the water, I cradled it with one arm whilst using the other to fend off more blows from the Caporal behind and ran to re-join the rest of the herd.

They pushed us along, the water up to our waists, firing blanks from the bank. When the adrenaline had worn off after several minutes, the fatigue set in, but of course it was far from over. We had to complete a long team-based obstacle course through the mud in the darkness. It was the type of thing where two men had to help a third mount a wooden wall using their knees as steps and help each other over, or we would crawl through a tiny concrete tunnel, pushing our bags in front of us and feeling blindly in the dark as muddy water sloshed around our chests. It's the typical sort of thing you think of when someone says basic training. What they don't tell you is that you'll be doing it all with fatigue, hunger and the cold sapping away at your morale and the easiest thing in the world would be to raise your hand and shout, 'civile! I want to quit!'

Someone did just that halfway through, and they were taken back to the farm, but the rest of us would have to suffer on through a long night. At the time it was horrible, it's only with the benefit of hindsight having now left the Legion that I'm able to appreciate that it was all character-building stuff. When something doesn't go to plan nowadays, I can say to myself, I have a roof over my head, I'm warm, dry and well rested and I have a full stomach, life could be worse! Life could be the farm.

I remember being constantly tired for that month. Once, a Sergeant was giving us a lesson outside on how to adjust the sights of the FAMAS. There were a number of us crowded around him in a circle, watching him fiddle with the rifle. I had been stood somewhere at the back, nodding off on my feet and stumbling every now and again. Finally, the Sergeant had seen me drooling, eyes half shut. 'Dempsey!' Shit, now I was awake. 'Come here.'

I came forward to stand before the Sergeant. Reaching into his pocket he took out a training grenade and removed the pin. I gulped. Taking my hand, he took the grenade and placed it into my palm, wrapping my fingers tightly around it. 'Voila!' He exclaimed, 'now you won't sleep.'

Now whilst it was only a training grenade, had it gone off it would not have taken my hand with it. They still make a fair bang and would, at the very least, have given me some nasty burns and would probably have shredded the skin of my palm. I held on, gripping the safety lever tightly, fighting against the spring inside. Needless to say, I was wide awake from then on, and the Sergeant was able to continue his lesson without further interruption.

We had been doing some combat drills one day, creeping through the woods with our faces painted. To my dismay, I had landed in the group with Mattei, and not wanting further conflict, I decided it would be best to try to stay as far away as possible from him. I would fail in that endeavour, however, for once the instructors set us on the course, I had been placed on the left flank, with Mattei beside me. As we patrolled the woods, Mattei began to whisper to me.

'Man you watch your back tonight. Don't sleep 'cause I'm gonna come up to your bunk and beat the shit out of you.'

Mattei had seemed to have taken a real disliking to me since our last encounter. Though I believed most of his threats were hollow, his hostility did give me reason to doubt.

'Don't sleep tonight man!' He cowed in hushed tones.

I turned to him in anger, 'hey, you know wha-'

Crack! Crack! Crack!

'Dempsey! What the fuck are you doing?' The Sergeant who had been hiding in the bushes to my left in ambush roared, and I turned to see his face purple with rage.

'We are in a hostile environment and you think its okay to be talking with your comrade? Because you're so relaxed, you and the rest of the group can run the course ten times with your rifles above your heads! Go!'

The rest of the guys groaned and gave me a sarcastic thanks as we all hoisted our rifles above our heads. Mattei cackled beside me.

'Fucking idiot!' He cooed.

I had to stop myself from responding by biting my tongue and tried with every fibre of my being to supress my rage.

As I mentioned before, one of the goals of the instructors was to turn us into a unit via group punishment, the mistakes of the individual were felt by the entire section. The hunger and fatigue meant we were at each other's throats; when one guy fucked up his mates would defend him and everyone else would curse them in disgust, or as best they could during their fifteenth lap around the farm with their rifles above their heads. I was guilty of the same. Up to that point, I had led a sheltered life: three square meals a day, eight hours of sleep, and I had lived comfortably at home with my parents who only very rarely made me iron my clothes, and never with the same vigour as Caporal Merino. I'm not ashamed to say that I found it very difficult, not because I had never known hunger or fatigue like that, but because working with the other guys, whose attitudes were often combative, made the whole ordeal twice as hard.

Sometimes however, our suffering would not be due to anyone's mistake, and was simply because the instructors felt we needed it. Unfortunately, things could be taken a little too far.

There was a new Romanian caporal filling in for several weeks. He was small and had beady eyes and a strange twitch. One of his favourite things to do was make us do 'position samurai'. The assembly point in front of the farm was on a gravel track, and if we were late we would be made to go into a press-up position with our hands clasped behind our backs and foreheads pressing into the gravel. It was extremely painful, especially when you had to do it for a few minutes at a time.

It was a Sunday evening when typically, the sous-officiers and lieutenant had gone home for the night, leaving a skeleton crew to watch over us until Monday morning. Anyway, this Romanian Caporal had managed to find himself a few grams of cocaine that he was sniffing that night and had decided it would be entertaining to fuck with us. It must have been the early hours of the morning when he came into the bunk house shouting at us to wake and to assemble outside.

I jumped out of bed, believing it was another exercise, and seeing the others scramble to put their clothes on I followed suit. Soon fifty of us were rushing down the stairs at once, the sheer amount of bodies blocking the path caused the guys behind to began to push and jostle those not fast enough, the Caporal screaming at us all the while.

Outside, the Caporal screamed some more, telling us we were too slow and to go into 'position samurai' on the gravel. There was a collective groan, but we complied, and assembling quickly, we knelt on the gravel, pressing our foreheads against the little stones and lifted our knees up off the ground, our hands clasped behind our backs.

Soon, everyone was hissing through their teeth in pain as the little gravel stones dug deep into the skin of our foreheads. The Romanian Caporal began to give us a long lecture about how useless we were and what poor soldiers we would make. The usual.

'You are all shit! Why do you take so long to get out of bed? I think you have too much sleep!'

I bared my teeth and clenched my eyes shut in pain.

'What? Does it hurt?'

'No Caporal!' Fifty voices shouted back in unison.

The Caporal scoffed. 'Stop pretending! I can see you are all just a bunch on pussies!' He spat on the ground before us.

But this apparently wasn't enough for the Caporal and all of a sudden, he strode over to the front row and began to viciously kick the exposed sides of the men with his heavy-duty combat boots. The night was filled with cries of pain and surprise, as half of the front row were left writhing on the ground, clutching their sides. No one quite knew what to do, this was our Caporal. We had been told to obey every command and it seemed the only thing for us to do was to bear the beating. Fortunately, I was at the back, having been one of the last outside, and was grateful for my position of relative safety.

It wasn't until the Caporal had felled several men that a couple of us thought to stop him and tackle him to the ground where a scuffle broke out. The Caporal fought back with a frenzied yell.

'Get your fucking hands off me! I'm a Caporal! I'll make you all do guard duty for the whole night after this I swear!'

Once the Caporal had been subdued, the duty Sergeant, with impeccable timing, came outside in his underwear, demanding to know what was going on. One of the Madagascans explained and the Sergeant frowned, demanding us to release the Caporal, who was then promptly dragged back inside by the Sergeant, still hissing and spitting at us.

Some of the guys were still writhing around on the ground, clutching their sides in pain. A few minutes later an ambulance had been called, and once the Sergeant had managed to calm the Caporal somewhat, we were eventually allowed to go back inside to get our well-needed rest. In the aftermath, there had been three guys sent to the infirmary with broken ribs. The lieutenant had tried to cover the whole thing up on Monday morning to protect the Caporal with only partial success and was himself punished for negligence and confined to office duties for a month or so, meaning Chef Raynaud was in charge of the section now.

That was fine by me, we hardly ever saw the lieutenant anyway and the section seemed to run like clockwork under Raynaud's careful supervision. I've never had a particularly high opinion of the officers found in the Legion. Once, it had been an honour to be an office, as only the best were selected to lead the French army's most elite fighting force.

Now, however, that didn't appear to be the case. Presently, it seemed as if a position in the Legion was more of a punishment. Most came from wealthy families and had not worked their way up from the bottom like the sous-officiers had. Instead they had gone to an officer training school, which was undoubtedly cushier than our own training. Moreover, they were often slim-built and effeminate, and their unjustified confidence far outstripped their abilities. Having said that, I did have a few excellent ones that I think were fine examples of what an officer ought to be, but they were unfortunately a minority. However, there were some rare examples of officers in the Legion that had worked their way up from the ranks of Legionnaire and passed the officer training course.

The sous-officiers in the Legion were far more respected, being able to claim to be true legionnaires. Raynaud was one such I held in high regard and who led by example, as I believe all leaders should. He could do just as well as any one of us on the physical tests, some feat, for there was no shortage of athletes amongst us. His firm but fair demeanour promised that he never made us suffer unnecessarily, but if we fucked up, we knew about it.

Marching behind the Chef was tough. Every week at the farm we would march in preparation for the famous Kepi march at the end of the month. The section would have to complete a two-day quick march at the end of which we would be presented with our kepis if we were successful, and officially become legionnaires. Chef Raynaud was tall and would take enormous strides, causing the little Venezuelan and Nepalese blokes in our section to jog to keep up. Marching like this hour after hour would mean that the section, almost fifty strong and marching as a column, would soon be spread out over the distance of a kilometre, and the Chef would become angry at those less fit who were lagging behind.

He was the first leader I looked up to in the Legion, however there would be many more like him. But there would also be just as many, if not more, that I disliked. I would see many types of leaders and would come to understand what made a good one and what didn't. In the Legion, your superiors are always right, they require total obedience, and those extra stripes on their uniform gave them power.

Often, this power could manifest itself spitefully, and those new Caporals or Sergeants who had never earned any respect of their own would be particularly vindictive to their subordinates, just to prove a point. They would also demand things of you that they could not do themselves. This, in my opinion, is poor leadership. But a good one will know to be just, and to lead by example, holding their charges to standards set by themselves.

Sunday evenings at the farm were the only brief periods of respite. The section would be given some meat to cook on a barbecue, and we would sit around tables in a field next to the farmhouse with the instructors having their own table. Chef Raynaud would make each mafia sing a traditional song from their homeland before the rest, which was very entertaining to watch and I learned a bit more about each culture as they did.

When it came to the Anglophones, Bailey, Steinrod, Hughes and I scratched our heads. Being from three different countries, we didn't quite know what traditional song we all knew that we could sing. So, we sang 'Carry on Wayward Son' by Kansas instead. As I remember, it went down rather well. After that we could eat. It was the only meal of the week we were allowed to eat in peace and actually finish. It's funny how even something as simple as eating a hot meal and being able to laugh and joke around a table without fear of punishment can raise your spirits dramatically when everything else is shit.

With a week to go at the farm, we focused more on the Kepi march to come. The kepi blanc is the traditional and formal headwear for legionnaires. It appeared during the initial colonisation of Algeria and was a cap, white as snow, designed to keep the hot sun from the soldiers' necks. Somehow, it developed into the more rigid and upright design that we have today. The Caporals would often inspect them for dirt. I've taken many a shower with my kepi, scrubbing at it with a toothbrush and wondering why it couldn't be a nice dull grey. The stark white was supposedly due to the fact that the original caps had been bleached by the sun. I didn't even know this at the time, it was only until after the farm that we were given a proper history lesson on the Legion and there were many things I was still in the dark about. This mysterious foreign military romanticised by so many was still a damn mystery even though I was in it!

In theory, we would have to complete a two-day quick march, upon the completion of which, a Colonel would formally present us with our kepis during a ceremony to officiate us as legionnaires. The marching was tough for some. The boots we had been issued had little to no padding, and after marching for a few hours, it felt like we had concrete blocks strapped to our feet. I had at least done hiking before my life in the legion and knew a little of what to expect, but others were already plagued by blisters and chafing with no time to dress their wounds behind the relentless pace of Chef Raynaud.

The day soon came that we had to pack up everything into the trucks again in preparation for the march, leaving with only a 24h pack with all the gear we'd need to camp out. Even though only four weeks had passed, it seemed much longer. I was looking forward to getting back to the relative comfort of the barracks at Castel, where we wouldn't have to do guard duty during the night. I wondered, before I drifted off to sleep, what it would be like to be able to call myself a Legionnaire…

When we woke the next morning, I think I was just relieved to be finally getting on with it. I still wasn't entirely sure how I felt about being a legionnaire, proud I suppose. It still intrigued me, this strange amalgamation of nations and cultures that formed this supposedly elite fighting force of men. How did that work exactly? I still didn't entirely see how a Belarusian and a South Korean could fight alongside each other for France, especially when they both barely spoke a word of French. All I knew was that I wanted to be a part of it, and I owed it to myself to finish basic training.

There was the usual hustle and bustle of the Caporals and Sergeants ordering us around and us engagé volontaires running back and forth with equipment and making last minute changes to our gear. We finally embarked into the JBC's with our heavy packs (around thirty kilograms of weight) and they took us high into the Pyrenees mountains where we were rewarded with fantastic views of distant snowy peaks and the flat plains far below. Chef Raynaud of course would be leading the march.

One curveball we had to contend with was the 12.7mm Browning machine guns that had been given in two pieces, each along with their solid steel tripods to carry on top of our own gear. The guns weighed around forty kilos each but it wasn't so bad when you consider that there were around forty-five of us to carry them, each man taking his turn for a few minutes.

The preparations we had done had always been marches of a few hours at the farm. Now, however, the terrain was steeper, and Raynaud seemed to have set a demonic speed. It wasn't long before there were a few stragglers at the back, and for once, Hughes wasn't the last one. An Italian guy, who claimed to have been in the Italian parachute regiment, had been struggling physically from day one. Stupidly, he had got French Foreign Legion tattoos before joining the legion, and upon their discovery, had been a favourite go-to for the caporals to harass.

If Merino was the 'bad cop', Goldberg was certainly the 'good cop'- being our favourite for he was the only caporal that treated us like human beings. Even he however, had lost patience with the Italian.

On the second morning, Chef Raynaud had halted the section to see what was taking so long. He strode back down the column past me to ask Goldberg what the hell was going on. Goldberg was at the rear with the limping Italian, apparently with blisters so painful they prevented him from marching.

'Hey!' The Chef barked, 'You will keep up or you will quit, I don't give a fuck which but you will not delay me for another minute is that clear?'

'But Chef, my blisters -' The Italian began, obviously forgetting that beginning any sentence with 'but' when addressing someone higher ranking than yourself is a bad idea. 'I don't give a shit!' Raynaud shouted. 'That's it, you quit right now because a pussy like you doesn't deserve to be a legionnaire!' The chef glared down at him and the Italian visibly quailed under his gaze.

'Ask me. Ask me to become a civilian.' Raynaud glared down at the Italian for a moment as most of the section had stopped to look back at the spectacle.

The Italian raised a hand and stammered, 'I wish to become a civilian, Sergeant Chef.'

'Good. Now get the fuck out of my sight.' And that was that. The Chef turned on his heel, not giving the Italian another glance and strode back to the front of the column. The Italian himself was embarked onto one of the JBC's and whisked away to Castel to begin the signing out process.

Progress was quicker after that. After two long and hard days marching under good weather conditions and fifty kilometres later, we had arrived at the old fort; our destination. In typical fashion, we had no time to rest. Instead, we had to change into our formal dress uniforms that had been loaded into the trucks beforehand for the ceremony. The colonel hadn't arrived yet, so once ready, we were given a little time to practice our legionnaire code d'honneur.

When the colonel arrived, we assembled in a field in front of the little fort. He gave us a long speech, of which I understood less than half, but got the gist that he was explaining to us the gravity of becoming a legionnaire; telling us the responsibility that would be upon our shoulders now that we wore the Kepi, to uphold the standards of the Legion and congratulate us for completing the first step of our careers.

Then it was up to us to chant as a unit the code d'honneur from memory. We shouted into the silence of the still afternoon with the Colonel and our instructors watching, finishing with, 'Legio Patria Nostra!', 'the Legion our homeland'. Words I have since had tattooed on my skin. Then, we put the kepis on our heads for the first time, knowing we had earned them.

Afterwards, we congratulated each other, shaking hands and smiling tiredly. In a month, I had made friends, and perhaps an enemy or two, learned how to handle a rifle, experienced hunger and fatigue like I had never known in my comfortable life in England and had begun to understand a little of the ethos that made up this mysterious army. There was no room here for weakness, and the highest level of discipline was demanded from recruits.

# CHAPTER 3

Though the Kepi march was complete, training was far from being over. There were another three months left before we would have to choose a regiment to go to. Yet it was with relief that we trudged back into Castelnaudary, fewer though we were. At Castel of course there is a lot of singing, 'chants' as we called them, in the Legion. I suppose I had a kind of love hate relationship with the singing because, on the one hand it was rich in the Legion's history, but on the other it was often used as a punishment. Now that we were Legionnaires back at Castel, we were finally given some insight into the Legion's history.

The French Foreign Legion was created on the 10th of March, 1831 by King Louis Phillipe of France with a dual purpose: to increase the French army's numbers (to aid with the great colonisation missions of the French royalty) and be a solution to the swell of migrants in mainland France by recruiting them. The Legion's first deployment was in the same year of its foundation and was sent to Algeria to aid with the colonisation efforts there.

Being comprised of foreign troops, the Legion was often used on the front lines; more expendable to the French army as it was preferred to sacrifice foreigners to Frenchmen. This bred a tough and disciplined culture within the legion. Some of its more iconic deployments are the Crimean War, the War of Indo-China, World Wars one and two, the Algerian War for independence, the conflicts of Iraq and Afghanistan and, of course, the current conflict in Mali, northern Africa.

During World War II, the Legion had various duties such as guarding transport ships as well as fighting in the Syria-Lebanon campaign. It was here where the 6th foreign infantry regiment of the Legion clashed with the 13th D.B.L.E, another Legion regiment, resulting in the 6ème REI being disbanded in 1941.

In the aftermath of the war, there were many German soldiers hoping to escape prosecution or to begin afresh. Many volunteered themselves to the Legion, knowing they would receive a new identity. Even today, there are many things that embody the spirit of these German soldiers in the Legion. For example, many of the songs (the best, in my opinion) are sung entirely in German and are incredibly catchy. Also, there are some German words that were incorporated into 'Legion-French' and that are still used today such as 'Archtung'.

Other universal words in 'Legion-French' are kurwa, blyat and suca which are all Polish or Russian swearwords; a result of the influx of eastern Europeans in more recent years. Popular phrases include 'j'ai plein les couilles' (my balls are full), 'je m'en branle' (I don't give a fuck) and, 'même pas la peine' (I don't even know what to say/it's not even worth bothering). If one were to walk into a Legion base one would undoubtedly hear some of these several times a minute. In fact, it might not be entirely inaccurate to estimate that a good fifty percent of communication between young legionnaires is comprised entirely of these words and phrases.

I would learn more on the history later, but as anyone can see, it is rich, interesting and often depicted in the traditional songs or chants. The songs tell the stories of the Legion; the little book of chants that each legionnaire is given is almost like a history book if you know what you're looking at. I suppose that's why I have never felt prouder of my service in the legion than when I sang in unison with fifty other men during my training at Castel - fifty strong voices reverberating deep tones off the buildings to the iconic slow rhythm of the Legion's march. We could spend four solid hours crammed into a little room, singing together, with a Caporal supervising us, ensuring that we weren't slacking off. At Castel of course, we had to sing on the way to the canteen and back or, if Merino felt like it, we would march around the barracks singing at the top of our lungs for a time.

The songs were also a good way to learn French. I translated some of them into English whenever I had free time. My favourite is probably 'Les Lansquenets,' it's a chant about 16th century German foot soldiers and mercenaries and their noble fighting code.

We settled back into the routine at Castel with all the usual bullshit. The Caporals would find new and interesting ways to punish us, and despite having done a month together at the farm, the section still felt very fractured. The fact that certain things tended to go missing every now and again didn't help the cohesion of the section. Whether that was theft or simply guys misplacing their belongings I couldn't say for sure, but I had my suspicions. I had myself 'misplaced' one or two things during the farm and wasn't entirely convinced that someone hadn't taken my gear to replace their own. The Legion is famous for recruiting petty criminals after all, so I kept my eyes open.

To my dismay, I had to share a wardrobe with the Polish guy, Maleski again. We argued constantly as to who ought to have the middle shelf in broken French and how everything ought to be arranged for the Sergeants' review. Maleski wasn't the only one I was at odds with, however. Mattei had not forgotten me and seemed to have taken a liking to calling me names every chance he got. Whenever he got a chance, passing me in the hallway or waiting in line for the canteen, he would say something like, 'Dempsey, you are useless man. Go home!' and sneer at me. If I'm completely honest, I didn't quite know how to react half the time and did nothing. Clearly he saw me as a victim, as easy pickings. I was the youngest in the entire section and the most baby-faced and, at the time, I had the slight frame of a runner, such as my training had been before the legion.

I had chosen to ignore it and do nothing, thinking that I didn't want to cause trouble in the section and be punished for fighting. Looking back that was a mistake. Every day Mattei would become bolder with his insults, hoping to provoke me and enjoying it when he got a reaction out of me.

'You are a useless fucker man, you need to ask to become a civilian because you're gonna be a shitty soldier.' Eventually it started to get to me more and more. I realised my tactic was not working. I had to do something; I wasn't going to be humiliated for the next three months.

Things came to a head a week later in the showers. The section was taken for sport in the morning and then had to run upstairs to the barracks to shower quickly before the next activity. If you were fast, you could get to the front of the queue and be out before everyone else. The showers themselves were five cubicles with no doors. The guys lined up in front of the cubicles to shower while the ones at the back yelled for the ones at the front to hurry the fuck up.

One morning after our usual run, I had hopped upstairs, stripped, and headed to the showers wearing only a towel and my flipflops. Mattei had beaten me there. He stood scrubbing himself, taking his sweet old time and laughing, 'you can fucking wait for me man! I'm gonna use all the hot water haha!'

I tutted, clenching my teeth, waiting for him to eventually get bored. Finally, he finished and stood in the doorway blocking my path.

'What? You want to use the shower? Ha!'

Sighing in exasperation, I tried to move past him, but he moved to cut me off.

'No no no! Not today! No shower for you.' He guffawed. I tried to move around the other side, but he blocked me again. The other guys waiting were silent, looking on in interest.

'Just let me through.' I said, trying to squeeze past him a third time.

'I said no!' He shouted, and shoved me, sending me flying into the wall behind with a thud.

That's when I saw red and snapped. Getting up, I yelled and charged at him with my hands outstretched. Mattei only had a moment to look surprised before my fingers had found his throat and shoving him up against the back of the cubicle, my rage gave me a new strength. Despite him being broader than I, he was unable to push me off him and was soon spluttering and clawing at my face, trying to shake my grip free. I wouldn't relent, and tightened my grip, squeezing the soft tissue, my fingers a vice around his neck.

Somewhere along the line, I had lost my towel, leaving me stark bollock naked, trying to choke the life out of this guy. I know I wouldn't have stopped had it not been for some of the others trying to pull me away, seeing that I was going a little too far and not wanting to be punished for letting me kill one of the other recruits.

It took three of them to hold me back and I was still cursing Mattei as he slumped to the floor, coughing and gasping for breath, his wide eyes clearly illustrating his shock. 'You're... *cough*... crazy man, you're... *cough*... fucking crazy!' I went back to my room to cool off. Mattei didn't bother me for the rest of basic training, hell, he didn't even look in my direction. I hope the look in my eyes scared him when I had my hands around his throat.

But it could all have been avoided if I had just punched him in the mouth the first time he had said something. Or done something along those lines. Maybe that was the lesson to be learned here.

In the ranking system of the French army, each rank has a symbol that, along with a name tag and a regimental patch, are velcroed onto your combat fatigues. Legionnaires have no symbol, just a bare patch of velcro. Only from the rank of 'premiere classe' does one receive a patch, a single diagonal green line. Perhaps for Legionnaires, the absence of any patch serves as a reminder that we are the lowest of the low, the very bottom rung of the Legion and to keep us humble. It certainly made us more vulnerable in a sense.

There was a Sergeant who joined the section a few weeks after the farm to replace a colleague. He was Romanian with a short enough temper and was quickly none too popular. On Sundays however, his attitude was different. Sundays were still the best days of the week, there were fewer instructors and no planned activities for the evening meaning we might even have a calm few hours of peace, depending on the Caporal on duty of course. This Romanian Sergeant gave us a speech one Sunday telling us that he was incredibly pleased with our progress and wanted to reward us, much to our bewilderment. Very graciously, he had offered to drive his car to a local takeaway and buy the entire section a kebab (which we would have to pay for of course). Excited chatter broke out in the hallway as all of us were always hungry and there was always a very strict ban on having extra food in the barracks.

'Sergeant kebab', as he soon became known, gave us leave to take cash out of our new French bank accounts at the cash point next to the canteen whilst someone else made a list of how many kebabs and drinks were needed. It wasn't until he had returned with the food and we had to pay him that I realised what his angle was. A kebab is around four euros each, he charged us eight. Let's imagine that most of us had two, being the hungry legionnaires that we were, which is about seventy in total. Sergeant kebab had just made almost three hundred euros from us, excluding any profit made on the drinks. Not bad for an hour's work. Being the lowly Legionnaires that we were, the prospect of questioning the methods of Sergeant Kebab's profits was a daunting one.

However, nobody said anything. We were happy just to eat. Nor do I think anyone would have said anything even if they had been particularly upset. One thing you don't want to do as a legionnaire is report a sous-officier for misconduct; your life would become immeasurably more miserable. My point is that it is easy for people in power to exploit those without and in the Legion, it was doubly so. It happened all the time but there was often nothing we could do about it. Perhaps that is just the way of the world.

The four months seemed to roll by slowly, the seasons changed, the air grew colder, and the sun climbed into the sky a little later in the morning. We, of course, were often awake long before it had made its first appearance. The Caporals and Sergeants hadn't seemed to ease up on us at all, and I remember feeling depressed during the last half of instruction. I was young, had all my freedom taken away, and often found myself with a guy, screaming in my face in a foreign language because my running shorts had a crease in them that morning. Even the 'Quartier Libre', orguy- a period of a few hours every couple of months when we were allowed into the town centre - seemed more trouble than it was worth. We had to iron to perfection our formal dress uniform and have it ready for inspection the day before.

Merino, the bastard, had found that the pleats on my chemise didn't quite align and to my horror had dunked it into a bucket full of water before my eyes, grinning all the while. I would have to start again. And so, I stayed up until 3am that night, having to wait for one of the two ironing boards that my room shared, and worked away with a head torch until it was pristine. I didn't want to be the guy that missed out on a rare QL because his shirt wasn't good enough.

Not only that but we were constantly tested, every week we had to do the standard fitness tests: running, swimming, the obstacle course, pull ups and push ups. The instructors usually threatened us with the prospect of having to stay at Castel an extra month if we failed to meet their requirements. For me, it wasn't a great worry because I was comfortably within the time constraints, but Hughes and I were often together and he had without a doubt, the worst physique in the entire section, and I was often punished by proxy. Hughes seemed to do nothing to help his case either, paying regularly the hefty price of ten euros per chocolate bar somehow smuggled into the barracks by the Russian mafia that kept his bodyweight at an excessive amount. It annoyed me, too, that despite me telling him he needed to wake up and get his act together, day by day he seemed to lose interest in keeping his fatigues clean and neat. The items in his wardrobe well-arranged did nothing to help his current standing within the section. Merino had an unhealthy fascination with Hughes, baiting him on a daily basis, loving the grimace he would receive when he made Hughes scrub the toilets with camouflage on his face and his marching pack on his back.

We were camping once out in the forest for some combat drills, and Hughes being Hughes had failed to complete some task. So, Merino set the two of us to doing press-ups with our rifles on top of our hands as I had the misfortune to be in the vicinity. Merino eventually allowed me to get up and waved me away with a hand.

'Go on Dempsey.' He had said, his full attention already turning to the panting Hughes. Merino then switched to English so Hughes could better understand him.

'You can't even do ten press-ups Hughes, you're so fat!' Merino began to apply pressure to Hughes rifle, still resting on Hughes's hands with his boot.

'Come on fat boy, up and down, up and down!' Merino laughed all the while and I think that's what finally sent Hughes over the edge.

Yelling, he got to his feet, and with a similar look in his eye to the one I must have had when trying to throttle Mattei, Hughes threw his rifle into the mud, barrel first, and lunged at Merino, who dodged with an excited whoop, finally having achieved his goal of goading him into doing something stupid. The already out of breath Hughes chased Merino through the woods, much to the amusement of the rest of the section, who had stopped the combat drills they were doing to watch in fascination, as the cackling Merino easily outran Hughes. Dodging behind trees and skipping this way and that, laughing all the more at the enraged state of Hughes as he stumbled after him, chasing with little success. It was like watching a rabbit dart around a seal.

The charade didn't stop until Chef Raynaud strode over and ordered an end to the nonsense. He demanded to know what was going on and, when he had learned what Hughes had done with his rifle, he turned purple. In the seventh article of the code d'honneur it is stated that a Legionnaire will never abandon his weapon, much less throw it into the dirt barrel first. It was an inadmissible blunder, and from that day on, Hughes would become a shell of his former self. He was assigned every guard duty, every cleaning duty, made to run around with his rifle above his head while everyone else walked, clean the already spotless toilets until 2am and a whole host of other wonderfully imaginative punishments Merino could think up. To be around Hughes was to make your life more complicated than it needed to be, so I stopped, not wanting to be roped into guarding the corridor of the barracks all night.

Towards the end of instruction, the section was taken for a week's training in the Pyrenees mountains where the Legion has a chalet. It turned out to be the best week of basic training by a long way. One day, a friendly adjutant chef even took us canyoning in a large gorge pitted with pools and waterfalls. We jumped from one pool to another with great splashes and turned to watch the other guys follow. Everyone splashed around laughing, and for once none of the caporals told us to shut up. We were well fed at the chalet, too, and were actually allowed to finish the meals and we only had to clean the toilets twice per day! But the best thing was the pay phone in the chalet that we were permitted to use for short periods of time. There was always a long queue, but I was determined to call home. When it was finally my turn, I pushed in the required coins and dialled the landline number to my childhood home back in Halifax, praying there was someone in, even if it was my brother. 'Hello?' a voice answered.

'Mum? Its me!'

'H-Harry? Is it really you? God I was so worried!' It was the first time I had spoken to her since I had left for France and I had no idea the next time we spoke would be almost four months later. We spoke very briefly, as the guy behind me was already tapping his foot and tutting with impatience. I told her I was fine and asked if anything had changed at home and she said everything was just as it was when I left. That comforted me. It seemed so long ago and like so much had happened already. I had met many people and learned so much but home was still the same, and it would be waiting for me when I got back. We said our goodbyes and I passed the phone along to the next guy, my spirits lifted.

Back at Castel the end of our four months of basic training was in sight. Of the ten or so other sections going through instruction, ours was now among the 'oldest'. I had met a few of the other rare anglophones there at the time, and we'd call out in greeting to each other in the queue canteen before our Caporals swore at us to stop fraternizing. We saw the other sections load the trucks with equipment and ship out to the farm, apprehensive looks on their camouflaged faces. When we saw the section ahead of ours have its passing out ceremony, we knew that our time would come in a couple of weeks. It was relieving to know that we were almost done, and the hope of a better life in our chosen regiment was tantalisingly close.

I was still undecided as to which regiment I wanted to spend the next four and a half years of my life, understanding perfectly how big a decision it would be. In the Legion, the combat regiments were 1ère REC-cavalry, 1ère REG-combat engineers, 2ème REP-parachutists, 2ème REI-infantry, 2ème REG-combat engineers, 3ème REI-infantry and 13ème DBLE-infantry. Sometimes however, places weren't always available for each regiment, 3ème REI was based in French Guyana,

South America, and the Legion only accepted candidates at certain times of the year for example, or, at least when I had joined, the 13ème DBLE was based in Mayotte, and was a cushy deployment, more of a reward that anything else. Because I wanted to be infantry, my choices were 2ème REI or 2ème REP.

2ème REP was based in Calvi, northern Corsica which made travelling to and from the mainland complicated, whereas 2ème REI was based in Nimes, much more practical. Plus, I liked the idea of being infantry, it just seemed like the right choice for me. During the last few weeks, I made friends with a Serbian in my room called Romaric. We had recently found that we were able to communicate in an albeit crude manner, having discovered that our French had improved sufficiently over the last few months. We discussed our choices and had both seemed to come to the same conclusion of 2ème REI. I knew Bailey and Steinrod had both chosen 2ème REG, the combat engineering regiment well known for its mountaineering training courses (it even had its own section of mountain commandos...). Steinrod, having come from the mountainous city of Boulder, Colorado, liked the idea of skiing in the Alps. But I wasn't entirely sure Bailey had ever seen any real snow, so maybe that was enough to sway him!

Before all this however, we had the 'raid march.' This was the final test before the passing out ceremony and consisted of a several-day march, twice as long as the Kepi march (around one hundred kilometres in total) with half practical, half theory tests at the end. I remember being more apprehensive at the time, but really, if you can do a two-day timed march, you can most likely do a three- or four-day timed march too. On top of the revision we had to do for the tests, we had to practice our chanting for the passing out ceremony along with a lot of ironing of our dress uniform. They kept us cooped up in a little room again for hours on end, singing the same chant over and over until our heads hurt and our throats were sore.

One thing I had noticed towards the end was that the guys had tended to argue less, and whether that was because we were finally starting to learn to work together and accept people of different cultures or because we were simply becoming accustomed to being stressed and under pressure, I couldn't say, but at least it felt somewhat like a military unit - even if it were a totally bizarre one.

At least with the language barrier somewhat lifted, we could all laugh together. Fuchs, the ex-German paratrooper, who always seemed to have a big grin on his face no matter the circumstances, was the first to make me laugh. He spoke good English too, but he really was a little crazy. Most of us were sad to see him go when he broke his ankle and was deemed unfit for military service. At least he was able to leave for Germany with his head held high not having quit.

Another slightly whacky character was Solo: an Algerian who had joined the Legion because he had been visited by a spirit at night who had told him to. That narrative appeared to fit because he always seemed so reluctant to do anything, as if he were not here of his own free will.

Horvath too was interesting; a short stocky Hungarian who had served five and a half years in a Hungarian prison for armed robbery. Whatever our stories, whether we were tall, short, brown, black or white, we had had seen each other every single day for the last four months of our new lives. Because of this, it was comforting to see these same faces and to hear the regular string of Legion swearwords, 'kurwa! J'ai pleine les couilles blyat', especially when the instructors planned some new and uncomfortable experiences to test us. We had become a unit that created, at least the impression of, a functional section.

We would march together one last time for the raid. In the days before, the atmosphere in the section was jovial as we knew things would be over in a week, one way or the other. Merino had found fewer excuses to punish us, so he invented them instead, but even that seemed to affect us less. When we did the usual sprints up and down the stairs to the assembly point, instead of shoving and shouting at one another in frustration, we began to laugh at the silliness of it all. After Merino someone eating in the room, the corridors of the barracks filled with giggling legionnaires in press up position for thirty minutes at a time.

When we began the march, I was even in a positive mood, for all that was left to do was put one foot in front of the other and enjoy the beautiful French countryside. The Autumnal rains were upon us and we were damp from intermittent showers. The leaves had a lovely golden-brown hue to them and dropped from the trees to fall majestically to the ground. There is one thing I remember quite distinctly during this march: the section was in single file on the side of a road, climbing yet another peak in the Pyrenees, when some civilian hikers passed us and, from one of the women among them, I smelled a whiff of perfume.

It was quite surreal, for the last five months or so, I had barely seen a girl, let alone spoken to or been in close proximity with one. When I smelled the perfume, my brain remembered a long-lost memory. 'Oh, I thought, so that's what women smell like!' Back in the civilian world I wouldn't have thought twice about it, but apparently I had been taking the presence of women for granted. It's funny how vivid a memory like that one is; in some ways it was like a breath of fresh air, a window into the rest of the world and the reality that this was not everything, that there was life outside of my training in the Legion. But for the moment, it might as well not have existed. It would be some time before I was allowed to roam free away from the constant supervision of the Caporals.

The march went without incident, at least until the last night. When at the campsite, Chef Raynaud had chosen someone who had been taking a shit in the woods at the wrong time and hadn't shown up for the assembly when it was called. And so, during a torrential downpour, we did squats with our rifles above our heads, rather than set up our tarpaulins for the night. Needless to say, everything was soaked in the morning for the march.

The weather was good the next day, and with the rapid pace of Chef Raynaud, we dried relatively quickly. The Chef, apparently having had a large breakfast and a good night's sleep, made us run the last few kilometres with our heavy marching packs. Only a handful of us managed to remain in his wake when we reached the end. The destination was a castle on a hillside somewhere, and tourists watched on in interest as a group of camouflaged legionnaires came running into the courtyard panting. I dropped my pack and sat down heavily on it to wait, congratulating my friends with a smile as they trickled in. Raynaud had given us the opportunity to rest, eat, drink and enjoy the view of the castle and the hills before we headed back to Castel.

We had to complete the theory tests in a fatigued state, but before I knew it, they were over. Soon we were showering back in the barracks, before practicing for the passing out ceremony the next day, asking each other which questions we'd fucked up as we scrubbed off. In the morning, we put on our dress uniforms and, before everyone was ordered out and into formation on the place d'arme, Romaric and I checked each other's ties, vests and shoes to make certain they were faultless. We cleared our throats before roaring the chant as we marched to the centre of the parade ground, our voices reverberating off the buildings and filling the still morning air. To be a part of it, forty something men singing in deep tones in perfect unison, felt quite incredible. I felt proud and, suddenly, it all felt worth it; all the sleepless nights and arguments and hunger - this was what it was for.

Of the fifty of us that had begun the training months ago, several had dropped out during the farm and several more in the training. We finished as forty-three, and that was after seven or eight had been weeded out before the training began. It was a long way to have come.

We came to a halt in silence before the same colonel that had given us the speech after the Kepi march some months before. Turning to him with a crisp stomp, he gave us another long-winded speech, of which I understood considerably more this time. Finishing, he congratulated us and we were dismissed, marching back the way we had come, chanting all the while.

There was one last thing to do before we left, we had to formally submit our choice for our future regiments. The often-absent lieutenant and the formidable Chef Raynaud summoned us, one by one, into the office to sit before them to discuss how we had done over the last four months and where we would like to be sent afterward. I told the lieutenant 2ème REI, infantry. After he looked me up and down, he said, 'Okay Dempsey, do you have any questions?'

'No, Lieutenant.'

'Very well. Dismissed!' So that was that, I thought leaving the room. The next few years of my life would be at Nimes, on the southern coast of France. I was okay with that.

We were allowed in the club that night. Every compagnie in every regiment has its own club - a kind of bar and rec room for all ranks to have a coffee during work, or a beer after. It was the first time we had been inside to relax, (I had cleaned it top to bottom a few times of course) and we cracked open a few beers and drank with our instructors, who were actually congratulating us! Even Merino had a beer in his hand and came over to cheers me, which I returned through narrowed eyes, half expecting it to be some kind of trick before he made me run around the building. 'Relax Dempsey, I won't make you do any more push ups today! Maybe there will be time in the morning…'

I wondered lying in bed that night what my life would be like when I got to regiment. Better, surely? It couldn't get much worse than this; in the cramped barracks with the caporals screaming in our faces for the slightest misdemeanour. I was optimistic, I think, and quite ready to move on to the next chapter, to see what the French Foreign Legion had in store for me next...

# CHAPTER 4

Sometimes life just doesn't go to plan. Romaric, myself and the others who had chosen 2ème Regiment Éntrangère d'Infanterie in Nimes, were getting the last of our things ready the day before the bus would take us, when a Caporal called us into an office where the Lieutenant was waiting. We all piled in one after the other, each giving the typical formal presentation rapidly, as the Lieutenant watched us impassively.

Once we were all present, he cleared his throat and said, 'unfortunately all the places to 2REI have been cancelled, you will all be going to different regiments instead.' I couldn't believe it, the one thing over which I had any say had just been yanked from under my feet. He began reading from a list of our names and our designated regiments. 'Romaric, 2REG, Dobson, 2REG...' At least Romaric and I would be together. When the lieutenant had finished giving each of us our new regiments, he said, 'report to your groups for the bus tomorrow. Dismissed.' And just like that, fate had sent us on a different course. Outside, Romaric and I exchanged a knowing glance. It was typical of the Legion - our careers would now be entirely different, and not out of choice, without so much as an explanation.

Nevertheless, I didn't dwell long on my misfortune, knowing that there are some factors that are simply out of my control. I decided, instead, to look at the silver lining. Bailey and Steinrod were also going to 2REG, so at least I would also have some good friends. Also, because it was a mountain regiment, it sounded interesting; I had skied in the Alps before and was taken with the stunning views of the epic landscape.

The bus took us all back to Aubagne first, the mother regiment, before we would be separated. It was strange being back after four months, and everyone peered curiously out of the window to see if we could spot the potential recruits who were in the same position as we had been, what seemed like a lifetime ago. The Caporals were quick to inform us that it was forbidden to talk to them. Anyone who broke this rule would incur serious punishments for the entire section.

Now that we were all Legionnaires, custom dictated that we must all pass by the Legion museum to see its history, along with the fabled wooden hand of Capitaine Danjou. He had lost his real hand when his musket exploded and designed the prosthetic one himself.

Capitaine Danjou had been an officer in the Legion during the latter half of the 19th century. He had commanded the sixty-five legionnaires when they faced off a Mexican army of almost two thousand on the 30th April, 1863. This was the battle of Camerone in Mexico, a defining moment in the history of the French Foreign Legion.

The sixty-five Legionnaires were beset upon by a vast Mexican force and were besieged in a farmhouse near the town of Camerone. During the eight-hour battle, the sixty-five legionnaires were killed almost to a man, the dead including Capitaine Danjou. But they put up such a stalwart defence that the Mexican commander implored the remaining three to surrender and lay down their arms. When he saw their number, he said, 'That's all what is left? These aren't men, they are devils!' The three of them, having put up such a defence, the Mexicans believed they had numbered many more. Supposedly, the Mexican commander had been so impressed the last three had refused to give up their weapons, he had let them leave with their lives and even fed and watered them.

The wooden hand of Capitaine Danjou had been collected and brought back to France, where it sits in a glass box for the Legionnaires to see in the museum. The battle of Camerone epitomised the attitude of the Legion - fighting to the death and refusing surrender, or at least it did back then. I'd like to believe a modern force of Legionnaires would give a similarly spectacular performance, but perhaps I'm being too optimistic.

In any case, the battle of Camerone is an especially important part of the Legion's history. So much so, that every year on the 30th of April, every regiment celebrates the event by opening its gates to family for several days and holds a parade, along with games and activities. Several boxing matches can be expected to occur, as they were always very popular, during which an incalculable amount of alcohol is consumed.

But we didn't know that yet. When we were outside there wasn't even time to say goodbye before new Caporals from our respective regiments began screaming at us to get our stuff and get on the different buses. We pulled away from Aubagne not having had the chance to bid farewell to the men that had been our lives for four months.

2ème Regiment Étrangère de Genie is part of the French army's mountain brigade. The 'Brigade de Montagne' is made up of seven regiments, including 2REG; the others being French regular regiments. The brigades are deployed together for tours of duty, but other than that, we rarely crossed paths with them back in France. Nor did it help that we at 2REG were the furthest from the mountains than any of the other mountain regiments. Truth be told, when we arrived, I was a little disappointed to find that the terrain was more hilly than mountainous, having imagined we would be based on some snowy peak somewhere. Still, at roughly one thousand metres of altitude, it got cold enough in the winter.

The base was a kilometre away from the small village of Saint Christol, and around an hour and a half from Avignon, the nearest substantial city. Essentially, we were in the middle of nowhere, and had only each other and sheep to console us. It became a bit of a running joke that the Legionnaires on the base would have to look to the sheep if they were lonely, for there were no single girls for miles around.

Until recent years, each Legion base had its own brothel with sex workers that were regularly checked by the regimental doctor for infections. All of the officers knew the legionnaires would go out on the weekend to the 'bordels', anyway. They figured if they're going to do it, they might as well be safe. A fantastic idea if you ask me. Unfortunately for us however, the wife of a colonel had taken offence in the late '90s and had demanded that her husband abolish them all. Clearly, she had not sympathised with the Legionnaires difficulties.

The base itself was once an old nuclear missile silo built in the '80s and had been repurposed to be a mountain regiment in the '90s. Everything was neat when we entered the gates. We were met with the pristine place d'arme, which dominates the main space before the administration buildings. It has well-trimmed bushes that form the shape of the flaming grenade and no stray leaves or pine needles were left about to create unsightly litter on the roads. The words 'honneur et fidelité' are written in big bold letters on the administration building where the 'Chef de Corps', the commander of the regiment, has his office.

There are always armed guards on the gate, twenty-four seven, and they eyed us with interest as we took in the surroundings of our new home. We were taken to our new lodgings where we were told we would be housed during our month and a half of 'instruction', during which we would specialise to become combat engineers.

Strangely enough, one of my clearest memories upon entering the rooms was that there must have been some kind of mistake. We had a single bed each, not bunks, and there were only four of us to a room - not ten or twelve - and each of us had three metal wardrobes for our things! I relayed this to the Caporal, disbelieving that we had all this to ourselves. He frowned at me and confirmed all of it is for us and that every room in the regiment is the same.

I remember literally almost weeping with joy. I had been sharing half a wardrobe and a bunk with a difficult Polish guy for four months, and something so small as having my own little space to use at my will was so incredibly relieving, it is hard to put into words.

We had arrived late on Friday, so going out on the weekend was not an option. Bailey, Steinrod and I stayed in our room and watched films on the laptop Steinrod had gotten back after it had been confiscated four months earlier. Gorging ourselves on shitty food from the foyer, the regimental shop and bar on the base, we revelled in our first weekend of freedom. Free from any Caporals or Sergeants telling us what to do. It felt fantastic. Apparently, I had been taking for granted the ability to put my feet up and do bugger all before the Legion. Some of the built-up stress of the last four months slipped away, as I had my first unbroken sleep in a long time.

It would not last long, however, for the following Monday we were broken into a new routine. We began what was called CP04 - the training course for combat engineering. There were several classes on the regiment doing this at any one time, with around ten legionnaires in each. We had a Belgian sergeant, Dufour, and a Belarusian Caporal to harass us daily to learn the ins and outs of basic 'genie' practice. We learned about clearing minefields, how to place minefields, rescuing stuck vehicles, clearing roads of IED's, how to look out for booby traps and the use of military explosives.

Everyone agreed that the explosives training was the best. The regiment, being ten kilometres square, had its own explosives 'shooting range,' in which we would practice the different chains Sergeant Dufour had taught us in the classrooms. We would light the fuse under careful supervision and then turn our backs on the primed charge, as the flammable chord hissed and spat with sparks, then walk calmly away; running on the explosives range was forbidden. Once we were at a safe distance, the carefully measured fuse would detonate the several kilos of explosives we had set that would send a great mushroom of black smoke into the air, along with a 'boom,' shaking the ground. I couldn't help grinning the first few times we did this.

The ten of us had revision in the classroom until 20:00 after 'soup' (as dinner was called) and we'd chat in the classroom or mess around a bit until our reluctant instructor, Dufour, showed up to supervise us. Unlike Castel, however, after 20:00 we were left to our own devices most nights to drink in the foyer, relax or meet any of the other legionnaires doing their CP04. Whilst I was still very conscious of being on the bottom rung, I certainly had a greater sense of freedom.

In some respects, joining the army is like being born again. Going through basic training, you are akin to (or perhaps even worse off than) a baby, in the sense that you will eat only when you are told, you will shit only when you are told, you will be exactly where your superiors demand that you be and be doing exactly what they order you to do at all times. Your life is essentially not your own. When you become a Caporal after several years, you progress to infancy. You can just about shit when you want, but you will still eat when you are told. Becoming Sergeant is the equivalent of adolescence - you can use the toilet anytime, eat whenever you want, or don't. Oh, and you'll still have to do as you're told, but at that rank some guys might choose to interpret some orders differently. The officers then, are the adults, telling everyone else what they must do.

Learning now felt much easier. Everything was still in French of course, but now I felt as though I could understand a greater portion of it. My friend Romaric had quickly found the Serbian mafia on the base. But when I hung out with them, we were able to communicate in French now, at least to a certain extent. Unfortunately, not everyone progressed at the same rate. In our group, there was a lovely South Korean chap named Na, who had real difficulty with French. We were friends for the whole five years, but even at the end it seemed as though he had barely progressed past the basics. It can't be easy learning French when your first language is Korean. There was Angarag, too - a Mongolian who had been in my section for basic training who had been another favourite of Merino because he had such a poor understanding of the orders in French. He would often look around gormlessly and blank eyed until Merino's malicious eyes had found him.

I'm sure any linguist would have a field day on a Legion base. There is a certain crude uniqueness to the Legion's version of French, usually with a heavy eastern European accent, that is far more satisfying to use than the proper version. I heard a good story about a group of Legionnaires kicking down the door to a known arms dealer's house in central Africa whilst shouting, 'Armee Francais blyat!' 'Blyat' being a Russian swearword meaning 'fuck.' The image of a group of Eastern Europeans battering down your door and shouting at you in French, whilst insulting you in Russian, is an incongruous but comical one. French is surely better this way.

Before our first weekend out of the regiment, all the new Legionnaires had to pass a 'review de tenue' to ensure our formal dress was pristine. If they weren't good enough, they would, of course, be dunked into a bucket of water. It also became a habit each Friday to be made to run around the barracks as a group several times for some minor infraction until we were sweaty and agitated. We would only have several more weekends of having to leave in formal dress, however.

In 2015, the people of France had lived through the Charlie Hebdo terrorist attacks, in which two gunmen had slaughtered twelve people for mocking the prophet Muhammed in a newspaper cartoon. On the 13th of November of the same year, whilst I was in CP04, there were a series of coordinated attacks, during which shootings and bomb blasts had killed one hundred and thirty and critically injured hundreds of others. This caused the French government to call for a 'state of emergency.' French troops would be sent to patrol cities, airports and train stations in an attempt to dissuade any further attacks. One side effect of this was that no French troops were allowed to be in military dress outside of the base, unless working or under special circumstances.

2016 held yet more terrorist attacks. Eighty-six people were killed by a nineteen-tonne truck as it ploughed through crowds on the Nice promenade on Bastille day. The Islamic State claimed responsibility for all of them, and their rapid rise to power in the Middle East was a worrying surprise to much of Europe. IS had begun to acquire territory in Syria, and from watching the news, I would see it grow over the coming months. It seemed to all of us watching from 2REG that the world was changing, and France's enemies were growing bolder by the day.

I awaited the end of CP04 with anticipation, hoping that perhaps life would improve a little more now that I had finished all the standard training required. When I got to the '2ème Compagnie du Combat,' however, I was sorely disappointed. I was in a room with two Caporals. I, of course, had to do all the cleaning, and was too often reprimanded for the smallest things; my mere presence seemed to irritate them. I found it easier not to be in there and went, instead, to the compagnie's club after work hours to drink with Bailey.

To my dismay, the days were filled, just like at basic training, with menial tasks, such as de-weeding the compagnies place d'arme with a teaspoon or cleaning the toilets for the fourth time that day. I remember a Romanian guy that spoke pretty good English tell me that the first two years of a Legionnaire's life is shit.

'You mean I have another year and a half of this?' I had asked him.

He laughed and said, 'at least!'

So now, I was a Legionnaire in the 2ème Compagnie du Combat of 2ème REG. But what was life actually like? Well, I have scrubbed many a square kilometre of surfaces during my career, most of which I have done in the 2ème compagnie. Even if everything was clean, we would clean again. Unless you were a Caporal or a Premiere Classe, you could safely bet that you would be roped into doing all the shit jobs. Often, it seemed as though we did most of them just to fill the day, so we wouldn't be sat on our arses-which I would have preferred over re-painting the compagnie emblem on the place d'arme.

We were treated unkindly, and without respect. We did as we were told, and at the slightest whiff of insubordination, the screws tightened further still. The Sergeants would dish out punishments to the culprits until the message had been well and truly hammered home, that to obey, was the path of least resistance. For those of us who were new to the compagnie, there was no hiding, we would have the worst of it. I came to learn that that was just the way it was and the way it would stay for years, until each man had earned his place.

To be completely honest, I expected there to be far more combat training and shooting. We had done combat drills during basic training, but not to the extent one would expect from a modern, professional army. Nor did it seem at all a priority for the Capitaine of the 2ème compagnie then. And shooting? Well, we were lucky if we would shoot as a compagnie more than once per year. Once per year! The regimental range had to be booked, paperwork had to be filed and ammunition was expensive. It all took effort on our superiors' part, whereas cutting the grass and sweeping the roads took only the sweat of Legionnaires.

If the chef de section was feeling particularly constructive, he might delegate some of the Sergeants to give us lessons on something to do with combat engineering, perhaps. Otherwise, the time between meals would be filled with something more creative, like working on the compagnie's new chant as a section. I was sorely disappointed, knowing it was fortunate there was not a significant war that involved France, for while the Legion had discipline in buckets, it was lacking in combat ability.

I would do a lot of physical activity too. We would be taken for sport by section each morning, (there are usually around four sections of twenty to thirty to a compagnie) which, nine times out of ten, would be running no matter what the weather was like.

I would also do my own sport after work hours, if we weren't being made to do something ridiculous. There was a boxing gym above the sports hall on the base and I quickly came to know the regulars there. The Legion has some serious talent when it comes to combat sports. In the ring on the regiment, I have had the pleasure to be beaten by ex-heavyweight professionals, ex-kickboxing national champions, budding professional MMA fighters and everything in-between. Most would be Eastern Europeans, and there were always one or two up for sparring.

I remember a Moldovan sergeant, who was an ex-heavyweight professional. He must have weighed an excess of 110kg with a height of 195cm, whilst I was about 75kg. Several of us would take a round in the ring each with him to see if we could last. I'd climb between the ropes with a grin on my face, having already accepted the inevitability of my downfall. It was only a matter of time before he was able to swat away my combinations and back me into a corner with a few jabs from his long, muscled arms. Then, he would drop me with a massive body shot to the ribs, leaving me gasping for breath on the floor, as he chuckled good-naturedly.

The boxing served me well, for we had a saying in the 2ème Compagnie: if you had a problem with someone, you would invite them 'behind the building.' Inviting someone 'behind the building' was essentially inviting them to fight out of sight of any prying eyes of the officers. It was widely accepted by the sous-officers, and they would turn a blind eye whilst the Caporals and Legionnaires resolved their differences with fists. In many ways, it made life wonderfully simple. If you were not prepared to follow through you kept your mouth shut and that was that.

Bailey and I met a few of the other English speakers on the regiment in the winter of 2015. There were two other Englishmen in the 3ème compagnie, Bax and Frank. Frank had served in the Rifles regiment of the British army for some years. After, he had found that civilian life wasn't for him, but couldn't re-join the British army because he now had a criminal record for fighting. Bax also had some run-ins with the law; I didn't learn his whole story, but the scars on his face certainly suggested there was one. Both Bax and Frank were tall, solidly built lads, Caporals already, and a great laugh.

There was an Irish sergeant in the 1ère compagnie, an easy going American, Griff, in the logistics company and several Scandinavians who all spoke very good English. In my own compagnie, however, there was another Englishman, Nait.

Nait was what we called a 'bannanier' in the Legion: someone who couldn't stay out of trouble. He wasn't a bad guy, but he just seemed to have a problem with authority from what I could tell. He had already done thirty days of 'taule,' or military prison.

There was a building next to the guard post at the front gate that housed the prisoners who would carry out their sentence by gardening and cleaning the regiment. Whether it was repainting the kerb, or watering the plants, or clearing away the snow, they would be outside in all weather conditions for twelve hours a day and locked up at night. Nait would soon rope Bailey (and almost myself) into his first stretch too.

The three of us had been drinking in Nait's room one night, which he shared with another Premiere Classe, a Madagascan. I had been willing to drink a couple of beers before lights out, but nothing too crazy, as we had a compagnie march the next morning. For a while it was great fun. We had a beer and talked about our new lives in the Legion, joking around a bit and cursing whichever Caporal and Sergeant we hated the most. At 22:30, I finished the rest of my drink, stood up and said, 'right, I'll see you boys tomorrow morning for the march!'

Nait had other ideas, however. He broke out a full bottle of rum, twisted it open and began pouring drinks. 'You're not going anywhere. Sit back down, have another drink.'

'Erm, you do realise we have to get up for a march at 06:00, right?'

Nait snorted in derision. 'So what? We're just having a couple more drinks and then that's it. Who cares about that stupid march anyway? Stop being such a pussy.'

I flat out refused and said I was calling it a night, turned on my heel and left the two of them to their rum. It turned out to be the right decision.

The next morning for the 05:50 assembly I was keen to see the state of Bailey and Nait, and searched for them in the other sections, craning my neck to see above the green berets of the other guys. But after searching the faces, I realised neither of them were there. When the duty Sergeant realised there were two missing, he turned to the 'Caporal de jour' (Corporal in command) of Nait and Bailey's respective sections and was promptly informed that both were in the infirmary, along with the Madagascan Nait shared his room with. What on earth had happened last night?

'Hey Dobson! You were with them, what's going on?' Someone shouted across the place d'arme. All eyes turned to me, but all I could do was shrug.

As it transpired, Bailey had been found the next morning passed out next to the toilet, with his phone inside it. Nait had beat the daylights out of his roommate for threatening to tell the duty Sergeant that he was making too much noise and that he couldn't sleep. The Madagascan had shown up to the ordinaire, or mess hall, with a swollen face the next day for lunch and told everyone the story. The result was around twenty days of prison for both Bailey and Nait, mainly because they had missed the march for being drunk. I think if they had still managed to go on the march, it would have mattered less that they were drunk.

Most of the guys in the compagnie found it hilarious, and Bailey seemed nonchalant about the whole thing too.

'Ah fuck it.' he said, when I saw him a few days later. 'I'll do a few weeks in taule, could be a good experience. Plus, they say you're not a real anglophone until you've been inside anyway!' He finished with a grin. As for Nait, it was nothing new to him anyway. After a series of other unfortunate events, he would become the only Legionnaire I personally knew to be forcibly discharged before his contract was fulfilled. Not an easy accomplishment in the Legion.

In early December, my entire compagnie was deployed on what they called 'mission sentinelle,' as part of the taskforce now assigned to guard public places nationwide from the terrorist threat. The upside of this mission was that we were paid almost double wages and had one day off in every four from guard. Romaric and I took this time to explore the city of Lyon, in which we were stationed. It's a beautiful city, built around the confluence of two rivers and has a wonderful cathedral high on a hill to the north from which fantastic views of the city below can be found. The French air force base we were staying on had a canteen that was like a restaurant compared to our own. Back in Saint Christol, the food was a running joke; especially the bread, which was so hard it was said you could beat someone over the head with it and knock them unconscious!

As for the meals, I had been put to work in the canteen on occasion and the 'cooking' consisted of heating huge tins of conserved vegetables that were mushy and tasteless. And the meat was too often sinewy and seemed to be mostly cartilage. On the base in Lyon however, we ate like kings! There was a choice of not two, but three different types of bread, and they were all soft! Then, a choice of main course too, and yoghurts and other cakes for dessert, as well as many different types of fruit. We were spoilt, it was not at all what I was used to. If I asked for a choice of main course back in saint Christol, the Polish Sergeant in charge of the ordinaire would have narrowed his eyes at me and told me to eat what was being served or go hungry, with 'kurwa' (a Polish swearword) thrown in a few times to properly emphasise his point.

The work was easy and boring, and consisted of guarding the train stations as well as synagogues and other parts of the Jewish community, as they were supposedly the most at risk from extremist militant groups (Al Qaeda or IS). There was a Ukrainian guy in my section that told anyone who would listen that the Jews paid money to the French government for this privilege, as we seemed to be guarding them disproportionately. How true this was, I have no idea.

We would spend Christmas there as a compagnie, too. Normally Christmas was the second largest Legion celebration after Camerone, but my first with the Legion was compacted as the 2ème Compagnie had its patrolling and guarding duties to carry out in the city of Lyon. We, nevertheless, had some celebrations. The Capitaine awarded us each with a couple of little Christmas gifts bought by the compagnie's treasurer, ironically paid for by ourselves, I might add, via the monthly 'cotisation', a tax of around twenty euros per head.

But the best bit of a Legionnaire's Christmas was the 'sketch noel.' It was just that, a sketch show performed by the Legionnaires, impersonating their superiors in a bit of playful mocking, only tolerated one day of the year: Christmas Eve.

All too often, however, the sketches would be taken what some believed to be too far, and the playful fun turned into downright slandering. As a result, the 'officier adjutant', the second officer in command, would review the sketches to ensure they were suitable to be performed in front of the entire compagnie. If the Legionnaires were feeling particularly brave, they would show the second officer in command one version, then perform entirely different one on Christmas Eve, much to the delight of everyone else.

Something of the sort happened for my first; there was a Polish Sergeant Chef in the 2ème Compagnie that all the Legionnaires shared a mutual hatred for. He was one of those men who completely abused his power over others and treated his subordinates like total dog shit. He was, to put it bluntly, an arsehole. The boys in his section hauled out the Legionnaire picked to play him on a 'throne,' being carried on their backs with Darth Vader's theme tune playing in the background, a hilarious symbol of the Chef's tyranny. The Legionnaire in the throne was dressed in a stuffed toga to imitate the Chef's rotund belly and had a laurel wreath upon his head, looking like quite the little emperor. But when he spoke with a perfect imitation of the Chef's lisp, the entire compagnie was in stitches, the Capitaine included. The actor began to delegate idiotic tasks to a group of Legionnaires pretending to carry them out with forced enthusiasm whilst he picked at a bunch of grapes. Glancing at the real chef, all could see his face turn bright red and there was practically steam coming from his ears! Apparently, the Chef didn't find it amusing as he turfed all the Legionnaires out of their beds that night and made them sleep on the hard concrete floor of the sports hall. Well worth it, I say.

In the new year, the 2ème Compagnie began preparation for something I was looking forward to: the winter mountain training course. This was one of the more interesting things our regiment did. There were some epic photographs dotted around the compagnie walls of entire sections scaling the side of a mountain or skiing down untouched-off-piste slopes. It looked pretty fun. At any one time there would be at least one section at the regimental chalet in the Alps doing their training and it was a couple of sections from the third compagnie that preceded ours whilst we trained with cross country skis of the lower slopes of Mont Ventoux. Our Sergeants and Sergeant Chefs would help us correct our technique of marching with the skis, and whack us with their ski poles when we got it wrong. There was a lot about knots to learn too and how to maintain ropes, harnesses and other bits of equipment that might help us abseil down a sheer rock face.

Yet, I found that, for perhaps the first time since arriving at the 2ème compagnie, I was enjoying myself. We were preparing to climb mountains in perilous conditions in the middle of winter, a real adventure! This was so much better than guarding the front gate or cleaning the toilets all day. Plus, I was one of the better skiers of the section, having been one of the only ones to have actually done it in his civilian life.

But there was much more than just skiing to learn. My chef de Section gave us a lesson on all the many dangers of the mountains: frostbite, altitude sickness, avalanches, glaciers. The list went on. Each year, there was always a foolish tourist or two who would underestimate the dangers and would disappear in the mountains, never to be found again. But surely we'd be fine, we were with professionals after all.

Then, calamity struck. The unthinkable had happened. There had been an avalanche whilst the detachment from the third compagnie had been climbing a path in the mountains, trapping a good four-fifths of them and submerging them in ice and snow. We were at the regiment at the time, but within a day it was all over the news and the compagnie club was full as Legionnaires peered at the television before morning assembly.

'Oh shit! Look, it must be the guys from the third compagnie!' Someone said, as the camera panned to the Legion chalet. Quiet fell as the reporter began to speak with the empty chalet in the background.

'Just a few hours ago, a detachment of military personnel called for local assistance when they were caught in an avalanche south east of the resort of Valloire. Rescue teams have been called in from other resorts to aid in the operation and are still on the mountain. We will have more information on this story in a few hours.'

We had a better idea of what happened when the news eventually trickled down from our own superiors and the story began to unravel.

Every time a section of Legionnaires enters the mountains, they must be accompanied by professionally qualified instructors with extensive mountaineering training. This was the case with the commander of the detachment of the 52 Legionnaires from the 3ème compagnie. But for whatever reason, he had very wrongly decided to commence the outing in the afternoon. This is an awful idea in the mountains, and I'll explain why. In the night, the snow will freeze and become hard, meaning that just before sunrise is an ideal time to trek, as the risk of avalanche is minimal. Every outing I have ever done in the mountains has commenced before sunrise.

As the sun comes out, however, it will begin to slowly melt the snow, making it soft and increasing the risk of avalanche, especially after midday. Even just one skier is capable of setting off an avalanche, but fifty-two...

Not only was the time of day wrong, but the detachment should have been better spread out over the side of the mountain. This is standard procedure for exactly the eventuality of avalanche. The theory is that the more spread out the troops are, the less are caught under the snow, meaning there are fewer victims and more men to help dig them out, saving crucial seconds. The inevitable tirade of snow, ice and rocks engulfed most of the section, burying them alive. Everyone is trained to locate and dig out avalanche victims before any of us are allowed on the mountains, but it still takes precious time. Meanwhile, those below the surface were slowly suffocating, trapped and unable to move, hemmed in by a claustrophobic, icy coffin.

For the rest of the evening, this was the talk of the Regiment. The club was full as everyone discussed what might have gone wrong. Why had the Legionnaires been caught by the avalanche despite all the training to avoid such an outcome? For a while no one knew, and rumour spread like wildfire. A Romanian guy, who knew a Caporal from the 4ème compagnie who had grown up in the same village as one of the Sergeant Chefs present on the mountain, came into the club told the Caporal that told the Romanian that there were still twenty guys stuck under the snow. An Italian from the first section was telling everyone that the Legionnaires from the 3ème compagnie were all safe and well, and that the Legion was just milking the story for publicity.

It was impossible to say, and it was not until the Chef de Corps called a regimental assembly the following afternoon that we finally had some reliable information.

He explained in grave tones that six Legionnaires, Premiere Classes and Caporals were still missing, their bodies not yet recovered and that it was almost certain they were dead. There was a sombre silence as all the men present digested the information. They had been friends to many and now they were gone.

But the commander survived, I thought. It would be a mistake he'd live with for the rest of his life. Thankfully Bax and Frank were not among them. Just to give you an idea of the amount of snow they were trapped under, it took the local authorities over a week to dig out all the bodies.

We held a ceremony for the dead several days after the incident, the atmosphere in the regiment was sombre. I was in the third compagnie the night of the ceremony; I could hear the wails of anguish as the guys mourned their fallen comrades. 'Why?' someone had kept calling out, 'why?'

I had assumed that after all that our training would have been cancelled, at least for the time being, but I was wrong. Things were going ahead as planned and before I knew it, I was in the very same mountains unloading all the equipment into the chalet where the Legionnaires of the third compagnie had stayed a week prior. Many of the guys felt apprehensive about this, some were downright cursing the Capitaine for pressing on with the training. Most had never skied a day in their lives, let alone set foot on wild and dangerous mountains such as the Alps. And just after six of their comrades had died in an avalanche... Surely to be here so soon after was tempting fate?

My chef de section wasted no time in getting us on the mountain. Even though eighty percent of the detachment had never skied before, we found ourselves climbing up the piste using special detachable skins on our cross-country skis that allowed the ski to travel in one direction but not the other. These skins would be taken off at the top and the ski boots locked into place, essentially turning them into downhill skis. The temperature was below freezing, but the mountain was steep and you could easily work up a sweat ascending five hundred metres with a heavy pack. Working up a sweat was inadvisable, however, for once your clothes were damp, as soon as you stopped, the moisture would make the cold worse. So, we tended to march in long sleeve t-shirts once we'd warmed up.

I was quick to work up a sweat. On the first few days, we marched up the piste instead of the wild slopes on either side to ease some of the less comfortable guys into the rhythm of putting one ski in front of the other. The slopes seemed so much steeper from below than above! I looked up to see the mountain stretching way upwards into the clouds above me, the summit not even visible. But it was so far! How could we make it all the way up there?

We had awoken at 04:30 and were marching in single file before the sun was up. The clacking of ski boots on the cross country skis and the heavy panting of Legionnaires was the only sound in the pre-dawn air. It can't have been more than fifteen minutes before our bodies were so warm that the Chef was ordering us to take off our jackets and hats as we had all broken into a sweat. A couple of hours later, we took a break by the side of the piste. But no sooner after I stopped, that I felt the biting cold of the wind pinch my torso and I quickly took my jacket and hat from my bag and wrapped myself up in them until we were told to continue. It was 11:00 when we finally reached the top, the other guys dripping with sweat and looking exhausted. We had just climbed five hundred metres and the views proved it; from up here we could see for miles!

From there, we could ski down and were divided into groups by our skiing competence. Since I had skied before, I was with the first group, and within twenty minutes we had skied to the bottom of the mountain that had taken us hours to climb.

It is unwise to underestimate the mountains because of all the extreme environments, the mountains will kill you the fastest. This was demonstrated to us with the next phase of the training.

There were a few cases of mild frostbite from guys who weren't paying attention, especially when we went to stay high in the mountains in some abandoned military outpost for several nights. Incredibly enough, the gear we were issued with at regiment we had been forbidden from using! When I arrived at 2ème Regiment Étranger de Genie, all the new Legionnaires were issued a mountain pack along with gloves, mittens, salopettes, jackets, socks and a sleeping bag. The irony was that the gear was awful quality and hypothermia and frostbite had been recorded whilst using them.

The instructors of the training course knew it too, and we were told we had to buy our own on the weekend. I dished out three hundred euros for a new sleeping bag alone!

Part of the course was to march up to these old military buildings that were located high in the mountains. Mostly abandoned, their windows broken and snowbanks covering half the rusty beds within, they provided little shelter. But we lived there for several days, nonetheless. We had some shooting drills, which was fun, but complicated by the fact that we had to stay wrapped up in several layers, as it was below zero and we dropped plenty of empty magazines in the snow due to our clumsy mittens.

The views were magnificent, though. From our vantage point on the summit of the highest mountain, there lay a vast expanse of white peaks stretching away into the distance. After climbed to the top before 10.00, the sun now shone off the snow, illuminating everything. It was breathtakingly beautiful. A landscape so wild and incredible, it was like something from a fantasy book. But it was deadly, too, in the mountains. If you had no shelter in winter when a storm raged, you would be dead in a matter of hours, as the temperatures would drop to twenty below.

We made 'igloos' too, not in the conventional sense, but carved out dome shaped hollows from snow drifts with little tunnels leading up to them, which slept three men a piece very snugly. There had to be a man outside on guard all night to look for the candlelight within each igloo, signifying it hadn't collapsed on the men inside. If the guard noticed there was no light, he would blow his whistle, and everyone would crawl out of their igloos and come to the rescue. They were surprisingly warm inside, which I suppose is the point, and I would have gotten a good night's sleep had I not had to get up in the night to do my guard shift in a sub-twenty-degree blizzard. After which, I crawled awkwardly back into my sleeping bag following an hour of being frozen to the bone.

There were a couple more shooting drills the next day. They taught us how to create a makeshift bipod with our ski poles upon which to rest our rifles to have the prefect shot, then to ski to a different position. Because of the cold, we had to do it all with thick gloves of course, making it all twice as hard to manipulate.

On the way back down the mountain, and to the delight of my Chef de section, someone had injured their ankle, giving him a chance to demonstrate the use the first aid sled. Because I was one of the better skiers - not because I'm particularly talented, but because I was one of the only ones on the training course to have actually skied previously - I was nominated to ski on one corner of the sled.

The poor guy was strapped in and left to our mercy. With one of us on each corner holding one end of a rope with the other attached to the sled, it should have been easy going with the weight split four ways. In practice, however, it was a nightmare. The sled moved this way and that, and coordinating ourselves to turn was extremely difficult. I seemed to be in a constant 'snow plough,' where your skies make a down-facing triangular position to slow your descent. To this day I have never felt my legs burn so horribly with muscle soreness. I could hardly let go and leave my injured comrade to plummet to his doom and so I gritted my teeth and wrestled with the sled.

The training course ended with a race, in which all the participants must walk up one mountain, ski to the bottom of another, then walk up that one to the finish line at the top. Even at a fast pace, it took most of the morning. I knew I had to play to my strengths; there were a few guys in the section who were cardio machines and would eat a mountain or two for breakfast, but were not so comfortable going downhill on their skis. I would have to beat them on the downhill journey between the two mountains. When the whistle blew we all set off, being directed by a Sergeant placed at intervals along the course so we didn't lose our way. Some guys were practically running uphill and I had to force myself to keep a fast but steady pace; it would not do to waste all my energy here.

I got into a rhythm, sticking my poles into the ground and pushing myself forward as I slid my skis upwards. There was a group ahead of me that were pulling away, but I let them knowing I would have to ski downhill at breakneck speed to win. After an hour, I reached the summit of the first mountain and unclipped myself rapidly to take the skins off the bottom of my skis. Looking around, I was still one of the first up. Once I had the skins around my neck and had clipped myself back in, I sped off downhill.

Not even bothering to turn, I shot downwards and passed a couple of the fitter guys who were now snow ploughing safely, but slowly, down. I zoomed past with a wave and a chuckle, still grinning when I reached the bottom after hearing them curse after me. Once my skins were reattached, I was away again, but this mountain was higher and steeper. I was soon out of breath and heard some of the guys I had passed hot on my heels. It took over an hour to get to the top of this one, and by that time I had been passed by two or three guys. But when I reached the summit, I was happy to claim fourth place as I dropped my pack to the ground panting, taking in the views whilst I waited for the others.

# CHAPTER 5

We were all a little glad to return back to the base to the usual routine of scrubbing floors, as it was considerably easier than climbing mountains, and we were all looking somewhat thinner and more tanned. In the earlier months of 2016, I was pleased to learn that some new Legionnaires would be joining the 2ème Compagnie, hoping that they would help, either willingly or not, to spread some of the workload. Being the youngest in the Compagnie, both in terms of age and military service, didn't seem to do me any favours. Among the ten or so newcomers would be Cabello, a Spaniard who spoke good English as well as Savelli, an always very cynical, tall, and ungainly Italian who had served in his country's army before, and, lastly, Kane Harley.

Cabello and Savelli would become my friends, but Kane would become much more than that to me; he would become a hero. He is the type of man that is difficult not to like, the perfect soldier, but a better friend.

Kane Harley was born in the United States, his father was out of the picture, and his mother was deemed unfit to raise him by the government as she had been addicted to drugs in Kane's infancy. As a result, he grew up in institutions. He did not come from a wealthy background and relied on the government and various foster homes to support him, some being better than others. Kane was moved around from foster home to foster home and was never able to form bonds with any one of the families. I can't imagine how disruptive that must have been for him as a young boy; he had no permanent parental figures in his life to look up to and was almost nomadic in the way of life he had been forced into. He had no home. It seemed inevitable for him that he would join the Marines. By that time, the rigorous discipline of boys institutions and foster homes had made the decision easy, and made the transition feel natural.

He joined the Marine Corps at sixteen, as soon as he was able, and would see eight years of service in a light armoured division, finishing at the rank of sergeant. He had served in Iraq twice, and finished a tour of Afghanistan. At twenty-four years old and already a veteran of many a gunfight, Kane tried his luck in the civilian world. Understandably, after having been in institutions his whole life he struggled. It got to him - that strange way of life and he began to spiral downwards, becoming addicted to drugs and losing his way. He needed the structure in his life again, he needed purpose. And he needed to fight, he was born for it. But one day when he was high on something again, he fired shots in the air at a house party and was arrested, blowing his chances of joining the US army.

He had told me that before he left for the Legion, he decided to reconnect with his estranged mother, and tracked her down to an off-the-grid trailer park. He described the encounter as an awkward and difficult one as his mother was the polar opposite to him. She, a peace-loving and carefree spirit and him, a veteran of several wars. It was not a long visit and it would be the last time Kane ever saw his mother.

Kane joined the Legion in late 2015, the same year as me. When I met him at the regiment, I saw a short, blonde haired and blue-eyed man, covered head to foot in tattoos and would not immediately have imagined us becoming friends. Yet Kane had a very pleasant demeanour, and his quiet confidence gave the impression of competence which proved to be quite accurate, as the man knew what he was talking about where warfare was concerned. What amazed me when I learned his story, was how after being dealt such a shitty hand by life, being downtrodden all those years in crappy institutions, he could be such a kind and enjoyable person to be around. Even the other Sergeants and Sergeant Chefs treated Kane with respect. Kane was the first one to help when you had difficulties, always seeming to have his shit together himself, and was ready to explain anything calmly to the guys who struggled.

Funnily enough, it was he who taught me the basics of combat first aid, how to prepare my equipment so everything was accessible in a firefight. And plenty of other useful little snippets of information, such as the correct time to hold down your finger over the trigger of a machine gun to fire a burst.

The 2ème Compagnie had been training at a French regular base in the spring so that we could shoot some larger calibres on the ranges there, namely the browning .50cal. For many of us, it was the first time we had ever used the gun. I recall myself struggling to remember the order in which to reassemble the pieces, and breaking into a sweat because the sergeant was coming back to the classroom we were in soon, expecting me to have it reassembled in time.

Seeing my frustration, Kane stepped in. 'That one first.' He pointed. 'Then that one, and you had it the wrong way around. It goes in the other way - yes that's it. Now the next one.'

Under Kane's supervision I had the gun reassembled in a minute. And just in time, too, because the Sergeant had entered, coming from one of the other classrooms where another group of guys were assembling their own. Looking over, he gave a 'hmph.' Not being able to find anything to fault and left once more.

'Thanks.' I said. Kane seemed to know his stuff. 'So what's it like to shoot?'

'It jumps up a bit. You have to fire it in bursts. Look,' He moved to grip the handle and pressed down on the trigger making a 'click' before releasing after a couple of seconds.

'Hold the trigger down for about that long. It's about the time it takes to say 'die motherfucker, die!" I laughed.

'Is that true?'

'Well, I'm sure it's not in the manual, but it works!' He said grinning.

In fact, Kane became an unofficial instructor for our section for when anyone wanted to know how to say, strip down the browning 12.7mm gun and clean it. Kane knew the ins and outs better than anyone, and would seldom snap at you for asking a silly question. Everyone came to appreciate the charisma of this newcomer and we avoided many a punishment from the Sergeants due to Kane's quick-thinking wit and his ability to break tensions with a joke, before getting the rest of us in line to appease the Sergeants. They even let him teach some of the lessons himself.

Unfortunately for us, Kane had been 'spoiled' by the US army, whose training, facilities and general quality of life was much better than our own, as the French budget simply didn't compare. Not only that, but I think Kane had been drawn in by the romantic ideal of the French Foreign Legion, the fraternity and adventure that it promised, and was disappointed that the modern reality didn't live up to his expectations. It must have been hard, having worked his way up the ranks of one army, only to find himself at the bottom of the pile in the Legion, having to do all the menial tasks that young Legionnaires have to put up with.

Moreover, Kane missed a fight. It's a feeling I have come to empathise with myself. War can make men combative, all that hyper aggression builds up after you've been taught for years to kill. Kane had done it too, he had seen countless gunfights during his eight years in the US army and it had made him tense, even if he did well to hide it from everyone else. Kane needed a fight, he needed something more worthwhile and fulfilling, not cleaning the barracks for the hundredth time.

I could sense his restlessness - he wanted to get away, find something with more action to sink his teeth into. He told me he needed to give his life more purpose, that scrubbing the floors was not enough for him. Only several months after his arrival to the regiment, Kane had found his excuse.

It started with the news, the only thing reported at the time seemed to be the rise of the Islamic state in Syria. Everyone agreed that we should be there, but we were never deployed. Kane took matters into his own hands. Via Facebook, he had managed to get in touch with the Kurdish rebels, who were attempting to recruit troops from anywhere and everywhere, to aid them with their desperate struggle against IS, with the hopes that some western fighters would join the fray. Luckily for them, Kane was one such man. And after a back-and-forth exchange, Kane was decided and his trip planned. They would sneak him across the Turkish border, illegally of course, where he would meet up with the Kurds.

In our conversations in the barracks, I told him I would be sad to see him go.

He had smiled and said, 'you should come with me, we could use all the help we can get.'

I seriously considered it, what an adventure that would have been! But I decided against it in the end. I had signed a contract for the Legion and meant to see it through for better or worse. It was the last time I would ever see Kane Harley in our all-too-brief friendship, as one Monday morning when the register was taken, Kane was absent. I smiled at my friends knowingly, as the duty Sergeant threw a fit, demanding to know if Kane would show up.

He wouldn't. Kane travelled to Turkey where he crossed over into Syria and would fight there until late 2017, over a year, becoming a team leader and playing a role in the battle for Raqqa, until the IS threat was all but extinguished. I would like to say that his story ended with a happily ever after.

It almost did. For when he returned to the US, he met a girl and fell in love. They were together until late 2018, when she broke up with him for reasons unknown to me and broke his heart. I think Kane had pinned his last hopes of happiness on this girl, a last chance of redemption perhaps. When she left him, it was the last nail in the coffin. When I spoke to the men in the 2ème compagnie, who had known him best, they shared a similar opinion. Kane was happy fighting a war in Syria. There, he had purpose, he was a leader. He knew what to do and did it well. But now he was back in the civilian world and the rules were completely different. He wasn't yet thirty, but had already lived many lifetimes. He would have felt as though it was too late for him to begin again, his second chance had melted away before his eyes. It was the spark that brought all the demons of his past back to torment him. He must have felt truly alone, in a world he didn't understand and did not appreciate him.

Turning on social media one day, I saw that Kane had made a strange post on Facebook. There was a picture of a board with all his military accolades stuck on with the words, 'I was a marine, I was a Legionnaire, I was a rebel commander in Syria, and I gave it all up for a girl. It seemed like a good idea at the time.'

I didn't know what I was looking at and assumed it was some weird kind of joke, but there was a nagging doubt in the back of my mind whose presence turned out to be justified. The next day Kane's body had been found by one of his old Marine brothers who had also seen the post and had feared the worst. He had shot himself and was dead.

Despite his suicide note, I don't believe that Kane had done it because of the girl. I believe there was a deep frustration with a world that had no place for him. The army and war had been all he had known, he had suffered and seen things that most civilians cannot even imagine. He worked hard to develop skills that a soldier needed, but outside the military and war, it counted for nothing and no one cared.

What is remarkable about Kane is that, despite it all, he had a truly good soul and a ready smile that I'll never forget. It seems completely ludicrous to me after having known him that people could ever idolise half the celebrities around today, as Kane far outshines them all, a true hero and an outstanding gunfighter. Those who had the honour to have known him will never forget him.

For me, it was an awful blow and hard to imagine the cheerful and amicable man I knew was gone forever. I would never see him again nor share a beer as he recounted tales from his tours of Iraq. It seemed entirely unfair that he was gone and so many others that were lesser men were still here. And I hated that he had taken his own life, he must have felt so alone and desperate, that the idea of going on and rebuilding his life was too painful. And yet, it had happened. There was nothing I could do now save honour his memory by telling his story. Kane Harley was a good man. Rest in peace brother.

Life as a young Legionnaire was difficult in more ways than one. I never had much free time on the base, and any time I did have, I tried to spend away from my room; away from the uncomfortable presence of the two Caporals living there. The weekends were something I always looked forward to: forty-eight hours of freedom before another shitty week began.

In the beginning, I'd go out every chance I got with Bailey, Steinrod or Romaric. We'd rent a crappy hotel room for a couple of nights and go out drinking in Avignon or Marseille in whichever bar would let us in. Most in Avignon didn't. They knew Legionnaires well, as it was the closest town to the regiment and Legionnaires with shaved heads and foreign looking faces were easy to spot. We were known for causing a bit of a ruckus, so most places had a 'no military personnel' policy.

During those weekends, we got drunk wherever we could. I got a few tattoos, and we did all the things one imagines soldiers on leave do. But after a while, the novelty wore off. I had no roots in France, I was foreign, in a country of people who seemed not to care what I was doing for it. Hell, most of them probably didn't even know we existed.

A year or so into my service, I was nineteen, bitter and angry. I thought I had made a big mistake, that I should have been more patient and joined the British army instead. At least then I would have been with my countrymen and not so far from family.

I finally managed to visit home in 2016. With two weeks of leave, I headed up to Paris to the British embassy and mumbled something about losing my passport (at that point it was still confiscated as I hadn't reclaimed my old identity yet) and was given a temporary one to get home with. Of course, this was all against the rules; until I had my old identity back I was supposed to stay in France. But that would mean that I would have to stay in a hotel alone for two weeks and I wasn't going to do that. Instead, I opted to risk heading home with the temporary passport, in the hopes that I could make a new one in time so that I could get back France before the end of my leave.

Stepping off the plane onto UK soil I realised it had almost been a year since I had last been here. I took a breath of air and closed my eyes. I was home! Whilst France is a wonderful place to visit, there is nothing quite like home and I had missed the English culture.

I visited my parents at home where nothing had changed, it was still the same old house. There, I had a new passport ordered and it was made with a few days to spare. I stayed with my brother Alfie in Sheffield too, where he was at university at the time. We partied hard with his flatmates and would stumble home at 6am after a long night out drinking. It was perfect for relieving the stress that I realised had built up over the last year. It is hard to describe how much I needed to 'let loose,' and how much better I felt afterward. Seeing the ridiculously easy life that students took for granted made me envious and bitter. Here I was, giving my golden years to the Legion on some shitty base in the middle of nowhere surrounded by foreigners and sheep when Alfie and his mates were living the good life, partying, meeting girls and probably not even bothering to attend half their lectures.

I could stay at home once my days of leave were up, effectively becoming a deserter. The thought crossed my mind more than once, especially as I woke in my own bed the morning of my return flight. I thought about how easy it would be for me to just roll over and go back to sleep. I'd tell my parents that I'd had enough. They'd understand. I could be at the same university as Alfie by the end of the summer, making friends, chasing girls and partying all night. All I had to do was go back to sleep…

But I couldn't. I was a man of my word and knew I would never forgive myself. I had made a promise to see it through and I was going to live up to it. I wanted to be an honourable man, like so many of the characters in my history books had been. What would they think if I gave up because it was too difficult? It was all a test. And it was that thought that got me up on those mornings and on many others.

Returning to France was difficult, too. It was easier, in a way, not to come home in the first place because going back was just so depressing. The last few days of leave would often be tainted with the looming return journey as I'd think about all the bullshit I'd be doing when I was back in 2ème REG.

In France, I was no better. I'd complain regularly to my friends, and the bitterness would eat away at me. What on earth was I doing here? Fighting for a country that was not my own, whose values I don't share. Why wasn't I at home in the UK? I had another four years of this, I reminded myself. Would they be four years wasted?

At the end of the day, I had signed a written contract, I had given my written word, even if I never truly understood what I was getting myself into back in Fort de Nogent.

Then, a beacon of hope came into my life when I least expected it. Romaric and I were out in Marseille one weekend, drinking at an Irish bar and enjoying a respite from the week when two girls came to our table giggling and one said, 'hey, we have a bet: I bet my friend here a drink that you two are in the army.' The girl that had spoken caught my eye, she was petite and pretty, with shoulder length dyed curly blonde hair and full, red lips.

Romaric and I exchanged a glance, knowing full well we looked every bit the Legionnaire, shaved heads and foreign looking. For some reason I said no, and that we were just tourists. Her friend whooped with delight having won and they ended up sitting down to join us. I asked the blonde what her name was. She told me. It began with 'M', so I'll call her 'M.'

M was from Georgia and had moved to France alone when she was eighteen in search of a better life. She was twenty-three when I met her and quite the linguist too, as she spoke several languages already, including flawless French. In fact, when she wasn't working in the restaurant where she was employed, she would translate official documents, like birth certificates, from Georgian into French.

After some while chatting, I told her and her friend that Romaric and I were in fact military and offered to get the next round of drinks for the ones she had lost. 'Ha! I knew it!' She had said, 'with a haircut like that, you must be!'

I rubbed my shaved head self-consciously and said, 'is it really that bad?'

She cocked her head to one side smiling. 'Hmm, I like it, you have a nicely shaped head.'

'Oh, do I? Remind me never to cover it.' I tried to give a good witty response, but was too lost in her smile and she laughed at my expression.

'Legionnaires are funny.' She said.

We chatted the night away, or as best Romaric and I could given our basic level of French. To my surprise, I ended up back at her apartment where, both quite intoxicated by that point, we wasted no time with any more chatting and hopped into bed together, fumbling at each other's clothes and laughing.

I had expected her to kick me out in the morning, but she didn't and after lying there talking softly for most of the morning we had breakfast together before I had to go back on the Sunday evening. She even agreed to see me again the next weekend, and I had left her apartment with a grin on my face and a spring in my step to go and find Romaric in our hotel room.

The next week everything seemed a little easier, I had something to look forward to at last! When Friday finally came around, I was a little nervous to say the least. I met M at a bar in Marseille and to my relief the conversation flowed well. Apparently, I gave a decent account of myself for, before I knew it, we were heading back to her place again. Before the door had fully closed behind us, we were all over each other. Breathing quickly with anticipation, I stripped off her clothes kissing her all the while, to reveal her gorgeous lithe body, and I laid her down on the bed. I made love to her, with all the stamina of a twenty-year-old, engaged rhythm and passion I had never experienced with another woman.

M and I slept with our legs entwined and our foreheads touching. I loved the way I could feel her warm breath on my chest as she exhaled and her small arm around my waist. I cradled her protectively, as if someone might try to take her away from me. I still couldn't believe my luck; this beautiful girl seemed to have taken an interest in me, but I was loathe to question it at the time. I simply wanted to enjoy the moment.

M was a fiery little thing. She wanted me to teach her some boxing and I was hesitant at first, not wanting to hurt her, but she quickly proved she was not to be trifled with as she wrestled me to the floor of her apartment in protest, as I cracked with laughter and gave in to her demands. How could I not? We went to the beach with a pair of my boxing gloves and I showed her some of the basics, holding my hands out for her to hit a few jabs on.

'Okay, just throw a jab at my left hand. Are you ready? He-' But I was cut off because M had ignored my instruction and had thumped me straight in the nose and had proceeded to double over in fits of giggles.

'Ow!'

'You're too slow for me, English boy!' She laughed, skipping out of the way as I tried to grab her.

'Ooh, I'm gonna get you for that! You should have pulled that dirty trick after the lesson, maybe then you'd have stood a chance!'

I circled her, grinning, my hands outstretched ready to grab her wrists. M laughed and threw another couple of punches and ducking under them I saw my chance. I grabbed her around the waist and pulled her to me as she tried to wriggle away.

'Got you!'

'Noo!' I pulled her down into the sand with me where we collapsed in a heap laughing.

M would tell people exactly what she thought of them too. If someone had done something to upset her, they would know about it. She had once punched her friend's boyfriend in the face, breaking his nose for calling her a 'bitch,' and that is just one example. She was like a honey badger, small but totally fearless and I found that I respected her strength of character more than most of my colleagues back in the regiment. Around M, there was never a dull moment.

The next few weekends were more of the same. I would spend them in bed with M, talking or making love. I was totally insatiable. It was glorious. Heaven even. When I was with her everything seemed perfect, like the stars had aligned for me. And when we were apart, she was all I'd think about.

Even back at regiment cleaning the toilets for hours on end didn't seem so bad. I could do it and laugh now. My friends, too, saw the difference and would ask, 'why are you in such a good mood?'

I would just shrug and smile. I had something keeping me going now. Surely, if I was with M I could do anything and everything. There are plenty of fucked up things in this world that seem contrived or don't make sense, but loving a beautiful woman is maybe one of the only things that does. Perhaps that is what makes everything worth it.

The life I was living was hard; I was on the very bottom rung of an organisation that was completely indifferent to my feelings, even seeming cruel on occasion. I had no family in France and no friends there outside of the Legion. No one thanked me for the work I was doing, no one made sure I and the other Legionnaires had what we needed and were happy. Besides my close friends, no one cared. But now there was a difference, I had something waiting for me on the outside of all that. It felt as though I had hope. To tell you the truth, I fell in love with M far quicker than I should have.

There was a nagging doubt at the back of my mind. When something feels too good to be true, it often is. It was as though I couldn't acknowledge it, or I wouldn't acknowledge it. My young and naïve mind was sure everything would work out, that we would somehow live happily ever after. The alternative had never even crossed my mind and I never saw it coming. The problem was, M didn't love me back.

One day at the regiment, I had a message from her saying she didn't want to meet up as we had planned that weekend. I had asked her why and she had said that she didn't want a relationship because, for years since leaving Georgia, she had been fiercely independent and had always been on her own. M hadn't wanted me to compromise her independence. That's what she told me anyway.

I was devastated; the one good thing keeping me going was gone. Beautiful little M didn't want to see me again and it hurt. Shit, I thought, what a fucking idiot I am. How could I ever have expected that to last any more than a few weeks? She was a girl I'd hooked up with in a bar. Besides, I was young, barely a man and I had much to learn.

I'm not sure if I ever meant that much to her and nor do I know if she ever knew what she had been to me. I was living in a hard world and she had been my light, a glimmer of hope that had been extinguished all too quickly. Maybe that was why I had been so upset by her leaving me. I suppose I had just wanted what everyone wants: to be loved.

# CHAPTER 6

I was as miserable as ever after losing M. I walked the halls of the 2ème Compagnie, cleaning, cutting grass and chanting like a zombie. The only thing keeping me going was the fact that I didn't know what else to do. I lay awake for long hours in bed despite tiring my body during the day with exercise. I kept wondering what I had done wrong, why had she thrown it away when it had been so sweet? I was angry and bitter and would snap at my comrades, finding myself arguing with my friends over the stupidest things. It took me long enough to figure out that I couldn't continue like that, I had to get my act together. Time heals all wounds, I told myself. But there would be something else that would appear on the horizons of my future, something much more reliable than love. An opportunity presented itself.

In the winter of 2016, it was announced that the 2ème Compagnie would be deployed to Mali, Africa, the following year. Mali was a significant deployment at the time of my service and the only way anyone could see any action. It was considered lucky to get a Mali under your belt, you'd have double pay for four months and a new experience to boot. Or at least most of us saw it that way, there was always the odd Legionnaire or two who scoffed at the idea of fighting for France and risking their lives for a foreign war. I didn't know what they expected they would be doing when they had joined the French Foreign Legion. I, on the other hand, was happy to do it, if not for France, then for myself.

The conflict had begun in 2012, with insurgent groups fighting for control of northern Mali. There had been a military coup in the capital, Bamako, where the president had been ousted before an election. When the military stepped in to retake control of the country, the rebels captured some northern cities. But because the rebel groups were quite numerous, and because they didn't always see eye to eye on how their new territories were to be run, there has been a back and forth ever since. When it became apparent that some of these rebel groups were supported by the likes of Al Qaeda and IS, they were labelled as terrorist organisations and European help was sought.

This is where the French army came in. Mali had been an ex-colony of France, and the Malian government had argued it was France's responsibility to help. In my time in the Legion, Mali had long since been a significant deployment for at any one time there were around five thousand troops stationed there. It was a whole military ecosystem of its own that required an enormous amount of resources from the French government in order to sustain it.

Luckily for me, the army's different brigades took it in turns to be deployed to Mali. And in 2017, the mountain brigade had been chosen. It was the talk of the compagnie, the 'Chef de sections' had to make their combat groups from Sergeants, Caporals and Legionnaires. There was plenty of paperwork work to do, including having my birth certificate translated so I could reclaim my old identity.

I had it done and became known once more as 'Harry Dobson.' It was always very confusing when this happened; one week I would know the names of all my friends, but once changed back to their old identities, I'd have to learn what they were called all over again.

So, William Dempsey was no more, and Harry Dobson would be deployed to Mali in his place. But which role I would play in Mali remained to be seen. One day, the Chef de section called me into his office and said, 'Dobson, I need an armoured vehicles driver for Mali. Are you up to the task?'

I looked at him blankly and said, 'Chef, I've never even driven a car before, I'm not sure I'm the best man for the job.'

'Nonsense!' He had said, 'You'll be fine, there are barely any roads in Mali anyway, so you can't swerve off them!' He chuckled, but I wasn't reassured.

The French army's standard armoured vehicle was the VAB (Véhicule d'Avant Blindée). It has four enormous wheels, weighs twelve tons and has a very small window from which the driver must peer through to see where he is driving. But to qualify for the VAB course, I would first have to complete the regular vehicles course and the heavy goods vehicles course, which were both at Castelnaudary. Shit. I had hoped I wouldn't be seeing that place again until my Caporal training.

So, back to Castel I went, and even though I was no longer an 'Engagé Volontaire', I was still incredibly reluctant to be there. It turned out to be just as shitty as I remembered. I had a nasty Romanian Caporal Chef who, during the heavy goods vehicle training, would wrap my knuckles with the steel insignia of his beret if I made a mistake or smack me round the back of the head. He was a real bastard of a man that you happened to find more often than is desirable in the Legion. There were three of us in the same vehicle doing our training. He would brag to us about how he beat his wife and I had to clench my teeth and remain silent; I wasn't going to do anything that jeopardised my place on the Mali deployment, and I needed this course to go.

'That's the way it is with women, I'm telling you.' He said once as I was driving us along. 'You have to discipline them, hit them every now and again so they know who's in char- Damnit Dobson! I said left at the next junction, didn't I? Idiot!'

And with that he hit my knuckles a couple of times with the metal insignia of the flaming grenade on his beret. He knew he had us, the bastard. We could do nothing. If I were to answer back, he would dangle the threat of failing me on the course over our heads which would mean a ten day stretch in prison. I knew that it would be no use appealing his decision either, the Adjutant running the course would always side with a Caporal Chef over a Premiere Class or Legionnaire. It was all I could do to grip the wheel tighter to stop my hand making a fist.

I actually managed to pass the course in the end, God knows how; I certainly wouldn't have approved my application. But I was glad not to have to do the mandatory ten-day minimum stay in the regimental prison for failing a training course.

It amuses me when I tell people about that, they are always rather shocked. However, I think it's a good idea; it certainly makes you think twice about fitting in that extra revision session! Perhaps they ought to apply a similar rule in the UK, ten days in a juvenile penitentiary for each failed GCSE. I'd be willing to bet that the national average result would increase significantly...

The Legion's method of discipline is certainly more stick than carrot. Guys in the Legion go to military prison for lots of things: failure to salute the regimental flag, being late to morning assembly or getting drunk when they weren't supposed to.

There is a wonderful story about a donkey who tried to escape from 2REI. At the 2nd infantry regiment there are some regimental animals, like there are at Castel - a couple of pigs, a deer or two, and a donkey. Now, the donkey has its own 'matricule', a unique service number like the ones given to each Legionnaire. This meant that technically, the donkey was an active service member of the French army, and even had its own salary and pension. A Caporal Chef at Castel was telling me how he knew someone who had to guard the donkey as a young Legionnaire, as was common practice for Legionnaires in instruction; it gave them something to do during the night other than sleep.

The inevitable, however, seemed to come to pass as the donkey took its chance to escape when a gate was left ajar in its paddock. The Legionnaire guarding him had apparently advised the donkey to stay in the field, but claimed he was in no position to stop it since they were both of the same rank, that the donkey was actually his senior in terms of service. Eventually, the alarm sounded, and the escaping donkey was caught. Both the donkey and the Legionnaire were brought before the 'Chef de corps,' the colonel in command of the regiment, and sentenced each to a thirty-day stretch, the donkey for desertion and the Legionnaire for negligence. Upon leaving the colonel's office, the donkey had failed to salute the regimental flag there and had received an extra fifteen days onto his sentence as a result. Also, the donkey would have no treats for a month!

It wasn't my time to visit 'la trou' (military prison) however, and I returned to regiment with the driving course under my belt. I had to bid goodbye to Bailey during that winter, as he had volunteered to join the 13ème DBLE, an infantry regiment re-joining the French mainland that would require its ranks to be greatly bolstered. Steinrod, too, had changed compagnies- he had been sent to the notorious 4ème compagnie, infamous for the awful conditions in the building; one working toilet for fifty men and cold showers! Poor Steinrod.

There was a surprise waiting for me at the regiment, too. Quite a few Legionnaires were up for promotion to 'Premiere Classe' and Romaric and I were among them! Finally, I thought, I had been waiting one and a half years for this. Even though life would not change much for me, and my salary certainly wouldn't, I would have certain privileges, such as being able to grow my hair past a certain length. For a Legionnaire, the rule was if you could pinch it, it was too long.

Before I could put my new 'galon,' a single green diagonal stipe on my chest however, there was of course a catch; I would first have to complete 'la casque.' 'Casque' means helmet, and a new Caporal Chef in the compagnie who we called 'Botch,' insisted each of us do 'la casque' as tradition demanded. Botch was Russian and had served a few years in the Russian army before joining the Legion. He was very fit and capable and at nine years' service was still a Caporal Chef because his promotion had supposedly been blocked due to fighting. He was a bit of a hard arse and wasn't immediately popular when he joined the compagnie.

'La casque' consisted of drinking a full combat helmet's worth of beer while we stood on a chair in the corridor with the section cheering us on. We had those 330ml bottles of Heineken that we'd bought from the foyer by the crate and each managed to fit eighteen of them into our helmets! To put that into perspective that's almost six litres, or ten pints! We had to drink from the helmet without stopping. If we paused for breath, a sergeant would pour another bottle of beer into the helmet.

There was a great atmosphere in the barracks as Botch organised the spectacle for half of the compagnie to watch in one of the corridors. The guys were already chanting, 'drink! drink! drink!' as chairs were brought out for the six of us to stand on. And then the helmets were handed out and the other guys gleefully helped us to fill them, laughing in delight as the helmet seemed to fit bottle after bottle. My eyes widened, how many had that been so far?

'Eighteen!' Someone who had been keeping count shouted, as the helmets were finally filled to the brim, and I struggled to keep the contents from sloshing out over the edges.

'Legionnaires!' Botch shouted over the din and silence fell. 'Are you ready to become Premiere Classes?'

'Oui, Caporal Chef!' We cried in unison and I brought the rim of the helmet to my lips and began to drink as the watching crowd roared their approval.

Inevitably, one cannot rapidly consume eighteen bottles of Heineken and hope to keep it all down. To that end, we each had a helper who would be holding a bucket out for us. Around halfway through, I remember vomiting an extraordinary amount of liquid into the bucket, some of which missed and found my poor helper to the delight of the watching crowd. Gasping for breath before vomiting some more I was soon being shouted at for slowing down and, eyes watering, raised the helmet once more.

Of the handful of us doing it I am not ashamed to have finished dead last, but was pleased to have survived the ordeal, eventually finding the little velcro patch at the bottom of the helmet and sticking it proudly to my chest to the cheers of the rest.

Christmas of that year came and went. I spent New Year's Day guarding the front gate on a twenty-four-hour shift, which was quite shit, but hey, you can't win 'em all. At least there was finally something worthwhile for me to look forward to. In June, we would be going to Mali! This was exactly the sort of thing I had signed up for. I was ready for it.

The compagnie preparations would begin in earnest now, we even knew whose group we would be in so we could begin to train together. My Chef de Section actually moved us around in the barracks to that effect and put me in a room with Horvath, a Hungarian, whom I had done my basic training with and Caporal chef Botch. Horvath was short, stocky and had an unfriendly demeanour if you didn't know him. He had spent five and a half years in a Hungarian prison for armed robbery of a bank and snored like a lawnmower. Horvath was one of those guys who had that look about him that suggested he would fight you with the slightest provocation. And win. The other guys in the section respected him and not many dared to poke fun at him.

Horvath had made his decision to join the Legion whilst he had been sitting inside a jail cell, at some point over the last five years, and had promised himself a fresh start when he got out. His ties to the criminal underworld of Budapest meant that he had certain privileges on the inside and was something of a 'leader.' As a result, he had an authoritative air about him.

We were good friends, however, brought together by the common enemy: Botch. He broke our balls in the beginning and I found it easier again to be out of the room when I could be, cursing my luck that I'd have to spend four months with him.

As time went on, though, my opinion changed. We got to know each other better and Botch relaxed the rules a little (that or Horvath and I simply got used to them) and the three of us were able to joke together, the atmosphere in the room actually becoming pleasant. Imagine that!

Romaric and I did our VAB course on the base and familiarised ourselves with the vehicle we would be driving for the four-month deployment. You had to step on the enormous wheels and haul yourself through an armoured hatch to enter the driver's seat. It was cool at first, there were all these buttons and switches that I had no idea what they were for. It felt a bit like driving the millennium falcon. The novelty wore off fairly quick however, as the engine block was a metre square solid mass of steel situated right behind the driver's seat and made one hell of a racket. During the mission's preparation and training, we would discover that communicating inside the VAB whilst driving was near impossible. They taught me to maintain and clean the VAB, too. This was no small task, especially in the desert, where the sand was prone to working its way into all the nooks and crannies.

The preparation also had the benefit of helping each group get into a working routine. I was happy with my group. The Sergeant was Del Campo, a small Spaniard who was an excellent runner and incidentally, my favourite Sergeant in the whole compagnie as he was fair and easy going. Then there was Caporal Chef Botch of course, the second in command, Horvath and myself, Iona, a Premiere Classe with a few months more service than me. He was Hungarian too and spoke very good English. Noh, the burly South Korean, who was very friendly but spoke almost no French despite having the same service as I. Caporal Karnowski was Polish, a calm guy who occasionally came out with the most brilliant jokes and finally Tessier, a half French half Japanese Legionnaire who would work the radio (because he spoke the best French out of all of us) and the 12.7mm gun on the VAB.

Del Campo took to the command easily and was very relaxed with us, probably because he knew Botch would give us a good old kick up the arse if he caught us slacking. Our compagnie met its French regular counterparts during the preparation at a training base, as we would be working together closely. We immediately felt a sense of competition between our superiors and the regulars and found ourselves doing 'extracurricular activities,' apparently to impress the French. While they'd all be relaxing in the barracks next to ours, we'd be scrubbing away at something outside with one of the Sergeants screaming at us for being useless, making sure the French could hear it. The sous-officiers ensured that the Legion zone was a constant bustle of activity. If everything was clean, we'd sing until the sun had set, or wash our clothes by hand in the concrete basins outside. The Legion has a reputation in the French army for being its most tough, disciplined division and certainly its craziest. One of the French guys had said to me, 'wow the Legion, it's tough, eh?' with a gleam of admiration in his eye.

I shrugged as if it were nothing and said, 'it's not so bad.' We had a reputation to uphold after all.

All the training would come to a standstill for a few days at the end of April 2017, however, as Camerone was upon us. Each Compagnie was expected to make an effort, whether they were being deployed or not. There were various challenges for which each compagnie had to put guys forward, as well as a regimental march during the night and a 'defilé' (a march on the place d'arme in front of a crowd) in parading clothes, because someone had decided that we hadn't suffered enough. That was the worst because the Sergeants and Caporals would break our balls for weeks before the actual parade, checking our shirts and trousers for the slightest crease or stain.

There was also the boxing match, which I was hoping to compete in. I knew the Sergeant in charge of organising it, the huge Moldovan ex-heavyweight whom I'd sparred with a few times. I put my name in along with my weight and he'd promised me a match. I still trained plenty in the regimental boxing gym, so I wasn't too worried; I'd done a couple of amateur bouts in my civilian life.

The boxing match took place the night of the official ceremony, when the families had already headed home and the front gates were shut. None of the Legionnaires wasted any time in getting drunk; the evening's entertainment promised to be stellar. Along with the boxing matches, there was the 'Miss Kepi Blanc' competition, during which either local girls, wives or girlfriends of officers, or even on one occasion, a semi-famous porn star someone had hired, would strut down a catwalk between the rounds in full view of the entire regiment wearing some very 'minimalist' outfits.

Traditionally, the Chef de Corps, the youngest serving Legionnaire, Caporal Chef and sous-officier on the base would vote for their favourite. Why on earth you'd be comfortable letting your girlfriend get whooped and whistled at by hundreds of Legionnaires was beyond me, or maybe I'm just the jealous type. It was good fun nevertheless, and backstage I had a great place from which to watch.

The fights took place in a ring that had temporarily been set up in the sports centre, the combatants duking it out before a sea of white kepi blancs; the Legionnaires going wild when someone was knocked down.

Seeing the huge crowd that had formed, I began to feel a little nervous. I hadn't eaten much before the fight so I was lighter on my feet and jogged up and down backstage practicing a bit of shadow boxing to distract me. I had sparred countless times, but not often before a crowd so big. I knew that once it began, I would be fine. It was just the waiting…

Finally, it was my turn. With a deep breath, I jogged up to the ring and climbed between the ropes to face my opponent. My ring man was Mark, the English Caporal from the 1ère Compagnie. Unfortunately, Mark didn't know the first thing about boxing, but it was alright. I reassured him. I knew more or less what I was doing, perhaps trying to reassure myself a bit, too. He draped the English flag I had brought with me around my neck and I made sure the crowd could see it. It was met mostly with 'boos' from the crowd.

Despo, my opponent, was a Serbian. I had seen him train in the gym several times; he wasn't bad. Once the bell had rung to start the fight, my nerves vanished, and I blocked everything out but my opponent. Despo was slightly taller than me and had better reach. He tested the waters with a few jabs that I swatted away and hit back with a short combination. I quickly got in the rhythm of punching and dodging, my head constantly ducking, weaving and moving. I was in my element here, and felt I had the better of him. The fight lasted a total three rounds, but in the third, I pulled an illegal move - a spinning backfist allowed in Muay Thai, but was of course illegal in boxing. Shit, I thought, I hadn't meant to do that, it was just instinct.

The crowd booed me. I cursed through my gum shield and held up a glove in apology. The judges voted in Despo's favour, in a unanimous decision, and I'd lost. I didn't mind, however. I feel that losing can often be more beneficial than winning. When you win, you learn nothing; when you lose, you learn plenty. And it keeps you humble. I had still had a blast, fighting in front of a big crowd is always exhilarating!

Despo met me after his countrymen had let him down from their shoulders and we shook hands with a smile, both still sweaty from the exertion.

'If you didn't pull that illegal move you might have won!' He said.

'Yea, I'm really sorry about that man, it was just instinct. I had fun though!'

'Ah, don't worry about it, me too!' Despo handed me a beer, which I raised to him before taking a swig as Romaric joined me.

'Who were you cheering for?' I asked him with a grin. 'Me or your countryman?'

'You, Dobson. I thought I better had because no one else was!' I laughed and put an arm around his shoulder as we went to find the rest of our friends from the section.

We had some unfortunate news after Camerone - the officers had reserved our medical check-ups until the last minute. The doctor would listen to our hearts, poke around our stomachs and feel our joints for anything untoward. I had passed fine, but that could not be said for everyone. One afternoon I was in the room and Horvath came and sat down heavily on the bed.

'What is it?' I asked him, looking up to see a very forlorn look on his face.

'They've just told me I'm inept medically,' he said in disbelief. Botch and I exchanged a glance.

'So, you won't be coming to Mali?' Botch asked.

Horvath shook his head. 'No, it's something to do with my old knee operation. For some reason it means I'm not fit to go on mission, even though I've already done both the winter and summer mountain training and it's been fine!' He tutted in exasperation.

'What will you do then?'

He looked at me and said, 'I'm going back to Budapest, what's the point of being a soldier if I can't go on mission?'

I was inclined to agree with him and I felt for the guy. His hopes had been dashed because some medical officer detected the slightest problem that he clearly hadn't wanted to bite him in the arse. He covered himself by marking a big red 'X' into Horvath's medical dossier, killing his career without a second thought.

'I'll go this weekend' he continued, 'I'll take a bag and I won't come back for Monday. That's it.'

There was a long silence in the room with each of us lost in his own thoughts. For a moment, we absorbed the gravity of the situation for poor Horvath.

It was finally broken when I said, 'so Horvath, what shoe size did you say you were?'

We all burst into laughter and Horvath opened his wardrobe for me to peruse. 'Take it all, it doesn't matter to me now.' I did not see him again after that Friday. I'd always assumed he'd worked his way back into the criminal underworld of Budapest, once more.

Horvath's place in our group was filled by Crecu, a Moldovan Premiere Classe who I was not particularly fond of at the time, but consigned myself to make an effort with as we would be spending four months together.

A week or so later I was on leave for the last time before we all went to Mali and spent a few days in a suburb outside of Novisad, Serbia with Romaric. It was a wonderful culture to experience, and I was readily welcomed by all his friends, as Romaric showed me the night life whilst we drank ourselves stupid.

I also spent a week in the Hungarian countryside with my friend DeVries, a big guy from the Netherlands, who I had recently met from one of the other sections in my compagnie. His father had a farm there and we hunted deer and boar with a crossbow to prevent them destroying the crops. There is a strange excitement you feel when stalking game, it's like something primal, instinctual even. We followed, as stealthily as we could, the tracks of wild pigs into the dusk until darkness had fallen around us and the only light came from a full moon above. After an hour of this, we could finally hear them feet away, rummaging and snorting into the undergrowth. DeVries put his arm out to stop me moving any farther and pointed.

'They're just on the other side of that bush, listen.' He took the crossbow slowly from his shoulder and placed a bolt into the flight groove. He brought the bow up to aim, not quite being able to make out his target.

DeVries took the shot and missed, cursing, the sudden noise sending them sprinting away squealing. It was a mixture of both excitement and fear as boar can maul you quite nastily given half the chance. We did get deer, however. Creeping through the meadows, we knew we were likely to startle one who had been sleeping in the long grass. They would awaken, jump up and run a short distance away and then stop, scanning the environment to see if the thing that had woken them was truly a threat. That was the best time to shoot.

And it was exactly in that way that I brought one down, firing a bolt through its centre mass as the barbed head of the arrow tore through organs, killing it in seconds. We brought the carcass back for DeVries' new puppies who wasted not a bite, stripping the bones of meat in a couple of days.

My thoughts turned to the coming deployment to Mali and I wondered what it would be like. It would be hot I knew that; northern Mali was right in the middle of the Sahara Desert, one of the largest expanses of nothing in the world. It was one of the poorest countries in the world too, a hard place to live for sure. I wondered if I would see any action. There was a war going on, after all; even if the French weren't as involved as the Malian army, we might see something. I hoped so. Is that not what I was there for anyway?

The time soon came for us to bid goodbye to the regiment and our friends to take the first leg of the journey as a section. There would be several waves of incoming French troops to Mali as the battalions changed over, so the process would not be so taxing logistically. Some sections of the compagnie had already departed several weeks earlier and just a couple of days before we left the regiment, we had some unwelcome news.

One of the Caporals from my compagnie had been stationed in Timbuktu with his section and had somehow managed to accidentally fire an AT4, an anti-vehicle rocket, next to an ammunitions container. Luckily, the AT4 is equipped with a minimum safety distance ensuring that if the rocket were to hit the ground before say fifty metres, it won't explode.

A good thing someone had thought to include that feature too, for if the munitions container had been hit, it would have exploded, killing the group of Legionnaires who were in it at the time. There had been a casualty of sorts, though. Another Caporal from my Compagnie had been hit by the metal wing of the rocket as it passed his inner thigh, cutting it open and requiring stiches. It was one hell of a blunder, and the culprit was sent home early, sure to spend a decent stretch of time in military prison. An annoying side effect of this was that every waking moment, until we actually left the regiment, was spent doing AT4 training. Clearly, someone higher up didn't want the same thing happening twice, but they needn't have worried, I wasn't even going to touch one of the damn things after that!

It wasn't a good start, but spirits were high nonetheless, as we made our way to the airport. We had all known each other for a while now and everyone had settled into their roles, which we knew more or less. Del Campo was easy going as usual, and Botch was both the disciplinarian and trickster. When I lay down to have a kip whilst we waited for the flight, he encouraged the others to balance as many random objects on me as possible, so I looked like some strange kind of homeless person wearing desert camouflage fatigues to passers-by.

As all the French troops piled onto the plane, I realised just how many of us there were. Several hundred filled every seat and I had to remind myself that there had been numerous waves of this. Thousands of French soldiers were being shipped off to the desert in a gargantuan effort to combat the terrorist insurgency. France had long been a favourite of terrorist attacks in Europe; it was time we took the fight to them.

It took us five hours to get to Niamey, southern Niger, the French command base of operations. When I stepped off the plane into the sun, I remember thinking, 'shit, these engines are hot'. But when I came down the steps and away from the aircraft, I realised that was the temperature of the air outside. In the high forties (degrees Celsius), it was an oppressive heat, the likes of which I had never known. And it would only get worse, as we were at the start of the rainy season - the hottest part of the year.

We had to wait in Niamey for twenty-four hours before we flew out to Gao, the largest FOB (forward operations base) for French troops in Mali. The Legionnaires stuck together in Niamey's waiting area, always feeling like the odd ones out amongst so many regulars, sweating and hoping we'd get used to the heat soon.

As the plane was coming in to land in Gao, a less comfortable military aircraft than the civilian one we had entered Africa with, we had the chance to see the terrain, and the city of Gao. What I saw was a vast expanse of sand, as far as I could see, broken up by small patches of green bushes and rocky outcrops protruding from the ground here and there. The earth seemed to have a reddish-brown hue to it and the landscape was monotonous. Looking closer, I could make out the trails of dirt roads that lead into town, with a couple of little specs far below that could have been a boy leading a donkey laden with plastic containers full of water.

Gao itself was unremarkable, too. All the buildings seemed to be made from earth, as they were the same reddish brown as the ground around them, often favouring simplistic square designs with flat rooftops. The wealthier districts were broken up into small walled compounds with two or three of these houses in each, the roads in the grid-like system all leading toward the river Niger, the city's life force.

As for the military base, it was truly vast from the air, being almost half the size of Gao itself. An enormous airstrip dominated the centre, either end of which was one half of the base for the UN and another half for the French and Malian forces. In the French half alone, walking around Gao was like walking around a small town in its own right. There were two huge mess halls at either side that would fill with troops during mealtimes, numerous outdoor gyms - as the one air conditioned indoor one was always full - an infirmary, several mechanics yards with vehicles in various states of disrepair baking out in the hot sun, antennas and satellite dishes dotted here and there, walls of metal shipping containers stretching out for hundreds of metres, hangars along the airstrip where the helicopters were stored and row upon row of heavy duty light brown tents, which were the standard accommodation for a group of soldiers.

When we landed, we were ushered out of the plane and away from the airstrip where the base was a hive of activity. People and vehicles were moving this way and that, more aircrafts were taxying into the runway and the beat of helicopter blades filled the air as they travelled overhead from the UN camp.

Del Campo searched the waiting crowd of faces and found our compagnie's Adjutant, who waved him over and shouted over the noise that once we had isolated our bags from the enormous pile being unloaded from the aircraft, we were to report to the Legion's own camp at one side of the base. He would send a truck for our bags later. One of the first things I noticed about the people already there was that their desert fatigues were all covered in the dusty reddish colour of the earth. Looking down at my own, I was conscious that they were still very clean.

I chatted to Istvan, the Hungarian Premiere Classe in my group, that I couldn't wait to see how the guys from the first section were doing with the compagnie Capitaine, the Adjutant Fonta and the Polish Sergeant Chef that everyone hated now that they were all living together in the same camp. It was never good to have too many higher-ranking individuals around because they would always find a way to break your balls, one way or another. We amused ourselves wondering just how bad it would be. When we got there, it was as bad as I had imagined.

I shouted out a greeting to some of the guys I knew, we bumped fists and they told me in grave tones what they had done since they got there. Apparently, they had re-arranged the whole Legion camp to a way that had suited the Adjutant. And then they began to make pyramids of rock on either side of the camp's entrance, meticulously painted the flaming grenade along with the Legion colours - red and green, as well as the gigantic wooden sign that read, 'Legion Étranger,' so the whole base would know we were there.

I had to laugh. It was typical Legion culture to show the rest of the French army that we were the best. It would be less amusing to me, however, when I discovered that I would be living in the same camp for the foreseeable future. Until there was a plane ready to take me and my team to Timbuktu, where we were supposed to be, we remained. As the day was almost over, there was no point in starting all the work we had to do. Instead, the eight of us in my group headed to the main bar, or foyer, to get a drink and discover a bit more of the base.

By the time the sun set at 6pm, (consistent all year round) the main bar was already full of troops chatting and drinking. We all sat down, once we had a beer paid for in our new Malian money, and I seemed to be in a constant state of wiping the sweat from my brow, despite the fact the sun was nowhere to be seen. Del Campo gave us a little pep talk, seeing that the news of our staying in the camp with all the unpopular officers and sous-officiers had disheartened us somewhat.

'Come on guys, it's only for a week or two, just until they find us a plane.'

Botch gave us a sly grin, 'in the meantime, look at some of the girls! Oh la la!' We laughed and I shook my head sceptically, for while the concept of girls in combat fatigues was new to us, army girls tended to be more masculine than most.

I was impressed by the sheer scale of the French operation in Mali when, at breakfast, we could see the number of people eating, the dining hall full of soldiers. I was quite enjoying being a part of it all, even if my role as a single armoured vehicle driver made me feel like a very tiny cog in an immense system. But there was work to do, I wouldn't be much of an armoured vehicles driver without a vehicle. My job for the day was to get my VAB from logistics and get it working.

I saw the sergeant there, filled out the necessary paperwork and climbed into my new VAB. Well, new to me at least. The VAB's had been in service since the 70's and this particular one seemed to have had a very long and eventful life already. It was rusty, some of the hatches didn't close properly and, because it was the older version, there was no air conditioning. This meant that behind the armoured glass the cockpit was like a greenhouse, the heat having nowhere to escape to, and at midday it was a furnace.

I drove it back to our camp where my team was waiting and we got to work on it. I checked the oil levels and made sure the steering was okay and then, over the next few days, we had the job of modifying the interior and exterior of the VAB, to make it capable of holding all the extra water and rations we would need to survive a two week patrol out in the desert. We used the bastion wall, a flat packable steel mesh that would fold out and then fill with a cubic metre of earth in each section to build the wall of a FOB, to make two heavy duty baskets on either side of the VAB. The steel of the bastion wall was good, and thick. We also made a kind of shaded roof for Tessier, my gunner, who would sit to my right on the 12.7mm gun operating the radio and would be the most exposed to the sun. As for the other six, they would be on two opposing benches in the belly of the vehicle, on the other side of the motor.

I played some ACDC through my speaker as Botch, Istvan, Noh and I worked on the vehicle, totally underestimating the power of the African sun. We were red as lobsters by the end of the morning. Most activity stopped on the FOB from 11am to 3pm, as the conditions were simply too hot to work under. The temperature could climb to over 50 degrees celsius; the hottest I ever saw on an exposed thermometer was sixty!

The tents we lived in had a layer of insulation and an air conditioning unit behind them in an attempt to keep them cool during the day. The only problem was that the units had been running non-stop since 2013 and had also been used in Afghanistan before that. The result was that they were not always the most reliable machines. The air-conditioning repair team on the base must have had their work cut out for them because they seemed to be called out to our camp every other day. Even when they were working, when it was over fifty outside, you can bet that inside it would still be at least thirty. We'd lie on the metal cots trying to move as little as possible, sweating into the mattresses. It was truly an abominable heat, one that you never really get used to. There were locals who came into the French base to work and they were all small, skinny and dark, well suited to dealing with the incredible sun and lack of water.

We must have been there a week before we heard we would finally be placed on the next convoy mission out to the north, escorting some vehicles to another destination. It would be the first time I would leave the safety of the great fortress of Gao. I had learned of certain attacks on the base at Gao. There was a bar called the 120, as that was the diameter in mm of the soviet mortar that had struck, taking the leg of a French soldier with it. There was also a 'night club' on the base called 'La Ruine,' which was exactly that: an old building there long before the French army, and was peppered with bullet holes. Attacks were still nonetheless rare; they were more common in the remote and northern French outposts like Kidal, or Tessalite.

Almost the entire combat engineer detachment of the Legion would be present on the convoy, a total of five groups of eight and a command group with the captain, too. We'd be inserted into the convoy with the infantry, the regulars from the different mountain regiments. It was something like one group of Genie to three groups of infantry, who were twelve to a group, not eight. That was already a sizeable force, but on top of that, there were the medics VABs, logistics trucks with extra water and rations for everyone, the CAESAR's, artillery trucks with 155mm cannons on the rear, mechanics trucks and more. It would be a massive operation.

Our Adjutant tightened the screws, beginning to micro-manage the Sergeants to make sure they were ready, and generally being a pain in everyone's arse. It was sometime at the end of June before we headed out, that I saw my first sandstorm. They come at roughly the same time in the year, give or take a week, and the first is truly magnificent. The sand is bone dry by then, easily picked up by the wind. One day, the Adjutant Fonta was out shouting at various people for not operating to his ridiculous standard when I spotted some guys stood on a bastion wall pointing into the distance. More guys joined them to see what the fuss was about. Soon, half the camp had stopped what they were doing or had ran toward the airstrip to get a better view. I followed, and when I climbed up onto a wall I stood with the rest, open mouthed in disbelief. Far in the distance, there was a colossal wall of sand moving slowly toward us, stretching out in either direction as far as the eye could see. A famous sandstorm of the Sahara, I thought excitedly.

Lightning flashed ominously behind the clouds, and the booming sound of thunder rumbled toward the camp. The sheer size of it became apparent the closer the storm came. It rose hundreds of metres into the sky, a dirty, reddish-brown, billowing angry cloud. It was like a titan, a biblical phenomenon, or the hand of God slowly reaching out to squash us all. As I watched in fascination, guys either side of me had taken out cameras to film as it got closer and closer, slowly moving toward us. It must have been ten kilometres away, then soon only several and then, it was upon the outer walls of the FOB, and moving far quicker than I had initially thought. My fascination turned to mild panic, as I saw other people sprint away from the cloud several hundreds of metres ahead, only to be swallowed up and disappear from view. I turned to run and felt the howling wind on my back as the grains of sand pelted me from every direction. Suddenly, I was blind. There was sand everywhere, the force of the wind sending it flying into my face, stinging the skin painfully.

I had to stumble back to the relative safety of my tent, relying more on my memory of the camp to navigate rather than my vision. I bumped off walls, tripped on the guide ropes fastening the tents to the earth and stretched out my arms blindly, I couldn't see a thing! Somehow, I did manage to find my way back to my tent. The first thing I did was try to scrape the sand out of my eyes. Looking down, I could see it was everywhere, I was completely plastered in it. The others had fought their way back, too and were in a similar state, our fatigues covered in a fine layer of red.

The wind battered the tent outside, and it felt as though it would rip it up at any given moment. Del Campo shouted at us to zip down the tent flap as the sand was already working its way inside. I peeked outside and saw only several metres in front of the entrance, the storm had created a unique kind of sand-fog that blotted out all sources of light; one could be forgiven for thinking it was the dead of night.

I remember reading a historical source on crusader armies in Egypt years ago that touched on African storm. Supposedly, they had been caught in the open in a particularly violent one and had even lost a chunk of their number to it. So, these storms, while beautiful to behold, could prove deadly if you didn't find shelter. It wasn't difficult to imagine either. The sand pelting my skin had been painful and disorienting, and it was all too easy to lose your way in the eerie darkness.

When the storm had passed, we were able to resume work, having to brush sand off everything. In the aftermath, we spent a considerable amount of time hunting rogue objects that the wind had picked up and strewn everywhere.

In the time leading to our departure in the convoy, my group and I had fallen into a routine: we would run in the morning, just as the sun came up as it was the coolest part of the day, shower, eat breakfast, work on our VAB or familiarise ourselves with the equipment, eat lunch, take a nap until 3pm, work another couple of hours and then finish with another workout of pull ups and dips by the bars next to our vehicle, before eating again. When the sun had gone down, I'd have a beer or two with my team. Del Campo, Botch, Karnowski, Tessier, Istvan, Noh, Crecu and myself would sit around a little table in the foyer, chatting away calmly and joking in a most agreeable way that the leadership of Del Campo and Botch seemed to produce. It was great fun, I have some fond memories of a few good evenings out in the desert, where there is nothing to do to pass the time but talk.

'If you could have a superpower, what would it be?' Karnowski had asked the group once, as we sat around on ammo crates and camp chairs one evening.

'The ability to be clean and cool in an instant.' I said wiping my dusty brow.

'How about the ability to make a pizza magically appear whenever you like with whatever topping you like.' Tessier piped up, attempting to squeeze every last drop of chocolate from a bar that had long since melted in its packet.

'I knew you were going to say something like that, you chubby little fucker.' Botch said. 'Lay off the chocolate! And how about the ability to read minds?'

Karnowski sucked air in through his teeth. 'Ooh, you don't want to see what's in my head Caporal Chef!' He grinned.

'Relax, I've already seen plenty of pictures of your sister.' Botch retorted. 'How about you, Sergeant? What would you have?'

Del Campo slapped at a mosquito on his neck before replying 'how about some bug spray that actually works?'

'Yea, one that doesn't melt my watch, look!' He held up his watch the plastic strap of which had been partially eroded by the corrosive spray.

'Ah, the mosquitoes could be worse.' Botch said. 'What about that French guy who got bitten by a scorpion last week and had to be airlifted out?'

Del campo snorted. 'Firstly, the mosquitos probably don't want your Russian blood. Secondly, that guy was prodding the scorpion for a good half hour with a stick. Zip up your nets and you'll be fine.'

'But my net has a huge hole in it!' Tessier complained.

'What happened, did you roll over in your sleep?' Karnowski laughed.

'No, it came like that. I swear, the logistics guys didn't want to give us Legionnaires to have the good ones.'

'Hm. Maybe.' Botch said. 'But they definitely kept all the good ration packs for themselves. All I've had is menu number twelve for three days now! There's only so much beef casserole a man can take.'

Noh sat smiling around at everyone as usual, laughing at all the jokes even if he didn't understand them.

It's all quite surreal when you think about it. In my group there was an Englishman, a Spaniard, a Ukrainian, a Pole, a French-Japanese, a Hungarian, a Moldovan and a South Korean, all working as a team, in theory to fight terrorists for France. They told us we were French soldiers and I suppose we were technically, but I always felt more like a mercenary. Let's face it, if they stopped paying us, we wouldn't be there. Ninety-nine percent of Legionnaires do not come to France for any particular love of the country, they were being paid for a service. And in this case that was war.

# CHAPTER 7

For the most part, everyone looks pretty similar in the army - the same clothes, the same haircut, individuality isn't generally a terribly widespread concept. That's why, when you see someone different, you know there is a special reason. Botch and I were eating one day in the canteen, when a group of men walked in wearing European camouflage. Everyone else had to wear the light browns of the desert, while they wore the darker greens and blacks of the European countryside. They wore their hair and beards long, the polar opposite of 'everything-shaved-but-the-eyebrows' Legionnaires, and each carried a glock at their hips.

'Who are they?' I asked Botch. Looking up, he told me the only people who could dress like that were the special forces or the commando units. I had to admit, I was jealous. When they passed our table I got a glimpse of the Velcro insignia on their shoulders: an owl upon a star.

'That's the GCM.' Botch said, pointing at the insignia. 'You know we have a section of them at our regiment, right?'

Of course I did, how could I not? 'GCM' stood for Groupement Commando Montagne, the mountain commandos. There were plenty of guys I knew who had tried the selection from my compagnie last December. I would have tried out myself, had I not been on that damn vehicles course. I didn't know a single person who had passed it because they had all been unsuccessful. I supposed that would have been the case for me too, as they all agreed that it was tough. But I couldn't help thinking how cool it would be to be part of a unit like that, the French elite, shock troops flown into battle on helicopters when the shooting started. For the moment, I could only be envious and consigned myself to my trusty VAB.

Before the big convoy mission, we got a chance to test the VAB when our compagnie headed out with the infantry to the local shooting range, which was more of a sandy berm several kilometres from the base. You must have explicit permission to leave the base and must travel in armoured vehicles when doing so. As a result, our little shooting party soon had made a convoy of its own as we left the FOB for the first time. The VAB grumbled as I wrestled with the steering wheel whilst I peered out of the front window, wiping the sweat from my brow. Tessier was sat in the turret to my right and called out the obstacles as we swerved around the carefully placed bastion walls leading out of the base. My field of vision was extremely poor and Tessier had to shout, 'slow down, slow down!' several times to prevent me colliding with some bollards on our first outing. Once outside the base however, there was nothing really to collide with. It was just open ground. And with the vast openness and gentle dunes meant, you could drive literally anywhere; that is just what we did as the convoy headed toward the range in neat single file.

The infantry always took the first position in the convoy, and Genie took the second. This way, if ever there was a threat of an IED, we would be near the front to deal with it. We had to be envious of the VBCI's (véhicule blindée du Combat, Infanterie), too- the infantrymen's vehicles. They were enormous beasts, four huge wheels on either side and a 20mm gun mounted into a turret on the top. They had come into service around 2010 and it showed. They outclassed the VAB's in every way; the extra wheels meant they seldom got stuck in the sand, there was extra protection in the form of a thick armoured plate protecting against IED's bolted to the underbelly. And most importantly, they had air conditioning!

I followed behind the front VBCI all the way to the range, cursing the fact that their vehicle, although twice the size of mine, seemed to be twice as fast, too. I had to floor the accelerator from time to time to keep up as we sped over the dunes.

There were already dark-skinned children waiting for us at the range; I had to break hard to avoid hitting one as they came running in delight up to the vehicles and was rewarded with a string of curses from the back. The children shouted, 'Chocolat! Chocolat!' or 'Argent! Argent!' holding out their hands hopefully. I watched as a guy standing on the VBCI threw down an energy bar from his ration pack and a swarm of barefoot children descended upon it, the older ones getting the better of the younger as they punched and kicked their way to the food. They must have been hungry.

They were soon shooed away by a sergeant, and the range was cleared so we could begin shooting. Tessier played with the 12.7mm gun on our VAB, which is tremendous fun and makes a great noise when you shoot it. I laughed as I saw one of the officers had let Karnowski shoot two 7.62mm machine guns at the same time, looking like Polish Rambo as he held them both at the hip with some difficulty, a big ole grin on his face.

When I stood on the roof of the VAB, I had a pretty good visual of the kind of terrain we would be working in and it struck me again how barren it was. Away from the river Niger, there was barely any green; it seemed impossible that there could be enough food for everyone. The city of Gao was big enough and they could not all be farmers. I had not seen any fat locals yet...

The day before we left for the patrol, I had to refuel my VAB and park it in its respective position in the convoy, with all the other vehicles so that, the next morning, all we had to do was embark and be on our way. There were an incredible number of armoured vehicles - it must have been close to a hundred! On the morning of our departure, I sat on the roof of my VAB, my legs dangling into the hatch just above the driver's seat. We were in the first third of the column and I had a good vantage point to watch the hub of activity around me as soldiers rushed this way and that. Group leaders tested communications, loaded equipment or made last minute changes to the vehicles, while some others were scoffing a quick breakfast. The Commandant in command met with each of the Capitaines of the respective entities present for the mission, giving them their final orders. Each vehicle was supposed to support its occupants for five days with food and water, and the vehicles looked as though they could have come straight from a scene from Mad Max. There were a plethora of mis-matched and homemade additions to make them capable of storing all the extra rations. Most had done as we had and added huge bastion wall baskets.

I watched guys load extra water and food into the backs of the vehicles. It was a lot of water when you added it up. We calculated that in a day each man would need eight litres. That sounds like an awful lot, but taking into account the horrendous temperatures it makes more sense.

So, there were eight of us needing eight litres a day - that's sixty-four litres for a day in total and times that by five and you get three hundred and twenty. In a bottle there were one and a half litres, so three hundred and twenty divided by one and a half, is two hundred and fourteen. Two hundred and fourteen bottles per VAB for five days. Now, imagine that there are one hundred vehicles in total, some with more occupants than ours. That is a lot of water.

The French had it shipped in by the container, and, for a mission like this predicted to last a little over two weeks, there had to be several trucks in the convoy carrying only water and rations. It was a logistics nightmare and it's easy to see how poor planning could screw you later on.

My thoughts were interrupted when Del Campo waved at me to get into the cockpit and fire up the engine after a voice on the radio asked each vehicle in order if it was ready to go. 'Pret!' Del Campo shouted when it was our turn. And soon we were pulling out of the safety of the bastion walls of Gao once more.

For the first few kilometres, we drove on what was probably one of the only tarmacked motorways in northern Mali. We made decent progress, but it wouldn't last long. A few hours in the convoy rolled to a halt. Tessier shouted to my right and I, of course, heard nothing over the sound of the engine. All I could see of him was his little legs sticking out of the bottom of the turret, so we developed a system whereby he would tap his feet twice on the dashboard next to the gear lever to signify 'stop', and once to signify 'go.'

Someone had mechanical problems already, so everyone had to stop and wait until it was resolved. It was somewhere behind us but when I opened my hatch to peek out, the column of vehicles stretched out back to the horizon. We each maintained at least fifty metres between each vehicle in case an IED was triggered, insuring only one vehicle would be hit by the blast. The result was not being able to see the last vehicle in the convoy. It was so far away from our position near the front.

Fortunately, it was resolved quickly, and we were on our way once more. We followed the motorway to the most northerly part of the river Niger, and then pulled away from it and onto sandy dirt roads that didn't seem like roads at all - just trails in the desert that a few vehicles and donkeys had come along before. The going was much slower now and, every now and again, the convoy would grind to a halt once more as one of the vehicles got stuck in the sand, wheels spinning uselessly. One of the VBCI's would have to come and pull them out.

It was hot, always so hot out there. I would be sweating constantly and there was never any respite from the heat. We stopped for lunch during the hottest few hours of the day - the convoy being ordered into a large square formation to defend from any attack the guns on the turrets all facing outwards - as everyone set up some fine netting or tarpaulin for shade. Even in the shade and with my shirt off, my body instantly made a sweaty puddle on the fabric of the cot I lay on. It was like being in a sauna I couldn't escape from. We all ate and tried to move as little as possible. I remember thinking that fifty below had to be better than fifty above, at least if you are cold, you can warm yourself up. Out in the desert you could only wait until the day became a little cooler and the sun dropped below the dunes.

The camp was soon still as everyone had tried to find some shade to hide in, most guys sitting shirtless or lying on cots with their eyes shut willing the heat to abate. It was hard to cope and sometimes it was too much to handle. On more than one occasion someone had to be airlifted out and taken back to the infirmary in Gao, having collapsed from heat stroke. And it wasn't as if any of us were doing anything particularly energetic either. During the patrols we carried out every now and again in local villages, we would walk around slowly and hoped that there would be some breeze that day.

Lying there, I was desperately thirsty but reluctant to drink because I knew the water would be scalding hot and would burn my throat as it passed. The constant glare of the sun reflecting off the sand all around was enough to make you dizzy if you didn't wear your sunglasses, too. I had to close my eyes and breathe deeply.

I think we were all glad to pack up and get back on the road, at least the journey would take our minds off the heat. The novelty of driving the VAB in the desert wore off quickly when it was hour after hour, day after day, and fatigued me much more than regular driving. You had to concentrate, avoid wet patches of sand that the rain from last week had soaked, so as not to get the vehicle stuck, and wrestle with the steering wheel of the VAB back and forth, doing your best to follow in the tracks of the vehicle ahead.

Every now and again the wheels would spin in the sand; I would worry that the VAB would get stuck and the entire convoy would have to stop to wait for us to pull out. The VAB ploughed on, however, managing to haul itself to safety as I floored the accelerator. For the night, we stopped at around 18:00 to set up the camp on high ground. Again we formed the gigantic armoured square of VAB's, VBCI's and trucks that would protect us against any enemy suicide vehicles. Even with all the vehicles neatly aligned nose to nose, the interior was still around the size of a football pitch and would have been a bizarre sight indeed for any passing locals.

There was soon a hub of activity in the square as everyone set up their cots and mosquito nets for the night, whilst some of us stood guard atop the wall of vehicles. There were a couple of jobs to do; because we were combat engineers (and Legionnaires), the Commandant in command of the convoy had delegated us the task of digging the latrines. This soon became a running joke that we were there so the rest of the French troops could shit. It was essentially a glorified trench with a couple of poles joined by a crude curtain for privacy, some fifty or so metres outside our square.

To the annoyance of the guys situated directly opposite the latrines, there were some who did not fully understand the concept of filling in the trench with sand once you had done your business. An adverse side effect of which was that the next gust of wind would send shitty toilet paper blowing into the camp over their feet. They would proceed to curse the culprit in loud voices until someone told them to shut up. We never dug them opposite our VAB.

I also had to clean the air filters in my VAB's engine almost daily as the amount of sand that accumulated inside could cause problems within. It was always a pain in the arse because, to access the engine, you had to unscrew these great big plaques and awkwardly lift them off, then fiddle around with your hand in the hot engine to unscrew the air filter and bring it outside, clean it and replace the whole lot. Once it was done, however, I was free to sort out my bed and eat something.

I cannot tell you how many of the standard French rations I have eaten, but it must be hundreds. They come in this rectangular cardboard box in which you get a couple of tinned meals, lots of hard biscuits - handily designed to block you up slightly so that when you shit, you'd only need a wipe or two: a packet of muesli, some paté, tinned cheese, a few little energy and chocolate bars, a heating kit to warm your meals, some tissues and some water purification tablets. No one has ever looked forward to eating them, so a lot of guys tried to find creative ways of improving the taste or brought pot noodles they had bought back at Gao.

Fortunately, Del Campo had planned ahead and had managed to scavenge a large pot, a propane tank and a bag of pasta from the kitchens before we left and began cooking us all a concoction of pasta, soy sauce and pate that actually turned out to be quite good. Using the empty 1.5L plastic water bottles, we could make bowls by cutting them in half down the middle, effectively making a long container into which Del Campo served the pasta pasta. We sat next to our VAB on ammo crates or camp beds and chatted away as the last rays of the sun disappeared, taking the piss out of Klimek's tattoo's or laughing at Botch's jokes, bathed in the bright glow of an unobstructed moon.

Showering was perhaps the best bit of the day. After sweating into the same set of clothes for a week, the daily shower was fantastically refreshing. You could get nasty sweat rashes and the shower was the one respite you might have. I'd strip off, make my way to the outside of the square wearing only my trendy blue Crocs with a couple of water bottles under my arm and a bar of soap in my hand. Looking left and right, I could see plenty of other naked pale bodies showering down under the stars too.

In our daily water ration, we had accounted for several litres with which to shower. Generally, one bottle poured over our heads to wet us and to soap up with, then a second to rinse down with. Drying naked in the night air, if there was a bit of a breeze, I might even feel something close to being cold. When it was thirty degrees after the sun had set, that sensation would never last long unfortunately. One thing I did enjoy doing once my little evening routine out in the desert was complete, was to climb into my cot and zip up the mosquito net, through which I could lie in and see every star in the Milky Way outlined perfectly. There was no light pollution to speak of in the middle of the Sahara. I would drift off to sleep looking up in wonder at the vastness that lies beyond our world, marvelling at just how small I was.

We continued like this, day after day. I would try to rub the fatigue out of my eyes as I followed the tracks of the lead vehicle, the loud droning of the engine ringing in my ears all the while. We were deep in the desert now and did not seem to be following any road or path at all, instead carving our own way through the great ocean of sand. Every now and again, in the middle of nowhere, we might pass a family living under a tarpaulin propped up by four sticks with a few donkeys around them. The children would wave and try to run alongside us for a while. I remember wondering how they managed to survive as there was no green, save for the occasional dry thorny bush, for miles and miles. There are easier places to live than northern Mali.

One week in, we had reached Tessalit, the northern most FOB under French control. The town nearby was small, the buildings all a uniform colour that matched the sand so that they seemed to blend in with the environment. There were rocky hills surrounding the FOB from which semi-regular mortar strikes were launched by the terrorists onto the town and military outpost that tended to be inaccurate and ineffective, for the most part. That was something I would experience first-hand the following year.

Once we had unloaded our cargo, whatever it was, we did not hang around. We headed south for the return journey where we would be taking a different route with the aim of patrolling a little more of the 'hot zones' in the desert. We would never find anything, however; the terrorists would have to be both mad and stupid to attack a convoy of this size, but that wasn't to say they weren't watching us.

You can always tell when a large storm is coming in the rainy season - the air becomes completely still and particularly hot and thick. It's much easier when the convoy was on the move, as that would be the only sort of cooling breeze you would get. When stopped, however, it was so hot and oppressive it was almost difficult to breathe. When we stopped for the night there were already dark clouds in the distance that screened the occasional flash of lightning.

In our square, we set up camp, but quickly realised the storm was moving toward us. Those brave enough attempted to make a kind of tent with a tarpaulin over the mosquito nets on their camp beds. But I now know, having done three rainy seasons in Mali, how futile that can be: the storms are violent. The wind will pick up and toss around anything not anchored firmly into the ground. As the wind began to blow stronger and large droplets of rain began to fall onto the still warm sand, I realised I'd have to give up on the idea of sleeping outside and tied my cot to the VAB, so that it didn't blow away, and clambered up into the driver's seat.

The VAB is not very comfortable on the best of days, nor did it help that it was parked on a slight dune so that the body was sloping downwards. The driver's seat was already at a ninety-degree angle on flat ground but now I was leaning forward and there was no way I was getting to sleep like that. I had a khaki-coloured shawl that I tried tying around my forehead with the other side tied around the back of the seat. It didn't really work, and my discomfort only intensified when water began to trickle onto my lap from the leaky hatch above my head, the rain now hammering on the steel. It was a long night, and I didn't sleep much. I was glad when the sun finally rose, and movement began in our camp. It wasn't long before we were on our way, but the torrential downpour during the night had caused other complications - the sand was now wet and trapped our vehicles far easier.

We all had sweat rashes by that point; the cheap material of our desert fatigues chafed against the skin. I was glad to be a driver when the convoy stopped at a village and disembarked to carry out a routine patrol, whilst I guarded the vehicle. It was easy to drink a litre an hour, or more, when on the move in the afternoon sun. I sat in my armoured greenhouse with both trapdoors open to try to encourage a through breeze without much success.

During the last few days of our mission, after around two weeks out in the desert, I detected a growing sense of longing amongst out team for a long cool shower and an air conditioned tent. The command seemed to have felt it, too, as the pace quickened and everyone managed to avoid getting their vehicles stuck on the last day, so as to re-enter Gao as soon as possible. Before long, we were back on the raised highway that followed the river Niger and took it back to Gao. I think we all breathed a sigh of relief when we saw the bastion walls with the little French soldiers stood upon them in the distance. Upon entering, the underbellies of our vehicles were checked by the guard with a mirror on a stick ensuring there were no IED's underneath. And then it was over, my first real mission. Nothing much had happened. We hadn't seen any real action, but it still felt like we had done something, worthwhile or not, and that had to be better than sitting on our arses in the base.

That night, after having cleaned and stored all the equipment, and showered of course, my team and I got drunk in the foyer and enjoyed a good night's sleep in an air conditioned tent.

In Gao, it was soon to be the 14th of July, the French national holiday, during which there would be magnificent military parades back in metropole (France). In Gao, too, there would be celebrations, albeit ones that we were told would all finish at 23:00 so as to keep the troops somewhat operational. As July came around however, Del Campo became increasingly anxious about leaving Gao and relocating to Timbuktu, as per our Chef de Sections promise. In fact, our group of eight was only supposed to be stationed in Gao for several days upon arrival, as the French FOB at Timbuktu had need of more combat engineer teams.

Yet, we had been absorbed into the Legionnaire camp at Gao and several days had already turned into weeks. Due to storms and higher priority missions, all the planes and helicopters taking soldiers from Gao to the other FOBs, and vice-versa, were seldom idle and had no space for us, or simply could not work at all when thunderous grey clouds were nearby. The rest of us were keen to get to Timbuktu as soon as possible because the Legionnaire camp had become more and more like the regiment. Adjutant Fonta seemed to feel the need to prove, either to the compagnie Capitaine or to the rest of us, how tight a grip he had over the men by micromanaging each group, getting us to do bullshit tasks and just being a pain in the arse in general.

One evening, we thought our prayers had been answered when the logistics sergeant came to inform Del Campo that there was a plane for us tomorrow morning. Excited, we all packed our things and prepared our equipment to head off to Timbuktu.

The next morning, a dusty and battered looking fifty-seater aircraft was waiting for us on the airstrip.

'Wow, they must really have run out of helicopters.' Karnowski said. 'That thing looks like it could fall apart at any minute.'

We climbed into the small plane nonetheless, and fastened our seatbelts as the pilot checked that everyone on his list was present and seated. Once complete, the door was closed and the pilot shut himself back in the cabin. Over the intercom system, he warned his twenty or so passengers of the risk of a storm blocking our route to Timbuktu, but added that we ought to make it anyway. I crossed my fingers that the fair weather would hold out long enough for us to reach the other FOB.

But half an hour into the journey, I realised that luck would not be on our side. Looking out of the window, the sky became greyer and greyer as we passed through several stormy clouds. Soon, all I could see from the little window was a dark grey mist. The turbulence light came on a moment later and the little plane began to shake fiercely. Tessier gripped the arms of the seat next to me so hard his knuckles were white and his eyes were shut tight.

A particularly violent gust of wind buffeted the aircraft threatening to pluck it from the sky, causing half of its passengers to shriek in panic.

'Jesus.' Tessier said, his eyes still screwed shut. 'I'm gonna die on this plane!'

'Ah, it'll be fine.' I tried to reassure him. 'Just think of it as a rollercoaster ride.'

'I hate rollercoasters!'

The plane shook again and banked sharply to the right. A couple of water bottles that had been left on the floor were thrown down the aisle and a bag fell from one of the overhead compartments.

'Shit!'

Fortunately, our pilot was not completely suicidal and wisely decided to make a U-turn out of the storm and to safety. The pilot apologised that he couldn't get us there and it would mean we would be stuck in Gao for another week, at the least, before any more aircraft became available. We groaned collectively. We must have been most of the way there.

Back at Gao, we trudged off the plane, thoroughly disheartened to find the Adjutant Fonta waiting for us at the entrance to the Legionnaire camp. 'Ah, so you're staying with us a while longer I hear. Excellent! I need someone to clean the barbeque grills for tomorrow. Del Campo, see to it that you and your boys get it done by the evening.' We all exchanged a look.

The evening of the 14th of July came and, when our work was done for the day and we had done our sport, there was a fantastic atmosphere around the military camp. The sun fell at Gao and everyone made their way to the bars. Botch, Karnowski, Tessier and I had decided to do a bar crawl, having a beer at each unit's respective bar. By each unit, I mean each collective group that worked together. For example, the logistics guys had one, the infantry and cavalry boys shared several and the medics had their own. Some bars were better than others - they had plenty of picnic benches and space with big walk-in refrigerators with a countertop built around them made from nice pine boards that they had paid the Africans to bring in from outside the FOB. Others were smaller, built from whatever anyone could find around the camp and the bars would be made of pallet wood surrounded by a few fold out chars.

There was no way we could do them all in one night, but we must have got though a good chunk before we ended up at the infamous 'la ruine' nightclub. Really, it was just a ruined old building tucked out of the way that some French regulars had put speakers in and a few chairs and tables. We were fantastically drunk by that point and sat around a table with some of the regulars talking about the differences between the Legion and the rest of the army.

It all came to an end when a commandant came yelling at 01:00 that we were all to bugger off that instant and to stop making so much noise. He was taking names, promising to have words with our superiors in the morning, which was when Botch decided we would make an escape by climbing through one of the back windows, giggling drunkenly as the Commandant shouted for us to stay where we were. The four of us headed back to the Legion camp, untroubled by the Commandant's threats, as Gao was big enough for us not to run into him any time soon. Sometimes, everyone looking the same in the army can work to your advantage.

Several days later, we finally had a plane to Timbuktu and this time we actually made it! Strangely enough, Timbuktu used to be a tourist destination before the conflict, mainly because of a semi-famous mosque and university. The mosque was said to be the world's largest mud building and almost seven hundred years old. But there were no tourists now, the war had kept any foreign visitors away for years.

The city was not enormous and was similar in many ways to Gao and every other Malian settlement. The streets were dusty and potholed, the buildings square and reddish-brown. The FOB was smaller too, at just a fraction of the size. The canteen was five air-conditioned tents, butted up against one another to make one long corridor and the foyer was just a fridge with a homemade wooden bar, a few tables and chairs. We got to see our friends from the 2ème compagnie that had got there before us and asked them how it had been so far. They were commanded by a Lieutenant who was by no means likeable, but was decidedly more relaxed than Adjutant Fonta. As a result, the atmosphere amongst the Legionnaires there was jovial enough. They had also mentioned that there had been a mortar strike on the base some weeks ago. My friend, who had not been in his bed at the time, had shrapnel tear through his sleeping bag exactly where his head would have been. Good job he hadn't decided to take a nap.

In fact, the only casualty so far was Djo, a Serb from the 1ère section, who had been a victim of the AT4 incident. The first time I met Djo (pronounced Jo) was some months ago back in the 2nd compagnie. He had just returned from his Caporal training having come second in his class and it was widely agreed that he was one of the fittest guys in the compagnie. Djo was of average height, muscular in an athletic way and was annoyingly competent. He could do anything the sergeants asked him to and did it well, whether that be leading a small team in a combat exercise, or delegating cleaning duties for the younger Legionnaires. I thought he seemed a little stern at first, but once I got to know him better, I found he was often quick to joke and he had a funny sort of chuckle when he laughed. Djo and I would go through a lot together in the coming years and, through all the shit we endured, I never once saw him break down or succumb to stress, fatigue or hunger. Djo didn't quit when we found ourselves in a dire situation. Instead, he'd say something like, 'well, I guess that's that, then. What's next?' And press on. Of all the guys I met during my time in the Legion, Djo is up there with the toughest.

He showed us all the scar on his leg where the guiding wings of the rocket had cut the flesh open and had to be stitched up. The culprit had long since returned to France and the damage, while it was insignificant to the FOB and its personnel, had tarnished our reputation there. Half of the French army seemed to have heard of the Legionnaire who fired an AT4 out of an ammunitions container. During one of my first nights in Timbuktu, some of the drunk regulars mocked us about it.

My friend, Cabello, was there, too. He was also a VAB driver and was showing me the VAB I would be driving my team around in.

'So, you have the VAB ultimate' he said, 'you know the version with extra armour, an automated gun turret and air conditioning?' He indicated the vehicle next to us.

'Of course,' I replied, 'I cannot wait to use the air conditioning inside!'

'Oh, the air conditioning is broken in this one' Cabello smirked, 'I did a patrol with it not so long ago' He said slapping the side of my new VAB. 'It's much worse because you can't have any of the trapdoors open whilst you're driving because of the extra armour.'

'Shit.' I said.

Cabello slapped me on the shoulder and laughed at my expression, 'You'll be fine, just drink lots of water!'

At least life on the FOB was easy going - the tempo seemed a little slower than that of Gao and everyone here seemed to know each other, it being far smaller. I had gotten used to the heat by now and didn't mind using the outdoor gym, sheltered from the sun by a mesh covering. There were also a couple of guys to train boxing here and we did a bit of sparring on the sandy ground below a guard tower.

There wasn't really a whole lot to do. We had to find other ways of entertaining ourselves, and there are only so many films I could watch at once. I've always been fond of making things. So, out of the bastion wall wire mesh, I managed to sculpt a pretty decent armchair. It took me a couple of days, my only tools being some wire cutters and a multi tool and I was red as a lobster when it was done. I brought it proudly into my little alveole in our eight-man tent.

Several days later, I was sat on the very same armchair playing a game on my laptop with my headphones on when there was a commotion out in the corridor. Crecu stuck his head into my alveole and said, 'Hey the FOB is being attacked, we need to get our equipment and head to the wall now.'

Now Crecu had a weird sense of humour and that, coupled with the fact that he said it so nonchalantly, led me to believe that he was having me on.

'Pssh, yeah whatever.' I said, sticking my headphones back over my ears and turning back to my game.

Crecu shrugged and said, 'suit yourself.' And was gone. I sighed and shook my head at the annoying disturbance.

Some fifteen or twenty minutes later, I decided I needed a piss, got up and strolled out of the tent wearing only my underwear and crocs, stretching as I blinked in the sunlight. When my eyes had adjusted to the glare, my heart stopped. The entire length of the bastion wall facing our tent was lined with French soldiers armed to the teeth, their rifles pointing out over the wall at what I could not tell, a definite sense of quiet tension in the air. Holy shit, we really were under attack! That bastard was telling the truth.

I ducked back into the tent and scrambled for my clothes, got dressed, grabbed my rifle, combat vest and helmet and sprinted outside. Where the fuck is my group? I panicked, running along the length of the wall until I spotted Tessier's short, chubby form in one of the guard towers, and then saw that the rest of them were there too.

'Where the fuck have you been?' Del Campo turned to me, questioningly.

'Ummm...' I started awkwardly. 'It doesn't matter now, get on that wall there and keep your eyes peeled.' I glared at Crecu next to me and he smirked.

'I did tell you.' He whispered.

We could hear a little gunfire in the distance, but could see nothing from our position on the wall. Apparently, one of the Malian army's outposts a kilometre away was being attacked, as they were easier pickings, but the firefight never made its way to our FOB. Botch, Karnowski and Istvan were aiming their rifles down the road in our field of fire. 'If someone comes down that road now, they're fucked.' Karnowski said, his eye looking down the sights of his FAMAS.

'Better make sure they're actually a terrorist first and not a civilian.' Botch chuckled.

'I'll just shoot anyone with a rifle.' Karnowski replied.

'But how do you tell?' Istvan chipped in. 'The terrorists and the Malian soldiers all look the same anyway.'

The three of them pondered that for a moment before Botch said, 'Shoot the one who shouts 'Allahu Akbar!''

'But they're all Muslims, the Malian soldiers could shout that too.' Istvan reasoned.

'Well, damn.' Karnowski turned to Istvan in frustration, 'I just want some action, tell me who I can shoot!'

'The Adjutant Fonta back at Gao.' Botch said with a grin. We all laughed.

It was true that we hadn't even seen the enemy since arriving a couple of months ago, but heard regular stories of attacks on Malian convoys and FOB's, during which there were frequent casualties and deaths. It seemed that the terrorists were not stupid, they picked their battles, knowing that the French army was far better equipped and organised. They avoided us at all costs and inflicted damage on the Malian army when they could. Perhaps they knew too that the French army would not be in Mali forever and saw our aid to the Malian forces a temporary disadvantage that they had to work around. In any case, it was frustrating to be here ready to fight and to put our training to use, only to find we hung around in the FOB not doing much at all; serving, apparently, as a passive deterrent.

In the end, the gunfire died down. An hour or so later, we were told that we could take off our equipment and go back to what we were doing, no one from our FOB having even fired a shot.

Some way through August, the Colonel on the FOB had a two-week patrol in the desert planned with several points of interest he wanted to visit. One of them was a suspected arms dealer's home in a town called Ber, east of Timbuktu. When we arrived there several days into our patrol, the fine red sand already in every nook and cranny imaginable, the Capitaine in command of our column established contact with the town's leader, who was known as 'the General.'

But general of what? There was fuck all there. He claimed he could summon a host of a hundred soldiers, but looking around the town it seemed more than likely that a good portion of that one hundred would be children or youths. Indeed, we saw a couple of lads zooming around on a motorbike as we entered the town with Kalashnikovs slung over their soldiers.

Supposedly, the Capitaine had asked 'the General' if he had given aid to al Quaeda or any of the other terrorist groups, accusations which he, apparently, vehemently denied. Del Campo relayed all of this to us over the radio, but I couldn't help feeling that 'Le General' would dance to the tune of any armoured convoy passing through his village, French or otherwise. He'd tell us whatever we wanted to hear, so long as he kept his position as leader of the town. This was no man's land after all, there was no law here; it was survival of the fittest.

The most desirable residence in the town belonged to the General, the walls of which were even plastered and painted. His wife was also the fattest woman in the village by a good stretch, a clear sign of wealth in this part of the world. As for the arms dealer, he was nowhere to be found. But we were directed to his property, which was walled off in a defensive compound. One of the other legionnaire groups began tearing the place apart and it was not long before there was a considerable weapons cache building up in the courtyard. There were AK's, PKM's, RPG's, Tokarev's, rockets, grenades and thousands of rounds of ammunition.

Our boys took it all several kilometres outside the town, while Tessier and I waited in the VAB chatting to pass the time. Eventually, we heard the thunderous boom of the explosives telling us the weapons cache had been destroyed in its entirety. I managed to persuade Del Campo to let me go on a patrol in the town, but soon regretted it because the air was particularly hot that afternoon and my camelback was shortly empty of water.

Ber was a miserable little place in truth. The houses were small and often consisted of a single room. The entrances were covered with a piece of fabric that waved in the breeze and the latrine was a hole dug behind them. Rubbish littered the street in front, where the children ran barefoot. Apart from the several old and worn vehicles, the only sign of modernisation was a single antenna that climbed ten metres into the air of a larger building that must have been the hospital. It was attached with several ropes, all of which had clothes drying on them. Here and there you could see women bashing grain to make flour with a rounded wooden branch and a stone basin, a process that would take up most of the working day. Some of the older children coerced tired looking donkeys along that pulled a cart load of recycled plastic containers filled with water from the river nearby.

We stuck around near the village in case the arms dealer showed up, having been promised by 'La General' that he would give him to us immediately should he learn of his whereabouts. Of course, he never did and several days later we were gone, our convoy moving out into the vast desert planes once more.

The halfway point of the mission had long since come and gone. Once we had finished our two-week patrol, it was almost time for the other two groups of Legionnaires in Timbuktu to leave for Gao and then return back to France as they had arrived in Mali around a month before us. We would be leaving for Gao several days after to be sent off to Ansongo where the rest of our section were stationed and where we would see out the rest of our opex (operation extérieure).

We bid goodbye to Djo, Cabello and the others as they boarded a cargo plane that left for Gao, leaving the rest of us quite envious. Del Campo had us pack our things once more and, like a band of little desert nomads, we found ourselves on the runway with all our gear waiting for our plane. It took us back to Gao where we stayed in the Legionnaire camp one night and caught up with the others.

A Caporal from one of the other sections had told me a funny story over a couple of drinks:

'So, whilst you guys were gone, there was a mortar strike on the base.'

'Oh shit, was everyone okay?'

'Yea, everyone was fine in the end. But you should have seen the Adjutant Fonta!' The Caporal had to control a fit of giggles before continuing.

'We were all sat outside the tents one night talking at around 21:00 and it was dark outside. Anyway, there was this massive 'BOOM' and the ground shook and everything! When we heard the siren wailing, we knew it was an attack and the Sergeants started shouting at everyone to get to the bunkers. And then we saw -' The Caporal stopped to laugh once more.

'What? What happened?' I asked.

'So, I was running down the tents here.' He indicated behind him. 'And just as I was passing the Adjutant Fonta's tent, he jumps out! And he's completely naked save for his flip flops and his rifle! He starts panicking, sprints for the bunker when this hugely fat black chick comes out right behind him, completely naked and shrieking! Louder than the siren!' The Caporal was cracking up as he told the story.

'And she starts running the wrong way and I'm like 'no, the bunker's over there!' and all the guys around me are wetting themselves while they run to the bunker. It's a miracle any of us made it. Once we were all crammed inside, it was so funny. The Adjutant and his whore are still completely naked and there are like fifty dudes waiting out this mortar strike!'

I was bent, doubled over with laughter and took a couple of minutes to compose myself before asking, 'So, what was Fonta like after that?'

'The bastard hasn't looked anyone in the eye since!'

We didn't linger long. The next day we were embarked on a Puma, a medium sized troop transport helicopter, and were flown out to Ansongo, where my chef de section greeted Del Campo and the rest of us. Romaric and Savelli were there too and I was glad to see their familiar faces. Ansongo was a similar size to the FOB at Timbuktu - there was only one bar and one canteen, and everyone seemed to know each other, but in typical Legion fashion the Legionnaires tended not to mix too much with the regulars.

Having said that, I did manage to get a few decent sparring sessions in with some of the Troupes de Marines. There was an empty shipping container that we used as a ring and I'd box my opponent inside, bouncing off the steel walls and leaving patches of sweat running down the hot metal as we panted from the exertion.

The rest of our opex was uneventful. Our attention soon turned to the three days of R&R in Crete that the army would pay for after our mission. Botch, Karnowski and I discussed over our food what the first thing we were going to do back in Europe was. 'Get drunk.' Karnowski had said, speaking like a true Pole.

'I heard there is a pool and a sauna in the hotel.' I said.

'You want to go in a sauna after four months in Mali? You're mad.' Botch chuckled.

'Well, maybe I'll give the sauna a miss. I certainly wouldn't mind an evening with a pretty barmaid though!' The others wholeheartedly agreed. After several months in the desert, we were as randy as a bunch of soldiers that you are ever likely to stumble across. It made me wonder how monks went a lifetime without sex, surely an unnatural state for any man?

We were given yet another VAB in Ansongo, which I managed to get well and truly stuck in some particularly wet sand, needing to be towed out by another vehicle using a heavy-duty cable. They pulled for several minutes to no avail, the wheels of the other VAB spinning uselessly in the sand and mud.

'What's wrong, why isn't it working? Do we need another vehicle to help?' came a voice in the radio and Tessier replied that we were doing all we could. One of the French sergeants ran up to my window, looked at me and said, 'did you take the hand brake off?'

I looked at the handbrake. It was engaged. I cursed. The sergeant sighed and told me not to worry about it. After I had wasted a good half hour of the convoy's time, we got back to the FOB for a late supper. Perhaps this was why the opexes were four months, you can only be at the head of your game for so long. I certainly had had enough at that point. Having to accept that we weren't going to see much action, the novelty of Mali had worn off. I was quite ready to go back to France, where the temperature is pleasant and there are considerably fewer bugs.

We saw the change in the landscape as a result of the rainy season three weeks later from the vantage point of our transport helicopter taking us back to Gao. There was now a lot of green mixed with the reddish-brown sand, as the rain had caused dormant seeds to germinate. During the last few weeks, we had had some powerful storms. So much rain had fallen, we had to dig irrigation trenches around our tents and the roads of the FOB had been churned into a muddy, wet mess. Wooden pallets had to be put down between the tents and the toilet so we wouldn't slip around in the middle of the night.

The water had also attracted great swarms of insects, the most annoying of which were mosquitos. The FOB commander had to insist that everyone wear long sleeves as soon as the sun had set, despite us all having had malaria injections back in France. I was still bitten plenty, however, and was often scratching at fresh bites on my body the next morning.

Gao was busier than ever. We were at the changeover period, another battalion would be replacing ours and there was often a hive of activity over by the airstrip as bags and crates were loaded and unloaded. Men shouted from the forklifts and wide-eyed fresh troops came down from the planes wearing pristine desert camouflage.

For our part, we had a week left and were 'technically' operational for a few days yet. But that didn't stop us drinking. The sous-officiers turned a blind eye or, like Del Campo, joined in and drank with the rest of us.

The evening was going great until a Ukrainian Legionnaire from the first section got drunk and started talking shit about Anglophones.

'Why is it that the Brits and the Americans have to stick their noses into everyone else's business, eh?'

'I don't know mate; I don't make the rules.' I turned away, but he poked me on the arm.

'No, you guys think you are so good and tell everyone you want peace, but it's you guys who are the real assholes. I'm telling you.'

'Why don't you just calm down and have a drink?' I said, starting to get a little annoyed.

'You are all a bunch of assholes!'

Having had too many beers myself at this point, and enough of the guys shit talking, I hit him square in the face and tackled him to the ground. We rolled around in the sand until the other lads pulled us apart. Fortunately, such things are forgotten fairly quickly, and the rest of the evening was spent recounting funny stories from the last few months.

I liked the one about a French Legionnaire from the third compagnie. Known for doing stupid stuff, he had gotten drunk, somehow managed to climb over the razor wire-topped bastion walls of the FOB without alerting the guards and stumbled the several kilometres into Gao city, where he supposedly drank at a local bar. Of course, for the morning assembly he was nowhere to be found and fearing the worst, the general in command had a helicopter in the air and an armoured patrol sent out to look for him. Soon, the whole base in Gao knew there was a Legionnaire suspected to have been kidnapped by Al Qaeda until he was found lying fast asleep in a drunken stupor several yards from the FOB walls, wrapped in a tarpaulin. He did plenty of jail time for that!

The last few days seemed to drag. And the eight of us, Del Campo, Botch, Karnowski, Crecu, Tessier, Istvan, Noh and myself, spent most of it in the foyer, just hanging around with not much else to do. As Karnowski explained to Botch the perfect shit he'd had the other day - Noh sat there smiling and nodding, understanding little as he always did - I thought of how fond I was of my group. After four months seeing the same faces day in, day out, we had formed a kind of bond. It is one of the more winning aspects of military life: the fraternity, and I supposed we had it at the end.

Before I knew it, we had left Gao for Niamey and were boarding the civilian aircraft that was to take us to Crete. I could sit back and breathe a sigh of relief. It was over. All there was to do now was relax. Stepping off the plane and smelling the scent of European pine in the fresh, cool evening air was reward enough. But the hotel was even fancier than we had imagined. Several hundred troops came off the bus and into the hotel lobby where we were ushered into an events room. The colonel in charge gave us all a speech, reminding us that we were to stay in the hotel during the night and under no circumstances were we to go to the bars in the local town. There would be serious consequences for anyone caught breaking this rule. Botch and I exchanged a grin and he whispered, 'better not get caught, then!'

Once we had put our bags in the room, we went to the hotel bar for some drinks and then slunk out to take a taxi to the town. A lot of dancing, laughing and beer later, I was spewing my guts up on the beach, thinking how nice it was to be out of the desert.

# CHAPTER 8

I dug my toes into the sand of Pa Tong beach in Phuket, Thailand, smiling to myself and enjoying the sun. We had returned from the three days of R&R to arrive back at 2REG for the hectic unloading, checking and cleaning of all the equipment we had taken with us for Mali. And a week after that, we had been allowed a month of leave. So, I had decided to take myself to Thailand. It was a completely different landscape from the one I had just absconded from and during my month off, I was treating myself to a well-earned period of rest. Well, sort of. I had once again come for the Muay Thai training camps. This time, I had volunteered myself for an amateur fight in a local stadium at the end of the month. I was doing several hours of boxing each day in preparation: running, hitting pads, sparring and grappling. It felt great putting my body through its paces.

There are all sorts of other fun distractions in Phuket, such as elephant sanctuaries or 'ping pong shows' that have nothing to do with playing ping pong. I had a great time. And when the night of my amateur bout came around, I had a feeling of excitement mingled with nerves. As I prepared in a back room, I peeked out and saw that there must have been several hundred spectators, at the least. It was the largest crowd I had fought before up to that point. Once I was in the ring, however, I knew the nerves would disappear.

My opponent was a local, and the Thai's, while they have phenomenal technique with their kicks, can be beaten with some solid boxing combinations. They are also known for their stamina and toughness, so I knew I'd be in for a challenge. But after having trained for five and a half hours every day for the last week, I too was a machine. I felt as though I could have done ten rounds, let alone five.

My ring man, one of the coaches that had trained me for the last month, rubbed a strong smelling ointment all over my skin that burned a little, as per Thai tradition, to warm the muscles up in preparation for the first round. I watched the fight before mine through the doorway of the changing room unravel as one opponent began to get the better of the other and managed to knock him down with a roundhouse kick to the jaw. The enthusiastic crowd roared their approval. He didn't get back up and the fight was over. It was my turn.

There were a few moments, during which the ring was prepared, when I had time to check the tape on my hand wraps before my coach was pulling my gloves on and tying the laces. Then, the event organizer was in the changing room and speaking to my coach in Thai, giving me the thumbs up. We were good to go. I took a shaky breath. There were a lot of people out there. I swallowed. Why did I always do this to myself?

My coach pushed me out of the door. The crowd applauded, as I made my way down the aisle between the spectators and climbed up to the ring. My opponent soon followed suit and I saw a lean, bronze skinned Thai a hair shorter than myself, jog up to the ring and climb in. He looked far more confident than I felt, I thought as the referee brought us together to check our gloves and gumshields. I looked him in the eye and held his gaze for a moment. We touched gloves before the bell rang and the fight had begun.

In Muay Thai, the first round is typically spent feeling each other out, throwing the odd jab and getting to know the style of your opponent. So I decided to go all out from the start. I advanced with a leg kick that was checked as my opponent replied in kind and then pushed me away with his other leg. I took the centre of the ring and advanced again with a couple of jabs and another kick. He checked me again and threw his own, which connected on my ribs with a resounding 'smack!' The crowd cheered and I growled. I kept the pace up for the first round, trying to back my opponent into the corners so

I could use my boxing, but I was learning that he was proficient with his kicks. He kept me at bay until the bell rang after three minutes and we returned to our corners.

I sat on the stool my coach provided and listened as he gave me advice and water.

'Use your boxing' he was saying.

The bell rang once more and the second round began. The Thai threw a couple of punches that I dodged easily and a kick that caught me in the gut. I tried to sweep his leg out of the way when he threw another, but was too slow. I grunted and the crowd cheered again. So far, he was getting the better of me. That's it, I thought, I've had enough of his damn kicks.

I jumped in with a long jab and caught him on the bridge of his nose, rocking his head back. I saw my chance and threw another jab, harder this time, and his head rocked back once more, dazing him. I threw one push kick that put him on the ropes and leapt into the air with a flying knee that connected perfectly. I hit the Thai with the entire weight of my body behind me as my knee sank into his stomach, causing him to double over and fall to the canvas, the wind knocked out of him.

As he lay attempting to suck oxygen back into his body, the ref called it off and I had won! I couldn't believe it. The crowd cheered me and I felt phenomenal. It's easy to see how that can become addictive.

All good things must come to an end, however, and in late October of 2017, I was re-entering the gates of 2ème Regiment Étranger de Genie with a despondent sigh. It was time to get back into the draining rhythm of the 2ème compagnie again. It was much the same as I had left it, with a few new faces arriving in my absence. Great, fresh Legionnaires meant I would be doing less cleaning. It wasn't only in the 2ème compagnie that there were new Legionnaires. In the Compagnie D'Appui there were two new Anglophones, an Englishman named Ross and an American, Christian. I met them soon after and we became good friends from then on.

Unfortunately, my time with the VAB's was not over. Every four years the regiment carries out a check on all of its vehicles over the course of a month to ensure that they are all operational. Of course, this meant that they had to be absolutely spotless as the inspector came from a French regular regiment and we had a reputation to uphold. As I was already an experienced VAB driver, I had my very own to clean. The damn thing was never good enough each time I showed it to the Sergeant Chef for inspection. I spent the best part of a week scrubbing away at every little nook and cranny.

One day in early November, my chef de section asked to see me in his office. Perplexed, and assuming I had done something wrong, I knocked on the door and presented myself formally. He asked me to sit and gave me a hard look before saying, 'Dobson, the GCM tests are coming up in December, I think you'd be a good candidate. What do you say?'

I was hesitant, I doubted myself. As I mentioned, there were a lot of quite capable guys from the 2ème compagnie I knew who had tried and failed in the past. Why should I succeed when they had not? My chef de section seemed to sense my hesitation.

'Come on, Dobson. What do you have to lose?'

An entire weeks' worth of sleep, I thought. But the idea did appeal to me; I imagined being able to count myself as an elite soldier, among the most revered in the Legion. In the end, I agreed, knowing that this was one of those moments in life, a pivotal point. An opportunity that, should I fail to grasp it I would never forgive myself. I had to try.

'I'll do it.' I told him.

With several weeks before the selection tests there was already a cold bite in the mountain air, when I began my preparation. It was great, having something to work towards, and I was quickly warming to the challenge. Every night after work, I would fill a pack with weights and run around the athletics track until I had done eight kilometres (the official length of the 'Marche Course'). Or practice shimmying up a three-metre rope and working on my pull ups and push ups. I'd follow this with some topography revision in my room. I'm not sure I honestly believed at that point I could pass, but I knew I would give everything during the tests. Besides, I had my honour to uphold. If Harry Dobson was going to volunteer his name for something, you can be damn sure he's going to give a decent account of himself. Pride is too often seen as a negative quality; I think it helped me greatly during those tests.

There were a couple of caporals from the 2ème compagnie who would be trying out for the GCM with me: Liska, a Czech boxer whom I liked and had sparred with plenty before, and Djo, the Serb who had been stationed in Timbuktu at the same time as myself. We discussed what challenges we could expect in December.

Since Djo and I would be in the same boat for the tests, he seemed to have done away with the usual stern exterior he used to relay the orders to the Legionnaires. Despite him outranking me, he insisted that I call him by his name instead of 'Caporal.'

There would be all the standard fitness tests, of course - shooting, and theory tests including general knowledge, topography, mathematics and French - they would also test our resilience during that week. We would be marching every night with our rucksacks and would sleep little, all the while battling against the elements. Whilst I didn't know it then, the most important thing the instructors would be looking out for was our strength of character.

In the last week before the tests, I was looking forward to getting the whole ordeal over and done with, one way or another. By now, everyone in the 2ème compagnie knew who was doing the tests. The Capitaine even wished the five or so of us luck one morning assembly, before giving us a list sent by the chef de section of the GCM, which included all the items we would need in our rucksacks. There were some weird ones, such as fishhooks that I assumed were for a survival kit, but didn't think it necessary to bring. We would have most of the weekend to prepare our things before beginning on the Sunday evening.

On the Friday, some of the guys from my section came into my room to wish me luck, including Botch and Iona. I thanked them and gave them all a reassuring smile that did nothing to aid my own anxiety. When the Sunday evening finally came around, all the potential candidates reported to the GCM section, a large building tucked away at the far edge of the regiment that they shared with the radio transmitters.

In the orange glow from the streetlights, I could already see a large group of guys waiting, some faces I knew from around the regiment and some I had never seen before. Soldiers from any regiment in the Legion were welcome to come to 2REG to try out for the GCM tests. During my selection, there were one or two each from the 13th and the 2nd infantry regiments. On top of that, French regulars from the mountain brigade were present. Because the tests in each regiment ran only once per year, any stragglers could be sent to us if they had missed their own selection. There must have been a little over thirty of us and most I didn't know, save for the boys from my compagnie. I decided it would be best for me to keep my head down for as long as possible.

It struck me that I knew no one from the GCM section itself, nor could I remember even seeing someone who was in it. They tended not to be in the regiment for any length of time, supposedly, as they were always either in Mali on opex, or training. As a result, they gave the impression of being quite secretive. Just then, the door to the building opened. A muscular bald man with an enormous jet-black beard stepped out and looked around at us all.

'I'm Chef Osorio, and I'm running the tests. Come inside and head up to the classroom for the briefing.' This was Ricky (I would later learn), the sous-officier in command of the GCM section under the lieutenant. He seemed quite pleasant, but at the same time gave the impression of being one of those men it would be a bad idea to cross.

We settled ourselves into the classroom, an atmosphere of obvious apprehension in the air. On the walls, I saw the emblem for the GCM painted on one wall: an owl on a five-pointed star within a circle. Ricky cleared his throat and we were immediately quiet and attentive. He bid us welcome and explained that the GCM section shared its building with the PCG: Plongeurs de Combat Genie, a team of elite divers that would bolster the ranks of the GCM in Mali. He let us know that at any point during the week we were welcome to ring the bell, to signify our surrender and it would all be over. The bell in question hung ominously in the corner of the room from a tripod.

Ricky also gave us a brief overview of what we could expect for the week and finished by taking questions. One guy wanted to know if by passing the tests meant we passed selections. Ricky told him no, you can pass all of the tests with full marks but that didn't guarantee you a place. Great, I thought, that wasn't exactly reassuring.

Ricky made it very clear before we left that we were to be present at 05:00am the next morning. I lay in bed that night knowing this was the last time I'd sleep on a mattress for a week, but even so, I didn't sleep a wink.

At 04:30, I was up and had already left the building to head over to the GCM section. The thirty candidates for the test assembled in the dark in silence, most of us looking around at the others nervously to try to gauge the 'competition.' We all wanted to be commandos, some of the most elite soldiers in the French army. Who wouldn't? But there was a long road of suffering before that could happen, and most knew it. This was simply the first hurdle in a long race.

The infamous bell was already waiting on a tripod, swaying silently in the morning breeze. It was December and already very cold. There had been snowfall several days ago and we shivered in silence. The lieutenant finally came out to give us a speech, the head of the GCM section. He too, had completed all the various training courses just like his subordinates, his place in the section won not given.

He gave us a similar speech to that of Ricky the night before, and indicated the bell behind him with a gesture, adding that we could ring it any time we wished. We were taken into the hangar by Ricky and another sergeant, David - a tall, muscular Hungarian, whom I would come to know much better in subsequent months - and the pair began by lining us against once wall, ordering us to take everything out of our bags. This was done in silence. Once I had finished, I looked around apprehensively to see what everyone else was doing. Numbers on laminated cards were placed in front of us and we were told to keep them safe, they would be our 'callsigns' for the week.

Upon inspection of our belongings, Ricky had already found several GPS watches and extra food that he quickly confiscated, scolding the culprits while noting down their respective numbers in a notebook before the fidgeting candidates. We were then given a standard French ration pack for the day, given the task of ensuring our packs weighed at least twelve kilograms, left only with a weighing scales. After this, we would begin the Marche Course: a timed eight kilometre run around the regiment with our helmets and packs. Outside, it had begun to rain.

Liska and Djo were helping each other with their bags whist Liska, forever the practical joker, had sneakily put his ration pack and helmet into Djo's bag whilst his back had been turned. Utterly perplexed at the numbers the scale was showing, Djo finally cottoned on when he saw Liska giggling to himself in the corner and proceeded to throw his kit back at him with a chuckle.

Someone behind me asked if I was an Anglophone and turning, I saw Oskari, a Fin who worked in the infirmary as a medic. I told him I was, and we spoke quietly in English until Ricky strode back into the hangar. There was silence again. He weighed our bags and told some guys to make some last-minute adjustments before reminding us that the bags would be weighed again after the test. Anyone who was caught lightening the load would immediately be disqualified. Then, we were to make our way to the beginning of the Marche Course. I shouldered my pack and took a deep breath, my heart fluttering nervously.

Whilst we had been in the hangar, the rain and wind outside had intensified from a drizzle to a shower, much to my dismay. The elements were now against us. All the candidates were lined up in a group by the starting line and, once we were ready, Ricky clicked his stopwatch and shouted, 'Go!'

I set off at a jog. Within a minute, the group had begun to thin out into a line. I stayed at the front, keeping a fast pace, cursing as the rain intensified and made my trousers stick to my thighs. My pack rubbed uncomfortably against my lower back, too but there was nothing to do but bear it.

Ten minutes in and I was already around the back half of the base, where I knew there was a long stretch of road that accounted for at least half the course. The mountainous terrain was undulating and I was soon panting. The rain now felt torrential and once I had mounted the next rise, I had the wind in my face, blowing a gale and actively seeming to slow me down. The conditions could not have been worse; I was absolutely drenched and was almost grateful for having to run for if I had stopped, the cold would surely have worked its way into my bones within minutes. As for my hands, they were completely numb.

I soon realised that I had begun the course too quickly and was beginning to fatigue. Several guys passed me. I gritted my teeth and pushed on, promising not to let anyone else pass me. The going was tough, but once we had rounded a bend the road took us toward the gymnasium, the end of the course. We were almost there, and to my dismay, a couple more guys passed me at the last minute. I ran over the line in around tenth place, sucking in air and shouting my number to a poncho-wearing sergeant shielding a clipboard from the rain.

Several minutes after I had finished and was waiting for the others, the rain died down to a drizzle again and I was not the only one who cursed aloud. I knew I was well within the maximum time, however, and those of us who had finished waited by the sergeant for further instruction. Djo had apparently finished first, with one of the French regulars finishing just after.

Sometime later, after most of the candidates had trickled in I heard the sergeant tutting to himself and say, 'a couple more minutes and they're gonna be out of the time limit.' He was referring to the three or so who remained. In the last seconds, one guy came limping over the line, apparently having rolled an ankle. Ricky and David had come to watch, too and, as we saw the last two appear in the distance the poncho wearing, sergeant announced that the time was up. We waited quietly for them both to come in.

When they had arrived gasping for air, Ricky wasted no time telling them they had failed and would not be welcome to try for the tests again because they couldn't be bothered to train for the Marche Course before arriving, something they knew would be part of the tests. One of them had come all the way from 2REI, too, and would have to get a bus back with all his bags that very day. As for the rest of us, we had passed, and were directed to the gymnasium for the next tests.

Next challenge was the 'Chorde', or rope - a thick 3m length of hemp rope we had to climb to the top of twice using only our hands. We were lined up in order of our numbers and I quickly discovered, to my horror, that my hands were still so frozen I couldn't even close them. I desperately tried to rub life into them, as the guys in line before me were summoned to complete the test. Shit, shit, shit, I thought, I'm up next and I still can't feel my fingers. Ricky stood with his clipboard and without looking up, called my number and prepared his stopwatch. 'Ready?' I confirmed with a nod even though I was a very long way from being ready. '3, 2, 1, go!'

I jumped and clasped the rope in both hands, but felt them slipping. I simply couldn't muster any amount of force, frozen as they were. I panicked and attempted to pull myself up, but the motion had only made me slip to the mats on the ground and I tried to jump up again, but slipped once more. It must have looked quite pathetic and it quickly became clear I wouldn't be able to complete the test. 'My fucking hands!' I shouted, sinking to my knees on the mat and bowing my head in shame. That was it. My dream of being known as the warrior elite had ended at the first hurdle because I couldn't even climb a fucking rope. How useless I felt. How pathetic. I dreaded going back to the compagnie and telling my friends how I had failed at the very beginning.

I realised it was quiet and Ricky had not yet said anything. I looked up at him with what must have been pleading eyes. He gave me a long hard look and the silence in the gymnasium seemed to stretch out forever until he finally said, 'go and warm your hand up and try again at the end. You have one more chance, if you can't climb the rope then, you're out.'

'Thank you, Chef!' I said and picked myself up to run to the bathroom. I let the scolding hot water from the tap practically burn my hands to life until the rest of the candidates had gone. Once more my number was called, and again I stepped up to the rope. Ricky looked at me and said, 'ready?' I gave him a nod once more, my heart beating as fast as it ever has.

'Go!' I flew up the rope, touched the top, let myself drop to the mats and climbed it again, as fast as a monkey. To this day, I'm sure that is the fastest rope climb I have ever done.

'Hm.' Ricky said looking down at his stopwatch, 'go and join the others.' Phew. It looked as though I had gotten away with it.

Next was an obstacle course we had to do as a group with a large tyre that wasn't allowed to touch the ground at any point (or we'd have to start all over again). It was wet and muddy and my boots slipped in the mud. But after lots of shouting and manoeuvring, we had finished it. And no sooner, there were four instructors screaming at us to get on our bellies and crawl. The instructors I didn't know, they must have been sergeants from the section that I had never seen. But I couldn't stop to look as the weight of the bag on my back and helmet on my head was pressing my face into the mud. We had to crawl the whole kilometre to the GCM hangar with the sergeants screaming at us all the while.

Back at the hangar, we quickly learned that free time was a luxury that we'd have to sacrifice for the week as we were directed straight to the classrooms for the theory and French tests. Each had a thirty-minute slot and there was barely a minute's pause between tests. Or the time it took for David to collect the test and hand out a new one.

I had no time to think how we'd done, before we were once more on our feet. We had ten minutes to eat before being directed back into the hangar, where tables had been set up with the armaments of the GCM laid upon them. There was the Glock 17, the H&K 416, H&K 417, H&K MP5 and the Benelli M4. We were shown how to disassemble and reassemble them and not to forget it either, as this would be one of the tests for tomorrow.

We were left to play with them for a while and given several sheets of A4 paper with various different armoured vehicles from around the world to memorise, which we were told would be yet another test for the next day. As for the evening, we were taken back to the classroom after a time where Ricky explained the mission for the night. There were ten 'balises' or topography markers dotted around the general area of Saint Christol, whose locations would be marked on a map given to each of us. We would have the whole night to find all ten of the markers and we were told not to come back into the regiment until we had. To stop us cheating, we would have to complete the course in a unique order. As an added bonus, there would be instructors patrolling the roads during the night who would immediately disqualify anyone they caught. We would have to be discreet, and were instructed not to work as a team, not to use a headtorch and not to use the roads, the penalty for which was also disqualification.

Ricky sent us off one at a time, every ten minutes and I was somewhere in the middle, waiting my turn. Studying my map with its plotted points, I became anxious to get going. When my number was called, I slung my FAMAS over my shoulder and headed out the door at a quick march, toward the cemetery at Saint Christol: where my first marker was to be found, according to the map. In twenty minutes I was there, but there was no sign of the marker and I hunted around frantically in the dark to no avail. Another twenty minutes had passed and I hadn't found a damn thing. A voice in my head was telling me if I were to quit and return to regiment I could spend the rest of the night on a comfy mattress in my room in the 2ème compagnie. For a moment I was tempted, but fortunately I came to my senses. Fuck that, I thought.

Just then, a figure came out of the darkness between the trees, his face painted with camouflage as mine was. 'Oskari? Is that you?'

'Yeah, it's me' came the whispered reply. I went over to him and pointed down at my map.

'Any idea where this fucking marker is?'

'Yeah, I found it by accident. It's not where the map says.' He pointed back in the direction he'd come from. 'Walk that way a hundred metres, you'll find it on a wall.'

'Thanks!' I whispered back.

'Good luck, bro.' Oskari slapped me on the shoulder and was gone again. Following his instructions, I found it and peering at my map using the light of the moon and a nearby streetlamp, I agreed that it was not where the map indicated and shrugged, assuming it was a mistake. Clamping the teeth of the plastic marker over my piece of paper to show I had found it, I moved on to the next one. Hours later, I had found eight of the ten, having given up on another two that were, again, not according to their position on the map. I didn't have them all, despite searching for hours and disobeyed Ricky's order, heading back to base. At 02:00am, I made camp at the bivouac site indicated and fell into a fitful sleep to await possible failure the next day.

Waking at 05:00, I was back in the GCM hangar ten minutes later and saw some of the other bleary-eyed candidates. I ended up chatting with a couple of the French regulars, Lulu and Alex Protin, to compare results. They had struggled too; one having found nine and the other seven markers. Our conversation was heard by the others and soon we were all having a discussion. The best of us, Alex, having found nine, whereas most had found five or six. 'They weren't where they were marked on the map.' someone complained.

'Yeah, I spent an hour looking for number 6!'

Ricky and David came in and the noise subsided. 'So, did you all find the markers?'

There was silence before someone piped up 'Chef, they weren't all according to where the map said.'

'So, who has ten?' No one raised their hands. 'No one? I thought I said not to come back until you had all ten. Nine?' Alex alone raised his hand. Ricky wrote notes on his clipboard. 'Eight?' Myself, Oskari and a couple of others raised our hands. 'Seven?' And so on, until Ricky got to four and everyone had raised their hands apart from one guy at the back of the group.

'Number fifteen.' Ricky said looking at his list, 'how many?'

'Two.' Number fifteen croaked. Ricky tutted.

'I think you ought to ring the bell.' The bell was standing to one side of the hangar. After a pause, candidate number fifteen went over to ring it into the silence. It was done, and fifteen left the room.

'Shooting is the next test.' Ricky declared. 'Get your gear and yourselves into the JBC.'

We all piled in and headed to the range where we had the shooting test. Whilst this was going on, they took us one by one to disassemble and reassemble the guns we had seen yesterday. I got the second fastest after Chef Zhang, the highest ranking and oldest candidate (from Tiawan, and in his forties!).

I met Lee, too, the crazy south African with the Plongeurs who had come to help out with the tests. Upon discovering I was from the UK, he switched to English and he gave me a bit of reassurance and advice on how to pass the rest of the week. I was actually beginning to think that perhaps, just maybe, I could do it.

But of course there was no time to ponder. We were quickly moved to the aggression tests in the gymnasium again, during which we had to spar and wrestle with another candidate. I did well against my opponent, already knowing how to box. And by the end of the third round, I think he was a little bruised. The evening was much the same. We had a couple of lessons and another mission for the night, ten more markers to find, but this time the course would be longer, so we had to move quicker.

During the night, I risked using the roads, only to find a set of headlights illuminate behind me as soon as I stepped onto the tarmac and the shouts of instructors behind me. It struck me that my face was camouflaged and it was dark outside, so they would have had no idea which candidate I was. Disregarding their shouts to stop, I sprinted off into the thick undergrowth without looking back, heading downhill at a rate of knots that could have been quite perilous had I fallen. By some miracle, I stayed on my feet, and the shouting behind me eventually faded away.

I finished with a similar time to the night before and had only a couple of hours sleep before the next day began. I found a spot in the armoured vehicles shed on one side of the base and lay down between two trucks. The concrete felt colder than the already sub-zero air. When I woke at 05:00, my body was rigid, cramped and shivering. Warming the life back into it by sprinting on the spot for a couple of minutes, I packed up my things and headed back to the hangar. I discovered that everyone present had done considerably better than the previous attempt, but a couple of candidates had quit or been caught on the roads during the night, as I almost had. Our number had been whittled down to around twenty.

The next few days were a blur and involved much of the same, with a forced march up one side of Mont Ventoux on the morning of the second to last day. I got to the top joint first with another candidate named Novotna: a Czech Caporal form 2REI who had been a world class kick boxer. I was still on form from my trip to Thailand and I gave a silent thanks that I enjoyed sport so much.

Hot on my heels was Djo, Liska, Alex and Lulu and it didn't go unnoticed. The Lieutenant had marched with us to the top and asked for our numbers upon arrival. After a few more physical activities during the day designed to drain us of energy, we had the last night of the tests to look forward to, and what the instructors called the

'Rallie.' This would consist of different stations dotted around the local area that we would first have to find and at each one we would have a test. This time, we were put into pairs as it was expected to take longer. I was paired with Novotna, and he seemed happy enough to let me find the first of the challenges. One of the sergeants from the Plongeurs, Katch, was waiting in the Ford Ranger and gave us a transmissions test. I did shit, but there was no time to dwell on it. As soon as it was over we headed off to the next test.

The next one was performing medical procedures on a wounded soldier, played by a Legionnaire from the 1ère compagnie. He writhed around on the ground in mock agony whilst we had to find the bullet wound and stop further blood loss using a tourniquet; I thought I had done much better. On the following test, at yet another location, we were given pictures of the armoured vehicles and weapons from around the world we had to revise and were to give names, nationalities and calibres.

Lastly, there was the English test taken by Lee. As English is in fact my first language, I dare say I didn't do too badly, and was mostly pleased with how I had performed overall. We finished in good time and returned to base, where at the designated bivouac point, I actually got more than four hours sleep.

There was only one more thing to do. The remaining candidates that had survived to this point, some seventeen or so, were to be interviewed by Ricky and the Lieutenant. We were to formally present ourselves and they would basically tell us how shit we were and how badly we had fucked up over the week. The guys before me left the interview room looking quite sick and utterly discouraged. When it was my turn, they grilled me on my shitty transmissions test and asked if I seriously believed I could be a commando with such an awful score. I tried to answer as best I could with an awful feeling in the pit of my stomach until I, too, was dismissed. A source of comfort was the fact that the others had all received a similar treatment, even some of the better guys, such as Djo and Novotna. Perhaps they said this to everyone?

Now, all that was left to do was clean our equipment and wait. The entire GCM section was present on regiment at the time of the tests. All ranks included, from Caporal to Lieutenant, would sit in a room and discuss which candidates they would take after having watched us closely throughout the week. Even the Premiere Classes could weigh in, giving his opinion and he would be listened to.

In the Legion, the hierarchal structure is usually incredibly strict and unbending; in the GCM however, it was possible for a Caporal to 'command' a Sergeant Chef if he had been in the section much longer. This tolerance and ability to see past the rank and work together is what makes the Groupement Commando Montagne unique within the French Foreign Legion. And why it is also so crucial that the section choose carefully which candidates to take and which to let go. We could be expected to operate under the harshest conditions for long periods of time, so a healthy atmosphere in the team was vital.

Amongst the hopefuls left in the hangar, there was certainly an air of apprehension. But also of relief. We had all made it to the end at least, and could hold our heads high no matter the outcome, having stuck it out. Everyone had bags under their eyes from lack of sleep and we were all happy to be in the warm shelter of the hangar, cleaning our rifles after having spent the week outside being battered by the elements. For my part, I was exhausted, and kept nodding off over my rifle, before jerking myself awake once more. Now that I had done it, I was grateful for not having wasted an opportunity, I could catch up on sleep some other time.

It was not until after lunch that we were called back upstairs into the classroom for the final verdict. First, Ricky called a group of guys in before us, and after some muffled voices we couldn't hear from outside, the group came out looking quite dejected. 'Did you pass?' someone whispered. They shook their heads. We were called in after. Myself, Djo, Novotna, Liska, Oskari and Zhang stood at ease before the Lieutenant and Ricky.

The Lieutenant cleared his throat: 'We have decided to give you all a place in the section.' I beamed. Holy shit! I thought, they actually chose me!

'There are aspects you will have to improve on, of course. And you will be under the guidance of the Chef here.' He gestured to Ricky. 'But make no mistake, this is only the first hurdle. From here on out, it will only get harder. And we will be watching you. If at any time we feel that you are not giving your best, or failing to work as a team, we'll get rid of you without hesitating. Otherwise, congratulations for passing the tests and I'll see you again next week to brief you on what will happen next. Any questions?'

Liska raised a hand, 'when will we actually be moved to the section?' He asked.

'In January' the Lieutenant said, 'then you will begin your preparation for the training courses.'

Training for the training, I thought. It's obviously not going to be easy.

Ricky stood and addressed us all, 'Remember, you are not Commandos yet, there is a long way to go and it won't be easy, you'll all have to give it your best. This is just the beginning. But well done for passing the tests.'

We all left the room in high spirits and were chatting excitedly, talking about how we'd done in the tests when we bumped into Lulu and Alex in the hallway. 'We passed!' They told us, clearly having been debriefed by a sous-officer from their regiment.

'We'll see you at the national training course then!' I said and gave them a wave before they had to return back to their regiment. It was the first time I had really worked alongside the regulars, even during my last opex there had been a bit of a divide between them and us, but I had found I quite liked these two.

I was still a little shocked when I returned to the 2ème compagnie and to sit on my bed to contemplate the last week. I had barely slept and had been half frozen for the entire ordeal, as my clothes had never dried from the first day. Looking in the mirror, I could see I had lost weight, too. My skin was taught over the muscles and a gaunt face upon a pale, wiry frame stared back at me. I had to smile, however. I had doubted myself, not even believing I would pass, but I had given it my best and done it. This would change my career in the Legion completely, for the better. But for now, I was shattered and lay down on the bed to sleep, quite content.

It was January, and time for me to move from the 2ème compagnie to the compagnie d'appui, where the GCM section was housed.

Ricky came to make sure everything went smoothly and to my shock, actually helped me with my bags by slinging a couple of them over his shoulder. This was unheard of: a Chef helping a Premiere Classe with his bags? It was the first sign of the change in mentality required for the GCM. The others were there already, and during the last month, Ricky had explained the challenges to come.

First, we would train for several months here, in 2REG, for the national test. That would then determine whether we were fit to take the commando basic training course that would last over two months. Then, two of us would be deployed to Mali very soon after to be injected into a commando group there, as the GCM section in 2REG was lacking personnel (usually, you would have many more months of training to complete first). Some might call that lucky, but it really depended on how you looked at it. In true Legion fashion, this was throwing someone in at the deep end on another scale. The fact that I could go from a premiere classe in the combat compagnie of 2REG to being on opex in Mali as part of one of the French military's most respected units in a matter of months was daunting.

There was so much to learn. We had an incredibly long list of weapons, vehicles, tanks, missile launchers, artillery and a whole host of other military related equipment from different countries to learn by heart and be able to identify. Then, there was advanced topography, transmissions, the GCM operational procedures, GCM combat tactics and French lessons, just to name a few topics. And that was only the theory. For the practicals we would have to transition from the FAMAS to the H&K 416 and Glock 17 and learn to shoot them effectively. Then, we had to have a basic grasp of the combat tactics that were completely new to us and different to anything we had done during our own basic training. It goes without saying that we had to learn all this whilst maintaining good physical form.

In addition to this epic workload, there were other great changes to everyday life that I had noticed. The GCM section was small; all the guys there had been handpicked during the tests and then had passed the national training course. One thing that I quickly realised was how capable they all were in comparison to any other section and how few 'militaire du rang' (ranks from Legionnaire to Caporal) there were. Instead, it seemed the majority were made up of sous-officiers, all of whom seemed to have a quiet confidence about them. Furthermore, they were friendly, despite outranking me, but spoke to me like an equal. Some even insisted I call them by their first names, something that would never in a thousand years have happened in the 2ème compagnie.

For example, when Ricky went to make himself a coffee in the little bar area we had meetings in, he would ask the rest of us, myself included, if we wanted one too! A Sergeant Chef making a Premiere Classe coffee? It was unheard of, and perhaps hard to explain to someone unfamiliar with the rigidity of military life. But this, I would learn, was commonplace in the GCM section. Everyone helped each other out and everyone pulled their weight. It was a true team.

I was treated well and with respect; but it came at a price. Ricky expected us all to give one hundred percent, all the time. We were also expected to revise in our free time, and it would become clear who had revised and who had not when Ricky gave us tests to do on subjects he had taught us. I soon had notebooks full of theory and found myself studying much more than I ever had for my A-levels. One would assume that military life would mean an end to academic tests. Not true.

Ricky and Chef Czurik, another large Hungarian, organised an infiltration for us candidates to complete one night, as this was something we would be tested on during the national course. We would be dropped off in the middle of the night by the JBC, at a point we were supposed to have revised, and then make our way using night vision goggles to another point, some ten kilometres away. Ten kilometres is not so far under normal circumstances, however there were other complications. First, our bags were weighted down to simulate those we would have for the real tests. These were in fact lighter, weighing here around forty kilos, whereas we could be expected to carry bags weighing up to sixty!

Moreover, all sources of light were strictly prohibited, as was making loud noise; this was supposed to be a stealth mission, an infiltration into enemy territory. Like the entry tests, the use of any main roads were prohibited and we were consigned to footpaths that wound around the hills and mountains, making our route that much longer and more difficult. But perhaps the most challenging aspect of all was the fact that we had to memorise our route. In theory, stopping to use the map would lose you points. So, you had to learn a stretch of the route and, while taking the navigation in turns, you had to know in your head exactly where to lead the group once the guy before you had finished.

In the darkness, it was not easy. We stumbled around for a bit and I, having used night vision goggles only once before, had an awful time getting them to focus. Since they were an old version, I couldn't see much even when they did. It ended up being a fiasco. Liska took a wrong turn, I had to keep checking the map and Oskari tripped and smashed his compass. By the end, the straps of the heavy packs were digging into our shoulders and Ricky was unimpressed to say the least.

During the debriefing, he told us how poorly we had prepared and performed, spending a good half hour grilling us. Reminding us that, if we were to give a similar performance during the national course, we would be ridiculed. There was still a long way to go.

Bad news came when we heard that Novotna, a volunteer for the Plongeurs, had had a medical evaluation during which a missing valve had been detected on his heart. He was therefore inept and would be unable to participate with any of the training. Bizarrely, he had been an ex-professional kickboxer with countless bouts under his belt and had never had any problem in his civilian life. We could all see that he was devastated by the news and reassured him that he could hold his head high having performed honourably.

# CHAPTER 9

In the Compagnie d'Appui, I had a whole room to myself, something that for a Premiere Classe was unheard off. It made all the difference to have some privacy, but there was always the nagging doubt that it would not be mine forever if I failed the upcoming course. The same tension stuck in the back of my mind, like a constant pressure. For if I failed, I would be returned to the 2ème compagnie de combat. Having seen the change in mentality and hearing about the past successful missions some of the guys in the section had done, I can never remember wanting anything more in my life and I worked for it.

Djo and Oskari seemed to share a similar ambition and drive. But Liska on the other hand, forever making jokes with a laid-back attitude, appeared less stressed than the rest of us. Unfortunately for him, Ricky picked up on this too and he soon became the first person Ricky would direct a question to. When Liska could not answer, he was scolded, reminded that this was no joke and that he had the reputation of the section to uphold during the national course.

I restrained myself from going out on weekends in favour of staying in my room to revise, spending long periods of time on base without leaving. The looming course was in March of 2018 and rapidly approaching. We had the national tests, which I passed without too much of a hitch. Our preparation thus far ensured that we all achieved a pass grade, on both the theory and physical tests.

When Ricky asked us to prepare the equipment for the course, I had a sudden sensation of butterflies in the pit of my stomach, realising just how close it was. The paperwork was finalised, the equipment all carefully noted and put into boxes with our rifles and pistols and loaded into a couple of vans. Zhang, Djo, Oskari, Liska and I would be on our own. The course was being run by the GCM section of the 27 BBC - the men of which we did not know.

When we arrived, we found that there were twenty-eight 'stagiaires' (soldiers on training courses), including ourselves, and around ten instructors. The chef de section of the GCM, 27 BCA introduced himself and the course, welcoming everyone. He then divided us into two groups with whom we would stick to for the next couple of months. Looking around at the other guys, I could see I was the youngest there by a decent stretch. As well as the lowest in rank, being one of only three Premiere Classes. The rest were mostly Sergeants and Sergeant Chef's, with a few Caporals in there too.

The structure of our day was often as follows: one group would spend the entire morning shooting whilst the other would do combat drills and in the afternoon we would swap. During the evening, we had a couple of classes once the light outside had faded. Liska was in my group and had a difficult time with some of the more dynamic shooting drills. I was pleased to see that I wasn't the worst shot there.

The combat drills were another story. I was not used to them and sometimes got confused as to where I should be placed in the formation. I was not the only one. Some of the other guys with less experience faltered, slowing down our progress. During the combat drills, we would practice with blank rounds as several of the instructors would ambush us or we would have to assault their position. A typical group of commandos consists of twelve men, and I soon learned how difficult it could be to manoeuvre twelve men on awkward terrain as one unit. The drills had to become second nature. When we fucked up, we would repeat them again and again and again, until we were all sick of them.

When the theory lessons in the classrooms began, I praised Ricky and his thorough preparation. Most of the content being taught we Legionnaires had already covered to a certain extent, and a good job too, for the instructors here did not use the Legion's version of simplified French. They all spoke quickly and with an unfamiliar vocabulary. After almost three years, my French was fairly decent, but I had rarely encountered 'real' French, as the only people in the Legion who spoke like that were officers, and a Premiere Class seldom had a long conversation with an officer. It was a far cry from the 'pompe kurwa!' (do pressups) and 'meme pas la peine blyat!' (it's too much for me) that I was used to hearing in military classrooms.

My ears had yet to adapt to this 'new' way of speaking. On top of that, I found that the regulars had a hard time understanding us Legionnaires, especially Chef Zhang with his thick Taiwanese accent. I often found myself mediating and translating Zhang's 'Legion French' into something comprehensible. Communication in combat is key for obvious reasons. And if my level was insufficient, I could say goodbye to joining the GCM.

Every few nights, we would have a special activity, too. One such night was the infamous 'Marche de l'Azimut.' We would each be dropped off in the night from the JBC at different locations with a small bag and our weapons, completely alone. All electronic equipment had been confiscated save for a radio, that we were to switch on only the next morning. There were a couple of other familiar rules, such as no lights and no using the roads, the penalty for this infraction of course being failure. But what made this march so awful, was the fact that we had no map and were required to reach a point six kilometres away - of which we had no knowledge - using only our compass.

The idea was, once we were given a bearing on our compass that was the only tool we had to help us reach our destinations. A six-kilometre march in a straight line sounds reasonable enough if the terrain were flat and bare. The reality, however, was that being mountain commandos, we trained in the mountains. A six-kilometre march in a straight line was impossible. There were rivers, dense woodlands, sheer drops, villages and a plethora of other obstacles we had to contend with.

We would be given a score out of twenty on how close we were to our respective points. Climbing into the JBC with the handful of other candidates that were with me, I felt quite out of my comfort zone, a feeling I was growing accustomed to recently. In the darkness, I gave a few last-minute checks to my equipment, especially my night vision goggles. As we sat there in the darkness, going God knows where, we cracked a few jokes to alleviate the tension. Lulu and Alex were in the same truck as me and Lulu said into the silence, 'I heard one guy had to switch his radio on early the last time they did this test because he was chased up a tree by a boar.'

Alex guffawed. 'Did the instructors have to come and save him from the boar?'

'Yeah they did. Turns out it was a badger though.'

I laughed. 'So, did he pass in the end?'

'Nah, I'm pretty sure they sent him packing.'

Then the JBC rolled to a halt and one of the instructors called my name from the cabin. It was my turn to go. The rest of them bid me good luck and I did likewise, shutting the tailgate behind me once I had climbed down. The JBC trundled away and I was left to my own devices, completely alone. Shouldering my bag and rifle, I used the moonlight to find the bearing on my compass and looked in the general direction it gave. I sighed. There was an enormous valley below me covered in dense woodland. This was not going to be easy.

The first obstacle I came across was the electric fence of a field I had to cross. I was zapped several times trying to climb between the wires, making me swear in several different languages under my breath. Until finally, I gave up, took off my bag and threw it over the wires, crushing them to the ground enabling me to step over safely. I used this technique for all the subsequent fields and was better for it. The challenge now was keeping the same bearing whilst not meandering left or right too much.

Another problem I had addressed with a little preparation before the march was the measuring of the six kilometres. I knew how many paces it took me to march one hundred metres, so the theory was: I would count that ten times to make a kilometre and I would need six of those to finish the march. I had a few beads on a string tied around my neck, so as not to lose count. In practice, however, it was a little more complicated; the ground was uneven and the terrain undulating. Moreover, there were so many obstacles to navigate: walls, fallen trees, streams, electric fences. It was so difficult to know when a kilometre had passed.

Once I had made my way into the bottom of the valley, a kilometre or so in, I was met with a wall of brambles. Shit, I thought looking around. The dense bramble woodland stretched out for hundreds of metres in both directions. What I ought to have done was march around it, counting my paces as I went, and then count the same number of paces back once I had cleared the obstacle. Rather foolishly though, I decided I would attempt to plough through them, worried I would lose count going too far left or right.

I regretted it within the first ten metres. The brambles tore my clothing and ripped the skin all over my legs, causing me to bleed all over my trousers. Fuck it, I thought, I may as well go through the whole damn thicket now. I pressed on, hacking my way through the dense scrub, cursing every now and again as the bushes tore into my skin. At some point, I realised my compass was no longer hanging from my neck as it usually was.

Fuck! I panicked, without that compass there was no way I was going to reach my designated point. I retraced my steps some way, but the brambles were still thick and dense, and finding anything on the forest floor was near impossible. After a long while of methodically searching and feeling around with gloved fingers, I decided to throw caution to the wind and use a red head torch to illuminate the surroundings and hope I wasn't seen.

Scanning the area, all I could see was just how dense a thicket I was hacking my way through was, and there was no compass in sight. I was conscious that I was wasting time and decided to try a different tactic. Lying on the ground, I shone my torch just above the leaves. To my relief, something reflected the light in the darkness and my little plastic compass presented itself hanging from a low branch. Yes! I was saved. Turning the torch off I checked my watch; I had spent over thirty minutes searching for the compass. At least this test was not timed.

Once I had cleared the brambles, the going got a little easier and I made decent progress. It was so hard to tell whether I was on course or not, and I had to simply trust my instincts. Upon clearing the valley, the terrain gave way to a hilly plateau with plenty of fields. It was easy until I realised some of the fields were completely waterlogged from the last rain. I was soon wading through freezing water up to my thighs, holding my bearing and attempting to count my steps accurately.

Hours later, all the beads around my neck had run out, signifying the end of my march. I looked around. I was in a patch of woodland with a dirt track some one hundred metres in front of me. I decided to make camp here, having no idea if I was where I was supposed to be.

I sighed. There was nothing more I could do. Either I was where I was supposed to be, which was unlikely, or I wasn't. The best thing I could do now was get a good night's sleep which was also rather unlikely. All we had been allowed to bring with us were our small twenty-four-hour packs. They had our night vision, a little water and food, extra magazines, a waterproof bivvy bag and a fleece. I yanked off my boots, pulled the fleece over my head and wriggled into the bivvy bag, my breath steaming a little in the air. I had no protection against the rain and little against the cold. The fatigue helped me to drift of, but I was woken several times from the cold, my body shivering and cramped. Fortunately, the night was still, and the weather held. I had the patch of forest all to myself and didn't hear any boars.

When the sun finally rose, I was ready. My radio switched on, waiting for the JBC to pass nearby, at which point I was supposed to radio in that I had seen them, and they would loop around. Hearing the engine, I called it in and the JBC came to a halt, allowing me to climb in the back. It was good to see some familiar, albeit fatigued, faces in the back. 'Alright fellas?' I said to them, grinning.

Back at the base, I took my trousers off to reveal hundreds upon hundreds of tiny cuts on my legs, it was like something from a horror film, as if I'd been tortured by some villain. Those damn brambles, I thought, and they had ruined a good pair of trousers. We had a debriefing later in the day. I had scored twelve out of twenty, having ended up over a kilometre from my destination. Fortunately, it seemed as though everyone else had struggled too, except for Djo. The bastard. He was the only one among us who had managed to get full marks. Liska and I approached him afterwards and asked discreetly, 'did you hide your GPS with you, Djo?' He insisted that he hadn't, and that ending up exactly on the mark was a fluke. We narrowed our eyes in mock disbelief and he waved us away, laughing.

The French regulars on the course we worked with were great guys, all capable and friendly. We had some good laughs along the way, but without a doubt, we all felt the pressure. Fortunately, there were a handful of guys already in the GCM doing their 'chef d'equipe,' which is essentially the same course as ours. But they would have to integrate leadership skills and their experience to successfully command the rest of us. They all knew what they were doing of course, having done several Mali deployments with their respective units already. And they would tell us about the way the GCM operated on mission. From the sounds of it, it was exactly as I'd imagined. The older guys recounted stories of firefights they had had, and near misses, how they'd attacked enemy encampments in the middle of the night and captured insurgents. It sounded like tremendous fun, and only served to motivate me more to succeed.

There were tests at the end of our several months stretch of training before the hardest part would come: the 'terrain qualification.' This consisted of two separate missions, each around a week long, during which we would have to march behind enemy lines and build a 'cache'- a hidden point from which we would observe an objective and report on the goings on, relaying it all via radio back to the base. We had to have everything we'd need for a week on our back: food, camera equipment, ammunition, radios, camping gear etc. The bags would be heavy.

First, I had the combat and shooting tests to worry about, as they were something I couldn't revise for. In the final test, I fucked up a few things and got only 14/20, but was awarded with 17/20 in shooting overall as my performance during the last few weeks had been much better. As for combat, I had 15/20 overall, something I could accept as I'd never been exposed to the way the GCM did it before. I must have shot several times the number of rounds during those few months than I had during my entire legion career.

Before the terrain qualification, we were given a weekend off, allowing us to catch up on some sleep before we were sent once more into the mountains. This time however, we would be working as a team of six, with one of the experienced guys (Steve in my case) doing his chef d'equipe in command. He alone would be briefed on the mission and would designate jobs for all of us once he knew what it was. Djo was in the same group as me, but we would be separated for the week because the group of six would be split into two cells: one for observation, and one for transmissions.

In the night, with bags in excess of fifty-five kilograms, we would have to march along footpaths completely committed to memory. Once we arrive at the designated point, we would dig our cache. It was essentially a hole in the ground, perfectly camouflaged, that the observation team would live in for the next week or so. And we'd have to dig it after having marched all night and not sleeping a wink. It was going to be tough to say the least. The itinerary our chef d'equipe had chosen was only perhaps ten to twelve kilometres when measured on the map, whereas in reality it would be considerably more due to the mountainous terrain.

We prepared in a military chalet up in the mountains where, although it was almost May, there were still patches of snow and a chill in the air at this altitude. Once briefed, there was a hub of activity, as each group prepared their respective missions. The instructors set up a command centre downstairs in the chalet's dining room, with tables full of computers, radios and maps of the surrounding areas. The Lieutenant had also enlisted the help of some extra muscle, who would have the role of the 'bad guys' that we would be observing.

Steve, our leader, took the five of us to one side and explained the mission. We were to infiltrate to a position suitable to conduct observation on a stretch of road. Once installed, the observation was to be constant until the lieutenant radioed in that the mission was over. We would report everything we saw, with as much detail as possible, all the while maintaining a discreet profile on the terrain. If we were spotted at any point, the mission would be failed, and we would have to exfiltrate as soon as possible.

It would be a difficult mission and to say that I was nervous was an understatement. Our greatest saving grace was Steve, he was the voice of experience in our group. He had several tours to Mali with the GCM under his belt and had been in the GCM six years already. He was a solid guy and knew his stuff. This was the kind of mission he had done countless times before and we were all grateful to have his experience.

I prayed that the mild weather held. During the practice we had done several weeks ago, there had been torrential rainfall as soon as our shovels had bit into the ground to dig the cache, which had soon been ankle deep in water. Steve divided up the equipment fairly, so we each had an equal amount, and began to prepare our bags. The bags themselves were interesting, they were made up of two compartments: a larger half and a smaller half. The smaller half could be broken away from the larger half in case of emergency and had straps of its own, containing all the essential things we could not afford to leave behind. The larger half had the more 'expendable' equipment inside, and a steel frame to support the weight of the entire thing.

Upon packing mine with everything I'd need - rations, batteries, shovel and pickaxe heads, sleeping bags, survival kits and more - the damn thing was difficult to get off the ground, let along put on my back. In fact, I tried, and couldn't physically shoulder it. I had to develop a technique whereby I sat, put my arms through, and roll into a kneeling position before standing up. It took a lot of effort, and I dreaded having to do it multiple times with the added complication of fatigue.

Once that was done, all that was left was to memorise our part of the topography, along with code words and the characteristics of certain points of interest on the terrain. It turned into a memory game. Closing my eyes, I could almost see the winding trail that made up my portion. Steve had shown me my portion on the satellite and we had talked through it.

'Okay, Dobson. You're up first. It's going to be pretty straightforward. On this first part you have to take us across this dried-up lake.' He pointed to the screen of his tablet.

'Are you sure it's dried up?' I asked him unsure. It looked like a grey mass to me, difficult to tell.

'Yeah, I'm sure, don't worry about it. On the other side of the lake, it should be pretty easy to find this dirt track which we'll join until we get out of the forest. At which point, we'll follow the treeline until we reach this farm that we'll have to go round...'

I sat down to study it in earnest. Closing my eyes, I thought to myself how the route went: north, north east for five hundred metres, stop, north for three hundred and fifty metres, stop, north, north west for a kilometre along the path... The better I knew it the easier it would be.

Whilst we marched, there would be a silent invigilator with us, grading us on several different aspects. I knew that if I fucked this up, I was done. For the next two weeks, I had to be at the top of my game. I was so tantalisingly close. If I passed this course, I would officially be a part of the Groupement Commando Montagne, to be able to call myself a Commando! Granted, there were many other courses to do before I got my stars (the five little stars often seen with the GCM emblem represented the training courses to be done before being considered 'complete'), but that was a worry for another time. In two weeks, I could be part of an elite unit, the most elite unit in the French Foreign Legion, in fact. There were just these last two missions in my way.

Right, let's focus on the first one, I thought to myself. The sun was falling in the sky, and at 22:00 we would have to be ready to embark into the JBC. From there, it would take us on an hour journey into the mountains. We camouflaged up, with more than a little trepidation, and made last minute checks to everything. Steve took out a list of equipment and called out the items whilst one of us raised our hand that we had it. It wouldn't do to run out of batteries for our radio.

Before our departure our invigilator would check with each of us that we knew our portion of the route and all the code words by heart. He also tested us on the operational procedure, ensuring that we knew what to do if the shit hit the fan. It all went smoothly, and we loaded our enormous bags into the back of the JBC with some difficulty. There was thirty minutes or so to mingle with all the other groups, chat quietly or revise a little more before we had the green light to go our separate ways.

I found Oskari across the car park and wandered over to him. 'That bag is fucking heavy, eh?' I said to him.

'It certainly is, mine is heavier than most, I've got a few extra snacks in there.' He winked at me conspiratorially. Oskari was short, but incredibly muscular - not built for running. I'd say he was well suited to marching with a heavy weight.

'Good luck, mate' I said, giving his shoulder a reassuring squeeze.

'See you on the other side, Dobson.' And we shook hands, parting ways as the Lieutenant called for everyone to embark in their trucks. We could begin when we were ready. I slung my rifle and climbed in, sitting down next to Djo in the darkness. As the JBC's engine rumbled into life, and the last of our team were embarked, the tailgate was shut upon us and I heard Djo chuckle to himself in the darkness.

'What is it?' I asked him.

'It's going to be a shitty week.'

I smiled, 'Yeah, I'm sure it will be.'

Steve's knuckles rapped on the rear metal partition on the cabin where he, the invigilator and the driver sat, signifying we were close to our drop off point. When the truck came to a halt, we had to work quickly and quietly to get everyone, and their bags, to the treeline; this was when we were at our most vulnerable. Myself, Djo and the others prepared to open the tailgate, and once Steve was outside, he caught it to prevent it slamming into the chassis and making noise.

'Let's go!' he whispered. We all clambered down while Steve scouted that the coast was clear, as we all ran for the trees (or ran as well as we could with fifty-five kilos worth of gear). The invigilator would be assessing us constantly, I knew. And I could see his green and black outline through my night vision goggles.

'Dobson!' Steve whispered once we were all there, 'you're up!'

I took a deep breath and led the way, knowing the dried-up lake was just a couple of hundred metres to the north. We crept through the trees in silence until they began to thin, and a moment later, we reached the shore. What I saw made me curse under my breath, and I lifted up my night vision goggles in disbelief, hoping it was just a trick of the lens. But no, my suspicions were confirmed. The supposedly dried-up lake was full of water. The weak half moon reflected on the surface and a little duck paddled close by, seeming to mock me with a little quack.

Bollocks. 'We have to go round' Steve whispered in my ear, 'follow the left edge of the lake and go around.'

I sighed and continued. The going was easy enough for a time, until thick, dense woodland slowed our progress. We had to break our way through countless branches, all the while trying to make as little noise as possible. Then, there was water everywhere - the ground around the lake apparently still waterlogged from the last rain. We had to wade through, wobbling slightly, trying not to fall in as we knew if that happened our gear would be wet for the entire week.

In the dark, it was hard to keep my bearing. After an hour of this, I whispered to Steve that I had to check the map, not having familiarised myself with the terrain on this side of the lake during the preparation. I knew it would lose me points with the invigilator, but it was better than stumbling around in the dark hoping to find the footpath.

After what seemed like an age, we were out of the marshy terrain and onto solid ground once more. We had found the raised path and followed it north east. I estimated that we had lost the best part of two hours navigating around the lake. It should have taken us twenty minutes to get to this point.

There was nothing to do but plough on. Another complication was the farmhouse we had to navigate around. We had to do it tactically, which took time. And it was not easy with our bags, the straps of which had already begun to dig into our shoulders.

Once we were past, I was done, and my group was behind schedule. We had to make it to the observation point before 06:00. Progress was painfully slow. We had to keep stopping to check crossroads that there wasn't some civilian out for a midnight stroll, or something else that would alert any would-be enemies of our position.

Up and down we went, hill after hill, and often over awkward ground, as we decided to avoid the footpaths for the most part in fear of being detected. Stopping for a drink halfway through was welcome, but getting going again was difficult. We had to help each other up as the bags were becoming increasingly heavy each hour. At least I could be thankful that the weather was fair, I thought, if a little cold.

Finally, after what felt like an age, the front man announced that we had reached our destination. Absolutely exhausted, I checked my watch: 05:50. We had made it with ten minutes to spare! Steve let us rest for ten minutes while he radioed in that we had arrived and were ready to begin construction of the cache.

Ten minutes was really all we had. As the sun rose above the horizon, Steve had already picked out a location to dig the cache with a good view of our target portion of road. We had all day to finish it, and would need all day; there was a lot to do. We needed a hole two metres by one metre by one metre - big enough for three men to crouch in, no, to live in for a few days. I left my bag hidden under some branches, keeping my rifle close by as Djo and I dug, piling the earth carefully as we would need it to camouflage the whole thing after.

It took most of the morning just to dig as the earth was full of stones, and we had to use the pickaxe on multiple occasions. Around midday, having been digging and shovelling for six hours, we heard voices nearby. Djo and I exchanged a horrified glance before Steve whispered, 'get down and stay down!'

We were on the ground in an instant, lying between the fir trees, waiting to see to whom the voices belonged. Two civilian women, hikers by the looks of it, were heading right towards our position. What the hell were they doing here? We were in the middle of nowhere with no path around, having picked this spot for its isolated nature. The two women approached, chatting quite amiably, apparently having noticed nothing. Djo and I hugged the earth as they passed metres from us and I held my breath and shut my eyes, expecting to hear a scream of shock at any moment. Eyes shut tight, I breathed into the soil, as if not seeing them would somehow mean they wouldn't see me. Please go past, I thought. If they spot us now, the mission will be over before it has even begun. A black mark against our names would seriously hurt our final grade.

Incredibly, I heard no cries of alarm, and they passed by Djo at a distance of what can't have been much more than two metres. All they had to do was glance to the right and they would see two men lying prone on the forest floor. But they did not. And then, they had gone. I lifted my head up to look around slowly, making sure it was true. They had, and I gave Djo a grin and a thumbs up. In fairness, we were kitted out head to toe in camouflage, having painted our faces too. I still felt quite lucky and had a chuckle to myself at the close encounter as we continued to dig.

Next, we needed to cut branches for the roof of the cache and drag them over. Having not slept for a minute, the fatigue made it all the more difficult. It wasn't until 16:00 that the cache was close to being finished. It required a few last-minute touches to make it truly perfect. When we stood back to admire our work an hour later, we were quite pleased. The earth had been carefully distributed over the area, a trapdoor had been placed onto the roof and a little slot was cut out for observation, the whole thing being covered with leaves to completely camouflage it. We added a couple of large, dead branches so no one would accidentally walk on top of it.

If you were walking in the woods, you would have no clue it was there. You could walk right next to it and never know there were three men living under your feet. Hell, even if you did know the general area of the cache and were looking for it, you still might never find it, so well was it camouflaged. It looked like any other patch of ground. Once that was done, I left Steve, Djo and one other to the observation cache and joined the others in the radio cell up the hill and away from the road. They had constructed a little hideout within a dense patch of thorny bushes and I was impressed at how impenetrable the whole thing looked. It was so dense you could not see more than a metre, and the barb like thorns would have discouraged anyone from looking.

I crawled in and greeted Jules and Donny, the two Frenchmen sharing the cache with me. Donny operated the radio and had an easy-going air about him. However he wouldn't stop farting in the cache, causing Jules and I to groan each time. The ration packs apparently made them more foul than usual and we couldn't escape them. Jules was a big lad and always joking around. He often had Donny and I in stitches about something or other.

Jules and I had the job of ensuring the antenna was unobstructed. We would also head out at night to fill the water container so we'd have enough for the next day. We had to talk very quietly, as the invigilator came back every now and again to ensure we were making as little noise as possible. We had a few good laughs over the next few days. They mocked my accent a little, and I mocked their culture, all in good fun, as we tried to pass the time.

I wondered about the three others down by the road and how they were getting on. All they had to do was always have one guy on observation while the other two slept. But I decided I preferred it here, as our cache seemed a little more spacious in comparison. The days went by slowly, and we relayed the information back to the command centre at the chalet as we were supposed to. We hadn't faced too many problems until Donny announced we had lost radio contact with the others. Despite his best efforts, he couldn't get it back. The solution was to send Jules or I down to the other cache every two hours to pick up the information physically and then bring it back up. We had to do this in our ghillie suits, which were camouflaged over jackets made to look like foliage. And it was hot work going up and down the steep hill.

At night, we could leave the cache to take a shit or refill our water. Otherwise, we were to stay hidden until further notice. The days passed slowly, and fortunately, without major incident. On the fifth day, Donny received a message that we were to quit the observation by 22:00, and exfiltrate out of the area. I relayed the message to Steve; apparently welcome news to the boys in the cache who couldn't wait to stretch their legs. We prepared to leave, collecting our bags from their hiding places as soon as the sun had set.

Then, in silence, with our omnipresent invigilator in tow, we marched away, leaving no trace that we were there at all. All in all, this first mission had gone fairly well, apart from my little fuck up at the beginning. Now, we were all looking forward to a good night's sleep.

Without five days' worth of rations, our bags were somewhat lighter, too, making the return journey a little easier. At 01:00, the JBC was in position and picked us up from the extraction point. The six of us collapsed in the back, not saying a word, grateful for the ability to stretch our legs out once more.

Back at the chalet, we were debriefed on the mission. Our invigilator said we'd done a decent job on the whole, giving us pointers of what we'd messed up and what we should improve on the second time. He also scolded me for screwing up my portion of the topography at the beginning of the infiltration. Oh well, it wasn't the end of the world.

After, we were allowed some much-needed rest and were able to talk to the other groups to compare stories. Talking to Oskari, I learned that, during his infiltration, their chef d'equipe had fallen ill with some freak sickness. I can't remember for the life of me what, but he had to be whisked off to hospital in the JBC, leaving his five inexperienced, would-be-commandos to fend for themselves. Commendably, they had managed to complete their infiltration to the observation point without a hitch and build the cache, conforming with all the operational procedures and radioing it in on time.

Unfortunately for them, the three guys in the cache took the discretion rule a little too far. Not having their Chef to advise them, they didn't leave their hole for five days, having each shat in the same plastic bag that was handed around! The silver lining was that their invigilator gave them extra points for 'dedication to the mission.'

Over that weekend, I had two fantastic nights of sleep, giving my aching body some well needed rest. One more week, I kept thinking to myself, and then I'll know if I'm in or out.

After the weekend, I had the general feeling that all of us were waiting to get stuck in. The sooner we started, the sooner we finished. One last push. The groups had switched around a little. I was still with Steve and Djo, but this time we had one of the regular Premiere Classes, Marc, whom I hadn't much confidence in. He had been at the bottom of the class in every aspect: shooting, combat and theory, and always seemed happy for others to do the leg work for him.

The mission planning felt easier the second time around at least. The mission itself was a little harder this time. Instead of watching vehicles go past on a stretch of road, we would watch a solitary property in the mountains in which 'terrorists' were conducting arms deals. Our job was to watch without being detected, again with a constant observation, and report everything that we saw every two hours via radio to command in the chalet. As we would have to see all angles of the house, there was no point in digging a cache for observation - we'd have to move quietly in our ghillie suits.

Steve hadn't many options for the route of infiltration here, as the terrain was more mountainous than ever. Funnelling us through several steep valleys -I suspect the Lieutenant had chosen the property specifically for that - we needed to march around fifteen kilometres, climbing five hundred metres from start to finish.

Again, the equipment was dished out and we began to revise our portions of the route. This time I was determined to have it perfect, there would be no more nasty surprises. I had satellite images up of the route and our objective, studying them intently in an attempt to commit them to memory. This time around, when the invigilator tested me on my route, he was impressed that I could recite it with such detail, and I was rewarded with a nod of approval.

Keen to get stuck in, I had my gear loaded into the truck early, and spent the last hour at the chalet revising the terrain once more before it was time to leave. I helped Djo and the others climb in and sat with my back against the side of the truck, waiting for the Lieutenant to give Steve and the driver up in the cabin the green light. Ten minutes later, we were off, the JBC working its way over winding mountain roads.

'Here we go again.' Djo said in the darkness.

'Last time.' I replied. 'At least after this, we'll know if we've passed or failed.'

He gave me a sideways grin, 'they'll take one look at that ugly English face of yours and send you packing!'

'Better hope they don't see you then, Serb!'

A couple of hours later, the truck stopped. We got out and made for the treeline, beginning the infiltration as soon as we were all off the road. Once Gott, one of the other candidates in our group, had finished his part, it was me. I strode ahead with confidence, knowing exactly where I was. For the next few kilometres I didn't even need to use my compass to navigate fields, woodlands and winding footpaths, despite never having been there and it being the dead of night. I was soon done and Djo took over, pleased that it had gone smoothly this time.

At 03:00, we had arrived on our mountain. We couldn't see it in the gloom, but our objective was a hundred metres or so below us at the bottom of the valley. Once Steve had radioed in that we had made it, we could sleep a little. I had my sleeping mat and bag rolled out on a rocky plateau in record time, and zipped it up to my nose, my rifle tucked in snugly by my side.

At 06:00, we were up and had eaten breakfast already - a little packet of muesli mixed with water - and Steve was divvying up the tasks. Gott and I had the job of finding a decent observation point on the mountainside, from which we would have a clear view of our objective whilst the others constructed a camouflaged hideout for Steve and his transmitter. We pulled on the ghillie suits and reapplied a layer of camouflage to our faces, checking each other before we went.

The mountainside had a thick covering of fir trees, shielding us from view of the insurgents played by the infantrymen down below. The steepness of it complicated things, however. Gott and I slipped and slid more than once, dislodging rocks that tumbled a short way, making us hold our breaths in fear that they would be heard. Whenever we found somewhere decent to set up, however, we found that the view would always be blocked by the branches. We found ourselves inching further down the slope, toward the danger, in an effort to find a clear vantage point. In the end, we found somewhere halfway suitable, closer to the objective than we would have liked. I left Gott there to commence the observation with a fancy camera and a huge lens to take pictures if he needed to, as I climbed back up the hill to report to Steve our progress.

Back at the top of the mountain, the invigilator who had been marching alongside us had left until the next morning. With the construction of the shelter well underway, Djo and Steve were sawing away at branches to make a roof in a little cleft in the rock whilst the transmitter was playing with his radio. 'Where's Marc?' I asked them, looking around but not seeing him.

'He went to go and cut more branches thirty minutes ago, haven't seen him since.' Steve replied, 'Go and look for him, will you. Tell him to hurry up.'

I left, heading further up the mountain in the direction Steve had indicated, taking a path that wound upwards. It was not long until I stumbled upon Marc, his back against a tree, a ration box open beside him to which he had clearly been helping himself.

'Oh, Dobson. I was just taking a little break, my shoulder had been hurting me a bit.' He rolled his shoulder and gave me a grimace to prove it.

'Where's your rifle?' I asked him, not seeing it on the ground next to him. He indicated a spot with his fork twenty metres away where I could see he had been cutting down saplings with a hand saw, his H&K propped up against one trunk.

'If the invigilator comes and sees you without your rifle, he'll fail you on principle.' I warned him.

Marc made a face. 'Steve said he probably won't come back until tomorrow.'

'Yeah, that's what he told Steve. Maybe he just wants to catch us off guard. But look, it's your choice. How much more wood do we need?'

'Just a few more logs. Can you cut them? It's my shoulder...' I sighed, shaking my head, wondering how he had wormed his way through the selection tests. I got on with it and threw the branches over my shoulder to head back to the others. Once their little hideout was complete, Steve and his transmitter installed themselves, leaving the rest of us to go and join Gott down below. Soon, it was just a case of taking it in turns and waiting from our vantage point, marking down all the activity in a little notebook.

There was a lot to see. The lieutenant had arranged to have at least 5 insurgents stay at the house, whilst several more came every now and again in a black SUV to pull large crates from the back that must have been the guns. We were a good three hundred metres from the property, or more, and could not hear what was being said. But using the enormous lens on the camera, we could take pictures of their faces that we would send up to Steve, so he could begin to make a mission dossier.

We had only a couple of branches to obscure us from view, so we could watch without being seen. The advantage of setting up on such a steep slope was that there was little danger of anyone passing our position on a stroll or discovering us by accident.

When there was a lull in the activity, Gott and I went off again to make a loop around the objective, whilst there was still some light in an attempt to take pictures of every façade. It was fun, crawling around on our bellies, trying to get as close as possible without being seen.

The next couple of days on the terrain went fairly smoothly and were much the same as the first. One pair would stay at our little observation point while the other would don the ghillie suit and work their way around the house, taking pictures of anyone and anything that we thought might be of use to Steve and his mission dossier. Once, Gott and I got so close to the driveway, we could actually hear the guards there talking, but were too afraid to go any further. We snapped some good pictures all the same.

That evening, Steve radioed in, summoning all four of us up to his radio cell. Djo asked, 'all four of us? But who is going to be on observation?'

It was unusual. When something like this happened, it was either because the mission was over, or we had been compromised. Gathering outside his cache, we waited for Steve to emerge and tell us what was going on. After some shuffling, Steve poked his head between the branches and glared at us.

'What the fuck have you been playing at? Some of the messages you've been sending on the radio are total shit.' (Some activity messages we could type using a special device attached to the radio).

'I need the exact time, followed by how many they are. What kind of weapons they have and what they're doing with them. Which one of you fools sent me this incoherent nonsense?' He fumed, speaking with the most aggressive whisper I've ever heard and gesturing to his radio. I exchanged a glance with Djo and Gott, but Marc couldn't meet our eyes. Steve went on.

'You idiots think I can send this stuff back to the Lieutenant? Do I have to remind you that you are training to be commandos? This isn't a fucking holiday camp; get your act together and give me detailed messages! Now, fuck off!'

We re-joined our original position down the mountainside in silence. As the sun set behind the mountains, I was beginning to feel as though some of us lacked the drive to finish the mission. That is to say, Marc. We hadn't eaten a lot, nor slept as much as we'd like, and the mountain air was always chilly. The temperatures often dropped below zero at night, even at this time of year. Looking through a thermal scope at the house down below, all I could see was the regular guard. It was quiet, as was usual for the hour, and we divvied up the shifts so one of us watched whilst the others slept.

An hour later, I saw movement down below. A vehicle had arrived at the compound and several men were getting out. Suddenly, there was a hive of activity and I began scribbling away in my notebook. But the group down below had just migrated around the corner of the building and, looking through the scope, I could see nothing.

'Shit.' I whispered to myself. I would have to move.

'What is it?' Djo asked, having been roused from sleep by my scribbling.

'There's something going on down there, but I can't see. They've gone round the other side of the house. I'll have to move around the mountainside to get a look.'

'We should all go.' Djo said and woke the other two. Quickly and quietly, we began preparing our equipment, and in a minute were ready to move.

Marc piped up. 'Umm, I'll stay here.' He said into the darkness. We all stopped what we were doing.

'You'll stay here? Why?'

'What if they come back round to this side? It will take you guys a lot longer to get back. This way we'll have eyes on three sides of the house.' I thought about it. In a way, it made sense. And to be quite frank, I was happy to be rid of Marc for a while, his constant winging didn't exactly make him a joy to be around. Apparently, the other two had similar thoughts and I saw Djo's outline shrug and say, 'You'd better stay in this exact spot then. We'll probably have to come back by morning.'

'I will, I will.' Marc reassured us. 'Go on or you'll miss what's going on.'

I suspected Marc had curled up into his sleeping bag as soon as we were out of earshot rather than watch. I sighed. It looked as though the three of us would have to do the legwork. We left him to his own devices and struggled to find our way across the hillside in the dark, breaking branches and slipping every now and again until we could see the opposite face of the house. Sitting down to watch, the three of us made a rota and marked the activity until we heard the car engine start up. The group of insurgents had left, leaving the house to the five guards.

'I suppose we'd better head back then.' Gott said. We picked ourselves up and headed back to our rocky outcrop where Marc would be waiting. When we knew we were close, Djo called out softly to him in the hopes that the sound of his voice would guide is to his exact location.

'Marc! Marc!' He said as loud as he dared. There was no answer.

'Where the hell is he? Is he asleep or something?' Gott tutted angrily in the darkness. After a while of fumbling around in the dark, Djo had found our vantage point, and clambering onto the rocky surface I heard him swear in Serbian.

'What?'

'He isn't here.' I came to look for myself and sure enough, Marc was nowhere to be seen.

'I told him not to bloody move.'

'Never mind,' I said, 'he knows where we'll be. Maybe he'll come back.'

'With any luck, he has abandoned us.' Gott muttered. I chuckled. Again, we sat down to wait, laying out our sleeping gear and having something to eat and drink to keep us going. Not five minutes later, just as I was climbing into my sleeping bag, I heard a great snapping of branches some fifty metres to our left. The three of us sat bolt upright, completely alert. Our eyes squinted into the darkness in an attempt to pierce the gloom and pinpoint the source of the noise.

'What the fuck is that?' Djo said, picking up the thermal binoculars. Snap! Crack! It sounded thunderous in the night air, surely the guards in the compound would hear.

'Holy shit.' Djo said, looking through the thermal scope. 'It's him.'

'Guys? Are you there?' Marc was practically shouting. I could hear the panic in his voice.

'Shhhh!' I whispered, but it did no good. He was too far away to hear, and I didn't want to shout.

'Damn, I can't find you. Wait, I'll just turn on my-'

'Nooo!' Too late. A brilliant white light erupted from the darkness and blinded the three of us, illuminating half the mountainside and forcing us to shield our eyes.

'-Torch.'

'Turn it off!' Djo cried, 'The guards will see it!' So bright was his lamp, I would not have been surprised if it could be seen from the other end of the valley, several kilometres away.

'It's just for a moment, I can't find my way.' Marc called back.

'Turn that fucking light off, now!'

'Fine, calm down.' The light cut out, and the area was plunged into darkness once more. But the damage had been done. Down below, we could hear shouting, the guard had seen the light and was rousing his companions. I heard dogs barking and looking through the thermal scope I saw the glowing forms of two dogs on a leash, held by one of the guards.

'Jesus, they have dogs.' I said. 'We have to go now!' The guards had bright torches of their own and were shining them up the hillside in our direction, shouting to one another. The exercise had become all too real as they began to scale the slope below us, hot on our heels.

'Move!' Djo shouted. There was no need for stealth now, and the four of us began to scramble up the mountain in a panicked haste, causing rocks to tumble down the slope below us. Despite the cold, when I reached Steve's position, I was sweating. I could just make out Steve's head poking from his hiding place.

'Dobson? Are those dogs I can hear?'

'Yea, they've spotted us.' Without another word, Steve and his transmitter hurried to pack up their things, knowing they couldn't leave any equipment behind. The rest of us prepared our heavy packs and shouldered them, the adrenaline giving us the strength to do it without the help of our comrades. A couple of minutes later, we were all on the path and ready to go. The barking was getting closer, and we could see the light from the guard's torches illuminating the tree trunks, not two hundred metres away.

'Listen' Steve addressed us all, 'the mission is already failed, but it's going to be a whole lot more embarrassing if we let those infantry boys catch us. Hear me, all of you. I will set the pace for the march and you will keep up, even if it bloody well kills you. Do you understand me?'

'Yes' we all said as one. With that, we were off. We took the winding path that would then take us through a cleft on the ridgeline to the other side of the mountain, and from there, back in the general direction we had come. We had the advantage of knowing the terrain far better than our pursuers, having scoured these very slopes for the past few days. It was not before long that the shouting faded away and the woodland soon blocked the torches from view.

An hour later, Steve had not relented with his manic pace causing the rest of us to pant heavily, having to work our lungs harder to pump in oxygen under the pressure from the straps of our bags.

'Chef- I can't...' Marc's voice sounded from the back of the column 'slow down!' He complained, sounding every bit a whiny teenager. I turned, he was already falling behind, his back bending forward from the weight of the bag.

Steve ignored him at first, but then seeing that Marc was out of sight, slowed the pace after a string of swearwords directed at our 'ball and chain.' Even after slowing, however, it was clear Marc was still struggling. He simply hadn't the willpower to keep up. Steve had to take him aside to give him a bollocking that no man would want to be on the receiving end of.

It was almost certain that we had lost our pursuers now. We had covered a distance of almost ten kilometres and were several valleys away from our objective. In the early hours of the morning, we had finally reached the point of extraction and settled down to wait twenty-four hours, a discouraging feeling of failure polluting the ambiance in the group.

Steve radioed in our position before demanding to know what had gone wrong. Gott, Djo and I turned to Marc. Djo said, 'go on, explain.'

'I... I was lost. I couldn't find the others, so I had to use my light.' Marc fidgeted, unable to meet anyone's gaze. Silently, we awaited Steve's reaction.

Steve looked at Marc with a disgusted face, as if Marc had just spat into his muesli. Steve shook his head in wonder.

'Wow. You're done.' Was all he said.

There was an uncomfortable silence until Gott broke it with a question, 'Does this mean we fail the course?'

Steve sighed. 'Well, it's not good for sure. But it doesn't necessarily mean you will be failed. We all followed the operational procedures despite being spotted, so there's still a chance.'

I exchanged a glance with Djo. Still a chance! It was more than I could have hoped for and it boosted my spirits a little. We would soon find out the results.

That night, the JBC picked us up and we were heading back to the chalet. The other teams had arrived on the same night too, and we exchanged stories again as we had the last time. It transpired that our group had been the only one to be compromised. All the others had completed their missions without a hitch. But there was nothing to be done about it now, tomorrow morning we would have the results. I would know whether I was a Mountain Commando or not.

The next day, I awoke with a tight knot of tension in my gut. Had I done enough? The official ceremony was in a few hours but first, all of the instructors had to sit in the command room and decide who would be taken and who wasn't up to their standards, going through all the candidates one by one. In the meantime, we had the equipment to clean and organise, a welcome distraction.

When the time finally came to assemble in the car park before the lieutenant, my heart was pounding as if I had run a mile, and I was anxious for him to get on with it.

He cleared his throat. 'Those I welcome into the Groupement Commando Montagne are as follows: ...Zhang...Alex Protin, Jeremy

Luesie... Djo..., Oskari...' I closed my eyes. Please, I thought, let him call my name too.

'...Dobson...' Dobson? I opened my eyes. Had he said my name? He had! I was in! I couldn't believe it, I was in! All the hard work had paid off. All of the revision until the early hours. All that marching, crawling, running and jumping; all those cold, hungry nights. It hadn't been for nothing, I was in.

The instructors were already coming round to hand us our Velcro patches that we could wear on our uniforms, congratulating us. I murmured a breathless 'thanks' as my patch was smacked onto my shoulder.

The lieutenant addressed us once more. 'For those of you whose names I haven't called out. I thank you for your efforts, but you will not be accepted at this time.' Marc was among those, as was my friend Liska. Poor Liska, it was hard to have come this far, to have completed everything only to be failed at the last moment. Supposedly, they had sensed that his heart had not been completely in it, something that had shown itself in his work. I couldn't say either way, but Liska seemed to have expected the decision and simply sighed and nodded sadly. But that was the game, it could not be any other way.

I still remember that as one of the best days in my life. It marked achievement. It was something that could never be taken away from me, no matter what happened in my life. From here on out, I would always be a mountain commando. The fact that I had fought for it, worked harder for it than I had with anything in my life before, made the victory all the sweeter. And I couldn't help grinning.

I soon found Djo and Oskari and slapped them both on the shoulder, smiling.

'We've done it boys. We are in. Can you believe that?'

They returned my smile. 'Not bad, eh?' Djo said, stroking his new patch.

'Not bad at all.'

'I'm gonna get so fucking drunk when we get back to regiment.' Oskari grinned at me. I laughed.

'Count me in!'

'Me too.' Djo said. With that, we all shook hands and went to congratulate our French comrades who were warming themselves by a bonfire, a crate of beer already opened on a nearby picnic bench. Steve was there talking to the Lieutenant.

'So, did you pass your leadership?' I asked him.

''Course I bloody passed.' He growled. 'Even despite you bastards screwing up that last mission for me.' He gave me a wink to show he didn't really care. 'And well done to you boys, you've earned that one.'

A week later, we had settled in back at 2REG where the other guys in the section had organised a little get together. Just a few drinks in congratulations, as we could finally get to know them a little better, our places secured for the moment.

Ricky took Djo and I aside. 'Listen,' he said, the serious look on his face immediately sobering the two of us up.

'I've chosen you two to go to Mali this summer. Over there it's no joke, you'll both have to be on form for the whole mission and I don't want to hear of either of you shaming the section, ok? You have two weeks to get yourselves sorted. I've organised for you to get a later plane over, so you'll have a little more time to relax and buy anything you need. Your groups will already be there waiting for you. Questions?' We shook our heads.

'Good lads. Congratulations by the way.' He left us and Djo and I exchanged a glance.

'So much for easing ourselves into it.' I said.

'Pfft, what did you expect? This is the Legion.'

I was twenty-one years old, had only three years military experience under my belt and in two weeks I would be deployed to Mali to operate in the most elite unit of the French Foreign Legion with a team I had never met, nor worked with. To say it was daunting was an understatement.

But that was a problem for tomorrow, I reasoned, sipping at my beer.

# CHAPTER 10

I stepped off the plane in Gao and was, once more, was blasted by the hot air. I thought it must surely have been the engines. But it was of course the thick, North African atmosphere. It was nearing the end of May and Mali was as hot as I remembered. However, this time around would be very different. Waiting in line to be processed, it was clear I was not like the other soldiers. I wore European camouflage, rather than desert - a privilege reserved for the commando units - and I wore the owl on my shoulder. So, I looked the part, but I was a long way from feeling it.

In truth, I was quite nervous. I had yet to meet my team; guys I knew had a wealth of experience and who would all have far more service than I and be much older to boot. I would have to be on the ball from day one. I spotted Zig at the end of the airstrip and he waved me over. Zig was a Polish Sergeant Chef and would be my 'binome', or partner, for the next four months. He was from my regiment, of course, and I knew him to be easy going and fair.

Zig was quite a religious guy, too. He always wore a necklace of a saint around his neck and over the next four months we'd have several long discussions about the existence of God and the purpose of mankind. I had asked him once how his religion allowed him to do this kind of work and he had shrugged and said, 'I'm not perfect.'

Fortunately for me, he was a good boss. He was always super laid back and seemed to understand that I was new to the GCM and still had much to learn. To my relief, he was surprisingly patient in the beginning, as I inevitably made mistakes. In hindsight, I realised that I was lucky to have landed Zig as a partner because, not only was he laid back, but he was also perhaps the most experienced sous-officier in the group. He was in his early forties and had around eight tours of both Mali and Afghanistan under his belt - a wealth of experience that I was able to tap into and learn from.

Zig also had an exceptionally sharp mind and his quiet confidence left me with no doubt that he knew exactly what he was doing. Yet, he was never the life of the party. He preferred reading in the quiet confines of our tent over drinking in the bar, but had a dry sense of humour and was able to laugh with the rest of us, nonetheless.

'Dobson, how was the trip?' We shook hands.

'Apart from being stuck in Niamey for three days because of a problem with the airstrip, it was fine, Chef. Where are our tents?' I knew that the parachute commandos had their own little compound within the FOB, whereas I didn't even know where the GCM had theirs.

'Come on, get your bags and I'll show you.'

Zig had a P4 he'd borrowed, a little 4x4 jeep, long past its best from the 60's, that the French army was apparently running into the ground in Mali, until they were all well and truly broken. We embarked and zoomed off, following the airstrip to the outer edge of the FOB. Zig explained on the way that we shared the area with the helicopter crews. Because, in the event that we were deployed, we would all be heading up to the hangars where the helicopters, were stored together.

There was row upon row of tents that were just as I remember them - all the same light brown colour and laid out in neat rows, the chunky air-conditioning units whirring away noisily. There was always a lot going on in Gao. In some ways, it was a comfort to be back and be a part of the operation. JBCs trundled by, helicopters and planes came in to land on the airstrips every few minutes. VBCIs and VABs headed over to the mechanics hangars to have repairs done and French soldiers walked this way and that.

The living zone at the edge of the FOB Zig was taking me to seemed no less busy. We had to wait for the road to clear, as men unloaded hundreds of packets of water bottles from a truck and into a shipping container. Zig brought the P4 to a stop outside the last row of tents, and I could see a group of guys sitting shirtless in the seating area between them.

'He's here!' Zig announced to the guys sat down, and they all stood up to greet me. First was Matt, the Sergeant Chef in command of our group, a short, athletic guy with a long, thick beard that came down to his chest. Matt was a great guy. Whilst everyone knew he called the shots, we all thought of him as a friend before a boss. Then Shishi, his second in command, a transmitter whose unassuming exterior would leave you perplexed at what he was doing in a commando group, until you gave him the equipment with which he was a genius.

Dub was one of the machine gunners and had grown up in some of the rougher areas of Paris. There was Martou, the tall and muscular transmitter. And then Val, the other machine gunner; both in their late thirties with over twenty years military experience between them. Val had left behind three children and a loving wife in France, of whom he spoke often and fondly. Then, there were the two sharpshooters Will and Franz. Will was short, athletic and sported a neatly trimmed beard. He was often the first to coerce the rest of us to the bar for a beer on an evening, or organise some fun activity for us to pass the time. There was never a dull moment around him. Franz was quieter and composed. I had never known anyone to take their work so seriously. He was always a professional.

Buss, the second youngest after myself, was bespectacled and friendly. He specialised in 'evidence gathering' after any engagement (weapons, DNA, sim cards on phones, etc). Then there was Alan: a laid-back chain-smoker. Finally, there was Kettle, another big bloke with a beard.

I introduced myself and they gave me a warm enough welcome, all seeming like good guys. Indeed they were, I would learn. All of us had been chosen by our respective sections because we were capable of working in a team, and a big part of being an effective team member is not being an arsehole.

We all chatted for a bit and I learned that most of them had ten years' experience under their belts and several deployments as commandos. I was painfully aware of being the 'weak link' and vowed to do everything in my power to pull my own weight.

It was good to see a couple of familiar faces in Djo, David and, of course Dam, another Serb from my section. Because we Legionnaires were from a combat engineering regiment, there was a pair of us inserted into each group of twelve to handle everything related to explosives. If there was a door that needed blowing off its hinges, we would be called. If there was a captured enemy vehicle that had to be destroyed, we were the guys to do it. Zig insisted that I have several kilos of military grade explosives in my bag at all times, just in case. By now, I knew how to use them, too. But Zig was good enough to give me advanced lessons on how to calculate how much explosives were needed to cut a steel cable or a concrete pillar, for example.

These were not the only new things I would learn. Every morning, our group would spend a couple of hours practicing our combat techniques, whether it be vehicle interception or close quarter battle, and re-visit all our various bits of equipment and how to use them. It was always such a pleasant atmosphere to work in, all the guys wanted to be there - they wanted to hone their skills. There had been one or two guys I had known back in the 2ème compagnie who would have moaned about doing extra work, but there was none of that here. We all got on with it and had a good laugh along the way. The training was taken seriously, we worked as a team. If there was something at which the collective was not as good as it could be, we would work out how we could improve and iron out the knots.

It goes without saying that it was hot work, of course, even if we began at 09:00. The rising sun still beat down upon us, and, by the time we finished, our combat fatigues were all drenched with sweat. We were all glad to re-enter the air-conditioned shade of our tents.

I loved working in that team, but at the same time I felt the pressure. These guys were all super capable, they knew how to do everything required of them and they did it well. Most had several tours under their belts already, and it showed. I had only just passed the GCM's basic training and my combat drills were still clunky and some of the equipment Matt had us practice with was the first time I had ever used it. It was clear that I was the least capable of them and I was beginning to understand just what I had gotten myself into.

As I saw it, there were two choices: either I wasn't good enough to earn my place as one of their number, or I would have to adapt. To do that, I realised I would have to change my whole mindset. For the first few years in the Legion, I had been broken down and taught to obey. You eat only when told, you sleep only when told, you shit only when told. But now, I found that if I did not take the initiative and think for myself, I would become a liability to my team. I would have to use my brain.

In the army in general, you can get away with being a little 'slow.' There is always a job for less capable people - you can clean vehicles or work in the regimental post office or a whole host of other jobs that required minimal mental exertion. But this was not one of those jobs. Sometimes we would have to think on the spot, under pressure, or in dangerous situations. It was the kind of work in which a wrong decision could literally cost lives.

Everyone was easy to get along with, and a good thing too, for we spent all day together. We woke, ate breakfast and then began our training. After that, we might do some sport, eat as a group again at midday, take the 'sieste' during the hottest hours, do sport again, eat again and end the day in the bar across the dirt road from our tents with a beer.

'Come on, Dobson!' Will shouted one evening after we had done exercise, 'the next round is on you!'

'Why is the next round on me?'

'Because I just kicked your arse in that last sparring session.'

'Oh, did you really? Is your jaw still hurting after that left hook I landed?'

'Pfft, that was one lucky shot. I had you and you know it.'

'Ha! We'll see who gets the better of who tomorrow!' I clapped him on the shoulder and we went to meet the others in the bar. Soon, the twelve of us had taken up two picnic benches which were laden with pringles and beer and we were chatting away amicably.

It was incredibly social. If I were to hide myself away in my tent instead of spend time with my group, it would be frowned upon to say the least. Not that it was any hardship, we had a great laugh together in the bar each night, and I got to know the guys and their quirks. Yet, we knew we had to be sensible, as we were technically 'on alert' twenty-four-seven and could, in theory, be called out at any hour of the day or night. Drinking excessively was therefore off the table.

It was easy to see that there was a real sense of brotherhood between everyone, not just in my group, but the others as well. It really felt as though I was part of something special - an excellent team in which everything ran like clockwork and everyone knew their role. We were doing good work here, it meant something, or so I wished to believe. The only thing that was missing now was a mission. I wanted to prove that I was worthy of place there.

The main focus of our mission here was the 'colonne', or column - which is what we called the commando convoys that penetrated deep into the desert in search of enemy insurgents that we were tasked with capturing or killing. The general in Gao wanted there to be at least one group of commandos in the desert at any one time, so our work would be cut out for us. When I had arrived in Gao, it had been the turn of the parachute commandos to patrol, giving us a chance to settle in. A couple of weeks later, one of our groups had already been deployed, and I had watched their departure with interest.

Instead of using the armoured vehicles of the French army I was accustomed to, we were using customised Toyota Hilux's, the most common vehicle in the north of Africa, supposedly. This was an attempt to blend in, as armoured vehicles with eight huge wheels and 20mm gun turrets were rather conspicuous. One downside of this ploy was that the Toyota's had no armour whatsoever. I had seen picture comparisons of armoured vehicles that had driven over IED's and unarmoured ones. The difference was stark. The armoured vehicles might be thrown twenty feet into the air by the sheer blast of the explosion, the shockwave ripping off the axel and wheels. But the body, being made from one solid piece of thick steel, would stay intact. More modern versions also had a reinforced underbelly, made in a 'V' shape, to deflect the blast toward the sides, lessening the blow.

Civilian vehicles were a different story. Before and after pictures show a vehicle on a road and then, poof! Like a magic trick, once the dust had settled, they were nowhere to be seen. This is because they had been blown into a million pieces. You would be lucky to find anything but scraps of hot metal. Anyone inside would be very dead. At least in the body of an armoured vehicle you had a fighting chance. Fortunately, the true wilderness of the Sahara provides little opportunity to catch a convoy with an IED. Anyone hoping to do so would have to find a natural funnel in the landscape through which any convoy wishing to pass would be forced into. Still, there had been plenty of French troops killed by IEDs and it would have been a little more comforting to have a VAB, knowing we could use it as cover from any small arms fire, too.

The first group were called 'Spartan 10,' 'Spartan' being the mountain commandos call-sign in Mali (mine was Spartan 30). They had two Toyota pick-ups for six guys, each with a .50cal machine gun mounted with custom fittings to the bed. There were four Toyotas in total, as on top of the twelve guys from Spartan 10. There was the Lieutenant from the 27 BCA in command of the GCM detachment, a couple of medics, and a team of regular French soldiers specialising in intercepting enemy transmissions and pinpointing their location.

The convoy would have to be autonomous, in terms of food and water for a good number of days. All of this needing to be stored somewhere on the pickup, in addition to all the other necessary equipment. The end result was that the vehicles represented something out of a post-apocalyptic war film as strange additions had been made to the vehicles to allow them to carry their payload. The guys from Spartan 10 had added large baskets made from bastion wall covered with hemp sacking to store and protect the hundreds of water bottles they would need.

When they had gone, the GCM camp was quieter and the rest of us continued our training as normal. In contrast to my previous Mali, this time we were kept in the loop about the goings on. Each evening after we had eaten, Matt, our Chef de Groupe, would gather us all in the little seating area in one of our tents to give us the orders for the next day as well as the news in the area. It seemed every other day there was a skirmish involving the Malian troops and the terrorists, often with fatalities on both sides. It had been the same last year: the terrorists preferred to attack the Malians, as they were easier targets.

The recent battles and firefights were not the only thing Matt relayed to us during those little briefings. We would also have word of various atrocities committed by different religious groups. Once, a church full of Christians had the door barred by an extremist Muslim faction one Sunday service and was set alight, burning all seventeen of them alive. During a different briefing, Matt relayed to us the story of a rival tribe storming into a local village, slaughtering all who lived there with apparently no response from the government.

It truly was a brutal country; especially in the north, where countless different factions and militant groups had taken advantage of the disorganised state of the government, imposing their own local laws with no one to stop them. Only the strong and canny survived in places like that.

One evening, Matt relayed orders that we were to head to the Malian encampment situated outside of the French bastion walls the next morning to teach the Malian soldiers some of the basics of close quarter battle. The twelve of us were sat in the tent when Matt delivered the orders and, to my surprise, it was met with a groan from the others. The guys shook their heads and frowned. It was the first time I had seen them react in such a way to Matt's orders. Matt was a good leader, and usually we were all happy to obey. I looked at him, but he was nodding sadly, apparently agreeing with the others.

'What?' I had asked. 'What is wrong with going to teach the Malian soldiers?'

'They tend to switch sides a lot. It's more common than you think, Al Qaeda pays them better. So, we have to be careful about what we teach them. The last thing we need is to teach the Malian soldiers all our techniques, only to have one of the bastards use our tactics against us a year later. The orders come from higher up of course, from some do-good officer wanting to appease the Malian general.' Matt finished.

We headed over the next morning to meet the trainees. They were a mismatched bunch, some didn't even have proper uniforms. And some wore sandals with their fatigues. Sandals. Their weapons did not look well maintained, either. I had to hold my breath on a number of occasions as the barrel of their AK's passed carelessly over their comrades once we had begun a few basic drills.

We didn't go into too much detail with the drills, for reasons previously discussed, and it was probably for the best, too. It soon became clear the Malians had quite poor training. In fact, Will, one of our snipers, had told me about a mission they had done last year during which a Malian translator had taken three AK rounds in the back whilst storming an enemy encampment. The bullets had come from the rifle of one of his comrades and I had an image in my head of them running this way and that, into each other's sectors of fire and making a general mess of the situation.

When it was done, there was a chance to chat to the Malian soldiers who had a chance to explain to us their feeling of resentment. They believed the French army was not doing enough, nor was the French government that had 'abandoned' them in the 1960's when Mali became an independent nation.

But that was sixty years ago, and it struck me that the kind of problems their government was facing now could only be solved internally. The terrorists in the north were a result of divided leadership, drawn by the weakness and chaos that recent political upheavals had caused. But then, it was none of my business for I was neither French nor Malian.

The first thing I got to do outside of the FOB was an 'EVM' mission, which stands for 'evacuation medicale.' News had come down the pipeline that Spartan 10 out on the terrain, had been involved in a firefight that had lasted most of the morning. They had been working with the Malians to find the terrorists when they had stumbled upon their encampment by chance. Both parties being as surprised by the other, a firefight broke out and the insurgents fled. During the ensuing chase, several Malian soldiers had been wounded. I was to accompany the medics in the NH90, a modern transport helicopter, as an extra security measure.

Within minutes of all this information coming from the boys on the ground, I was running to the helicopter with my gear and the medics' bags. The pilots were already in the cockpit preparing the engines, as myself and the gunner helped the medics inside with all their gear. Checking I had a round in the chamber of my Glock and H&K, I strapped myself in using a special lanyard attached to my belt. That, in turn, was fixed to a steel ring on the floor of the helicopter with a carabiner. With the gunner looking out on one side, I sat with my legs dangling over the other as the engines started up, and the blades began to turn above my head.

The engine made an awful racket, nothing could be heard over it, and I had to shut my eyes as the power of the blades kicked up a cloud of dust and sand as we took off. Then, we were in the air and zooming away. It was great fun watching the tiny square houses of Gao zoom by under my feet. I could see everything from up here: the river Niger and the little settlements lining its banks and the vast expanse of nothingness that stretched out to the horizon and beyond.

As we approached the zone in which Spartan 10 and the Malian troops were waiting, the pilots approached the ground to begin their evasive manoeuvres in case any insurgents had us within the sights of a rocket launcher. They brought the helicopter to what couldn't have been ten metres from the ground, and slalomed around the dunes with incredible skill. More than once my heart was in my mouth, surely we would collide with the next hillock! But we never did. The pilots darted around at the last minute and I got the sense they were thoroughly enjoying themselves.

Watching the earth whiz past underneath, I was so close I could just about make out individual stones on the ground. It felt as though I was on a rollercoaster ride for the helicopter leaned into the turns so much, I would surely have slipped of the edge had it not been for the G-force keeping me in. I must have had a permanent grin on my face for most of the journey.

It soon came to an end, however, as the pilots spotted our guys on the ground who had marked the area with red smoke. We circled once, and came in to land, the blades kicking up a great cloud of sand once more. As soon as it had cleared, three stretchers were being brought up to the helicopter with the wounded in them. We had a policy of having the helicopters on the ground for as little time as possible, as they are at their most vulnerable.

As I helped the Malian soldiers to position, their comrades in the body of the helicopter, I saw how badly wounded some of them were. One had crude splints supporting an arm and a leg. I would later learn that he had been run over by a vehicle during the chaos. Another had taken a round to a leg and was covered in his own blood. And the other had bandages over one eye that was apparently still bleeding underneath, as a patch of crimson was spreading to contrast the white of the bandage.

As I loaded a stretcher into the belly of the helicopter with one of the medics, its occupant groaned in pain and raised a thin, sandy arm to cover his face where the bloody bandages seemed to be bothering him. The medic firmly took his hand away and spoke clearly in French not to touch them. Looking around it seemed as though the other two were not even conscious. Lying prone in their respective stretchers, they didn't even flinch when the medics inserted the needle for their IV lines. Outside, Spartan 10 were clearing the area in preparation.

We could not have been there for more than five minutes. I never even got the chance to speak to the other guys from Spartan 10 to see how they were doing, just exchange a friendly wave, glad it was not one of them being loaded into the NH90. I clambered back to the opened doors of the helicopter and regained my position on the edge. Once I was strapped in, I showed the gunner the thumbs up. I watched as the boys from Spartan 10 turned away and ran for cover as the engine picked up speed, throwing sand into the air. They were blocked from view momentarily until we had risen upwards a good distance. But they soon faded from view as we zoomed away once more.

Looking over my shoulder at the wounded, I watched the medics work their magic. The guy who had been run over by the truck was in worst shape. Apparently, there was some internal damage to his torso and he was barely conscious. Because he had lost so much blood, it was difficult for the medics to find a vein to set up an IV line. They decided to punch a hole through his shin. Our own medic, Kettle, had shown the group the little gun used for this during a lesson. The gun uses a high-pressured trigger to shoot a brutal looking needle deep into the bone, so the IV line would have no chance of failing to reach the blood stream. I am told it is extremely painful. Luckily for the Malian soldier, the only noise he elicited was a small grunt, so weak and delirious he was from blood loss already.

When the pilots brought the NH90 to land back at Gao airstrip, there was already an ambulance waiting, and we had the wounded loaded in as soon as it was safe to do so. My work was done. Sweating profusely, I made the long walk down the airstrip back to my tent, having completed my first successful mission as a commando, albeit an easy one.

A week or so later, Spartan 10 returned to Gao after having been out on the terrain for a total of twenty-eight days. That was an incredibly long time when you consider they were eating rations, drinking scalding water from bottles that had been sitting under the sun all day, showering with a couple of litres and having to contend with the unnatural heat of the Sahara all the while. They looked more than a little rough when we saw their pickups roll up to our zone. Their skin was burned and peeling, their lips cracked and their beards scraggly, everything covered with a fine layer of sand. In Mali, you seemed to battle more with the elements than you do with the enemy.

The rest of us gave them a hand with unloading their equipment. Tired as they were, we gave them a chance to have their first proper shower in a month. Despite my rough looking and worn-out comrades, I was keen to get stuck in myself, and was particularly happy when Matt announced that I would be on the next convoy with Spartan 20 to bolster their numbers a little. That wouldn't be for a couple of weeks, though, so I consigned myself to the regular routine of training and exercise twice per day.

Fortunately, there are often guys in the army who practice combat sports. I made it known that I was willing to have some friendly sparring sessions. Pretty soon I had a handful of regulars to practice with. Will and Dub from my group were two of them and I had some quite surreal sessions near the airstrip, dodging and ducking punches in the red sand within a crudely made ring of four old tyres whilst cargo planes and helicopters took off in the background and armoured vehicles navigated the dirt tracks around us.

There was a lot of downtime, too. I slept rather well, so the siesta at midday was not always necessary and I found that I had several hours to kill. I had decided to fill them by carving a chess set out of scrap pieces of wood I found lying around the FOB. I soon had a little workstation set up outside my tent and could often be seen carving away in the shade quite happily. I must have spent a good couple of weeks making all the pieces and the board and painting it all, too. The end result was surprisingly good, and I found a fellow chess enthusiast in my binome Zig.

I found Zig reading outside the tent one morning and clapped my hands together. 'Ready for another game, Chef?'

He looked up and smiled. 'Sure.'

'I'll go and get the board.' We played. As usual, I gave the game my undivided attention while Zig read on with his book at the same time.

'Damn!' I said as he took my queen. 'I didn't even see that one coming.'

'Ahh well, your problem is you never plan ahead. You can't just go charging in with your knight and hope to catch me off guard. You make each move impulsively.' He chided me with a grin.

'Story of my life.' I mumbled.

In another four moves it was checkmate. 'What does that bring us to?'

I sighed. 'Six to zero in your favour.' Knowing full well he hadn't forgotten.

'Well, the good news is we have a few more months. You'll win one day.' He said with a wink.

Sometime in July, the first storms came, and they were always the most impressive. One day, a large crowd of people were gathered by the airstrip looking toward the horizon. I already suspected I knew what they were looking at as I poked my head from my tent to see what all the fuss was about. My suspicions were confirmed as I rounded the corner and saw the epic wall of sand approaching like an angry leviathan, stretching out as far as the eye could see in both directions. It was biblical in its size and I couldn't help but admire, as a flash of thunder momentarily illuminated the eye of the storm. Truly, it was a sight to behold, and I am glad for having seen one of the most awesome natural phenomenons that our planet has to offer.

From previous experience, I knew from last year how quickly the storm could approach and safely stowed myself in the entrance to my tent. From here, I watched the first timers awe turn to panic, as they realised they were about to be engulfed and chuckled to myself. Closing the tent firmly, I waited as the wind battered and shook the whole thing, threatening to rip it from the ground.

But the storms also meant that the rainy season was upon us, bringing the complication of heavy rainfall. Nor did it bode well, for it meant this opex we would be spending a lot of time in the vehicles out in the desert. We were sure to have problems with the weather.

In June and the weeks leading up to it, the football world cup was on the television. France won game after game and the French soldiers in Gao became more and more invested. Most of the guys from my group and the other Spartan groups, crowded round the television in the shaded outdoor living area, often sat in their underwear due to the heat. Football fans tended to get very involved in their team's games, and this world cup was no exception. In fact, it appeared as though most of the guys had become fanatical having little else to distract them.

I must have been the only soldier in Gao to be supporting England. When we were knocked out by Croatia, I was disappointed but not surprised. Everyone was grouped around the TV in the outdoor living area for the final, and no one cared that it was on during the hottest hours of the day. Around thirty of us were packed into the little deck area between our tents, chatting excitedly before the game and sipping at cool drinks. Of course, I had to cheer. Once the game was underway, there was silence save for the occasional, 'What the fuck are you doing? Pass the ball idiot!'

Or 'come on! Who hired that ref?'

The score was four to two, in the final minutes, and it soon became clear that Croatia could not close the gap in time. France had won! At the end of the game, all the guys broke into shouts of joy, whooping and hugging as if they'd just won the lottery. The atmosphere in Gao that night was electric. All the bars must have sold a record amount of alcohol and everyone drank more than they should have. The military police zoomed around angrily on their P4s, attempting to disperse the merry bands of soldiers happily chanting into the night. It was a good distraction for everyone and seemed to have raised the spirits of the FOB for a time.

But for us, there was work to be getting on with. The preparations for the departure of Spartan 20 began a week before we left. I was with Dam for the duration and not unhappy about it. He had always seemed like a relaxed, patient guy and proved to be so as we worked together to prepare the pick-ups for the convoy. Once our equipment was loaded along with all the water and rations we would need, there wasn't a whole lot of room left for personal belongings. The essentials of course were a foldable camp bed and a mosquito net each. On top of this, I brought a tarpaulin, a bar of soap, a spork, a change of socks and underwear, some sun cream and of course, my trusty blue crocs. With any luck, we would be on the terrain a couple of weeks and not an entire month like the last bunch.

Accompanying us commandos, were the transmitters whose job it was to intercept enemy signals. They drove in VBLs, 'Véhicule d'Avant Blindée': small, armoured vehicles that were speedy and nimble, coated in the typical European camouflage of the French army. I thought that this rather nullified our efforts of using the Toyotas to blend in. Because of the presence of the VBLs, any fool could see from miles away that we were French troops. But as a humble Legionnaire, one learns to keep one's mouth shut when decisions of higher-ups come into question.

We had kitted out the bed of the Toyotas with a large plywood board that sat snugly on top, secured with a rope to form a platform that guys could sit on comfortably, their legs dangling over the side. On the day of our departure, I had done my final gear check, ensuring I had everything I needed before replying affirmatively to the radio check that I could hear through the comms on my helmet. There was much shouting and activity as we all embarked. Dam and I seated on the second pick up sitting side by side. I gave my friends a mock salute goodbye and they came to see us off, including Matt, Zig, Will and the others.

'Good luck!' They shouted. 'Don't forget your sun cream, you pasty Englishman!'

'Thanks, mum!' I shouted back.

Whilst I was not with my own group, Spartan 30, the guys from Spartan 20 welcomed me readily enough, and we were soon joking together as the convoy left the safety and comfort of Gao. We were heading north and east, to a location at which would meet the parachute commandos to relieve them, a journey of at least a day and a bit. It felt good to be finally doing a real mission, and I secretly hoped we would see a bit of action.

The mission was to relieve the GCP ('Groupement Commando Parachutiste' or parachute commandos), link up with a friendly local militia who knew the area, and patrol near the eastern boarder that Mali shared with Niger, visiting a few points of interest along the way. Our biggest assets, apart from the locals themselves, were the signal interceptors. Without them, we hadn't a hope of finding anyone on our own so good were the terrorists at using the terrain to hide themselves. Moreover, they knew the terrain like the backs of their hands. We were foreign and, whilst we could withstand the heat to a certain degree, there was no way any of us could operate at a hundred percent during the hot hours where the temperature rose over fifty degrees Celsius.

During that time, even sitting in the shade was not enough and the only saving grace was being on the move, the breeze from the movement of the pickup cooling us ever so slightly. If I have not emphasised it enough already, I will do so again: it was hot, incredibly hot.

Drinking water that had been out in the sun was like drinking scalding tea and did nothing to help cool us. Some of the guys had developed a technique whereby they used an old, standard issue army sock that was so long it came up to the knee, put a water bottle inside it, soaked the exterior, and finished by tying it to the side of the Toyota. The idea was that the wind would cool the damp sock, and by extension the water inside. It worked fairly well too; you could drink warm water as opposed to hot water using this technique.

Even by the end of our first day, our fresh fatigues were soaked in sweat and the sand had begun to work its way into everything already. That meant we had to maintain our weaponry well, cleaning our rifles once we had stopped to make camp for the evening.

It was different from the convoys I had done last year. This time we were far fewer in number and the atmosphere between the lieutenant, Seb - the Chef de Groupe of Spartan 20 - and the rest of us was casual and informal. That is not to say we were casual in our work. Out there in no man's land, we had to be vigilant. A guard patrolled the exterior of our little encampment peering through his night vision goggles at the surrounding dunes at all times, leaving nothing to chance. It was wonderful to work with a team of professionals that took their work seriously and did it to a high standard. At the same time, they could stay calm and collected, but were always ready to have a laugh.

We set up our camp beds on a dune, the sun having just set on the horizon, bathing the sky in a bright orange glow and the air had finally cooled to an acceptable temperature. Sitting on our camp beds, I chatted with Dam and the others about previous missions and how the politics of the Generals dictated our role in Mali. Most of them shared the opinion that the convoys in the desert were ineffective and rarely yielded good results. They were in favour of the old method, a drone would pinpoint an enemy encampment and a 'Tigre,' the French attack helicopter, would fly over and pin them in place with gunfire from its 20mm cannons, whilst the GCM would be flown in nearby to clean up the remainder on foot. Nevertheless, we were here and had to make the best of it.

Once again, I had the pleasure of lying on my cot and staring through the mosquito net at the millions of stars in a clear, unpolluted sky. Out there it was almost magical, as if it had all been zoomed in on and brightened for me alone. There are worse ways to drift off to sleep.

The next day, we met the GCP late in the morning, and after a quick exchange between our lieutenant and theirs, they were away. Clearly, they were eager to get back to the showers and air-conditioning of Gao, leaving us with the detachment from the local militia. After a quick introduction, the lieutenant suggested we get on our way to which the militia's leader was in accord, but suggested his men finish drinking the tea they were brewing under the shade of a nearby tree. I chuckled at the visible frown on the lieutenant's face, clearly these guys worked a little differently.

There were several pickups worth of them, all driving the same Toyotas as us but with far less equipment. They were Tuareg tribesmen of the Berber people. Small and very slim in build, they were not black but Arab, and had lined, weather-beaten faces often covered with the cheche, or turban, that wrapped around their heads and could protect them from the sandstorms. All of them were either barefoot or wore sandals, and carried battered looking AK's, with the larger DSHK crudely mounted to their trucks.

They seemed perfectly suited to this terrain, their forefathers having lived there for generations, passing down all the information required to survive one of the harshest environments on the globe. They seemed to drink very little too, and the food they ate, apart from the flour they kept in sacks to bake bread in the evening, was found opportunistically. In addition to the handful of pickups they had, there were twice as many motorbikes. Apparently the youngest of the lot, mere adolescents, zoomed around on them and would dart this way and that, often disappearing for long periods of time before returning hours later with a dead goat they had shot strapped to the back.

While the blacks ruled from Bamako in the south, the Tuaregs roamed free in the north. Many believed themselves to be superior to the blacks and would not have taken kindly to be classified the same. But between the two peoples, there was a divide that was more than just race. The Tuaregs had thrived under French rule. Tuareg warriors had fought beside the French during the Algerian War for independence. I wondered if some of the young lads I saw on their motorbikes were descendants of these men.

They held hands often, too. In their culture, two men holding hands was a sign of deep, fraternal affection. But I could not believe they were soft, on the contrary. I had the impression that they were as tough as old leather, some of them were scarred, and the few of them that could speak a little broken French told us of their regular, perhaps weekly skirmishes with the extremist Muslim terrorists.

I understood that their war was far different to our own. We had the latest in military equipment: exemplary training facilities, air support in the form of attack helicopters and drones and superbly competent medics with an excellent knowledge of their craft. It was almost as if we could not lose. They, on the other hand, were alone. What you see is what you get. The merry little band of tribesmen defended their villages with no help save a rare French detachment. The tools of their trade were fifty-year-old Russian firearms, likely to have passed from hand to hand over the last half century. It was a far cry from our western European army.

When we were finally underway with the Malians leading from the front, I sat watching the desert slide by, munching on a biscuit as we passed villages. Boys whipped donkeys along laden with plastic containers full of water they had collected from a local source. Men guided herds of skinny cows to a fresh patch of thorny scrubland they could pick at whilst women crouched outside their homes, beating grain into flour. Children from the villages would try to follow along with the convoy on foot, shouting and pointing in excitement. Every now and again, we would see a camel or two being pulled along with a hemp rope by its turbaned owner.

We had turned south and could see that here the recent rainfall was already turning the landscape a little greener, but thankfully the ground was still generally firm and easy to drive on. The encampment we set up that night could not be called discreet. The first thing the Malians did was light fires to heat their tea and bake their bread. We stayed separate, forming our own little cordon with our vehicles and kept our own guard too, still a little unsure of our new allies.

The next day, the signal interceptors in our convoy got to work. Their VBL's had large antenna linked to a computer that was operated by a guy sat in the back who would wait for a signal to appear. We had been driving in the desert for at least an hour without seeing any kind of settlement. Following the militia's leader to where he believed we would encounter some of the enemy, the convoy was finally ordered to halt as some radio transmissions came in. The translator that we had brought from Gao listened in the back of a VBL.

'The French are heading east and have now changed direction to follow the border north. Now, the French have stopped.' The translator relayed this as he heard it through the radio, a pair of headphones pressed to his ear. They were watching us.

From my vantage point on the gun of the pickup, I looked around at the horizon in all directions. I could see nothing. Dam climbed up beside me to peer through a pair of binoculars, and guys on the other pickups were doing the same.

'See anything?' I asked, squinting at any potential hiding places. There was nothing, bar a few shrubs and thin looking thorny trees; the landscape was barren. Where on earth were they?

'You try.' He said, handing me the binoculars. But I was no more successful than he, seeing nothing but sand. So, they knew we were here. No more messages had come through and the transmitters were finding it difficult to triangulate the enemy position. The militia leader suggested we continue north to see if we could find any tracks. As soon as we were underway, it came over the radio that there had been another message: 'the French are on the move.' Again, I looked around but could see nothing.

Half an hour later, the Malians picked up the trail of at least three motorbikes, the tracks of which were fresh and heading north. We continued on their trail for a couple more hours, stopping every now and again to see if we could triangulate the more frequent enemy radio chatter of our movements. There was a noticeable tension in the air now. They knew we were following them and we could come across them at any moment. I sensed Luc, the guy sat to my left, check his H&K, and Dam tightened the straps on his helmet. The Malians began to pick up the speed slightly, and we followed, sensing the enemy was close.

The tension seemed to steadily rise throughout the next hour. The tribesmen would hop from their motorbikes at the head of the column every now and again to check the tracks they were following and shout excitedly. Reassured that we were on the right path, they would hop back on behind the driver and slap him on the shoulder to continue.

'Keep your eyes open lads.' The lieutenant kept saying in the radio. Gripping the .50cal tighter, I kept turning my head left and right, squinting into the distance or at the ridges of nearby sandy hillocks, but saw nothing.

Once more, progress had been halted up ahead, as the Malians had stopped. A couple of them dismounted from their motorbikes to point at something in the dirt. There was some whooping as they remounted and zoomed off again. As we approached, I saw the remnants of a campfire still smoking and a couple of bedrolls, the whole thing having an air of being hastily abandoned.

And then, once over the next rise I could hear the Malian tribesmen up ahead whooping and pointing with much excitement. There they were! Two motorbikes speeding off into the distance, at least several kilometres away.

This was it, the -

Whiz! Tak tak tak! I didn't get to finish my train of thought as I heard something zip through the air to my left followed by the harsh chatter of rifle fire.

'There! At nine o'clock!' Someone shouted, pointing at a dune a hundred metres away. Swinging the big gun around to face the new menace, I caught only a glimpse of two turbaned heads as they disappeared from view on the other side of the dune.

My radio exploded in my ear, 'CONTACT LEFT! CONTACT LEFT! Go fucking get 'em!' Our pickups all turned left, and some of the militia's motorbikes, too. We all raced to clear the hillock, spotting the enemy motorbike already several hundred metres away.

'Damn they're fast!' I shouted. The young men of the militia were screaming and shouting in delight again, quickly passing us on their bikes. Some of the passengers, gripping the bike with one hand, fired a few rounds from their AK's into the air with their other, smelling the fear of our prey.

The race was on! We were flying over the sand, quicker than ever before. The pickup bucked and rocked violently, somehow managing to stay on four wheels.

'What's going on, who's who?' Dam shouted from my right, leaning to see around the front of the pickup, as he clung on for dear life with his long arms. Looking ahead, I could see the bikes all pulling away from us, the occasional pop of gunfire reaching my ears as the Malians took optimistic shots on the move.

'I have no idea!' I shouted back. Other motorbikes had joined the fray as the insurgents were now heading in the same general direction as their comrades. Ahead there were a swarm of motorbikes, each with a couple of riders. The bikes kicked up dust and slalomed left and right, intermingling and criss-crossing. But one looked much like the other, I had no way of telling who was who. And even if I did know, there was no way I could have thrown down any fire at this speed, it was all I could do to hold on to the pick-up for dear life. I was all too aware that we were not driving on roads. With each little bump, my feet seemed to leave the bed of the pickup for a second as I was thrown into the air, before coming back down to be buffeted into the side of the gun turret.

'What's that ahead?' Someone asked in the radio. There was something lying in the sand up ahead and I squinted to see what.

'It's a body, leave it!' Came the reply. I saw a bundle of brown cloth. As we approached, an outstretched, lifeless arm was visible. Our Toyota was soon passing the dead man and I caught a glimpse of a face half covered in sand. A dead eye was staring vacantly into the sun, a pool of deep, crimson blood soaking into the sand from several bullet holes in his torso.

The disadvantages of having enormous amounts of equipment soon became apparent. The French pick-ups were lagging behind, laden as we were with men, rations, ammunition and water, keeping up with the militia was near impossible. They were far ahead now, a kilometre at least, I estimated.

Following their tracks, we were still holding a wicked pace, and most of my efforts were put into trying to stay on my feet. Suddenly, the pickup flew over a deceptively large lump in the ground, and I was thrown feet into the air before crashing back down on my arse with an 'oof!' Straightening, I shouted, 'you okay, Dam?' expecting a confirmation from the big Serbian Sergeant. But none came. Glancing over my shoulder, I could see a figure from the corner of my eye rolling in the dirt, already fifty metres from the pickup.

'Oh shit! Dam!' Clearly, he had fallen out. As I slapped on the roof over the drivers' head, I saw his body come to rest face down in the sand over my shoulder.

'Dam is down, Dam is down!' I yelled, 'Turn around now!' The Toyota was already turning as the driver had clearly cottoned on to what was going on. For one heart stopping moment, Dam's figure lay motionless. Suddenly, he seemed to spring to life, picking himself up and looking around, disoriented. Seeing us, he shouldered his rifle and began running over. We met him halfway and he hopped back on as if nothing had happened.

'Jesus, Dam. Are you all right?'

'Yea, I'm fine, just lost my grip that's all!' I had to laugh, having feared the worst for a moment.

'You could have chosen a better time to practice your roly-polys!' We chuckled at the absurdity of it all.

The setback had cost us our position in the column; we were now dead last behind our commando brothers. Now, I could not even see what was going on in the distance. The insurgents and the Malians must have been continuing the chase, for we maintained the same reckless speed for a solid twenty minutes without seeing anything.

Thump, thump, thump, I heard behind me. Turning my head just in time, I saw a Tigre - the predatory looking attack helicopter, all hard angles and menacing - as it flew towards us and then over our heads. I caught a glimpse of the underbelly mere metres above my head and whooped as it zoomed up the column at incredible speed. Everyone cheered as it flew fast, the pilot seeming to slalom in salute, showing off his skills as he stayed low to the ground. The lieutenant must have called it in as soon as we had contact with the insurgents.

It almost seemed as if there was not much else for us to do now. We couldn't keep up with the militia and the Tigre, and knew the insurgents weren't about to slow down and wait for us. The lieutenant must have known it, too because before long, we had slowed to a still fast, but more sustainable pace. Several kilometres later, our little convoy of French pickups and the two VBLs were in sight of a small settlement, before which we spotted the cluster of militia vehicles. The Tigre was somewhere in the distance, now just a speck.

We approached and formed a defensive circle, as our lieutenant spoke with the leader of the militia tribesmen. I learned in the aftermath that another couple had been killed - their motorbike commandeered - a man captured, and the last pair had absconded, which must have been what the Tigre was searching for in the distance. Gesturing to the small figure sat cross-legged on the ground with a sack over his head and his hands tied, the lieutenant had asked the militia leader if he wanted us to take the prisoner off his hands and return him to Gao where he could be questioned. The militia leader politely refused, insisting he would handle it.

That was the last we saw of the prisoner. When we made camp that evening, well after the sun had set, he was nowhere to be seen. The Malians could be seen laughing and joking excitedly together around their fires after a day's hard work, and even offered us some of their food as a token of friendship.

It had been a long day and I was exhausted, as I think we all were. I slept well, waking for an hour at 03:00 to mount the guard, enjoying the peacefulness of the desert.

For the rest of the week there was nothing quite as exciting, save for the storms. After spending the day following the Malians again, this time heading west and doing not much of anything, frustrating the lieutenant. We made camp early in the shadow of great, black clouds. The stillness and heat of the day indicated a turbulent night; it was the calm before the storm. Dam and I set up our cots together, optimistically believing that if we tied a tarpaulin over the thin aluminium poles of our mosquito nets, it might be enough to shelter us from the elements. I placed my bag, rifle, and armour under my cot in the hopes that they would stay dry there.

It was not until 23:00 that the wind began to pick up, blowing lightly and tugging at our tarpaulin gently. I remember thinking that if it stayed like this, we would be fine. Unfortunately for us, the storm was heading straight for our encampment. Not long after, the wind began to blow in earnest as the first drops of rain fell. The tarpaulin above our heads was soon billowing and flapping violently, it was all Dam and I could do to hold it in place. The wind was soon so strong that it tore the loop of one corner of the tarpaulin, causing it to flap over our heads uselessly. When I stood up out of my cot to try and catch it, the wind was strong enough to flip my cot and shear the other corner of the tarp. Suddenly, Dam and I were exposed, being pelted with torrential rain. Acting quick, we had to pile our gear on my cot to weigh it down, our rifles covered with our bags and armour in an attempt to stop the sand penetrating too deep into their mechanisms. Even with the dust cover up on the ejection port and a rubber cap over the barrels, I knew the sand would still manage to find a way in.

There was nothing we could, do but wait until the storm subsided. Dam and I huddled together on his bed, wrapped in the tarpaulin, trying to keep warm. The temperature had dropped to around ten degrees. Coupled with the fact that we were absolutely soaked and had the wind constantly battering us, we were soon shivering violently. The storm raged for several hours and we spent a long sleepless night huddled together. So heavy was the downfall that the water had now come up past our ankles, submerging our bare feet.

When the storm finally broke and the first rays of the sun lit up the eastern sky, we rubbed the life back into our limbs and took an inventory of our gear. There was activity around the camp as my bleary-eyed comrades blinked the tiredness from their eyes, looking as if they had been punished by the storm as badly as I had. There were rations, cots, water bottles, sandals and clothes strewn everywhere. Anything that had not been tied down had been tossed into the air by the wind, and the rain had soaked everything else.

But as the sun rose, I was reminded once more of the brutal heat of the Sahara and knew by midday I would be bone dry, save for the sweat that left my body.

The last few days of the convoy were less eventful. We spent them following the tribesmen's lead, breaking camp late in the morning, despite having been ready at 06:00 because the militia woke late and drank tea. There was one memorable event when we happened across several men riding camels with donkeys in tow laden with goods. As we were more local to the militia's own territory, some among them even knew the camel riders and progress was halted once more as they stopped to talk, asking for any news that might be of use to us.

Some of the younger Malians took the opportunity to hop up into the saddle and ride the camels around gleefully.

'Luc, I think you should give it a try after!' Someone piped up, causing the rest of us to laugh. Luc, one of the machine gunners had been the butt of several practical jokes in the past, and the image of him riding around on a camel made me smile.

Evidently, the rest of the guys from Spartan 20 liked the idea too, as they were waving the young Malian lad over. The young man turned the camel skilfully and trotted over to see what the fuss was about. Luc was shaking his head saying, 'you must be mad if you think I'm getting on that thing. Stop asking me to. I'm not going to!'

'Do it!' We all cried, 'stop being a baby, get on the camel!'

One of the other guys was trying to communicate with hand gestures to the Malian in the saddle, pointing at Luc, then at the camel. His frown turned into a smile as he understood, and dismounted from the wooden saddle, nodding in assent. The camel moaned in protest, as if it knew what was about to happen and snorted.

'Guys, I'm not doing it!' Luc held up his hands in protest, but the others from Spartan 20 were already pushing him towards the beast. I was laughing already, Luc must have weighed twice what the young Malian lad did. And on top of that, he had his helmet and body armour on. Everyone had gathered round by now and was egging him on.

Finally, Luc caved to peer pressure and said, 'fine! if it will shut you all up.' We cheered and laughed as we watched Luc try to figure out how to get his stocky frame into the saddle. After a minute of fumbling with the stirrups, he finally managed to haul himself up and swing his leg over. The camel groaned again, unaccustomed to the unusually large load and tottered a little, before straightening itself, seeming to grumble with displeasure.

Luc took a hold of the reins and we clapped as he pumped a fist into the air in triumph, beaming down at us. But after only a few steps, the camel had decided it had had enough of this unfamiliar and heavy human and began to groan and fold its front legs under itself, tipping Luc forward. Luc's grinning face seemed to change to a look of horror and panic as he saw what the beast was attempting to do. But he was powerless to stop it.

Almost as if in slow motion, the camel tilted forward. There was a great splintering of wood as Luc was forced onto the wooden saddle pommel, snapping it in two before tumbling forward over the camel's long neck into the sand with a very feminine shriek. Everyone who saw it roared with laughter as the camel straightened itself and trotted away, the ill-tempered creature having rid itself of its unwanted rider.

I was in stitches! So, too, were all the guys from Spartan 20. Most of them doubled up in laughter, as were the Malian militia who saw it. Luc swore after the camel who was eyeing him suspiciously from a safe distance, as he massaged his shoulder which only caused me to laugh even harder. I was crying, my face hurting from smiling so much. We all needed a good ten minutes to recover from that before we could apologise to the traders for breaking their saddle.

We soon had to bid goodbye to the militia once our orders had come through the next day and left for Gao. We had been on this terrain for twelve days.

# CHAPTER 11

The air conditioning of our tent was incredibly refreshing, and I let out an audible sigh of pleasure as I stepped inside. Some of the guys were playing Call of Duty on a PlayStation someone had brought from France.

'Hey, Dobson! Still alive?'

I caught up with them for a bit, telling them of my little adventure without them before insisting that I must take a long, cool shower. Air conditioning, proper showers and good food were the quickest ways to boost morale in the desert. And there was plenty of each at Gao, as well as a well-earned beer or two; I drank in our bar, as I thought about the mission. I had seen a little action at least and had begun to understand a bit more of this part of the world.

Once back into the rhythm of day-to-day life at Gao, I was disheartened to learn this was one of the 'slower' missions that the guys in my group had done. Because the General insisted we work with the local friendly militias on the pick-up trucks, good results were few and far between. Matt, Zig and the others complained that we ought to be using the drones and helicopters to pinpoint and attack enemy encampments, as they were less active during the rainy season, and the likelihood of us stumbling upon them was slim. Supposedly, this had all been relayed up the chain by the lieutenant, but had fallen on deaf ears - the mode of operation would remain the same. We would continue the convoys until further notice.

Again, the weather had begun to complicate things. There seemed to have been far more rain this year than the previous one. Now that we were well into the rainy season, the roads of the FOB had been churned up into a reddish-brown sludge, becoming impossible to keep anything clean. There were more stories of vehicles being stuck, and certain parts of the desert becoming inaccessible due to the 'wadis' (which was the Arabic word for ravines that were dry nine months of the year, but became saturated for the rainy season). Coupled with the temperature, which was at an annual high point through July and August, we were surely in for a treat.

In the meantime, however, there was one thing for me to look forward to. There was word that the British air force was sending two Chinook helicopters. All personnel required to go with them to Gao, for at least two years as a goodwill gesture, to help the French with the colossal logistical nightmare of supplying everything five thousand troops needed. It was nearing the end of July when they arrived. Because we were living next to the helicopter aircrews of Gao, the Brits were welcomed to use our bar so they could mingle with their French counterparts.

It was, of course, especially intriguing for me, as I knew that it could very easily have been me wearing their uniform. There were a lot of jokes from the French guys asking if I would abandon them in favour of my countrymen. On Sunday, the kitchens shut in the evening for cleaning, and the different units amongst the aircrew and ourselves took turns to cook a barbecue. Graciously, the Brits had offered to help the aircrew this week, wanting to do their bit to help out.

None of them spoke any French of course, the UK's education system is seriously lacking where foreign languages are concerned. As dinner was being served, one moustachioed Sergeant in British fatigues was shouting, 'come and get your fish and chips!' Tapping a ladle on the size of a large pot at the head of the line, dishing it out to the Frenchmen in turn, none of whom had any idea what he was saying.

When it was my turn, I grinned at him, and pointed at the food, feigning incomprehension. As I was wearing French fatigues and had a French rank on my breast, he would have assumed I was French.

'Would you like any more rice?' The sergeant spoke very slowly and clearly, in an obvious effort to help me understand, gesturing with his other hand to the pot of rice.

'Oh, yeah go on then mate, that looks brilliant.' I replied nonchalantly in perfect English. The Sergeant stood dumbfounded, his mouth agape in surprise. I had to smile.

'Wow, you speak really good English!'

'I should bloody hope so, I am English!' I laughed, and left the sergeant scratching his head, even more confused than before. After eating, I went to join the table of Brits to introduce myself. The Sergeant from before piped up and said, 'this is him! the Englishman in the French army!'

'Are you in the French Foreign Legion?' someone else asked. I was happy to indulge them all for a bit, clearly being somewhat of an oddity, and I was grateful for the chance to speak my own language. Sitting down and laughing with the Brits, it did occur to me just how odd it was having a beer with my countrymen out in the desert whilst we were serving different militaries. They all seemed like a great bunch and I wondered if I had stuck with my application for the British army, would I be sitting there wearing British fatigues instead of French ones?

There had been a lull in activity for a number of weeks. One of our Spartan groups was out on the terrain whilst the rest of us focused on training, our sport and finding various other ways to pass the time. We had been sitting in the tent one morning bitching about the colonel of the aircrew because he had given one of us an official reprimand for going to the toilets with his shirt off, despite the heat. He had also given me a bollocking for having my cap on back to front whilst I had been outside working on one of the Toyotas, listening to a bit of music.

'The man must have nothing to do all day.' Will was saying, 'can he really expect us to-'

Just then, Matt stuck his head in the door. 'Will, Franz, Buss! There's been an IED attack in Gao. I'm sending you three in the EVM helicopters to help out. Get your stuff ready now, the helico's leave in ten minutes!'

Without another word, the boys ran to their alveoles (what we called our individual portioned-off areas of the tent) to throw on their equipment. As Buss was dragging his bag into the cramped corridor, he asked, 'who got hit? Was it the Malians or ours?' Nine times out of ten it would be the Malians; French troops knew to avoid using the same route twice, as potential attackers might think to boobytrap the road in the hopes they would return using the same stretch. This, however, was that one time in ten.

'It's ours.' Matt said gravely.

Unless we were called out, there was nothing left for the rest of us to do but wait. I watched Franz, Will and Buss jog to the helicopter hangars on the opposite side of the runway. The birds had already been pulled out in preparation and their crews were milling around them.

It was not until several hours later, in the early afternoon, that the three of them returned. Crowding around our sweaty and fatigued companions, the rest of the group listened as Will gave his account of the affair.

Some of the infantrymen from the combat compagnies had been carrying out a routine patrol through the city centre in Gao. They had already commenced the return journey when a massive explosion had flipped not one, but two VBCIs. It is hard to describe the force required to achieve such a thing. To put it into perspective: each VBCI is three metres in height, over seven in length and weighs almost thirty metric tonnes.

Apparently, a suicide bomber had driven a vehicle laden with explosives between the VBCI's and detonated his payload, killing two civilians instantly and wounding many more. As for the French soldiers, miraculously, none had lost their lives, owing this to the excellently armoured and well-designed VBCIs. When Will, Franz and Buss had arrived on scene, there was a large crater in the ground where the bomb had exploded; rubble, debris and smoke everywhere.

A second suicide bomber had been neutralised soon after the first one had detonated, saving the local population from the death of more innocent lives. The whole thing was a mess. One had to wonder if the situation could have been avoided. But of course, it is easy to say in hindsight. During the patrols, one local pickup laden with goods looks much the same as another. It was all too easy for the enemy to load their vehicles full of explosives and cover them with a few bags of rice; searching every vehicle upon entry to the city was hardly a practical, nor sustainable, solution.

That year in 2018, there had been twice as many IED attacks as 2017. Another French soldier had lost his life after I had left Mali that year, a VAB driver taking the brunt of an explosion after driving over one. Frank and Bax, from the third compagnie back at 2REG, had told me an IED story of their last deployment. The third compagnie had been escorting a cargo convoy north when they heard an ominous 'boom' in the distance and saw a mushroom of black smoke rise into the air, visible for miles around. It was on the same highway I had used last year, and the smoke had been directly in their path.

Upon approaching, it was clear what had happened: two insurgents had anticipated their arrival and had dug a suitable hole in the dirt next to the road to plant a plastic tub full of explosives. Fortunately, due to their incompetence, upon arming the explosive they had set it off a little too early, a mistake that cost them their lives. Frank told me of how one of the guys had been reduced to bloody chunks, with nothing identifiable left, save a few scraps of flesh. The other had not been so lucky. The shockwave had cut him in half, his legs some twenty feet from his shredded torso. Apparently, he had still been alive, or perhaps it was simply the last motor functions of his brain that was making his arms twitch and his head seem to shake almost in disbelief. The third company had left him to his own devices and continued with their mission after the near miss.

But to label the entire bunch of these extremists as fools would be a mistake; many of them were not stupid. They knew that to target Malian troops over French would destabilise the country more. They knew how to avoid detection, and some knew how to make explosives. This last bunch must have been amongst their most valuable assets - cooking homemade explosives was a tricky and dangerous process. The men that knew how to do it would have been well guarded, most likely having been brought over from the recent conflict in Syria, and would not have been planting them themselves. They had soldiers to do that for them, fresh recruits who were more expendable.

The hard truth was, if they were really determined to get you, they probably could. Despite modern militaries spending millions of dollars on vehicles and equipment that could detect the hated IEDs after Afghanistan, terrorists had adapted, coming up with their own methods, usually being far less expensive. In the case of metal detectors, the casings of IEDs could be made from wood or plastic with only a few tiny metal parts within - about as much as a bottle cap - making them difficult to distinguish from all the other bits of metal debris strewn around as decoys. Some might even have been designed to be detected, built with a sensor picking up sunlight so that as soon as a bomb squad brushed the earth from its surface it would explode.

The threat of IEDs was constant. When using roads, you had to be vigilant, even after all the developments in technology the best tool to detect them was still a pair of eyes. We had been taught to look out for signs, something as insignificant as a plastic bag in a tree by the road could be a marker for a terrorist sitting on a nearby hill in wait. It was not an honourable way to make war. But then, at least as far as war was concerned, being honourable had often been an advantage awarded to the winning side.

When our turn came to ride the convoy mission with the militia, it was met with a little reluctance. Even the last time out, our Toyotas had been getting stuck occasionally in the sand. Now, however, there had been regular storms and much rainfall; we were likely to have a hard time doing much of anything on the terrain. It was also probable that most enemy insurgents had gone to ground, waiting for the weather to become more favourable. The last two convoy missions had yielded no results whatsoever and seemed to be more of a drain on French resources than time well spent.

But complain was all we did. We readied the vehicles, loading them up with rations, water and ammo once more, consoling ourselves with the fact that this would likely be the last convoy we did this year. The idea was much the same as the last time: we would patrol with the militia, following their lead and looking to intercept any signals at the same time.

The day of departure came and I spent a couple of minutes enjoying the air conditioning in our tent for the last time in a while. And then, we were all embarked and our handful of vehicles was leaving Gao once more. The atmosphere in the group was jovial, despite our scepticism of the mission. We would link up with the tribal militia in several days, as the lieutenant had a couple of points of interest he wanted to explore. A drone had picked up images of a villager who had driven out to a remote location to dig, before returning to a local settlement. We headed south and east to investigate. The first few hours were going well, until great black clouds could be seen on the horizon, threatening our progress.

The lieutenant ordered a halt to the convoy as it began to rain. We set up a defensive cordon, hiding under tarpaulins as we were battered by strong winds. Will, our sharpshooter, had managed to find himself a baby desert hare that had sought refuge under the chassis of our Toyota. Once the storm had subsided, we all crowded round the little creature nestled in his gloved hands. At this time of the year, it was clear to see that there was more life in what was usually a barren wasteland. Oases sprang up and wildlife could risk travelling further north without fear of going thirsty. The foliage, too, seemed greener and more frequent, with some areas actually having little patches of long grass.

This also had the added consequence of a greater quantity of bugs. Setting up camp on the first night, we had to swat away mosquitoes and douse ourselves in the corrosive anti-bug spray strong enough to melt some plastics. It did not seem to bother most of the bolder mosquitoes, however, and the next morning we were scratching at numerous bites. The dreaded camel spiders were bold, too. As soon as the sun had set, they seemed to be everywhere. Revolting little creatures. Instead of running away from us, they seemed to run directly for us, pincers outstretched as if they were going to attack. Scorpions were another worry. Some were quite venomous and, if we were bitten, we would have to hope that the skies were clear so we could be airlifted out to the infirmary at Gao, where the medics had antidotes for things like that.

On the second day, we had an awful time with the water and sand, having to traverse, at speed, several wadis that barred our path. The water came up to around waist height in some places. When the Toyotas hit them at speed, they caused a great wave of spray to fly into the air. More than once, the wheels of one of our pickups spun uselessly, and the rear axle dug deep into the sodden sand. We had to jump out, ankle deep in thick, wet mud, and use specially designed textured plastic planks to put under the wheels, giving them something solid to grip on after we had dug away the sodden earth.

It was hard work, and we were all too aware of the fact that this is the hottest part of the year. We drank many litres a day and sweated most of it out, our clothes becoming sweat and sand stained by the end of the third day.

When we eventually reached the lieutenants point of interest on the fourth, Zig and I disembarked with our metal detectors to shed some light on what the images of the lone man digging in the area could have been. But, after a few hours of searching, we found nothing - no weapons, no explosives. Disheartened, we returned to the pickups and climbed aboard. The lieutenant decided we would head further north to link up with the militia and see if they could shake the tree, so to speak, until something of value showed itself.

What ought to have been a several hour journey on the fourth day quickly turned into a nightmare. Waking at six and breaking camp at seven, we had a wadi before us that we had no choice but to traverse. On the face of it, it looked innocent enough, there was not even any visible water on the surface, but once the convoy had engaged upon it, every single vehicle amongst us became stuck in the thick, damp sand. Soon, the sound of revving engines and tyres spinning uselessly filled the air, as each vehicle's team tried fruitlessly to dig, push, pull and coerce the Toyotas through. By 09:00 we had come to the conclusion that the vehicles were simply too heavy. So, ShiShi, Val, Zig, Franz and I unloaded everything from our Toyota. The sandy ground was soon covered in ammo boxes, rations, water bottles, radio batteries, bolt cutters, rocket launchers, mechanics kits and a plethora of other objects, strewn around the vehicles that were now well and truly embedded to their chassis.

We were sitting ducks, and everyone knew it. Matt had our machine gunners, Val and Dub on watch, searching the nearby dunes for movement, whilst the rest of us hacked away at the sand under the vehicle. We must have removed a metric tonne of it until the empty vehicle began to move. As soon as it had, we cheered, only to curse seconds later as the Toyota became stuck in yet more wet sand metres away. It was hellish work, digging under the hot sun in fifty-degree heat, all the while wearing body armour. It caused me to sweat as if I were in a sauna. I consistently drank a litre of water an hour and didn't even care that it was so hot it almost scalded my throat. The air seemed thin, too, as if I needed to suck down more of it to have enough oxygen to fuel my muscles.

It was too late to turn back and try to find another way now; we had committed. We pressed on. Digging the Toyota out, driving it forward once more until it got stuck again and then digging it out again. In the afternoon, we might have been around halfway and were close to some thorny bushes and small trees that we attached the cable and winch on the nose of the Toyota to. Wrapping the cable around the thin trunks and then reeling it in, we hoped it would pull us through the mud and out to safety. Sometimes it worked, and we would get ten metres or so until there was no more cable to pull. Sometimes, the weight of the pickup and force of the winch would uproot the tree entirely, leaving us to dig once more.

All the other vehicles had the same problems, and soon we were all attempting to find our own paths out to the other side of the wadi. There was a cheer as the first of our vehicles made it to the other side, one of the VBL's with the transmitters inside, and they all came back to help us with ours. With the extra manpower the work went a little quicker, and we were able to move at an average of a metre or so per several minutes. Eventually, after much debating and shouting, pushing and digging, our Toyota was free and back on solid ground once more. Now, all that was left to do was reclaim the equipment and our machine gunners that we had left in the middle of the wadi.

Like ants, we soon formed little lines of men ferrying equipment and supplies back to the pick-ups, loading them up once more. We made camp on a nearby dune, as the sun had already set. Looking back the way we had come, I could see the spot we had made camp the night before. In around thirteen hours of solid work, we had travelled only several kilometres.

There was another storm in the night again, preventing us from a good sleep as we had to worry about waking up to save precious equipment. We probably would not have slept anyway, as the wind picked up and the rain saturated the ground anew. My tarpaulin finally gave up in the night, having been sheered in two by the force of the wind and was whisked away to be lost in the desert forever.

We were due a resupply the next day, anyway. Once the lieutenant had chosen a decent spot on a dry gentle hill, we marked the spot with smoke grenades. The resupply was effectuated by a cargo plane that slid out a couple of cratefuls of supplies attached to a parachute. We watched as the plane flew high overhead, seeing the little specks fall from their rears and white chutes unfurl a moment later. The pallets landed a couple of hundred metres from our position and we raced down to them, pulling the netting and parachute free. There were several barrels of well needed fuel, a spare part or two for the Toyotas that needed replacing and a whole lot of water and rations. Some kind soul had thought to include some vanilla yoghurts from the canteen, but the majority had burst upon impact with the ground, coating our ration boxes with sweet goo. I spent a few moments licking each box clean before loading it into the Toyota, a welcome change from the blandness of the rations.

Matt laughed as he pulled a porno magazine from between two bottles. 'Look, the guys in logistics are teasing us!'

Will snatched it from his hands. 'I'll keep this safe.' He said, tucking it into the cargo pocket on his trousers.

'I bet you will.' Kettel grinned.

'Hey, when I want to use it the pages had better not be stuck together!' Buss piped up.

Will made a face. 'I'm not promising anything.'

Matt seized his opportunity whilst Will was distracted and plucked the magazine from his pocket. 'Excuse me, but I'm in charge here.' He reminded us with a stern look. 'I get first dibs.'

We were already late to meet the militia, and the lieutenant had set a time for later in the day. Yet again, it was not to be. An hour or so later, we had mounted the next rise and saw a great waterlogged plain criss-crossed with little wadis blocking our path. Far in the distance, we could see a small mountain with sheer rock formations rising into the air, indicating solid ground. But first, we had the plane to traverse. This time, we decided to try our utmost to navigate around the wadis, finding the thinnest points to cross and driving up between them, sticking to what was relatively solid ground. It was easier this way, but by no means quick. Even between the wadis the sand was thick and wet. We were stuck several times crossing and had a heart-wrenching moment when our pickup stalled and refused to start up again. It finally came back to life, to our relief. Hours later, with more frustrating setbacks and delays, we finally made it to the other side and wound our way through the little mountain range. On the other side, we made camp after another long day.

Apparently, there was a hole in my mosquito net because the next morning, I was scratching uncontrollably and was grateful to get going again for the distraction. We met with our militia friends after several days delay and the Lieutenant and their leader discussed the plan of action. We would head a little further north, toward the point where the borders of Mali, Algeria and Niger met, where hopefully we could shake a few insurgents loose.

This far north, the terrain was a little drier. Yet we still got stuck several times throughout the day. The Malians seemed much more at ease, not in the least because they travelled light. We were out in no man's land again, where settlements were few and far between. Anyone wealthy enough to own a vehicle was suspicious.

One such vehicle was spotted heading straight for our position one morning, as we were stopping to listen for signals. One of the guys shot a warning shot into the sand to halt the vehicle, the driver apparently not having spotted us. Taking the vehicle and its occupants to one side, Zig and I were left with the task of searching it. Approaching we conducted an initial check of the exterior, finding nothing and, upon looking inside, exchanged a glance. The SUV was filled to the brim with stuff. There were suitcases, clothes, shoes and even a skinned camel's leg thrown in with it all, not even wrapped up-possibly food for the evening meal.

I sighed, dropped my bag and got to work opposite Zig.

'Remember, we're looking for anything electronic, too. Phones, sim cards and things like that.' Zig reminded me.

'Chef, are you hungry?' I grinned, holding up the camel's leg.

Zig made a disgusted face. 'Put that thing down before you contract some kind of illness.'

'What if they're hiding a sim card in here?' I dangled the leg in mid-air and shook it.

Zig raised his eyebrows. 'If that's the case they're smarter than they look. You go ahead if you like.'

I gave the leg a final poke before tossing it onto the growing pile of items we had searched already.

I remember thinking finding a lone sim card in that mess would be like finding a needle in a haystack and said as much to Zig.

'We can only do so much' he said.

It took us a couple of hours to empty the damn thing and we found nothing. I was disappointed. We had to reluctantly conclude that the driver and his passenger were innocent and let them go. I went over to my bag and knelt, sucking the entire camelback dry without pausing. Then, I downed half a bottle of water too, effectively replacing all the liquid I had lost through sweat.

Just as soon as we had finished, black clouds could be seen quickly approaching and the rumblings of thunder reached our ears from across the plain. We had several minutes to set up a cordon and hide under the tarpaulins, as a particularly violent storm shook the pickups under us. It was all I could do to hold onto the tarpaulin with Val, the two of us huddled together on one side of the Toyota, Zig on the other, sarcastically hoping that our comrades in the cabin in front were dry and having a good nap.

We pressed on north and, as the terrain became a little rockier, we picked up our first signals. The militia leader suspected that there had been enemy activity in the area and, lo and behold, the transmitters were soon relaying through the radio what they had intercepted. It was similar to the last time, we were being watched, but looking around could see nothing and no one. Franz, one of our sharpshooters, stepped up to the .50cal and was staring at the terrain like a hawk, watching for any sign of movement.

It was not long before the Malians found some motorbike tracks in the sand and we picked up the pace, the familiar feeling of excitement making my heart beat a little faster in anticipation. Again, the tension began to build, and we intercepted several more transmissions; the enemy was tracking our movement. Unfortunately, the sky began to darken before we were able to close the gap and the militia leader suggested we pick up the trail again at first light. It was eerie making camp. I sat on my cot eating a paella flavoured ration (one of the better ones), whilst the transmitters nearby in their VBL continued to pick up signals.

The messages they intercepted might be as follows: 'They are making camp to the south.' Or 'How many can you see? Are there French troops with them?'

They were watching, always watching. The only comfort was that, as they would surely have discovered by now, there were French with the convoy and the insurgents were always hesitant to attack the French. Regardless, I did not sleep as soundly as I could have, and the lieutenant doubled up the guard for the night.

As morning broke, we were away before the sun had fully risen, hoping to get a head start on our prey. The Malians, once again, found some tracks and followed them north with us in tow. The transmitters were soon receiving more frequent signals and we all had the impression of getting closer. The militia leader reported that one of his motorbikes in the vanguard had spotted what might have been a vehicle far to the north. Now, the chase was on.

The pace quickened significantly, and this time I found my arse being buffeted by the seats we had installed on the plywood board that covered the bed of the pickup. As there was nothing for my feet to wedge onto, they were simply dangling over the side. I had to use my arms to keep myself from falling off, as each bump caused me to momentarily fly into the air.

But our weight and the ground were still against us. One of the vehicles got stuck, and the rest of us had to stop and wait as Kettle and Dub got down to push. We were underway again, but then my own pickup became stuck in a dip in the land that had retained some of the moisture from the last rainfall. We lost crucial minutes, and the Malians had soon disappeared over the next dune. Following their tracks, we came upon them an hour later, where the ground seemed elevated and smooth. Bedrock broke the surface, making driving far quicker.

'Why have you stopped?' The lieutenant had asked impatiently, seeing that the Malians had caught no one. The militia leader had to explain that they could go no farther north. They were on the border with another Tuareg tribe who would not take too kindly to us crossing it. The lieutenant, understanding that there would be wider political ramifications if he was to upset another tribe, was reluctantly forced to accept that our quarry had escaped.

Heading back south, the transmission crew intercepted nothing more. All was quiet. We set up camp early with the Malians, and they let some of our guys ride their motorbikes for some fun. We all had a good laugh watching as Dub zoomed around our camp, wobbling precariously before he fell off.

The Malians showed us how they cooked bread in the desert, too. It was a strange technique that required no pan but was cooked directly in the sand. The dough was kneaded and spread into a flat, circular shape whilst a patch of hard ground was selected, brushed a little and the dough was placed on top. The cook would then spread embers from the fire onto the bread and wait for it to bake. The result was a little hard, but surprisingly free of sand. We even had our own campfire that night, for which I was grateful as it gave us a little respite from the mosquitos.

We had a last resupply before heading back to Gao, and the Brits had decided to make themselves useful. A Chinook flew in, carrying a net strapped to its underbelly full of fuel and water. They were fantastic machines. Weighing almost three times as much as the NH90's, they had two 'turrets' upon which there was a set of blades and a motor. Together they were able to achieve the force needed to lift the thing from the ground. We had to stand well back, for the sheer force of the Chinook engines and blades would send small rocks shooting at great speed that were incredibly painful if they hit you. Despite our distance, we were covered in sand once it had left us and Val cursed them, having just cleaned his minimi (the standard issue light machine gun).

The militia's leader was gracious enough to offer to show us a way to avoid the more saturated areas of the desert for our return journey to Gao. Within a day, he had led us around or in-between them, knowing the terrain only as a local could, and we had done within a day what had taken us several on our own.

They left us soon after, and the lieutenant wanted to take a look at one more point of interest before we made camp for the night. There was a nearby village that was suspected to be housing some hostiles. A perfect rocky ridgeline bordered the village and our sharpshooters. Will and Franz set up there, as Buss sent down the drone to investigate. The drones were a new addition to our kit, and could be used to reconnoitre an area from the sky without having to risk sending a man in. Again, we found nothing. However, to add insult to injury, the steering linked to the front axle of one of the VBL's shattered navigating the boulderous terrain near the base of the ridge, and the second VBL was forced to tow it.

For all of the next day progress was painfully slow, and the lieutenant was forced to make camp half a day from Gao, our column being slowed too greatly by the broken VBL. That night, we were caught by yet another storm and I cursed my bad luck, squatting next to the Toyota with Zig to wait it out.

After thirteen days, re-entering Gao was incredibly satisfying. The mission had been extremely disappointing and there had been setback after setback. I had sand covering me that would take days to wash out of my hair. My skin was burned and flaking, and my lips cracked. Looking in the mirror by the toilet in our living zone, I realised I would need a shave too, my beard had grown unruly and dirty. Taking a shower that evening, after everything had been cleaned and put away, was one of the most satisfying things I had ever felt. I washed two weeks' worth of sweat and sand from my tired body and closed my eyes in relief, letting the water wash over me until someone pounded on the cubicle door for me to hurry up.

Even after the lieutenant had relayed our awful results up the command chain, the General in Gao still would not relent with convoys and we warned the other groups what to expect now. At least for the time being, we could rest up and get back into our comfortable daily routine at Gao.

One day, as we filled up on good food in the canteen, Matt told us all that there was a possibility of a mission up in Tessalit (the most northerly French FOB, and the most vulnerable). There had been regular mortar strikes on the town and the FOB. To the east, there was a range of rocky hills elevated above the town from which the attacks could be launched and gave a good vantage point. Our job would be to wait for the drone to pick up images of the cell, at which point we would be deployed in the helicopter to hunt them down.

Everyone was pleased to finally be doing something with the helicopters. When the mission finally came to fruition a week later, the news was received with a little cheer. We took everything we would need for a week with us, not knowing how long we would be there.

On the helicopter ride over, it was clear as we travelled further north just how barren this part of the desert was. At least in the areas around Gao there was scrubland, thorny bushes that looked as though they were only just clinging to life. Yet, they were there. Here around Tessalit, there was nothing growing, just sand and rocks. It was hard to imagine a place more hostile and it made me wonder just what the motivation for founding a town in such an awful place could have been. The FOB there was smaller than Gao and it, too, had a half dedicated to the French and a half dedicated to the UN.

Zig knew a guy named Carlos who was working in the UN half as a contractor. Once we had settled in after the helicopter had dropped our team off, Carlos invited us all for a barbeque over on his side of the fence. Carlos had been in our unit before my time and Zig knew him well. He introduced the rest of us and we sat down to eat in their little zone Carlos shared with a South African and a couple of Russian helicopter pilots.

We had a good laugh. Limiting ourselves to a couple of beers, as we could be on call at any minute, we finished the evening in good spirits and headed back to our tents on the far edge of the French base.

In the first couple of days, we were hopeful of some action, but saw none. Passing the time with sport in the morning, we watched films or slept during the hot hours. Halfway through the week, we became less and less optimistic of anything happening and began to relax a little, perhaps letting our guard down more than we should have.

I remember one day at around 13:00, I was lying on my bed in the hot tent, sweating, watching a film on my laptop to take my mind off the heat. Then, out of nowhere there was a colossal 'BOOM!' and the ground shook beneath me. Anyone who had been sleeping was now wide awake, and we all sat bolt upright in our beds. There was a moment of hesitation as we all looked at each other. It could only have been an explosion, and it had felt uncomfortably close. Was the enemy attacking us?

'What the fuck was that?' Val asked into the silence.

BOOM! Another explosion jolted us all into action, sounding even closer than the first. The tent came alive with activity as Will shouted, 'Attack! Attack!'

Trying to remain calm I pulled on my trousers and stuffed my feet into my boots as fast as I could, not bothering to put on my plate carrier. I took it, along with my helmet and rifle, in a bundle in my arms and ran after the others who had left the tent.

In each FOB, there are various bunkers constructed from bastion walls for just such an occasion. Myself, and the other boys of Spartan 30, sprinted for the nearest one. To say it was nerve wracking was an understatement. We could not say when or where the next mortar or rocket would strike and could only hope it would not be on our heads. At least in a gun fight you can return fire, but now there was nothing we could do, save run for the bunker. It was frightening. I imagined a projectile whistling past my ear, slamming into the earth beside my feet and everything going black. The thought of waking up in a hospital bed, or not at all, was horrific and I managed to cover the two hundred or so metres to the bunker at break-neck speed.

Safety! We all piled inside, one after the other, ushering the last in until we were all safe.

BOOM! The last blast seemed further away. Looking around, I saw that the bunker was crammed full of soldiers. In the gloom, I could make out plenty of anxious faces. Sirens wailed from the guard tower in the centre of the base and I imagined all the bunkers must have been filled by now. I pulled on my gear just in case there was a follow up attack.

Boom! It sounded further still. After the fourth blast we waited for a fifth that never came. The siren was switched off after ten minutes or so, but we were ordered to stay in the bunker until further notice.

Franz said into the silence that followed, 'shit, I forgot to pause my film!'

'Yeah, they could have waited until I had wiped my arse.' Dub piped up, having been sat on the toilet at the time of the attack. I laughed.

'How could they be so inconsiderate?'

'Bastards!' We had a good chuckle, and soon the jokes served to mask a little of the fear that hung in the air I had felt upon entering the bunker. Sometimes, all you can do is laugh.

We were let out an hour later. A couple of helicopters were put in the air to circle the FOB in defence, but our attackers were long gone by now, and no one knew where. It transpired that the second blast had been only fifty metres from our tent, but on the outside of the bastion wall. It was closer than I would have liked, though I was grateful to still be in one piece. The idea of having my legs blown off is a nasty one, a fate that, for me, had to be worse than quick death. Luckily, the insurgents had not perfected accurate mortar fire, and none of the explosions had killed or injured anyone.

We were all dying to get out there after this, but since the drone had found nothing, we had no idea where to go. Our sharpshooters, Will and Franz, got to go up in a helicopter to circle the rocky hills to the east. Again, they found no trace of them. It was incredibly frustrating.

The next day was back to normal. We did much of what we had for the first half of the week, albeit a little more disheartened now, almost knowing nothing else would happen. By the end, the colonel on the FOB decided we would be of more use elsewhere. So, we were once again piling into two helicopters that would this time take the twelve of us to Menaka - a FOB that lay near the south eastern corner of the country. Again, the mission would be opportunistic. Until the drone had images of the enemy, we would sit and wait.

Menaka was the worst of all the FOB's I had been to. The living zone, which we shared with the helicopter pilots, was basic. There was no air conditioning in the tents, and the toilets consisted of two portable cubicles stained with shit and long since blocked up. It was easier to go and dig a hole in a barren corner near a bastion wall and squat, rather than to use the cubicles. The shower was a single tap on a raised water butt and there were often queues for it in the evening.

There was not even a canteen in Menaka. All the troops had to eat were the ration packs, which we were already sick of. The only consolation was a 'restaurant' run by the locals inside an air-conditioned container in the FOB. The twelve of us, along with the helicopter crews, ate there. A day later most of us had fallen ill.

'What the fuck have they given us?' Val wailed as he ran off with a shovel to dig yet another hole to shit into. I, too, had a nasty case of food poisoning and spent the best part of two days shitting my guts out and eating nothing. The fact that there was no air conditioning during the hot hours - meaning we had to find some shade to wait out the oppressive heat - didn't help our conditions improve. There was no chance we could operate like this.

The heat, too, caused problems for the helicopters, as the temperature rose higher than usual. If you imagine, helicopters are able to fly because the blades spin fast enough to push down on the air, lifting the bird into the sky. But, when the air reaches a certain temperature, a 'no fly' order is given as the particles in the air vibrate against one another from the heat, spreading and causing the air to become thinner. This in turn would mean that the blades of the helicopter would have less matter to push down upon, thus having to spin much faster in order to take off. Such was the case for the hottest part of the next few days.

By now, I was sure it would be an uneventful mission, and consigned myself to whatever entertainment I could find. It soon became a waiting game.

One of the Tigre pilots had found an empty ammo box and some clear perspex. One brave soul had captured several camel spiders and a large scorpion, placing them all in the box. There must have been around thirty shirtless and burned French soldiers crowding round this ammo box one evening, all shouting and placing bets with our Malian currency.

'Ten thousand CFA's say the spiders win!' Someone shouted.

'You're on! My scorpion is gonna have them all!' A Tigre pilot replied.

We all crowded over the box to see what would happen. The creatures had first tried to find a way out, scrambling at the side of the box, but eventually realised they were stuck. The scorpion flexed its pincers menacingly, but two camel spiders were already tussling with each other. The scorpion took advantage of the chaos, darting over and catching the third spider with its pincers. The camel spider struggled to break free, but the scorpion had deployed its stinger and had skewered the spider brutally. The bug was no more.

A great cheer rose from the spectators, and more camel spiders were found to be put in the box. The scorpion soon became a favourite. Dominating the little arena, it soon was surrounded by the carcasses of dead spiders, their eight hairy legs curled upwards in the throes of death. Then, one of the excited crowd had nudged the table upon which the box was set, displacing the Perspex and a couple of camel spiders took their chance to climb out to safety. Most of the guys shrieked like little girls and went running back a good twenty metres. I laughed and clapped at their reaction.

A week later, we were heading back to Gao, the whole excursion feeling quite pointless. I still felt weak after the bout of food poisoning from Menaka and rested several days in my air-conditioned tent before returning to normal.

We were weeks away from the end now. And after what the other guys had said was their least eventful Mali yet, we were all keen to get back to France. There were yet more storms, perpetual puddles seeming to fill the dips in the earth all around the FOB, and we had to dig irrigation ditches as our tents were beginning to fill with water.

Ours would be the last Spartan group to leave the terrain, the relief process being staggered so that there was always an active group ready in case something were to happen. When the first of our GCM brothers arrived in Gao, it felt like we were now on the last stretch. We greeted them, some I knew, too. Chef Jouk was there, as was my good friend Oskari and Peter, a Sergeant Chef from our section.

'Hey, Oskari!' I shouted when I saw him down at the airstrip. Oskari was about as wide as he was tall, one of the strongest guys I knew and always kept his head shaved. He was never the loudest in the room, but was as tough as they came.

'Dobson! How's it been? Seen any action?' I gave him a hand loading his bags into the P4 and made a face.

'Yea, a little bit, I guess there would have been more, but the storms were bad this season. Everyone went to ground to wait out the bad weather. What's changed back at 2REG?'

'Not much, really. New Chef de Corps, that's it. Oh, and the lieutenant has you down for the Commando spécialisé course in October.' He grinned.

'Ah, shit.'

'Commando spécialisé' was one of the most difficult and notorious training courses the French army had to offer. Up in the Pyrenees mountains at a place called Mont Louis. The course consisted of a month of being outdoors, learning to traverse difficult obstacle courses - some of which were water-based - and carry out complex missions each night, no matter the weather. It had an exceptionally high dropout rate supposedly, and I would be doing it in winter.

'Ah well, better to get it out of the way!'

'That's not everything. The lieutenant also says you're doing your Caporal training in Castel in January.' He laughed at my expression

'Oh, for fucks sake! Well, this winter is shaping up to be great so far.'

Caporal training was another notorious course within the ranks of the Legion. Considered by many to be two months of wasted time, most agreed that the only thing you learned was how to suffer.

'I'll worry about that later. Let me show you to our tents.'

Once I had shown Oskari to his tent, I returned to my own. Some of the guys were listening to music and giving their equipment a final scrub down, before we would pack it all away in a weeks' time.

'Who else is doing the commando spécialisé?'

The majority of them raised their hands, their expressions turning glum.

'Thanks for killing the mood Dobson. I was just daydreaming about how nice Crete is going to be in a few days and you have to remind me about that.' Will joked.

Franz laughed. 'Ha! I've already done it! You guys are gonna have a great time. In October, too!' He sucked air in through his teeth. 'Better bring a winter hat boys!'

We gave him the finger.

A week later, my team and I were hauling crates down to the airstrip with our weapons, armour and other bits of equipment we had used over the last four months. As we waited for the logistics team to load them up, we chatted amongst ourselves and cracked a few jokes. Spirits were high. The mission was over, and we were heading home after several days in Crete with our feet up. At the beginning of the mission, I distinctly remember feeling apprehensive and out of my depth, like a weak link.

But somewhere along the line, that feeling had faded away and I had begun to feel as if I had a place amongst them, despite being English, a Legionnaire and speaking a version of French that they must have found quite alien. Nevertheless, I had found friends here, and felt much more like a capable soldier than I had been at the beginning. I suppose that life is just one big learning curve.

Crete was a blur. The first night we ended up at the local bars, of course, despite the usual warning for us to stay at the hotel. The army had also been forced to change hotels after the last had refused to host them after one drunken soldier had shat in the pool. But the food was still fantastic. Unfortunately, however, I threw most of it up just before getting on the bus for the airport, having drank the hotel tap water that was apparently full of nasty bacteria. The coach journey was longer than it perhaps could have been, as other soldiers took it in turns to spew their guts up in the little cubicle next to the stairs, filling the coach with the smell of vomit.

Once I had bid farewell to the guys of Spartan 30, I took the train from Paris airport back to the south, back to 2REG, which I was starting to think of as home, in a weird way. I shut my eyes and thought of the little room I had left back in the Compagnie D'Appui, and looked forward to telling my friends, Romaric, Botch and the others from the 2eme Compagnie all about my adventures.

# CHAPTER 12

I had just arrived back at 2REG after several weeks of leave and was already preparing to leave again. The following Sunday, we would begin the commando spécialisé course, and I wasn't particularly looking forward to it. But I had no choice, I had to do as I was told.

There was a knock at my door and Djo poked his head in. He had beaten me back to regiment, having driven all the way from Serbia in his pride and joy, a black Audi, which he liked to drive incredibly fast.

'I've got the exact list of things to pack here.' He said, handing me a sheet of paper.

'Thanks. How was your holiday?'

He shrugged. 'Pretty good. The girls like my tan!' He winked and I shook my head with a smile, as he returned to his room. I was glad to have Djo with me. We had been together since the very first day of the tests which, despite feeling as though that was an age ago, was not so long in my past. Djo was of a similar height to myself and muscular. He was one of those guys who had a naturally hostile look until you got to know him. Amongst friends he would smile often. Yet, I knew him to be a particularly hard bastard. I had never seen him show any weakness and the average person would do well not to cross him. Djo was a rock, and I was happy to have him with me for the course to come.

David, too, would be joining us, making us three Legionnaires in a total of twenty-one candidates. David was Hungarian. Being tall and broad with naturally bronze skin, green eyes and a chiselled jaw, he was considered attractive to say the least. In fact, I had never known anyone to be so popular with girls. What made things worse was that David knew the effect he had on them, too. I was often left rolling my eyes whenever I was with him, as girls would walk past and try to catch his eye, not even noticing my existence. Unfortunately for them, David was married.

Like so many others in the section, David was also an extremely competent soldier. He had passed his sergeant training in the top three of his class and aced every course he had been sent on. Some of the other guys in the section had taken to calling him, 'golden boy.' Yet, it didn't go to his head; David never took himself too seriously.

The rest were all the guys from the French GCM units - all commandos and reliable men. Whilst a regular unit of French soldiers could afford to have dropouts (guys that opted to quit the stage if their morale broke), we knew that there could be no such option for ourselves. We were some of the best soldiers in the army; we had a reputation to uphold. It would not do if word spread that a member of the GCM had quit the course because it was too tough, so not even a single one of us could give up.

Time seems to go rather quickly when there is an event in the near future that you are dreading, and commando spécialisé was no exception. Before I knew it, David, Djo and I were in one of the section's vans, taking the winding mountain roads up and up, climbing higher and deeper into the Pyrenees. Even in October, at this altitude, the snow was already thick on the ground.

The fort was called Mont-Louis and was one of those early-modern era ones. Back from the time when cannonballs were used to batter down walls and the black powder of musket fire would have dirtied the air of a battlefield. The fortifications were constructed of a network of deep trenches and thick walls. With great triangular shaped protrusions on each corner of the fort, it was designed so defenders could pour down fire upon besiegers from a number of different angles. Atop a hill, it had a spectacular view of the mountain valley below that stretched away into the distance before it.

The snow was ankle deep when we got out, and the air was bitterly cold. It did not help a bit that our bodies were so used to the excessive heat of the desert. Now, we had been plunged into the polar opposite, and it must have been close to zero, even at midday.

As we passed under the ominous archway leading into the courtyard, where all the barracks houses were situated, we met up with some of the other guys who had already arrived. Will, Val, Kettle, and a bunch of others from Spartan 20 were there, and we greeted them cordially.

'Ah, the Legionnaires are here! We're saved!' Will grinned, shaking my hand.

'Good holiday?'

'I only took a week. I'm saving the rest for when this shit is over, I think we'll probably need it!'

We ended up waiting in the van for the rest to arrive because snow had begun to fall outside. And as the sun began to set, the temperature began to plummet. When we were shown to our barracks by one of the instructors, a Frenchmen with olive skin that looked as though he might have had Moroccan origins, he told us not to get too comfortable. Apart from the weekends, we would be spending the next month outside, he explained. He introduced himself as Raph and mentioned that we would meet the rest of the instructors in the morning, along with a brief overlay of the course.

I slept fitfully that night. Probably because I knew it was the last time I would have a proper sleep for a while. At 06:00, we were up and getting ready. The morning assembly was at 07:00, for which we had been instructed to have camouflage paint already on our faces.

The head instructor was an Adjutant Chef named Bossard, and he seemed an amicable enough fellow. He briefly explained that there were several modules to the course. The first was all the various obstacle courses we had to practice in preparation for a timed run. There was explosive training, something I was not a complete stranger to, at least. Again there was a final test, a self defence module and a rope safety course. After two weeks, we would be relocated to a different fort by the sea. There we would have a water-based module, with yet more obstacle courses. The final week would have a culmination of a bit of everything. It involved several exercises, along with some close quarter combat and a 'surprise' that I was sure would not be a particularly enjoyable one. On top of all that, there would be a tactical exercise organised for each evening, often involving an infiltration of a good number of kilometres. By the sounds of it, good night's sleep would be few and far between.

But before all of this, we would have to do some physical tests to ensure we were up for the task. They were not difficult. The twenty-one of us passed the push ups, pull ups and rope climbing tests with relative ease, and were soon heading over to the obstacle courses, where the instructor, Raph, would show us how to set up the harness. Because many sections of the obstacle course spanned the various walls and trenches of the fort, candidates might often find themselves shimmying across a single rope suspended over a drop of twenty metres or so, and had to be strapped in. We would also have to learn to recover in the eventuality that we did fall from the rope and were left dangling in mid-air.

Then, there were the safety precautions to take: attached to our harness, we had two thick rope lanyards with carabiners on the ends, which would secure us to a supporting cable. At all times there must be at least one of these lanyards attached, or we would lose points in the final test.

We practiced tying the lanyards on a grassy embankment, on one thick portion of the impressive walls, our breaths steaming in the cold mountain air. I fucked up the knot a few times and asked one of the other guys for help - something that did not go unnoticed by Raph. He tutted at me, making some comment about needing my hand held before moving on.

When it came to rescuing someone who had fallen from the cable and was dangling in mid-air, I was paired with Djo, but had forgotten how to untie the tangled knot. This resulted in Djo being suspended in mid-air by his lanyard, whist I fiddled with his harness. It was not long before Raph spotted me struggling, as all the other pairs had finished by now, their binomes safely on the ground.

'Hey, what's your name?'

'Dobson, mon Adjutant.'

'Are you retarded Dobson? I showed you how to do this two fucking minutes ago and you've already forgotten!' At the instructor's raised and angry voice, most of the others had stopped what they were doing to watch.

'You know, it's no surprise to me that you are a Legionnaire. Most of you Legionnaires are stupid!' In my peripheral vision, I saw Djo raise an eyebrow as Raph continued to shout from below.

'So, are you going to answer my question? Are you retarded or not?'

After several years in the Legion, I had learned that there is never usually a correct answer for a question such as this and decided to go with the one that was the most diplomatic.

'No, mon Adjutant.'

'Then explain to me how it is that you are incapable of following instructions? I'll tell you something else Dobson, it'll be a fucking miracle if you pass this course.'

I wondered if the instructor taking a disliking to me had anything to do with the fact that I was clearly the youngest on the course, and the only Premiere Classe. In fact, there were only two Caporals, one of whom was Djo. All of the rest held the rank of at least Caporal Chef. Perhaps he thought I was unworthy for the course, as it must have been rare that a Premiere Classe was put forward for something like this. Or maybe I just have one of those faces...

There was silence for a moment, as Raph glared up at me. Djo swayed gently in the breeze, still suspended underneath me by his lanyard.

'Umm... so could you please explain to me just one more time how to get Djo down, mon Adjutant? I think he's starting to lose his circulation...'

Once we had all learned the necessary safety precautions, some picking it up quicker than others, we could progress to practicing the obstacle course itself. My immediate thought was that it was not for anyone who was even a little afraid of heights. The first obstacle was to shimmy along a rounded ledge on a turret built into the wall. A sheer drop of fifteen metres below and only ten centimetres of stone on which to place your feet. Even with the safety lanyards, it was not for the faint of heart.

First, Raph showed us how to cross each one, after which the rest of us would follow suit; practicing the technique to cross the fastest. The course took us all around one side of the fort - climbing walls, gutters, crawling through trenches and even flying down a hundred metre zipline at one point.

We continued until midday, at which point we were allowed to take a ration pack from our bags and eat on the grass with our backs against the wall. Thirty minutes was all we were given before we were joined by another instructor who took us for the self-defence module. There was a dojo in one of the barracks buildings with padded mats. The room was soon filled with the sound of twenty men tossing each other around, panting heavily and eliciting the occasional, 'oof!' as we were thrown down. It was hard work, and I was sweating profusely by the time the sun fell behind the mountains at the end of the lesson.

'Right, that is it from me for the day! Report to the classroom where you'll prepare for tonight's mission!' And with that, our instructor left us to change on the mats.

Just to make things harder, we only had one bag for all our gear. And only two sets of fatigues, one dirty set and one less dirty set. It had to be crammed in on top of our camping gear and warm clothing, which resulted in a very full rucksack. We hoisted them onto our backs and, picking up our rifles, headed over to the classroom.

Every night of the course we would have a mission to complete. They were often similar in nature. First, there was an infiltration, which would be followed by an assault on an enemy position, securing an objective or freeing 'hostages.' Every man amongst us would take it in turns to take the lead on a mission, myself included. The thought of commanding twenty other commandos with far more experience than me was more than a little daunting.

I breathed a sigh of relief when the lead instructor delegated the command of the first mission to one of our Sergeant Chefs, leaving us in capable hands, after he had explained the mission. We were soon poring over maps and satellite images of the surrounding terrain on tablets, plotting the point of attack and preparing our gear. By the looks of it, we would have a long night ahead of us. The head instructor, Adjutant Chef Bossard, had ensured that our drop off point was sufficiently far away from the objective, that we would not have too long a sleep. Because once the mission was over, we would have to march back to the fort.

Tonight, all we would have to do was reconnoitre an old fort the military had long since abandoned. When we were dropped off by the JBC onto a dirt track high in the mountains, I was already feeling the cold. The temperature must have been below zero as there had been snow the day before. Marching soon warmed us up, however. Up one valley, down another, the twenty-one of us plodded along in silence, our boots crunching in the snow.

We reached the old fort somewhere around 01:00, finished our reconnoitre and were in the JBC sent to pick us up once we had radioed in that the mission was complete by 02:00. We marched away back to Mont Louis, where one of the instructors showed us our bivouac spot - a hidden hollow in the valley some five hundred metres from the fort. I had three hours of fitful sleep, sandwiched in between Djo and Val for warmth.

I wondered how many shitty nights I had spent sleeping in the cold or rain over the past few years. Many, was the answer. There was always a few seconds between the end of a dream and the moment I opened my eyes. I was not truly awake, but nor was I asleep. I had a few stolen seconds of bliss when I believed I was a child again. Back at my family home in Halifax, curled up and cosy in bed before my mother would come to knock on my bedroom door to wake me for school. I would roll over and think, just a few seconds more.

But then she was shaking me awake violently, and I opened my eyes to see that it wasn't my mother at all, but Djo shaking my shoulder and passing me my boots.

'Come on, Dobson. We have to be up at the fort by 06:00.' I looked around and my heart sank. Alas, the carefree joy of my schooldays were long since over. Instead, I found myself sat on hard ground, my body stiff and cramped from the cold. I would have to begin the day on an empty stomach. I had eaten the breakfast from the ration pack the night before to fuel myself for the march and I doubted the instructors would take pity on me. Come on then boy, I thought, time to get a move on.

Despite my sleeping bag being rated for minus twenty, I had been woken several times in the night from the cold and was glad to be able to shake some warmth into my limbs. I soon worked up a sweat, as the instructors wasted no time at 07:00 getting us warmed up for the obstacle course as soon as the sun had risen. We had our first timed run though and I, to my shame, was one of only two who technically failed it.

The course took around fifteen minutes to run in total, but by the time we began, we were all tired, hungry and cold already. And if that wasn't enough of a challenge, most of the obstacles were covered in a fine layer of snow and ice.

There was an obstacle called, 'the gutter', where you had to shimmy up a thick pipe bolted to a wall by pressing your boots into the wall, either side, and hooking your hands behind the pipe. I had made it all the way up, reached to grab the railing at the top - already panting as I had done half the course - when I slipped, my fingers just grazing the railing before I fell four metres, being saved from a jarring impact with the ground by my lanyard.

Picking myself up, I found I simply hadn't the strength for a second attempt. I tried pathetically to plant my boots on the wall and haul myself again, but to no avail; my biceps felt as though they were on fire and refused to co-operate. Raph saw it all and tutted almost in pleasure.

'Go around, Dobson. You're getting in everyone's way!'

Damn it, I thought. I was cold, tired and hungry and ready to snap at anyone. I felt weak. Had I been fresh, it would have been a different story. I was sure of it. But then, everyone else was in the same boat. I gritted my teeth and hurried on, trying not to dwell on my failure. Fortunately, I would have another chance later in the week.

Upon seeing that I was miserable afterwards, David put a hand on my shoulder and said, 'don't worry about it Dobson. You'll get another go in a couple of days.'

'I had it!' I blurted out in exasperation. 'My fingers were literally touching the railing at the top! I can't believe I let go. Now that arsehole thinks I'm fucking useless.' I gestured in Raph's direction.

'There's nothing you can do right now, so put it out of your mind. Try and eat something, we won't have much free time.'

As grey clouds approached from the distance, I was fearful that the night's mission would be further complicated by the weather. We ate from a new ration pack we had received for lunch and tried to warm our fingers over our little propane stoves. Lunch was quick, but we were soon warm again as we were put back into the dojo and were practicing more self-defence techniques.

Apparently, the temperature must have risen above zero at some point during the day. For when the heavens finally opened above us that evening, it was rain, not snow, that fell on our heads as we made our way back to the classroom to prepare the mission for the night. This time, we would have the task of setting an ambush for an enemy convoy along a stretch of mountain road.

I crossed my fingers in the hopes that the rain would subside whilst we were preparing the mission, but it was not to be. A steady downpour turned torrential several hours into the night, and we were pelted with freezing droplets of water. Somehow soaking us to the bone even with our waterproof jackets, and the only way to keep warm was to keep marching. The wind and rain were so powerful and violent that, at one point, several of the guys suggest we head back and wait it out. But our designated leader declined, rightly pointing that it was now too far to go back.

When we got to the ambush point, where we knew the enemy convoy would pass at 02:00, we prepared training grenades. Sitting down to wait, we shivered, huddling together on a grassy embankment to keep warm.

'Finally, here they come!' someone said with relief, as several vehicles approached from the south. We were all too happy to 'destroy' the convoy; the terrorists being played by the instructors. Upon taking inventory of my equipment, I realised my night vision goggles had water in the lenses, rendering them useless. Clearly, the storm had taken its toll, and Djo had the same problem with his.

It probably had something to do with the fact that we had the OB70 goggles, a very old version. All the other guys had MINIE-D's or LITTON's, the newer generation of night vision that was better suited to all-weather conditions. There was only one spare, the instructors said, and gave it to Djo, leaving me with nothing for the following night.

Luckily, I managed to pass the obstacle course the second try, easily climbing the gutter this time around and scoring a decent time. However, it did not lift my spirits for long as all of us were hungry. The only food we had came from the ration packs, which provided a couple of thousand calories - not nearly enough as we were burning far beyond what we would during an ordinary day. We were on the go all day and slept little. On top of that, we had to keep our bodies warm. It all required energy and must have been doubly difficult for the larger among us, like David who was over six foot and broad.

Heating up our rations he said, 'during the weekend we have to get some extra food. They'll want to search our packs, but we can put it in a plastic bag, bury it somewhere and collect it when we leave for the infiltration during the night.'

Strictly speaking of course, we weren't allowed our own food, but I imagined all previous groups of candidates would have found a way around the rule.

The last night of the first week I had been chosen to lead the group for our mission. It was fairly standard, we had to assault an objective where there would be a handful of enemy insurgents. The complication was, as is typical of mountainous terrain, that we had a significant climb to complete for our stealthy infiltration. Although I would have to choose the route and make the tactical decisions, I learned that being the boss did have its advantages. I could designate the topography to a few of the other guys and I was being advised by my fellow commandos, many of whom were experienced and capable.

Fortunately, that night the moon was bright, and I could see fairly well without my night vision goggles. The general consensus within the group, at this point, was one of mild indifference. Sure, we wanted the mission to be a success, but were not going to lose any sleep if we were not being as stealthy as we otherwise could be. It would not result in failure, and all anyone cared about was getting this damn course over and done with.

Some of the guys were even marching side by side and chatting softly, something we were able to get away with as the instructors were not marching with us but waiting at the point of ambush. In the end, it unravelled perfectly. We snuck up on the 'insurgents', having done a big loop around the hillside and attacking from above, taking our enemy completely by surprise. The exercise was soon wrapped up and we were allowed to trudge back to our little camping spot by the fort, arriving uncharacteristically early at 01:30, giving us a fantastic four hours sleep.

I autopiloted until Friday afternoon, at which point we were free until 06:00 the following Monday. The first thing I needed was food. After a quick shower, Djo drove David and I to a local pizzeria where we feasted until our bellies could fit no more. Upon collapsing into bed at the barracks, I slept like a stone for fourteen hours solid, waking only to take a piss before curling back up into my sleeping bag in hibernation.

Monday, of course, came around all too quickly, especially because I felt like I had spent most of the weekend sleeping. This week we would be working on the explosives module, as well as a couple of different obstacle courses and the self-defence classes. Fortunately, being from a combat engineering regiment, I knew most of the material already and could manipulate the explosives safely and to the instructor's satisfaction.

There was a shooting range up in the mountains, some ten kilometres from Mont Louis, and we were taken there to practice. To me, I never got tired of hearing the thunderous, deep boom of explosives and seeing the earth thrown into the air. What can I say, blowing shit up is just a whole lot of fun.

Once we had left the prying eyes of the instructors behind, David whispered to Djo and I that he had hidden a bin bag full of food behind one of the bins near the entrance of the fort. We gleefully made our way over only to find that the bin bag was nowhere to be seen. Apparently, Monday morning was the day that the bins were emptied. One good Samaritan had clearly thought to pull them away from the wall and reach into the little alcove David had stashed the care package inside to throw away what he must have thought was waste. In hindsight, we ought to have taken the time to bury it. But it was too late for that now, we would have to make do with the ration packs.

That night the instructors seemed to have stepped it up a notch, giving us a drop off point much further from our designated objective, most likely to fatigue us even more for the week. To make matters worse, I still had no night vision and there was a thick coverage of clouds blocking the light from the moon.

In the night, I found myself stumbling after the rest, as the twenty-one of us navigated a winding path through dense woodland. Outside, there is always a source of external light, whether it be the moon or streetlights, or something else. Rarely is it 'pitch black', but that night was as close as I had ever seen, and the thick canopy of the forest helped not a bit. I fell countless times, and shuffled along after my comrades with my arms outstretched for hours on end, tripping over branches and rocks, totally blind.

At one point, there was a dangerous stream crossing, and, in the silent darkness, I could hear the fast-flowing mass of water and the others as they leapt from one bank to the other. Even they were struggling to see through their goggles, as night vision works by amplifying what light there already is, and many of them had to switch on their infa-red torches. That was no use to me, of course. I was completely blind. I had to edge my way to the steep bank and wait for the guy on the other side to whisper that I was good to go. Then, I jumped into oblivion.

I do not think I had ever been so glad to see the moon once the clouds had parted a little and we were free of the forest. And then it began to snow. What began as an intermittent trickle became a thick downfall, and there was soon a fresh blanket of snow beneath our boots. It was still better than the rain, but the air was cold and I could feel the difference. We stopped once for a quick break, before picking up the march again - during which time I threw on an extra layer - but still felt the penetrating chill of the air. It was not long before my fingers and toes had gone quite numb.

The mission turned out to be a bit of a fiasco. The 'insurgents', at the position we had been sent to assault, spotted us when we were still five hundred metres away because someone had taken the decision to cross open fields, instead of stick to cover. They fired blanks at us and we had no choice but to advance, aware that had the blanks been real bullets there would surely have been casualties. We received a bollocking for it, and rightly so. The fatigue and weather had made us sloppy.

Disheartened, we had to march all the way back to the fort. The snowfall intensified to the point of becoming a blizzard, just as we arrived at our camping spot at 03:00.

'We can't stay here; we need shelter or we'll freeze!' Someone shouted over the noise of the wind. The twenty-one of us stood in a pack like penguins, huddled in indecision. The prospect of setting up my mat and sleeping bag on powder snow in the middle of a snowstorm was madness, a view the others clearly shared.

David piped up, 'There are tunnels near the obstacle course, we can sneak around the side of the fort and sleep in there!'

It was quickly agreed upon as no one had a better idea, and we all set off around the edge of the fortifications. The tunnels had clearly been built for the defenders to pass from one layer of the great fortifications to another, discreetly. As such, they had been built for men to pass in single file and were so small and narrow, we had to walk hunched over so as not to bang our heads.

We all piled in, grateful to be out of the thick snow and howling wind that blew outside. Yet, I was still bitterly cold, even squashed between two of my comrades, my back against the wall with every layer of clothing I had around me. I barely slept for the three short hours we had and every time my body tried to drift off to sleep, my own shivering woke me - I'd feel my teeth chatter in my skull.

The next day there was no respite. We had moved on to the team-based obstacle courses, which involved a series of obstacles that forced us to think before engaging upon them, impossible to complete as an individual. There was much hesitation and discussion as our fatigued minds tried to come up with a good solution, until the instructors shouted at us to get a move on.

It was followed by more self-defence techniques, this time using our rifles as weapons. Our hearts were not in it; at this point, it was survival. At lunch, some guys opted to spend the thirty minutes or so we had sleeping, after having wolfed down the rations cold.

And just when we thought it could not get any worse, the instructors had decided to draw our itinerary for the march that night themselves. The mission was, they said, to reach the end of the march. That was all.

Upon studying the map, I realised what the bastards had done. The itinerary, as the crow flies, was around twenty-five kilometres. A distance one could traverse within around five hours, if travelling on flat ground and in a straight line. However, we were far from flat ground, and the mountain passes had steep, winding paths. And we were tired and hungry already. The actual distance would have been closer to forty kilometres, rather than twenty-five, with a climb of over six hundred metres thrown in. The instructors assured us we had all night to do it, but expected us at the pick-up point at 06:00.

Once they had left us to our own devices, before we would all pile into the JBC at 21:30, there were more than a few sighs and mutterings of, 'pleine les couilles'- meaning they were totally fed up.

There was nothing for it but to load up on calories now. There was no sense in making this march any harder than it needed to be, and I devoured everything that was left of my ration pack, even the 'fromage fondu' that in times of plenty I would have left unopened.

We put on our camouflage and headed outside to the truck, piling in without a word and resting our chins on our chests in the hopes catching a few minutes of sleep.

At 22:00, we were dropped off and left alone in the darkness.

'Come on then, lads. Let's get to work, the sooner we finish, the sooner we can rest. Try to keep up.' One of the more experienced guys said. We all shouldered our bags and tightened the straps, clutching our H&Ks to our chest.

'See you all on the other side of the Pyrenees!' Another voice said in the dark, making us all chuckle. According to the instructors, we ought to be doing the march tactically. But to hell with them, we all thought, there was no way we could reach the extraction point by 06:00 if we were stopping at every junction to check for enemies. It seemed like one of those tasks that was designed for us to fail, like they never really expected us to arrive in the given time anyway.

We marched 'bite au cul', as we had back in basic training-so close to the man in front that, when the progress was halted for whatever reason, we would bump into him, causing a little domino effect. The first few hours went steadily enough. The weather was on our side, at least. It was cold, but dry and our progress was quick enough. At 01:00 we took a break, and someone suggested that we pair up so we would not get lost in the dark, as the guys at the front were setting a wicked pace.

In the Legion we have a saying, 'le diable marche avec nous': the devil marches with us. We knew how to march quick and I would not become a burden to the rest. Nor would David or Djo, I was sure.

As the night wore on, the weariness weighed upon us, and each step became harder and harder. The path steepened a little and the going became yet more difficult. Upwards, always upwards, we climbed, until somewhere around 03:00 exhaustion got the better of us. And it was agreed that we would take another break.

Not even bothering to take my bag off my shoulders, I collapsed by the side of the track with Djo beside me, both of us too tired to speak. I was so tired that within seconds I could feel myself drifting off to sleep, my chin touching my combat vest. I had to fight against it, willing my eyes to stay open. I couldn't for the life of me say how long we were sat there, it couldn't have been more than a few minutes, but it might as well have been hours.

And then the guys were getting to their feet, and I looked up at Djo and asked him what was going on. As he hauled me to my feet he said, 'we're moving, last couple of hours left.'

We marched another twenty or so minutes, before we met a fork in the track and the progress was halted whilst the guys in front checked the maps.

Then, Will's panicked voice broke the silence, 'wait! Where's Val? We've lost Val!'

Everyone peered at each other's faces in the dark, trying to discern if it could be Val's features hidden in the shadows. There were mutterings up and down the line of 'I can't see him' and 'He's not over here.'

'Count yourselves!' The front man called, raising his arm and beginning with himself, 'un!'

'Deux!' Cried the second. 'Trois!' And so on until the twentieth had been called. We all waited with bated breath for the twenty first. But there was only silence.

'Shit! We have to go back.'

It would not do for a section of Commandos to lose one of their numbers during an exercise. It would surely become a joke directed at our unit and people would whisper about it for a long time to come. Such is the reality of elite units - they have far to fall and there are plenty who would revel in any errors we might make.

And so, with sighs of resignation, we backtracked downhill for a quarter hour until the progress was halted once more. 'Can you hear that?' Someone in front said and we all stood with our ears pricked up, listening.

'Guys! Guys, where are you?' The faintest of voices could be heard in the darkness.

'Val! Over here!' Will shouted back, flashing an infa-red strobe so Val could follow it to our position. Seconds later, Val came running towards us up the track and flipped his goggles up so all I could see were the whites of his eyes, wide in panic.

Poor Val had clearly fallen asleep at the last pause and having been at the back, had been left behind by the side of the path. It must have been quite the shock when he came to, to find all of his comrades had disappeared.

'Sorry' Will said, 'I forgot to wake you.'

'Thank God I found you all. I just shut my eyes for one second and you were all gone! I swear it was just a second.' Val panted, and there were a few chuckles of relief as the guys crowded round him and slapped him on the back.

'Did you have a good nap Val?' Someone asked.

'Damnit!' David smiled, 'We almost got rid of him!'

'Right, keep an eye out for your binomes. Let's get a move on.' The front man said. And with that, we were away once more.

At 05:00, it was announced up ahead that there were only two kilometres left, to which there were sighs of relief. It would almost be over. But then the path became increasingly steep and I found myself slipping over rocks, sending them tumbling downhill, causing the guys below to curse.

'There's the road! That's where we need to be.' Someone was pointing upwards and we all followed his gaze. Eventually, I made out a point where the tree line was broken high up on the mountainside that could have been a road carved into it. It was difficult to tell, and even if it were the road, it seemed such a long way. And the mountain was so steep!

To make matters worse, as the mountainside became steeper still, the path became less and less established. In the darkness, it was hard to tell where it led through the small trees, it could have been several different directions. Or perhaps those were several different forks? Progress faltered as the guys up front tried to decide which was the correct path to take. Ten minutes later, they were shouting for us to go back down for there was no way through the dense undergrowth up ahead, it must have been one of the others.

The rest of us cursed, retraced our steps and someone chose one of the other paths. But only after a couple of minutes we had to turn back again and we were becoming more and more frustrated.

'Wait, it's this way, I think that's a marker.' Came a voice and we tried the new path. But that too yielded no results. We had to split up to search for the right one, until someone cried out in the darkness above me that they had found it.

'Finally!' And we climbed, the slope becoming so steep we had to use our hands to pull ourselves upwards on bushes and tree trunks. It felt much harder than it ought to have been. An uphill battle that seemed to have been fought more within our heads than with the mountainside.

And finally, at 05:58, we emerged onto a tarmacked surface - a little lay-by on a twisting mountain road upon which the JBC was waiting. I fell to my arse with relief to wait for everyone else to mount the rise, whilst one of the instructors hopped down from the trucks cabin to acknowledge our presence.

'Right on time.' He said as the last of us appeared.

We piled into the rear and had arrived back at Mont-Louis for 06:30, just as the sun was rising, not having slept a wink during an eight-hour march.

'Right, all of you to the dojo, I'm going to show you how you can use your rifles to defend against an attacker armed with a knife.' One of the instructors said.

So it was business as usual, and we trudged slowly away in single file, like the living dead themselves. It must have been comical to watch us. So slow the fatigue and hunger had made us, all I wanted to do was curl up on the mats of the dojo and sleep. I almost got my wish as my partner had somehow managed to find the strength to throw me over his shoulder, but the instructor was soon ordering me to my feet.

Later in the day we had a theory lesson on explosives in the classroom, that must have been equally comical. Inside it was wonderfully stuffy and warm, and the lead instructor's voice bounced off the walls of the room falling on deaf ears. Well sat with our eyes fluttering half open, heads lolling on our shoulders and then snapping back up as we looked bleary eyed toward the instructor to see if he had noticed us dozing.

Of course he must have, and graciously scolded no one. Obviously, he used to his students falling asleep and ploughed on with the lesson, regardless. I can guarantee that not a single person amongst us had taken any notes by the time we had left the classroom.

The rest of the day was a blur and I can't for the life of me remember what we did, save for the mission that night. It must have been clear we were all nearing our limit and were given a straightforward, short march up to the explosives shooting range. From there, we were to lie in ambush for the instructors' vehicles when they were due to arrive in the morning. It took us only several hours, but progress was slow, nonetheless.

I was so tired I was dozing off whilst marching, sometimes slipping out of the single file formation and falling over in the road. I had to pick myself up and shake my head as if that would do something to alleviate the fatigue. Eventually, we had found our positions and lay down to sleep, having arrived at 01:00 with five hours ahead of us. I was a log until 06:00, waking to the sound of alarms buzzed on watches.

We had our final explosives test and all managed to pass, despite having been asleep for most of the theory lessons. And then it was the weekend again. Just like the last, once I had showered and eaten, I lay on my bed and fell into what might as well have been a coma.

# CHAPTER 13

We had only completed two weeks of the course, but it felt like two months. Nevertheless, the end was in sight. All I had to do was survive for fourteen more days. Unfortunately, for the third week I would find that we had been tossed out of the frying pan and into the fire.

We would be moved down to a fort, in a town called Collioures, by the Mediterranean at the foothills of the Pyrenees. It was the same type of early modern fort that we had seen at Mont-Louis and was built on top of a sheer cliff, just by the water on the outskirts of the town. There would be yet more obstacle courses with sheer drops over the water, and we would have to shimmy along ropes and cables with the waves lapping against the jagged rocks fifty metres below.

But what made the third week so awful was all the exercise we had to do in the sea. It was Monday, and the instructors wasted no time in giving us each a wet suit, some goggles and a pair of flippers. They escorted us to a sealed off cave that served as a changing room, where we struggled to pull the neoprene suits over our extremities. The water was, thankfully, not as cold as it would have been in January, as it supposedly retained some of the heat from the summer. But neither was it warm. As we waded into the Mediterranean, the cold water seeped into our suits causing us to shiver until it had warmed up a little.

I was not at all at home in the water and would have much preferred to stay in the mountains where, granted it was colder, I was more at ease. One of the first challenges we would have to face was a two-kilometre swim within fifty minutes, swimming from one side of the bay to the other and back again. We were told that if we were to fail the test, then we would fail the course. No pressure.

The instructors spent the rest of the morning teaching us how to use the flippers and the goggles and snorkel, all items with which I was quite unfamiliar and not in the least bit comfortable. After lunch, we headed back down, having to pull on the cold and sandy wetsuits once more, before heading to a concrete pier to begin the test.

They set us off all together, and after several minutes, I found myself one of the last. I couldn't get my damn snorkel to work without inhaling mouthfuls of seawater and choking. I kicked for all I was worth and gasped for air, demoralised after some time to see that my friends were already on the return journey and were passing me. Eventually, I touched the pier at the far end of the bay where I shouted my name to a waiting instructor before turning one hundred and eighty degrees, turning back the way I had come.

The choppy little waves lapped at me constantly and I felt as though I were permanently stopping to empty my snorkel of water before fitting it back into my mouth. At one point, I felt one of my flippers beginning to come loose and had to tread water for valuable seconds to re-attach the strap so as not to lose the damn thing.

I did not have any way to tell the time, but I knew I must have been cutting it close. The others were quite a way ahead now and I even saw the first of them climb up onto the concrete banks of the pier in the distance. Come on, I thought, I can't let them down after coming this far. I think it was the thought of having to do the first two weeks all over again that really spurred me on to kick even harder.

The guys on the bank had turned to cheer the rest of us on, each helping the next guy climb out of the water and onto the pier. 'Come on!' They shouted, tapping their wrists to signal that those of us still in the water were cutting it close. Looking around, I could only see two or three other bodies beside myself. Shit, I thought, I might not make it.

'Move your arse Dobson!' Djo was calling from the shore. He still seemed so far away and it was as if the closer I got, the slower my progress became. Was there a current in the water? I paddled harder still and felt the right flipper coming loose again. I cursed, only to inhale a snorkel full of sea water and had to stop and tread water, as I choked and spat.

Come on, I thought, another fifty metres, that's only two lengths of a pool. I swam for all I was worth, until my lungs were gasping for air and my muscles were on fire. Then I was reaching out for the rocks with my fingers.

Yes! I had made it! But as two of my comrades hauled me out and onto dry land, I wondered if I actually had made it.

Being the second to last to finish, I gave my name and learned I had two minutes to spare on the clock. I was safe.

Without so much as a break, we were already heading off to the next challenge. Ditching the flippers and donning some fatigues, we would have to jump from a boat with a heavy pack and swim a hundred metres to the shore. When I launched myself from the bow clutching the weighted bag, I felt it drag me far below the surface, and I had to kick vigorously to bring myself back up, spluttering for air as my head broke the water.

This time, we didn't have the flippers or snorkel, but the yoke of the heavy bag instead. I felt it drag me back down under the surface and my eyes widened in panic. I kicked hard and gasped for air once more. I couldn't let the bag go or I would fail.

The shore was fifty metres away and I set my sights on it. Unable to use my arms as they were occupied with the bag, it would be up to my legs to provide the power. I kicked and kicked, but again it felt as if I were moving at snail's pace, with the bag dragging me down all the while. I redoubled my efforts and little by little, the shore approached. When I finally reached it I was sucking in air as though my life depended on it.

After a long day's trials, I was already tired and we hadn't even begun the mission for the night. The catch was this time, however, we would practice our infiltrations from the water. We had all been issued with a waterproof bag into which we had placed a fresh set of fatigues, our boots, packs and whatever else we needed for the evening, whilst we would use the bag as a floatation device.

As a section, we would hop off a boat a kilometre offshore and paddle inwards, our rifles balanced in front of us on our bags. Guided by a couple of glow sticks, placed strategically on shore by two guys who had paddled ahead, the rest of us would have to land on the beach in complete silence, change quickly, and be ready to finish the rest of the infiltration on foot.

Unfortunately for us, not everything went to plan the first night. As we neared the shore, the only sound was the water lapping gently against our bags, and we made directly for the nearest glow stick. But as we approached in the darkness, I heard someone swear.

'Shit! It's a fisherman!' They whispered.

Peering in the direction of the glow stick, I could see that it was in fact attached to the line of a fishing rod, marking in the water where the fisherman's bait was.

'Who the hell goes fishing at midnight?' Someone else said.

'We need to go around, there!' David pointed at another tiny light source much further up the beach. Our 'decoy' had taken us a good several hundred metres off course. We had to turn around and make a loop. We couldn't exit the water where we were as the fisherman would surely have seen us. What a fright that would be - twenty something camouflaged commandos armed to the teeth ascending from the depths!

By the time we arrived, the two that had gone on ahead were already changed and came down the beach to meet us.

'Where the hell have you guys been?' They hissed.

'Fishing.' Someone said.

We had already lost a half hour and changed quickly to make up for it. The night was young, and we had a climb ahead of us. There was a fort we had to assault up the mountain and had a climb of five hundred metres before we would even reach it. For the moment, we were still relatively fresh. Upon our arrival at the fort, we had to use rope to scale the walls with all our gear.

Then, of course, there were the insurgents to neutralise within. We did so perhaps a little quicker than might have been advisable, as we knew that the sooner we finished, the sooner we could sleep.

That week was more of the same: the days were spent mostly in the water, training stealthy infiltrations, doing water-based obstacle courses and a little free diving. The nights were long and arduous, but also considerably warmer. And the weather seemed to be much more agreeable at this lower altitude. In any case, by the time that week was over I was as exhausted as I had been after the first two. After we had eaten at a restaurant in the town of Collioures, I collapsed into bed again.

The last week was set to be the most interesting. We had our last land-based obstacle course, an exercise that would test our close quarter battle techniques, and of course the 'surprise,'- whatever that was.

This time, I had no issues with the obstacle course, and ended up doing rather well (giving my favourite instructor Raph a surprise at the end when he saw me crawling out of the tunnel on the final obstacle causing him to check his stopwatch).

With that squared away, there was the CQB test. The exercise was set up in a ruinous building outside of the base. All we knew for sure was that we would be fighting, for it was certain we would have to demonstrate the self-defence techniques that we had been learning over the previous few weeks.

I was paired with Djo and we entered the building. Our senses tingled on full alert, fully expecting someone to jump out at us. We had our rifles loaded with 'simunition', little paintball pellets and had them pointed before us. It was hard with just the two of us to cover every angle and we found ourselves having to improvise.

I could sense something was about to happen, it was too quiet. Our boots stepping softly on the stone floor was the only sound in the building. And then, when we entered the next room together, I saw in my peripheral vision that there was a black shape lurking behind the door.

'Contact!' I cried, firing my rifle. ZAP!

'AArgh!' I doubled over in pain.

They had given the bastards a cattle prod! The enemy in front of me was wearing a thickly padded black suit with a full-face visor and helmet to protect him. Good, that meant I could beat him senseless.

I shot again, but through the thick suit he clearly did not feel a thing and zapped me again with the cattle prod.

I was vaguely aware that Djo had his own opponent to contend with on the other side of the door and had already been backed into a corner by a dark shape wielding another electric baton.

I had been zapped twice now and it had hurt. I was pissed off. I charged at my opponent and thrust the barrel of my rifle directly into his visor, snapping his head backwards and leaving his body open. I followed up with a vicious roundhouse kick to his thigh which I'm sure he felt even through the suit. As he staggered, I flung him to the ground and knelt upon him, wrestling the cattle prod from his gloved fingers.

I was just about to start using it on him when an instructor shouted from behind us, 'next room!' seeing that both Djo and I had dealt with our opponents. I handed back the cattle prod to my adversary and whispered, 'lucky.'

Getting to my feet and readying my rifle, I was shoulder to shoulder with Djo once more. He gave my arm a squeeze, signalling he was ready, and we moved out into the corridor.

There were several more pairs of enemy combatants hidden in the building, but I could sense that the fight was starting to leave a few of them. Several pairs of my comrades had already gone before us, each time whacking our suit-wearing enemies with their rifles. By the time Djo and I had gotten to the end, I was sure we had given a decent account of ourselves and the attackers behind us would surely have a good number of fresh bruises.

Somehow, the final night seemed to have come around after what was, without a doubt, one of the most arduous months of my life. If we passed this, we were done. It would be over.

All the other guys, including myself, were anxious to see what the surprise was. We had to wait until darkness fell outside before the twenty-one of us were summoned by the instructors. When we were all present, without so much as an explanation, we were told to leave our bags and rifles in a locked classroom whilst we were ushered away to a dungeon like room underneath the fort that had to be accessed by a tunnel. Once inside, one of the instructors told us to keep our mouths shut or there would be consequences. The great oak door was shut behind us and locked, sealing us in pitch darkness.

We all sat down to wait on the stone floor, talking in whispers about what was in store for us. It seemed that the instructors were deliberately keeping us waiting for effect, in the hopes that it might rattle our nerves. It did not because after an hour or so, someone began to sing a Christmas carol to which we all joined in, quite incongruously filling the damp, cold dungeon with merry Christmas cheer.

Once we had finished, we all burst into fits of giggles at the absurdity of it all. The guys then began cracking a few jokes and laughter reverberated around the room.

Suddenly, the door was flung open and a blinding white light was shone into our faces. There was a lot of shouting as the instructors burst into the room and grabbed several of our number by the scruff of our necks, myself included, hauled us to our feet and shoved us out the door into the corridor beyond.

In the corridor, I saw that there were five of us before we were being shouted at to strip.

'What?' I said.

'Strip! Take off your fucking clothes and put them there in front of you. All of them!'

I did as I was told, quite perplexed and saw that the others were following suit. Once the five of us were completely naked, the instructors began to rummage through the bundles of clothes before us. They confiscated items like GPS watches, compasses and maps, before shoving them back at us and telling us to get dressed once more. I saw that they had left me nothing of use, save a length of paracord that I'd had in my pocket. After being so used to the familiar weight of my rifle around my neck, I felt as naked as before.

As soon as it was done, I saw the instructors cuff my comrades and place sacks over their heads, one by one, until I had handcuffs and a sack of my own thrust down over my eyes, turning my world into darkness. We were frogmarched outside a good distance and then shoved unceremoniously into the back of a van, the doors slamming shut behind us and the engine starting up after a few moments.

Fortunately, I had my friends Val and Will there with me and I appreciated their familiar voices.

'I can't see shit!' Will said, his voice slightly muffled by the sack. 'Couldn't they have tied my hands in front of me rather than behind? I think I'm getting cramp already.'

'Poor Will!' Val mocked. 'We'd better ask them to stop.'

'Ask them if we can stop for a coffee before we get stuck into whatever this is, too.' We chuckled.

We discussed what the night might have in store for us for around thirty minutes, as we could feel the van driving to some unknown destination.

'Maybe it's going to be one of those nice surprises.' Will was saying, 'maybe they figure we're at the end of the course and want to reward us with an all-you-can-eat-buffet.'

Suddenly, the van had screeched to a halt, sending us all flying forward and slamming into the steel division between the cabin and the rear. We could hear shouting and the sound of blanks firing outside. We waited with bated breath as footsteps could be heard coming closer and closer. Then, I heard the sliding door of the van being thrown open, and the jangling of keys as someone was uncuffing us one by one.

As my own were unlocked, I threw them aside and tore off my sack to lay eyes upon our saviour. A balaclava clad figure was freeing the last of my fellows before addressing us in an urgent tone. 'The mission is this: you have to get to the extraction point without being captured.'

He proceeded to pull out a burned fragment of map from his pocket and lay it down in the bed of the van so we could all crowd around to see it. There was not a whole lot to see. A red dot signified the extraction point, but most of the area around it had been reduced to charred paper, leaving us with little useable surface.

'You have to get here.' Our saviour continued. 'Avoid the patrols on the ground and the helicopters.'

'The helicopters?' I said. And almost as if I had summoned it myself, the beating blades of a helicopter could be heard in the distance and we turned our heads to see a Gazelle flying over the countryside with a brilliant spotlight shining down upon the ground below.

'Damn, they really went all out for this one.' Val said, sounding rather impressed.

'I have to leave you now, good luck.' And with that, our saviour had disappeared into the night.

'Look at the state of this fucking thing.' Will said, pouring over the map once more with the others. Looking around, I could see that our captors had clearly been 'killed' and were playing dead in the front seats. We were on a departmental road, which seemed quiet enough, and I could see the lights of Collioures behind us several kilometres away.

'Right, let's make a move. I think we must be somewhere here, so that means we have to go this way.' Will said, indicating the direction with his arm.

'And we can't use the roads.' One of the other guys piped up. 'He said there would be patrols.' Nor did I doubt it. If the army had gone to the trouble of putting a bird in the air for the exercise, you could be damn sure they had vehicles everywhere searching for us.

The five of us moved away from the road at a jog, through a field and onto a dirt track that had the occasional tree for cover. We made good progress, as we had no bags or equipment to slow us down, and the terrain was not as mountainous here. Using the light of the moon, and the occasional street lamp, we had to keep checking the map to try to figure out exactly where we were, as we had now entered one of the burned away sections.

After a while, we heard the Gazelle swing round the valley again and saw that it was heading right for us, the beam of light scouring the vegetation like the eye of Sauron. 'Get down!'

We all jumped for the nearest bush and made ourselves as small as possible feeling the light pass right over us, the helicopter so low the displaced air from its blades disturbed the tops of nearby trees. And then it had passed overhead, flying away into the distance once more. We waited several minutes just to be sure it hadn't spotted us and wouldn't swing back around. Fortunately it had gone, and I gave a quick thought for the other groups who must surely be on the terrain, too, by now.

We pressed on. Coming to a main road crossing, we waited on a grassy verge, watching and waiting. One of the instructor's camouflaged trucks rolled by slowly, its lights on full beam, the driver most likely searching the undergrowth. We scuttled back down the bank until the danger had passed and figured now would be the best time to cross. Moving stealthily in twos, we made the crossing without a hiccup and were soon in the safety of the trees on the other side.

Using back roads and pathways was of course slower, but also much safer. Nevertheless, after several hours we had the objective in sight. What looked like an old wooden shack stood by the treeline of a meadow. As we watched from a distance, we could see no activity; the place seemed deserted.

We waited twenty or so minutes, just to be certain, before we decided that we could not wait forever. Using the treadmill, we made a loop around the shack until we were feet from it, stepping cautiously, careful not to break a single twig. Exchanging uncertain glances, Val reached for the handle, looking back at the rest of us for a final confirmation that we were ready for whatever lay behind the door. I nodded, licking my lips nervously, my heart hammering in my chest.

Then, Val yanked the door open in one fluid motion and stepped inside.

'Oh.' I heard from within. Stepping through myself, I saw our instructor, Raph, sitting on a crate reading a book by the light of a torch.

'You've made it.' He frowned, sounding more than a little disappointed that we hadn't been caught. He took a sheet of paper and a pen from his pocket and marked down our names with the time of our arrival, whilst the rest of us shook hands, somewhat surprised that it had gone so smoothly.

We sat down to wait for the others, and the groups trickled in one by one, none of whom had been caught - much to the frustration of Raph. In the early hours of the morning, we were all present, and there was plenty of chatter and laughter as we all realised we had just finished the course.

As the JBC came to pick us up, I was chatting with Djo and David, mentioning how glad I was not to have do the course again.

'What was the worst part?'

'All the stuff we did in the sea for me.' I said. 'You?'

'I wasn't too fond of that cattle prod.' Djo replied with a chuckle.

We had a good five hours of sleep that night. In the morning, the passing out ceremony was the last thing to do before we could all go our separate ways, returning to our respective regiments. We lined up formally on the parade ground and the instructors came one by one, placing the brevets on our chests. The brevets were little metal badges of an eagle upon a sword and were fixed with two steel pins that would penetrate the material of our fatigues, before caps were placed on the other ends. The instructors, as a last trial, hammered the pins home with forceful strike, the little metal spikes puncturing our skin.

Raph came straight for me with a smirk and slammed the brevet with a punch and I felt a stab of pain as the pins dug deep into my pectoral muscle. I did not give him the satisfaction of flinching. Later, upon inspection, I found I had two bloody holes in my chest after I had pulled the brevet delicately out. Bastard.

And then it was over. We had all passed and no one had quit. It was a great result, and we all shook hands, feeling that our friendships had only been solidified by the ordeal.

Back at 2REG, nothing much had changed. Djo and I were to learn that, as the only two 'militaire du rang' present in the section, it was up to us to do the 'sketch noel',: the playful mockery of our superiors. Fortunately, we were allowed to make a video for it, for which Djo was the camera man. Using cut scenes and different camera angles, I was able to play all the characters.

There were a few scenes in which I acted as a couple of the Sergeants from our section, poking a bit of playful fun at their mannerisms. In another scene, I mocked the Major from the military police section on the base for how he seemed to find excuses to put Legionnaires in the jail on base so that they could cut the grass for him. When it was shown at the formal dinner before the whole compagnie, it was met with raucous laughter and I was pleased that it went down rather well.

I had no more than a week off after Christmas, for which I returned home briefly. I even had to cut New Year's celebrations with my brother and his friends short, as I would begin the fated Caporal training on the 2nd of January.

I had around three and a half years' service at this point and would normally have been sent on the course sooner, had I not been occupied with the GCM's own training regimen.

Looking at the list of other 'Elève Caporals' whom I would be on the course with in January, I knew only Savelli- the tall, lanky Italian from my days in the 2ème compagnie. The course would be a total of two months and would, thankfully, be the last time in my career in the Legion that I would go to Castelnaudary.

I met Savelli down by the front gates of 2REG with my considerable baggage to wait for the bus that would take us to Castel. There were a few others from our regiment that would be on our course that I would come to know. Petchsky, a bespectacled Ukranian and Vetikin, another Ukrainian, short and athletic, were among them.

The sign, 'Ici, c'est comme ca...' 'here, that's just the way it is...' stood as always in the entrance to Castel and made me smile a little when I saw it. I wasn't worried for this course. I had already done harder ones, notably the 'commando spécialisé', and would find it relatively easy. The difference was here, instead of letting us get on with it, the instructors would micromanage us like they had during basic training, forcing us to act as one unit and punishing the collective when the individual fucked up. It was a far cry from working with the GCM that I had gotten used to. Here, using your initiative was a punishable offence. The silver lining to this was that toeing the line did not require much mental exertion to carry out. I could essentially 'auto-pilot' my way through the entire course, which is what I did for the most part.

The only other good thing to come out of Caporal training, in addition to getting it over and done with, was my friend Tony. I met Tony as we were waiting in a hallway outside of a classroom for our introduction to the course. I heard him speaking English with an American accent to one of the Ukrainian lads and went over to introduce myself.

I learned that Tony was Mexican/American and had served eight years in the US army, before being discharged for drunk driving and joining the Legion after finding that civilian life was not for him. Tony is one of those guys that has a natural charm and is very easy to get along with. We became fast friends and could often be seen giggling together like a couple of schoolboys throughout the Caporal training - laughing at some punishment an instructor was dishing out or goofing around when the instructors weren't looking. Neither of us took it particularly seriously, nor did I feel that any of our instructors were greatly invested in the betterment of their charges. The whole thing felt a little half arsed.

Most of the course was spent at 'the farm,' the same ones that the Legion used for basic training. It was the middle of January and there was often snow on the ground in 'Camp Bravo.' There were forty of us 'Elève Caporals' and the instructors usually liked us to sing at 6am, bright and early, for an hour whilst marching around the little encampment. No one, of course, was particularly motivated to sing in sub-zero temperatures. We would often hear one of our instructors' shout, 'louder!' from their heated cabin on one edge of the camp.

On a Legion course like this, there is always a funny bunch of lads. Several little groups had formed within a few days. There were the Moldovans and Romanians, a crowd of Ukrainians and other eastern Europeans, the Nepalese, several Madagascans, a couple of Asians and then there were a group of misfits with me, Tony, Savelli and a Sri Lankan included.

As for the instructors, there were a couple in particular that made me laugh. There was a Spanish sergeant we called 'motherfucker' because that is what he would say every time anyone fucked up. One of the Nepalese guys would drop his rifle and the sergeant would put his head in his hands and groan, 'Motherfucker!' before making him run loops around the camp with the aforementioned rifle above his head, much to the amusement of the rest of us.

Then there was Caporal Chef Popa. A strange fellow that had a pentagram tattoo on the back of his hand and was said to be a devil worshipper. It was easy to believe too. He was tall, thin and incredibly pale, and if someone asked him a stupid question, he would turn his head very slowly to stare at them in silence. With an expression devoid of all emotion, his eyes seemed to bore holes into the soul. For my part, I found it easy to stay off their radar. I was in good shape physically and did as I was told, giving them no reason to chastise me.

It also helped that their attention was often directed elsewhere. Of all the races and nationalities in the Legion, the Nepalese are perhaps the least respected and, unfortunately, suffer for it. Most of them are small in stature and have a hard time speaking and understanding French. Coupled with their mild and often timid demeanour, they usually become the victims of not only their superiors, but the rest of the trainees too. 'Motherfucker' had it in for them after they had fucked up one too many times and took to punishing them as a collective, making them do all the menial tasks.

'Okay, all the Nepalese come here!' The five or so little Nepalese chaps would step forward out of formation, with anxious expressions on their faces.

'Go and refill the jerry cans!' Or it would be, 'clean the toilets!' or 'run, run! Get out of my sight!'

And the Nepalese soon became the butt of every joke.

Motherfucker liked to run. He once said to us, 'there are only two real sports. One is boxing and the other is running. All the rest are shit.' And since we didn't have the facilities to box at camp bravo, he made us run. What he promised would be 'just a little run' one morning turned into more than a half marathon. He told us after that we had run more than twenty-six kilometres. I had considerable chafing by the end and had been dying for a shit for the last quarter.

It was with ordeals such as this that motherfucker liked to separate the weak from the strong, and anyone lagging behind holding us up would be on his shit list. It was better to be at the front.

We often had orienteering challenges during the night, but they were child's play compared to the night missions of the commando spécialisé course I had done this winter. We were each given a map with ten markers to search for what we would use to puncture a piece of paper with, each with a unique pattern of teeth. I found that if

I jogged the course I could finish sooner and was often among the first to arrive back at camp. This meant I had more sleep and, as a result, felt relatively fresh each morning. Some of the lazier guys had not used the same logic, and spent hours trudging along at their own pace, becoming crankier by the day from lack of sleep.

We had a couple of weekends off over the course of the two months, too. Tony and I would go out into Toulouse together to drink in the local Irish bars, each sporting a freshly shaved head and a tired, hungry look on our faces, as the freezing temperatures at camp Bravo had shed away some of the excess fat.

We were walking down a street discussing the differences between the US army and the Legion.

'There's just no comparison,' Tony was saying when he stopped abruptly, took out a pocketknife and stooped to scrape a politically oriented sticker from the nearest bollard. 'The US army has a budget that is literally ten times that of the French army. And then the Legion only sees a tiny portion of it. You know how they keep all the good equipment for the regulars.'

It was true. I had seen it first-hand during my interactions with the regulars of the GCM. I noted how all the legionnaires seemed to have night vision that was a couple of generations behind, for example. Tony stopped once again to scrape away more socialist propaganda, before continuing.

'You should have seen the canteens in the US army, the food was magnificent! There was so much choice. It's not like all the tinned crap we get here. Ours was fresh.'

'Maybe that's why you're all so fat.' I countered.

He laughed, 'better to be fat than a skinny Englishman like you!'

We let loose on the bars, like only fun-starved soldiers can do. The next day, we nursed hangovers with a full English breakfast and a pint in an Irish bar, before we had to head back to Castel.

In-between practicing our chanting, disassembling and reassembling various weapons and revising for tests, we had to amuse ourselves wherever we could and there was one such character among us that Tony and I found hilarious.

His name was Ziggo and he was a Ukrainian. Ziggo had a very 'abstract' sense of humour and could often be seen doing bizarre impressions of who knows what. Making the strangest sounds, laughing to himself, he seemed to be completely absorbed in a little world of his own. Most of the other guys thought he was tapped in the head, and gave him a wide berth. But Tony and I could not get enough of his antics, and we found ourselves joining in with his ridiculous impressions, bursting into fits of laughter when we could no longer keep a straight face - very much to the annoyance of the rest of the guys.

One day, when an Albanian Elève Caporal was taking charge of the section and issuing orders, Ziggo- in his usual fashion let out a shrill warbling sound, like a turkey might. It stopped the Albanian dead in his tracks and there was silence as he looked up from his list and into the ranks of the section before him to see who had made the noise. Tony and I were already in fits of laughter.

'Hey, be quiet! I'm trying to give you all the orders! Stop mucking about. We have to practice our chanting in five minutes.' He shook his head in exasperation and continued reading out the orders once more. Tony left it a few seconds before giving me a conspiratorial wink before taking a deep breath and warbling at the top of his lungs. Ziggo followed suit and I joined in too, warbling and flapping about like a turkey. Before long, half the guys present had joined in. The Albanian had gone beet red with anger as the section he had been trying to control had apparently turned into a gaggle of turkeys, hopping around on the spot and warbling like lunatics.

'Stop it! The Sergeants are going to hear you!'

There was another entertaining Ukrainian, Bodnard, tall and lanky. He had served on the frontline trenches bordering Russia and Ukraine and had shown me videos of him sat in a foxhole, nonchalantly enduring a mortar strike with a grin on his face.

Once, when each of us had to take command of the rest to practice our marching orders, Bodnard had taken the rest of the Elève Caporals in a U-turn away from Caporal Chef Popa and made us do roly-polies on the ground. We completed this task amidst fits of giggles, knowing it would annoy Popa.

'Bodnard, what the fuck are you doing?'

Bodnard cocked his head to the side and regarded Pop for a moment with his typical intense gaze before replying, 'Caporal Chef, I was experimenting,' causing the rest of us to burst into laughter and even making Popa display a slight frown on his otherwise impassive face.

Fortunately, the time went much quicker than I expected, probably because I was not taking it at all seriously and was enjoying myself far more than I ought to have been. Savelli, Tony and I all agreed that most of it was bollocks, especially since I would have to unlearn all of the out-dated combat techniques that were taught instead of the GCM ones. Still, if the point of the course was to achieve some sort of unity through common struggle, I supposed they had managed it to a degree.

We had all gotten to know each other over the last two months. And while there were still the definite 'mafias,' I still found I could chat to any group. If nothing else had improved, our singing certainly had. I had several new Legion chants in my arsenal, for whatever that was worth. At the end of it all, I was sad to say goodbye to a few new friends, but pleased to leave Castelnaudary behind me for the last time.

For now, I had greater things to turn my attention to. My third and final opex to Mali was looming, and what an opex it would be...

# CHAPTER 14

I f my time in the Legion was a play, then my last deployment to Mali would be the climactic final act - a dramatic crescendo that everything before had been building up to. I would see some things that would change my perspective of the world forever. That, perhaps, also helped me to understand it a little better. I would learn that it can be a dark, brutal place and I would see just how thin the veneer of decorum coating our cosy western way of life really was. For just beneath the surface lurks the uglier side of human nature, and out in desert it was plain to see, raw and honest.

But I would also experience something more positive: the bonds of fraternity that can only be built as strong as they were through strife and turmoil. When you have your friend's back and know that he has yours, and either one of you could die at any moment, there is a special kind of trust that is formed. Just having them next to you is a great comfort. You know that if shit goes down, he'll have your six. They are your brothers. And while you're completely unrelated, they are men you'd die for nonetheless.

I would meet my team during the mission preparation phase for a couple of months of shooting and combat drills before the deployment. Most of them I already knew - they had been in the other groups on my last Mali. As for my binome, I was with David, the tall, muscular Hungarian who seemed to be good at just about everything. He was competent, quick to joke, but a total pro when he needed to be.

I knew Alexi, the 'pretty boy', whose hair always seemed to be on point no matter where we were. Even out in the desert he could be found peering into the wing mirror with a tub of gel in one hand and a comb in the other. Joyce, a muscular transmitter, was a budding artist in his spare time. Meme, the wild and hairy Corsican, who had endless stories of hilarious situations he often found himself in. There was Santo - our sensitive medic who was also the best mario cart player in the group. Big Max was the 'heavyweight'. One hundred and twenty kilos of solid muscle machine gunner, a monster by anyone's standards, he would support the group with his minimi chambered in 7.62mm and had the strength to fire it standing. Little Max, short and tattooed, was one of our group's sharp shooters. He was a tough little dude, and didn't take shit from anyone, giving back as good as he got. Sipp, the 'Turk,' was half French and half Turkish. He had dark skin and a hooked nose with a balding head of hair. He could do a fantastic impersonation of anyone. Serge, stocky with black hair and beard, managed everything 'evidence' related (I'll explain that later. Basto, tall and blonde, he was the second in command and the other sharp shooter. Basto was fair and often went out of his way to make sure all the guys in the group were happy. And finally, Seb, the boss and also the eldest. He was a balding Adjutant that always stayed cool as a cucumber in the shittiest situations.

It was a fantastic team - all the guys were super competent, fit and hungry for the action. Even in the early stages of the mission preparation, we worked well together and this time around I felt more confident in my role. I felt ready.

We headed to a helicopter base in northern France to train with the birds and practiced rappelling down from forty metres or more, whilst the pilots held the machine steady in the air. We also did a whole lot of shooting and close quarter battle training, until the drills were muscle memory.

It was after one of these days in the evening when we were all hanging out in the barracks chatting before dinner, making a few adjustments to our gear, when I received a little unfortunate news. Ricky came striding into the room towards me. Ricky was paired with

Fich for the mission, whilst Djo was with Sergeant Katch in the other Spartan groups.

He stopped at the foot of the bed upon which I was sat, fiddling with my plate carrier. I looked up at him and by his expression could tell there was something wrong. I swallowed.

'Chef?'

'Dobson, did you go back to the UK in 2016?' He got straight to the point, raising his eyebrows expectantly but already seeming to know the answer. When I saw that there would be no pulling the wool over his eyes, I sighed and nodded in confirmation.

Of course I had been back. More than once. In 2016, I had gone to the British embassy to claim that I had lost my passport to get a temporary one to get home for the holidays. My own having been confiscated all those years ago, when I'd joined and had been given a new identity. Whilst back home, I had a new one made and I had long since reclaimed my old identity. I had received my old passport, which I had promptly proceeded to throw out as it was now useless.

Ricky went on to explain that someone in the OPSR (military police office) back at 2REG had noticed the date, 2016, on a photocopy of my new passport and had realised that I had been breaking the rules. In the Legion, it is considered quite a grave offence. As the Legion provides ex-convicts and criminals a new identity, to cross international borders with this new identity without permission is to diminish it in some regards. It is also a rule that almost every single Legionnaire has broken. Whether it be to cross the Pyrenees to visit the infamous brothels of northern Spain, head to a casino in Monte Carlo for a weekend or go home to see the family as I did. It was for that reason that Ricky looked down at me without anger, but empathy instead.

'I did the same thing when I was a young Legionnaire, too.' He said. 'The only difference is I didn't get caught. And now you're in the shit, Dobson.'

My immediate fear was that I would be taken off the mission, and after mumbling an apology I asked Ricky what would happen.

'The lieutenant has spoken to the Colonel and it has been agreed that you can stay on the list for Mali.' Phew.

'But, you'll have a month of jail time when you get back.'

Shit, a whole month? That was nearly as much as the guy who fired the rocket into the munitions container almost taking Djo's leg off got. All I had done was see my family.

'So, the whole month of November?'

'Something like that. Just count yourself lucky you're still with us.'

And I did. I sighed and thought November is a long way away yet. And besides, there was a saying amongst the Anglophone mafia that you were not a true Anglophone until you had done jail time. So, I supposed no one could hold it against me anymore. I could not focus on that now. My mind had to be on Mali, for I would need to have my wits about me.

Before embarking on my final tour, we Legionnaires were obligated to attend the Camerone celebrations - something many of us would rather have skipped in preference of a week or two with our families. Nonetheless, we were there. And, once again, there were the boxing matches to be displayed before the entire regiment along with the 'Miss Kepi Blanc's.' I thought I might as well give it a go, despite not having boxed for months and having a currently poor level of conditioning. Still, it would be good practice. I went to see the Moldovan ex-heavyweight who had since been promoted to Sergeant Chef in my absence and signed myself up.

Luck was not on my side, however. I had been matched with an ex-European kickboxing champion- a Serbian Legionnaire recently joined. I had seen him spar a couple of times too and knew I was done for. If I had been training for a month or two beforehand, I might have put up a decent fight. But on the night of the 30th of April, it was likely to be a massacre.

An enormous tent had been set up outside the gymnasium to house the ring and a bar, around which there was already a large crowd of Legionnaires trying to attract the flustered barman's attention. Others were pouring in from the mess hall from the formal meal we had eaten and by 20:00 the tent was nearly full. I, along with the other fighters waited in a portioned off dressing room. I could hear the noise of excitement growing outside as everyone knew the first fight was soon to be underway.

The Serb I was set to fight was there too and I watched with dismay as he practiced some clinical shadow boxing, not being able to fault his technique one bit. We exchanged a long glance and his eyes let me know he would be unyielding. I sighed and began to tap my foot impatiently. The odds were against me and all I wanted now was to get it over with.

There was a roar from the crowd as the first pair entered the ring and started going at each other. Before I knew it there was only one pair left before I would have to go. Then, the Moldovan Chef poked his head around the entrance and beckoned us both out. We headed to the ring with hundreds of eyes upon us. I climbed in between the ropes and faced my opponent. Any minute now the bell would sound and everything else would fade away. The Chef asked if we were both ready. I nodded. So did the Serb. And then the bell went.

In the first round, he came at me swinging, throwing punches that connected, rocking my head back and forcing me to the ropes. It was all I could do just to throw a few jabs to try to keep him at bay. Even by the end of the first round I could feel myself getting tired - a little disconcerting as there were two more to go. The second round was more of the same. I don't think there was a single point at which I had control of the ring. And by the third, absolutely shattered, I stood in the corner with my guard barely covering my face, absorbing punch after punch that the Serbian threw to the delight of the watching crowd.

I was exceedingly grateful when the bell finally rang, signifying the end of the fight. I wasn't even too bothered that I had been beaten badly, just happy to have made it out in one piece. I reasoned that it was good to lose every now and again. It was certainly a humbling experience. Once I had recovered the energy to walk around, I found my friends and shared a beer with them, making the most of the chance to get drunk and have a laugh. I said my goodbyes to O'Callaghan, Harrison, Bax, Frank, Romaric and all the other friends I had at 2REG before the end of the night. The morning would mark the beginning of a short period of leave before Mali, which I used to go back to England and see my family, relaxing away from the pressures of the Legion.

Home was the same as it had always been. I spent a rare few weeks with my family and enjoyed the weekends with my brother and his friends. It was another brief window into civilian life and I remarked how much easier that was. Three square meals a day, finish work at 17:00, the weekend to do whatever you liked and eight hours of sleep a night. It could not have been more different to what I was doing. Although my work was fulfilling, I couldn't help but be a little envious of the simple lives that the average man appeared to lead.

I would soon find out, I thought. My five years in the Legion was coming to an end; there was only one last major obstacle: this last tour of Mali. It would all be downhill after that. This was the last bend until the light at the end of the tunnel would appear and I was looking forward to finally having some freedom. Yet at the same time, I knew there would be certain aspects I would miss. I would likely never work again with such a concentration of capable guys in the civilian world, and there would be far less action for sure. I would have to make the most of this last deployment.

This year, for whatever logistical reason, I was sent ahead of the rest of the group in the first wave of arrivals to Mali. Even the third time around I was surprised by the heat, my body seeming to have forgotten the hot, heavy air during a cold European winter - most of which I had spent outdoors. Once I was off the plane at the airstrip, sweating profusely already even at 10:00, I made my way to the GCM camp to see the guys I would be relieving. I knew some of them from my commando training. Seeing some familiar faces like Lulu, Gott, Steve and others, I shook their hands and gave them a friendly wave.

'How's it been?' I asked them in the shelter of their air conditioned tents.

'Ah, not so good.' Lulu replied. 'We didn't do a lot the first half, things were starting to get a little more interesting towards the end. Maybe one or two good missions the entire opex. But the command is switching over, maybe you guys will get luckier.'

There are a lot of politics in the army, increasingly so the higher up the ranks you travel. Your missions, and perhaps even your life, could depend on the men in charge of the Mali operation. You might, for example, fall under the command of a general who is a year away from retirement and is loath to put troops at risk - unwilling to take the gamble of a potential failure and the deaths of his men that would leave a stain upon his career. Or maybe the new General would be younger, looking to make a name for himself and willing to take all the risks for glory and to have military victories under his belt to boast about during his future career in French government. Of course, it was not his health he would be risking, only his career. But I still would prefer someone like that, as I craved some action.

Fortunately for this last tour, the stars had aligned. Not only was the new General hungry for success on the terrain, but our own commander was a force to be reckoned with, too. Lieutenant Pat, an officer in one of the other French mountain regiments, commanded the GCM detachment this opex. Like me, it would be his last and he wanted it to be one to remember. Pat had worked his way up through the ranks to become an officer. In my opinion, the best officers are always the ones who have worked their way up from the bottom. He was of average height, had short, dark hair and a large, chiselled jaw. He was a fighter for sure, and the finest example of a French officer I have ever seen.

Pat was always firm but fair with his guys and really had our backs. Moreover, we had the utmost respect for him; he would never ask us to do anything he wasn't prepared to do himself and always led by example.

Pat arrived in Mali at the same time as me. He wasted no time catching up with the current officer in command, disappearing off to the little GCM command tent to begin the installation process. As for myself, there was not much to do other than wait around for a few days for the rest of my team, and our equipment, to arrive. It was easy to tell which guys were leaving and which had just arrived at a glance. I must have looked fresh, clean shaven with pale skin and a neat haircut, whilst the others were tanned, with unkempt beards and long, curly hair. They would have to at least have a trim before heading back to regiment. I remember thinking if I showed up to the gates of 2REG looking like that I would have been refused entry.

We Legionnaires were held to a higher standard, and only a select few, with Ricky included, were allowed to keep a beard permanently.

This could only be achieved with our Colonel's express permission, but our hair had to be no longer than a few centimetres and neat. However, here in Mali, no one would make me shave and I liked to use the opportunity to grow my hair and beard long, making the most of the perks of being in a commando unit - knowing it would have to be cut short upon re-entry to France.

Another perk of being a commando on opex was that, as long as we weren't on mission, we were left to our own devices. We answered only to the 'big bosses' and Pat could command us the way he saw fit. Again, we trained in the morning. Whether it be combat drills, close quarter battle, medical training or something else, it was always on our terms. Once done, I could do my sport or go to the café and bar at the other side of the FOB for a drink, as long as I kept my radio on me.

Whilst options for entertainment were as limited as you would imagine them to be, being a military base in the middle of the desert, we had everything we needed. And once the rest of my team arrived, the ambiance was jovial and optimistic. I greeted them by the airstrip and showed them to our recently vacated tents.

There was the usual rush to try to find the best alveoles, like kids choosing bunk beds, as we all began to get settled in. David blasted some music in the corridor of our tent while we all unpacked our gear and prepared our equipment, cracking a few jokes and wondering what the next four months would have in store for us.

One thing David and I were looking forward to, having come from a Legion base was the food. And walking up to the canteen with the rest of the guys for dinner we were not disappointed.

'Wow. The bread here is actually fresh.' I said.

'Yeah, and look, we actually get a choice! I think we can take two desserts, too.'

Something else I noticed in the canteen were the British uniforms dotted around the place. It had been eight months since I had last been here and there must have been a new rotation of British air force crewmen. I made a mental note to go and introduce myself in the bar that night.

Of the camp itself, not much seemed to have changed. I saw the regular bustle of activity on the dusty red tracks of the FOB: soldiers walking this way and that in their desert camo shorts, JBCs and armoured vehicles navigating between the light brown tents and shipping containers, small planes taxying down the runway and the familiar dusty haze in the air, bringing that awful heat that will have you sweating at all hours of the day.

The GCM tents were unchanged as I was Spartan 30 for another tour. Again, we had the last two tents of the bunch, nearest the showers and toilets. Handy for getting up to take a piss in the night and not having to walk a hundred metres.

I remember walking over to the bar that first night, with David and the others, after spending the day preparing our gear. We were operational and ready for a fight, and I was feeling good. If this would be my last Mali, I wanted to make it a good one.

I didn't have to wait long for some action. After only several days in the country, there was a voice shouting into our walkie talkies one morning after our daily training session.

'Alert! Alert!' Seb's voice came a little muffled as I was sat I the tent with the others. We exchanged a glance before scrambling for our gear, pulling on socks, boots and armour, pulling out our 24hour bags, helmets and rifles, before leaving the tent for the helicopter hangars. Outside, we saw Seb running toward us from the command tent.

'The drone has picked up images of around ten insurgents camping in some woodland to the north east. The Tigres are going ahead first to provide some overhead cover. Get yourselves to the helicopters and I'll join you as soon as I'm ready.'

With that, he ducked into his own tent and the rest of us made our way across the airstrip. The late morning sun was already high in the sky above us. The other Spartan groups had answered the call, too. Spartan 10 and 20 joined us walking to the helicopters.

That was something I loved: walking to the helicopters across the airstrip with thirty of France's finest troops, total professionals, readying themselves for combat and whatever else awaited. And I was proud to be one of them. It struck me that I was a very different person from the eighteen-year-old that had passed under the archway of Fort De Nogent four years ago.

The air crews were already preparing the machines for flight, running this way and that with cables. The gunner was already strapped in, checking the MAG58 mounted on the side of the bird. As the pilots fiddled with the controls in the cockpit, my team crowded around one of the NH90's. Seb joined us at a jog and took out a tablet to show us the terrain on the ground.

He pointed at a long, thin stretch of 'woodland'- the trees were sparse, thin and thorny, but still provided enough cover. So, anyone hiding beneath could not be seen from above.

'We think there are ten or so insurgents hiding under these trees here. As I said, the Tigres are going on ahead to pin them in place until we can get on the ground.'

Right on cue, two of the streamlined machines taxied down the runway behind us to take off at the far end.

'We will be dropped off here.' Seb indicated a point on the map. 'And then form a line so we can rake the forest south to north. We will be on the right flank; Spartan 10 will be on the left and Spartan 20, along with Pat, will take the centre. Questions?' Seb looked around at the rest of us as we shook our heads.

'Right, then. Get yourselves strapped in. Let's go!'

I jumped into the back of the helicopter with David at my side, sat down on the floor and hooked my lanyard onto a 'D' ring built into a floor panel. I could see Pat striding toward the NH90 with Momo, the little transmitter for the detachment, and the Doc in tow. The three of them always stuck together for our missions, forming the command unit. All in all, we were around forty and took up at least three helicopters. Our collective weight having been precisely calculated to ensure the birds could actually fly. Where any flying machines are concerned, weight has to be carefully considered and the NH90 troop transport helicopters were no different.

Before the blades began to turn above us creating a refreshing draft, along with the less agreeable cacophony of the whining motor and spinning blades, we carried out our radio checks through the comms system on our helmets.

Seb gave his affirmative over the radio to Pat to signify that we were ready and the birds rolled into action. The other two machines taxied over to the take off point at the end of the runway, before us. I watched through the open door as Spartan 10 and 20 took off into the air and then it was our turn. The blades beat faster still, and the engine whined as I felt us leave the ground and begin to fly up into the sky. The scenery rushed past below, the buildings of Gao becoming smaller and smaller as we gained height.

With the twelve of us crammed into the back, there was not much room. I was cross legged and, after five minutes, had to adjust my legs so that they were either side of Serge, who was sat before me. Cramped, I shook them to get the blood flowing as Alexi tapped me on the shoulder, offering me a stick of gum and signalling for me to take the packet to hand out. I stuffed it into my mouth and passed the rest over Serge's shoulder to him. I then checked, for the seventh time, that I had a round in the chamber of my H&K, and that my EOTECH optic was at the right intensity.

The journey lasted around thirty minutes, and I knew we were close when I could hear the Tigres 20mm cannons firing in the distance. They would be shooting warning shots into the earth around the wooded area to prevent anyone from leaving - circling like a pair of hawks high in the sky, ready to destroy anything that moved below.

The NH90's flew lower to the ground and began the familiar evasive slalom to avoid any rockets that might be shot at us. And then Seb was holding up a single finger to signify that we would land in a minute's time. I unhooked my lanyard and got myself into a crouching position, ready to jump down from the helicopter as soon as I was able.

The nose of our NH90 angled upwards and slowed to a halt, hovering just above the ground as the pilots laid it down gently on the sand. The blades kicked up plenty of fine, red sand. The gunner gave Seb the thumbs up who then slapped big Max on the back. Max, having had his legs dangling over the edge, pushed himself off and ran to take up a defensive position twenty metres from the bird. The rest of us followed suit, forming a defensive line with David and I on the outer flank. We crouched and shielded our eyes as the pilots took off once more, kicking up yet more sand.

The other two groups had been set down too, and the three helicopters pulled away almost in unison. The sound of their engines quickly faded away, as they flew back the way we had come. The Tigres had stopped shooting, but we could see them circling overhead. In the newfound quiet, Seb called for us to spread the line further to the east over the radio. David and I moved off to the right and Basto, on my left, followed suit.

'We have confirmation that they are still in the forest and armed.' Seb's voice crackled in my ear. 'Keep your eyes open. If you see any fucker with a gun pointed at you, you shoot. No questions asked.'

I licked my lips and looked at the sparse woodland before us. It had grown around a natural shallow trench in the landscape that had clearly collected enough water in the rainy season to sustain a few trees and bushes. They grew quite dense in the centre, and we would have to get closer to be able to see anything. As there were already plenty of guns pointed toward the forest, it was up to David and I to protect our flank, being positioned on the edge of the formation. I could see for several kilometres or so toward the east and scanned the horizons, but saw nothing move.

'Here we go.' Seb said, and the line began to advance slowly. The forty of us moved in unison, slowly, as to maintain a perfect line. Then, Spartan 20 had reached the beginning of the wooded zone. I saw out of the corner of my eye, what might have been Djo and Katch, stepping over vegetation and then disappear from view.

'Go slower' Seb said over the radio. The bushes would be slowing Spartan 20 down. David and I advanced at a snail's pace, glancing regularly over to our left to make sure we were not getting ahead of the others. Now, as the wooded area widened, some of my own team disappeared behind bushes - Seb, Joyce and Santo among them. I advanced. The stock of my rifle tucked tightly into my shoulder, knowing that we must be close to whoever was hiding amongst the trees, and expected gunfire to break out at any moment.

And then I heard a voice in the distance shout, 'Don't move! Don't you fucking move! Get your hands above your head! Now!' I glanced left, but of course could see nothing. The vegetation obscured my view.

'Halt!' Seb ordered through the radio. We stopped and dropped to one knee as more loud voices came through the trees.

'Put your weapons down. Get your hands in the air!'

'One bad guy taken in. There'll be more, stay alert. Alright, let's get moving again.'

We advanced once more and the forest was widening to the point where David and I were in amongst the trees and bushes ourselves, just on the outer edge.

I could hear Pat yelling in the distance, 'Hold the line! Stay in line for fucks sake Momo or I'll kick you up the arse!'

I had to smile. Momo and the Doc were the only ones amongst us that were not technically a part of the GCM and had not had the same training. It did not help Momo's case that he seemed to annoy Pat, either, and Pat was often overheard giving him a bollocking for something or other.

Despite the slow pace, I was sweating profusely. The weight of my pack, armour, rifle and my tenseness added to the heat of the African sun, making my undershirt wet with perspiration. Moving forward, I kept my eyes forward and right, glancing occasionally to the left toward the dangerous zone. David was next to me and pulled on my elbow every now and again if he thought I was getting too far ahead or behind, trying to keep the both of us in a perfect line with the others.

'Don't move, don't move!' More shouting to the left, closer this time. And I could make out Alexi and Meme tackling a kneeling man to the ground, his hands in the air above his head.

'Halt!' Seb called it in over the radio to Pat as Alexi cuffed the man, while Meme picked up his AK and strapped it to his bag. It seemed that the enemy was not fighting us, instead allowing themselves to be captured peacefully. As we advanced deeper into the forest, there was yet more shouting. We stopped several more times to subdue insurgents that had wisely chosen capture over a firefight that would not have been in their favour.

'Take the prisoners behind the line.' A voice came from somewhere in the trees. 'One man to every prisoner and everyone else, eyes forward.'

We had captured around eight or so by now. They had all seemed to be sat waiting in the shallow trench, apparently too afraid to leave the relative safety of the trees, lest they incur the wrath of the circling Tigres and their 20mm cannons. It was hot work, and we had to move slowly and methodically. Searching the denser bushes to ensure we left no armed insurgents behind us, we spent an hour scouring the five hundred metre long stretch of forest until it began to thin out once more. I could see my comrades emerge from the trees on my left, some frogmarching cuffed insurgents as they went.

Looking over, there was a mixture of African and Arab men, all slim and small, wearing turbans and cotton tunics of neutral light brown colours with sandals upon their feet. By the time we had finished, there were eleven captured in total, without anyone having fired a single shot. We would need an extra bird to carry them all. Momo called it in for Pat, who wanted us to make one quicker pass of the forest to check for anything of value that might have been hidden, such as phones or weapons.

As we made our way back through the forest, I sucked on the nozzle of my camelback to fill up on some lost liquid and drank a litre without pausing. Once out on the other side, we lined up our captured charges and knelt them in the sand to wait. Ricky and Fich took a couple of motorbikes we had found a safe distance away, so they could set a couple of explosive charges to destroy them. Pat was very thorough, and insisted we leave nothing of value on the terrain for the enemy.

We kept the prisoners blind and deaf. Mufflers were put over their ears and blindfolds covered their eyes, their hands bound before them. The rest of us set up a defensive cordon and tried to find a little shade under which to plonk ourselves down to wait. I sat with David beside me, as he took off his helmet briefly to adjust the straps.

'Oh shit, look!' He pointed a gloved finger into the bowl of his helmet. Nestled between the padding, I could make out a little scorpion curled up, trying to make itself as small as possible.

'Wow, how the hell did that get in there?'

'No idea, maybe it dropped down from one of the trees and crawled in.' He flicked it out unceremoniously.

'Bloody lucky it didn't sting you, David. I hear the smaller ones are more poisonous.'

'Yea, this little guy came closer to killing me than they did today.' He gestured back at the captives. 'I wonder why they didn't fight back.'

Seb's voice came through my radio. 'Right, Ricky is going to blow up those bikes, try not to shit yourselves.'

And a few minutes later, there was the familiar earth trembling boom of several kilos of explosives as the motorbikes were destroyed. A great plume of black smoke rose into the sky.

Some minutes later our rides could be heard in the distance. Once the helicopters had landed, kicking up sand, we jogged over to them and shoved the captives inside first before clambering up one by one and strapping ourselves in. As soon as the birds were in the air, our job was more or less over, and there were a few fist bumps inside for a job well done. It was certainly a good start.

We would not have to wait long to find out why the mission had gone so smoothly. Once the captives had been dropped off at the 'chateau' back in Gao for interrogation (something we were never involved with), the intelligence trickled down to our level. Seb was then able to give us a debriefing one evening in the tent, several days later.

As it transpired, the eleven we had captured had been fresh recruits in training and inexperienced. Perhaps the Tigres' guns had taken the fight right out of them. Apparently, there had been one motorcycle that had braved the gunfire to escape and it was assumed that this was their 'instructor.' Nevertheless, eleven potential insurgents taken off the terrain was a good result for anyone, and it gave us confidence for the next mission.

I do not know what happened to the eleven we captured afterwards. Once we bring prisoners back to Gao, they are taken off our hands for interrogation. If it can be proven they are linked to a terrorist organisation, they are likely to be handed over to the Malian government and imprisoned.

The time between missions was spent training and working out, as usual. I'd train twice per day when I could, weightlifting in the mornings and some form of cardio in the evenings, whether it be boxing or CrossFit. Ricky and David were also big fans of CrossFit. To pass the time, and to serve as a distraction, they decided to set up a CrossFit competition in Gao. Finally, something we could sink our teeth into. The Brits were going to get involved, too. And in the first couple of weeks I had made friends with a few of them sharing a beer occasionally at the bar their Chinook crews had made by the hangars that they had called, 'The Queens Head.' It was fantastic. Made from pallet wood and other bits and pieces found or donated, it was a great little place to hang out. Trust the Brits to make the best bar on the FOB after a few months of their arrival.

They were intrigued by my situation. Unlike civilians, most of them had heard of the Foreign Legion, but knew little and I had to answer more than a few questions. The most common of which is always, 'Why didn't you join the British army?' I never have a suitable answer for that myself. I could have taken the time to wait for my application for the Parachute regiment and I would likely have got in. The truth was, I didn't know for sure what pushed me to abandon that in favour of the Legion. Perhaps it was just my sense of adventure, the desire to throw myself out into the world and experience it. I sometimes stopped to think of how odd it was... Here I was, an Englishman out I the middle of the desert, fighting for the French army with my Hungarian binome David alongside my French comrades. How on earth had that happened?

Djo and I had decided to pair up for the CrossFit, never having done much of it ourselves. Neither of us, however, are guys that do things half arsed and quickly found ourselves becoming more and more invested in the competition with each set of challenges. A lot of other people in Gao were enjoying the CrossFit competition, too. The events soon became a spectator sport with people egging on their favourites or representatives of their respective units.

As the competition wore on, Djo and I surprised ourselves by doing rather well. Because the other pairs from the GCM were eliminated, it soon became clear that we would be representing our commando brothers in the coming final. Neither of us had expected to get so far, and we knew now that we would have to get to the final. We would have to give a hundred percent to not shame the unit. The picnic tables had been cleared away from the bar near our tents for the final, leaving a large open space that Ricky and David had cleared and filled with a few Olympic bars and a rower. Unfortunately for Djo and I, seconds into the final against two other pairs, Djo somehow rolled his ankle doing box jumps and fell to the ground, clutching his foot and seething in pain. The moment I saw him, I knew we had lost. There was no way he could continue like that, and there was no sense in him pushing on despite the injury, as he had to be operational for the next mission.

It was much to the dismay of our GCM brothers that they had to watch two Tigre pilots take home the victory, while Djo was escorted to the Doc's tent. Still, I had enjoyed the challenge and was clapped on the back by my team for getting that far.

The next day, we enjoyed some music. David had managed to wangle a huge speaker from the logistics guys for the competition and took his time giving it back. Between the two tents of Spartan 30, the big Hungarian was often seen tanning with his shirt off, blasting dance music and grinning behind a pair of sunglasses. We played chess with the set I had laboriously spent so many hours carving the year before - I had found it in one corner of the bar, unused and collecting dust. The afternoons we had free were great. We would all sit around on the benches lining the tents and chat and laugh, listening to music all the while. Little Max would regale us with a tale of how he got into a fight with a few Arabs in the streets of Marseille. Joyce would show us pictures on his phone of the digital artwork he was selling. And Sipp's long term girlfriend, who happened to be on deployment from one of the helicopter regiments, would join us and treat us to some Cognac that had been shipped over by a relative.

Having little care packages sent over was always nice. The guys back at regiment would usually send one for us full of sweets, whisky and a few porn magazines to share, a reminder that there were people who cared about us back home. It made me wonder how the guys with families did it. Some of them were married with young children and with more on the way. Indeed, David's wife knew she was pregnant with their child before David's departure. But she refrained from telling him the news until he was safely back home as she thought, perhaps wisely, that it would be too great a distraction for him whilst he was away on mission.

As for myself, I had no one that directly depended on me. If I were to die on an operation, I would like to think my family members would be at least a little upset. But they would be able to continue their lives as they had been before. I can imagine that when you become a parent your own mortality is put into perspective. Should you not return, your infant son or daughter would have to grow up without a father. I suppose it could create a kind of nagging doubt, fear, in the back of your mind that could cause you to hesitate. And hesitation in this line of work could cost lives. For once, I was grateful for the relentless, nomadic lifestyle of the Legion that had not allowed me to put down roots.

In Gao, there were other Legionnaires based there at the same time as us. Different brigades took it in turns to be deployed in Mali. And whilst we were there, it was the parachutists. This meant that there were Legionnaires from 2REP, the Legion's parachute regiment based in Calvi, Corsica. Now in the French army, Legionnaires have a reputation for being the toughest and most disciplined, which often came close to being borderline crazy. Within the Legion itself, 2REP was known to be the 'maddest' of all the regiments. It was almost as if they had something to prove, and the Legionnaires I saw in Gao were no different.

I remember one day I was running an errand for Pat, acting as a go-between and translator for himself and the British Chinook crews, and I had taken one of the pickups to drive over to their hangars when I had spotted something quite bizarre happening in one remote part of the FOB. Out of curiosity, I made a diversion and brought the truck up to watch. There were six men running around a shipping container holding an inflatable boat above their heads, whilst a seventh was shouting abuse at them I couldn't quite hear.

Upon closer inspection, I saw that they were fully kitted out - plate carriers, rifles and all - wearing the green beret of the Legion and knew they must have been from 2REP. Bear in mind that it was later morning, and the temperature was already in the forties. And why on earth had the detachment from 2REP thought to bring an inflatable boat to the middle of the desert? I had no idea, but at least they were getting some use out of it. I amused myself for a while watching my airborne counterparts sweat under the sun. Poor bastards, I thought.

The parachutists in the Legion have an interesting history. The Algerian War for independence was fought from 1954 to 1962, during which there was bitter fighting against the Muslim rebels. Legionnaires were at the forefront of many of the military operations and, as such, saw the greatest loss of life. But politics would soon undo all the efforts of the French forces in Algeria. In 1958, the French government made the transition from the Fourth Republic to the Fifth Republic. It was established by their new President, Charles De Gaulle, who was at first an advocate for keeping Algeria as a colony of France. But as time went on, and to the dismay of both the French settlers in Algeria and the troops stationed there, De Gaulle's views changed. He stated that the Algerians ought to have free choice over who ruled them.

To the armed forces who had fought and died for years in the war, it was a great betrayal. To them, it meant that all the fighting and dying had been for nothing. When the Algerians finally voted for their independence in 1961, officers of the Legion's primary parachute regiment, 1REP, revolted. The coup, led by General Challe in April, 1961, took Algiers with the use of an elite unit of Legionnaires from 1REP. They were soon joined by other Legions and French regular forces alike, including 2REP. They were cheered by the French settlers of Algiers, who saw them as their saviours.

Charles De Gaulle made a speech on national television in response, asking for the support of the French people and French troops. The famous speech caused many of the French conscripts at the time to stop their support of the coup, refusing to work. A naval base was ordered to be seized by General Challe, but some of the troops revolted against his own rule and the mission was quickly abandoned.

Soon, there was great division amongst the French ranks. There were those who feared to disobey the government and those who could not accept that all those years of fighting the rebels would go to waste. Eventually, General Challe capitulated, not wanting to see French soldiers fighting one another. The forces of the French Foreign Legion had been integral pieces of the attempted coup, and some of its most loyal supporters. 1REP and 2REP had been especially instrumental.

In the aftermath, one hundred and ten officers were arrested, including General Challe who was sentenced to fifteen years in prison. Supposedly, there had been an attempt to assassinate De Gaulle, using one of the 1REP snipers sent to the mainland. Ultimately, it was unsuccessful. I do not know how true this is, but when you consider that there were around thirty attempts on De Gaulle's life, it doesn't seem implausible.

In any case, because 1REP was so crucial to the coup, the unit was disbanded. Since then, all other Legion parachute regiments have been 'banished' to Corsica, where 2REP now resides, and where they can cause the least amount of trouble. Another knock-on effect of the coup can still be seen in the structure of the Legion today. Because of the 1961 coup, no officer in the Legion can hold a position for more than two years, for fear of them becoming too attached to their men. As a result, they are rotated and will rarely get to know the soldiers serving under them.

We had soon gotten ourselves into the rhythm of life in Gao: sport, training and missions that were, this time around, frequent. Not all of them were action packed, though. Sometimes we would release prisoners back out into the desert, or act as a security escort in the helicopters. And sometimes there were alerts that never came to fruition. The drone would pick up images and we would run to the helicopters in all our gear, only to be told the drone had lost them and we'd have to return to the tents in frustration.

But there was one mission early on in our opex that was truly epic. In fact, the French have since made a documentary on that fateful night called, 'Nuit D'enfer,' 'Night from Hell.' The mission was called 'Azabara.'

Initially, I had wanted my account of events to be completely raw and truthful, with no unsettling details left out - a true portrayal of war and its effects on soldiers. I believe I have done a decent job of this here, enough to make my point. However, upon putting words to paper, I found that some things I had seen and done were far too personal and make me quite uncomfortable to speak about. Not only from the night of Azabara, but other missions during that deployment, too. So, I will skip over them. Yet even after having done things that are only considered acceptable in times of war, or for some perhaps not even then, know that I have never lost a moment of sleep over it. I was a good soldier, and did as I was told.

One morning, we were over by the Tigre helicopter hangars receiving a bit of a run down on the machines from the pilots as it was useful information to know out on the terrain.

'Look here,' the pilot was saying, pointing to a hatch on the side of the helicopter. Me and my team, excluding Little Max who was running an errand at the time of the lesson, crowded around the side of the machine.

'You can use this hatch to store things in. Let's say, for example, you've all been on the terrain for twenty-four hours and need an emergency resupply of water. We can keep it here and land the helicopter temporarily for you guys to get it out. Equally, you can put things in for us to take away, such as an important piece of evidence that needs to come back to Gao ASAP.'

The pilot continued his tour of the Tigre. 'Here we have the guided missiles.' He indicated towards the 'wings' that protruded from the body of the aircraft on either side - usually with an assortment of weapon systems attached underneath. He moved on to the cockpit.

'In the event of us crash-landing, there is a way to access the cockpit from the exterior, like so...' He demonstrated.

'And in the event, if any one of you need an emergency extraction, there is, in theory, a method of attaching yourself to the outside of the helicopter on top of the wheel, using your safety lanyards, of course.'

There were three wheels on the Tigre: one small one at the back and two larger ones just beneath the cockpit, attached to the body on hydraulic arms that were designed to cushion the impact of landing.

Just above each of the larger wheels, there was a protruding step that was around twenty centimetres by twenty centimetres - an aide to enable the pilots to clamber up to the cockpit.

'Sit on there while the helicopters flying?' Sipp scoffed. 'Fuck that.'

'The only one who's small enough to fit on there is Little Max!' Alexi joked as the rest of us laughed. 'He's not even here. We've probably just jinxed him and he'll be using it the next mission we do!'

The pilot smiled and shook his head. 'I don't think so' he said. ' No one has ever used this method before, not even in training. It's far too dangerous and only to be used in absolute emergencies. Besides, the odds are very slim. I wouldn't worry about it.'

And so our little lesson was concluded, none of us expecting to ever have to use the 'emergency extraction' method. We headed back to our tent for another Mario Cart tournament.

# CHAPTER 15

Several days later, on an evening just like any other, David and I had just got back from the bar, after having drunk a beer. I'd taken off my clothes and was lying in bed watching a film, winding down for the day. I heard big Max, Alexi, Serge and the others come into the tent, laughing, and duck into their own individual alveoles to conduct their end of day rituals. It must have been around 21:45 when I heard the tent door burst open once more and Seb shout, 'Alert! Get ready!'

I sat up in bed to make sure I had heard correctly when David said from across the corridor, 'bloody hell, nice timing. I was just about to fall asleep!'

I scrambled to my feet and began pulling on my gear, doing the usual checks for my equipment, and was ready within a couple of minutes. Some of the other guys were already heading out the door into the night and I followed, slinging my rifle strap over my head.

The airstrip was soon full of commandos that had answered the call. Making our way down to the helicopters, we had the usual rapid mission brief as the air crews prepared the machines for flight. We all crowded around Seb, once more, as he showed us satellite images on his tablet.

'Right, we have drone images of at least twenty insurgents in a wooded zone of Azabara, here. We'll land east of this forest.' He indicated an area five hundred metres by five hundred metres. 'And scour it from east to west. We'll be on the right flank again. Also,

Little Max will be staying behind to provide cover from the Gazelle later on.'

Each commando group had a couple of sharpshooters in it. One sharpshooter from the detachment might be kept behind to provide cover from the air when the Tigre's fuel reserves ran out. Having air support was an essential component to superiority on the ground. Little Max would sit on the side of the Gazelle, the French army's smallest helicopter, and lay down some precise fire from above.

Once briefed, we wasted no time dawdling, and gave our weapons, night vision and communication systems a final check. Before embarking in the NH90, we put a round in the chamber of our rifles and side arms. The familiar sound of the engines fired up, the blades beginning to turn as the air crew made the final checks. We were given the thumbs up and our little procession taxied down the runway to the take off point.

In the air, I clutched the familiar weight of my H&K like a comforting teddy bear and took a last sip from my camelback before the action started. Whatever happened, it was sure to be a long night.

The journey lasted an hour as we headed east of Gao. We did not even need Seb to hold up the three-minute warning as I could already see flashes of light from the Tigre guns. The beasts circled in the distance, laying down fire ahead of us. The noise soon reached our ears and I licked my lips in anticipation while Seb gave the one-minute warning. Flipping my night vision goggles down over my eyes, my world became green and black, and I adjusted the dial until everything was in focus. Unclipping my lanyard, I prepared to jump down, clutching onto David's bag in front of me as I knelt.

I felt the NH90 slow and lower to the ground, hitting the earth a little harder than usual, causing me to have to brace myself against the window. Big Max and Basto were already out and we were emptying the helicopter, forming a defensive line as soon as we had our bearings on the ground. Within seconds, the birds were taking off once more, leaving us alone on the desert floor.

The night was clear, which meant I could see sufficiently well with the night vision. The landscape a mass of green and black shadow, vast, open and familiar - it looked like any other part of Mali.

It was mostly flat, with occasional undulating dunes and sad looking bushes to break up the monotony. My eyes found the forest in which the insurgents were supposedly lurking.

Above, the Tigres were still firing, flashes of green light indicated their position high up in the sky momentarily. We could see the lit bullets slam into the trees ahead, the 20mm cartridges making a deep, reverberating 'thud' as they left the barrels.

This was it. There was sure to be a decent scrap this time around. 'Alright, let's start forming that line. Meme, Santo, keep eyes on Spartan 20 and Pat to your left, make sure we stay in line with them. We are going to check the smaller wood to the south of the main forest first before we make our way to the main one.'

Glancing left as the detachment mounted the next rise, I could see our detachment of forty commandos stretched over the space of a few hundred metres and grinned at my comrades. They looked like wolves of war. Helmeted spectres with night vision goggles pulled over their eyes and buffs on their faces, armoured and armed to the teeth, advancing confidently toward the danger. Woe betide all who would dare to oppose them. The terrorists were caught like rats in a trap, and my brothers were the hammer blow that would crush the life from them.

There was a lull in the gunfire from above as we moved. I stuck close to David and kept my eyes peeled, focusing on the bushes that were large enough to hide a man. Then, without warning, I heard a cry from somewhere to my left. 'Motorbike!' someone roared, and the warning was being repeated in my ear via the radio. Where? I hadn't seen a thing.

'There, there!' Someone else shouted and I looked, suddenly seeing a bike zoom over a dune some two hundred metres away, heading directly for us. I could clearly make out two green and black shapes atop the vehicle, armed with AKs.

'Shoot.' Seb gave the simple order over the radio and my eyes were presented with an image I will never forget. Forty guns opened fire. Innumerable flashes of green light erupted from their barrels all at once, and the sound filled the air as hundreds of rounds were poured onto the driver and passenger. A few hit the dirt around the bike, causing puffs of sand to jump momentarily into the air. Others pinged off the chassis to whiz off at a tangent, but more sunk into the bodies of the riders. For a second the bike teetered, attempted to turn away and then fell into the earth. Yet more rounds found their marks and the bodies convulsed when hit, like grotesque puppets jerked around again and again by their puppeteer. I fired my own rifle, and felt the recoil rock my shoulder back as I pointed my infrared laser on the target.

'Ceasefire!' Came the order through my ear and the shooting stopped at once.

'Advance.'

We moved toward the insurgents, unfortunate enough to have escaped the Tigres withering hail of fire only to find themselves out of the frying pan and into the fire. I suspect it was just bad luck they had chosen the path they did, and clearly hadn't even known we were on the ground.

The line was halted once more as two men were sent up to confirm the kills with their sidearms, leaving no chance for the insurgents to shoot us in the backs as we advanced once more. By now, the rest of them must know we were here. We cleared the bushes to the south of the forest before turning to deal with the main threat.

We went slowly and steadily, advancing sometimes a pair at a time to check any bushes. There were a few moments where my heart skipped a beat, as my mind imagined man-shaped shadows lying in the dark, only to find upon closer inspection it was a branch. I adjusted my night vision goggles again in the hopes that I could see better.

We neared the forest, approaching steadily and with caution. Gunfire erupted from somewhere on the left flank, so far away I couldn't see, and I heard Spartan 10 return fire as the line was halted. Then, another flash of green erupted from some bushes ahead of us, aimed in our general direction.

'Contact!' The response was immediate, we shot back. Big Max was soon laying down a storm of 7.62mm rounds from his minimi, aiming at the bush with an infrared laser that was clear to see through the night vision. 'Taktaktaktaktak!' went the gun as leaves and branches were ripped apart. Once the bush had been well and truly saturated and the return fire had stopped, we could advance once more, paying particular attention to the larger bushes from then on.

'Okay, we have a reaper in the air!' Seb's voice called over the radio. The reaper - a drone flying high in the sky - had excellent thermal imagery and could pinpoint the exact location of the enemy's position on the ground. A minute later, an enormously powerful infrared beam shone down from the black heavens (almost like the light you would imagine a comic book UFO to have), illuminating a bush three hundred metres away to the right.

'Shoot that bush!' Seb called and we laid down yet more fire, enough to be sure that whatever or whoever was in it was no more. The beam switched focus to something further away, over the next little dune.

'Advance!'

We moved off once more, and continued in the same manner for some time, occasionally stopping to neutralise the threat the reaper was illuminating for us. The Tigres continued to circle overhead, shooting sporadic bursts into the forest. So far, it had been a totally one-sided fight. We had the technology, the training, and the element of surprise. At no point did I feel as though there was any danger of us being checked by the insurgent force. Modern warfare, it seems, is all about technology. The night vision was a total game changer, especially considering the enemy was largely without.

Pat soon gave the order for us to turn our attention to the main forest, and the line swung around once we were sure the other dangers had been dealt with. After the Tigres had pelted the forest with fire, it was quiet as we approached cautiously from the east. Perhaps they had all been killed already? We were less than a hundred metres from the tree line, my pupils were wide, staring into the lenses of my goggles to scour the shadows in the forest.

'Allahu Akbar!' a voice cried, followed by the chatter of what must have been a PKM and several other AKs. They must have been shooting blind, at best seeing a few dark shapes illuminated by the moonlight. But some rounds came close to their marks. Sand was kicked into the air inches from the feet of some guys from Spartan 20 as the bullets slammed into the ground. Everyone hit the deck, trying to make themselves as small as possible as they returned fire. We were out in the open and there was no real cover, save for the treeline in which the enemy were situated.

I clearly heard an inhuman gurgling sound, as one terrorist was shot from the branches of a tree, and I watched as his lifeless figure fell to the ground. But advancing was still difficult. More gunfire was being directed at us from the treeline, the shooters concealing themselves well amongst the foliage. Then, the moon came out from behind a cloud, naked and bright, and we must have been quite visible to the enemy. Pat gave the order to retreat group by group, while the rest provided cover fire to the nearest dune behind us, feeling exposed all the way.

Once in safety, Pat made the decision to call in a couple of JBUs rather than risk losing a man with another attack. 'JBU's' were 250KG bombs, launched from planes that flew all the way from Niamey. As it happened, the planes had been readied as soon as the fighting had begun and were waiting on the runway for an eventual deployment. From the moment Pat called it in, it must have been thirty minutes until the planes arrived. In the meantime, a sort of stalemate silence fell over the area, and gave both sides a chance for a break amidst the fighting. We could reload and take a drink, having lost a lot of liquid through sweat even in the dead of night. It must have been around 00:30 when I gave David's shoulder a reassuring squeeze and we spoke in whispers in the dark.

We did not have to wait long before we got a five-minute warning for the JBU's. We were told to shield our eyes and keep our heads down. It would be a 'danger close' scenario. We were only a couple of hundred metres from the target and when the bombs exploded they would send thousands of shards of hot metal flying through the air.

'One minute!' Seb called over the radio. I shimmied down into the sand, lying flat, part of me wanting to curl into a ball and shield my head in my hands. Another part wanted to watch out of sheer curiosity. The planes whooshed past and I heard a distinct whistle that must have been the bomb as it came rushing through the air to the earth. Upon impact, it exploded with a tremendous 'BOOM,' followed a second later by two more in quick succession. BOOM, BOOM!

The ground shook under the almighty blasts and I looked up in wonder to see vast mushrooms of fire erupting into the sky, illuminating the desert for miles around. For a few seconds it might as well have been daylight, as the flames and smoke rose into the night sky like a fiery titan. Or perhaps it was the devil himself, come to claim the souls of wrongdoers. It was biblical, truly a sight to behold. A perfect display of the terrifying destructive power of a modern army, and I think we were all awestruck to have been so close. There was a pause as we all watched for a moment. The great fiery mushrooms began to collapse in on themselves, plunging the desert into darkness once more.

Intending to take full advantage of the disarray the bombs must have caused amongst the ranks of the enemy, Pat wasted no time in giving the order to advance once more. But surely nothing could have survived those blasts? I was wrong, they had. But this time the resistance was minimal - the JBUs had done their job. We were able to advance into the treeline after clearing up a few stragglers.

Once in the forest, the danger was far from passed; here there were plenty of hiding places. The line was more difficult to maintain amongst the trees, but it was imperative that we did so. We stopped regularly as there were several small exchanges of gunfire, and more kills were confirmed. Not only did we have to look on the ground, but upwards too. There had been one man shot down from a tree and I could see plenty of other branches capable of holding a man's weight.

In amongst the trees was a small pond, the source of life for the little forest - another obstacle to contend with. As the Tigres continued to circle overhead, our progress through the forest was slow and laborious. The trees and bushes were seemingly endless, and my biceps were soon on fire from holding my rifle up, pointed forwards. We stopped to check each tree because shots could be heard up and down the line as hidden enemies were uncovered.

Every now and again someone would shout, 'Reloading!'

And his binome would reply, 'covering!'

We were on high alert. Scanning the foliage with wide-eyed intensity, we made our way slowly through the trees.

In the early hours of the morning, we broke through to the other side of the forest and set up a cordon to wait for daybreak. The Tigres had left us a short while earlier and, for a time, an eerie quiet fell upon the battlefield. We all took the opportunity to take a long drink and eat whatever snack we had with us in our packs. As soon as I sat down in the sand, I felt a wave of fatigue wash over me. I hadn't slept and my senses had been on overdrive for hours. I was quite ready to collapse and sleep, but it was not to be. An hour later, at around 05:00, Pat got the intel that some of the insurgents were escaping to the north east and we were ordered to pursue on foot.

Dawn was breaking, and the first rays of sunlight turned the sky a fitting blood red in the east. Forty commandos marched toward it, tired and weary, yet determined still. It was not long before we were joined in pursuit by two Gazelles flying past overhead. We cheered knowing one of the figures who sat with his feet resting on one of the steel supports of the small helicopter must be Little Max. Unlike the Tigres, the Gazelles flew much lower, and stopped on occasion so their sharpshooters could get a good shot. They were soon circling a kilometre away and we could hear the occasional shot at an enemy we could not see.

The dunes were a little more undulating this side of the forest and blocked our vision. Pat pushed on, urging us to pick up the pace. I felt it was unlikely that we would catch them at this point, now it was all down to the helicopters. A familiar beating of blades made me look over my shoulder to see another Tigre flying toward us to join the Gazelles in combat. Apparently having quickly refuelled, the pilots were keen to re-join the fray.

By now, the sun had risen enough so that we could turn off our night vision and see quite clearly. Ahead, the comforting thud of the Tigres guns could be heard, occasionally broken up by the crack of what might have been Max's H&K 417. With the rising sun came a rising temperature. Even in the former half of the morning, the heat was uncomfortable. David and I trudged on, placing one foot in front of the other on the sand. Spartan 30 was now holding the left flank, and we soon saw the handiwork of the 20mm guns in the form of a lifeless corpse bleeding into the ground. Great chunks of flesh had been rendered from the torso and a large pool of blood had been absorbed by the sands of the Sahara, staining it a dark red. There was no need to check if the man was dead, it was quite clear that he was.

Before us lay a hillock, a dune larger than the rest. Seb had us all climb it so he could get a good vantage point of the chase in the distance. I peered ahead, but could not see a great deal. From this point, the dunes seemed to rise higher from the earth, and it seemed that the insurgents had taken full advantage of the time between the Tigres refuelling to get a head start. I readjusted my pack on my back and rubbed my peeling lips with a gloved hand. It seemed we would have a long march ahead of us if we were to catch them.

'Hey!' Santo shouted from my right. 'Weren't there two gazelles in the sky a minute ago?' All of us craned our necks upwards and squinted in the sun to search the clear blue sky. We could quite clearly see one gazelle circling in the distance. But where was the other? There had been two, I was sure of it.

'Holy shit. Look.' David was pointing a spot several kilometres away where great plumes of black smoke were rising from between two dunes, the sand obscuring our view of what lay between them. Surely it couldn't be?

Seb touched his ear to listen, his mouth forming a little 'o' of surprise and all of us turned to look. 'Pat's just confirmed it. One of the Gazelle's is down.' The rest of us exchanged looks of open-mouthed shock; was it Max? Were he and the pilots still alive?

'They took fire from a PKM. Looks like a lucky burst hit the engine.' Seb went on, looking as though he could not quite believe it himself. Judging by the growing cloud of black smoke rising constantly from the horizon, the Gazelle must be on fire. All of us knew the chances of surviving a crash landing were incredibly slim. I could see Pat with Spartan 20 gesturing with his arm. He must have said something through the radio because a moment later Seb was ordering us to move.

If they had crash landed near the enemy at whom Max had been shooting, there was no way we could get to them first. Even if we sprinted all the way, it was simply too far. Nevertheless, we pressed on, fearing for our friend's life.

Then, Seb stopped to listen again, shaking his head incredulously.

'What?' Alexi demanded.

'There are survivors! Tigre is going down to get them!'

'But how?'

'They'll have to hold on to the legs until the Tigre puts them down behind our line.'

'Jesus.'

We stopped to watch, and could actually see the Tigre dip gracefully from the sky, coming in to land somewhere near the black plume. It, too, disappeared from view. For a few incredibly tense minutes our hearts were in our mouths, until the machine reappeared and climbed into the sky once more, flying straight toward us.

'Are they holding on to the legs?' Basto muttered in wonder.

Amazingly, I could make out a little figure clutching onto the hydraulic legs of the Tigre on the outside of the helicopter, holding on for dear life. As it neared, I could see that it was indeed Max. And the two pilots were holding on to the other side too!

'I can't believe they all survived!' David exclaimed. 'That's incredible!'

The Tigre kicked up a wall of sand as it landed and we turned away to shield our eyes. The guys from Spartan 10 were running over, pulling Max and the two Gazelle pilots from the side of the Tigre and to safety. All the guys on the ground gave the Tigre pilots a roaring cheer and they saluted us with a grin from the cockpit before we had to turn away once more, the blades throwing more sand into the air as the machine took flight again. As soon as it had gone, half of the guys from Spartan 10, including the Doc, rushed over to aid the three wounded men. We all waited impatiently to hear if they were okay. A few minutes later, once an NH90 had been called from Gao, Seb informed us through the radio that the Doc was optimistic that they would all make it, having shooed everyone else out of the way. Thank fuck for that, I thought.

We would later learn from Little Max himself that, when the Gazelle had been hit, he truly believed he was about to die. The

Gazelle had swerved and then spun to the ground at a terrifying speed, slamming into the earth with almighty force. His world had gone black for a moment and when he came to, he was suspended upside down by his safety lanyard attached to the floor. He felt an awful pain in his lower back, and it transpired later, that upon impact, he had broken two vertebrae. Max cut himself free with his combat knife, falling with a thud to the ground.

Picking himself up and taking in his surroundings, he saw that one of the pilots had been ejected through the front windshield, shattering it and lying several metres away in the sand, motionless. The other was trying to free himself from the wrecked cockpit. Max knew he had to act fast as naked flames were licking their way up the sides of the aircraft.

Max jumped out and yanked open the door of the cockpit, despite the pain in his back, and pulled the pilot out onto the ground. He was dazed still, and unable to move of his own accord. The great beating of the Tigre engine made Max turn to look at the attack helicopter setting itself down in the sand thirty metres away. A video taken by a drone shows him pulling the first pilot toward the Tigre as the second, who had now regained consciousness but was unable to get up, began to roll his body as best he could in the same direction.

Fortunately, the two pilots had their safety lanyards intact. Max, not even having been present for the 'emergency extraction' lesson, knew that he had to get them both strapped to the legs after the two Tigre pilots gesticulated from their cockpit, pointing at the little step and the hydraulic legs below them. Once the first one was safe, Max went back for the second and helped him to his feet, taking an arm around his neck. He had soon pulled both men to the Tigre and had them clutch on to the outside of the machine using whatever they could, wrapping the lanyards around the legs just in case.

As for Max: he had cut away his own lanyard to free himself from the wreckage of the Gazelle. Moving around to the other side of the Tigre, he had to use only the strength of his arms to keep him from falling. Once secure, he had slapped the side of the cockpit and the Tigre flew them all to safety. The whole ordeal had not lasted more than a few minutes.

It was miraculous to say the least; incredibly lucky that the three of them had survived the crash and that the Tigre pilots had then had the balls to put their aircraft down behind enemy lines, making themselves incredibly vulnerable to attack to save their comrades. All three survivors have since made a full recovery and are currently in active service.

The rest of us maintained the security cordon, as the Doc took charge of the injured men. An NH90 was already on its way to extract the wounded, and in the meantime the Doc did all he could. Forty minutes later, after hearing Max laugh and joke with the Doc from his makeshift stretcher, the NH90 had arrived. More medics jumped down, taking the three men to safety. It was with great relief that I watched the bird fly away, knowing Little Max was in the most capable hands. They would be all right.

The mission, however, was not yet over. The insurgents had used the mayhem to escape and were long gone. The next job now was to gather what intel we could from the corpses of the men we had already killed. Retracing our steps, the sun beat down on us. It was not until around 09:00 that we were back at the forest we had spent most of the night clearing. Now seeing it in the light of day, it seemed far less sinister. We were able to relax a little knowing that the immediate danger had now passed.

Yet there was much work to do. The intel we had received all those hours ago had been incomplete. In the forest alone there were twenty-five dead, and more in the distance. The total inhabiting the encampment, we would later learn, had been closer to fifty.

Because there were so many bodies, each pair was assigned a corpse. David and I were given one on the treeline and took pictures of what was left of his face. The top half of his head had been split open like a watermelon, most likely the work of a big calibre gun. There was a mess of brains, bits of skull and blood around him.

In my head, I imagine there to be a command centre somewhere, where the images of known and suspected terrorists are pinned to a wall with a big, red 'X' on them. We would, therefore, need DNA samples and pictures of our fallen enemies that we would take with us and hand in to Pat back at Gao. They would then, presumably, relay it all to intelligence.

David was pulling on a pair of rubber gloves, as I took a few pictures.

'Here.' he said, handing me what looked like a cotton earbud in a plastic tube. 'Get some DNA.'

Kneeling, I took the earbud and squashed it deep into the dead man's brain matter with a wince, giving it a swirl for good measure before putting it back into the tube. David chuckled at my expression.

'We need to get his combat vest off, too.'

He gestured to the camouflaged vest holding a handful of AK magazines. I tried to lift a lifeless arm and bend it at the elbow, but the body was completely stiff. David watched me wrestle with the corpse for a moment before snorting with laughter and adding, 'why don't you just cut it off?'

'What, the arm?' I gave him an incredulous look.

'No, you idiot, the vest!'

'Ah, right. Yeah, probably a good idea.'

Taking out my knife, I cut away the vest to take the ammo that would be collected. Most of the weapons and vehicles we found would be destroyed on sight. Ricky was somewhere near the pond - the responsibility of amassing everything Pat wanted destroyed resting on his shoulders, as he was the lead combat engineer of the detachment. For everyone to finish collecting the data - DNA, simcards, radios and whatever else might be of value - took another few hours. It was midday when all the Legionnaires, Ricky, Fich, Djo, Katch, David and I were crowded around the pile of guns, rockets, ammo boxes, grenades and motorbikes that needed to be destroyed.

Ricky handed out plastic explosives that we moulded into balls and stuck with explosive wire, linking it all in a great chain that would explode simultaneously when detonated. When it was done, we stepped back to admire our handiwork, wiping our brows.

'Right, someone tell Pat he can pull the rest of the boys back. Dobson, would you like the honours?'

'Absolutely!' I grinned, taking the detonator from his hand.

'Wait for my signal.' Ricky said, as he and the others picked up their bags and rifles and moved several hundred metres away to a safe distance. A few moments later I saw him give the thumbs up and pushed on the little button that sent a crackling, sparkling flame to travel slowly down the explosive cord to the C4. Turning my back and walking away, I trusted Ricky had correctly calculated the time needed for me to get to safety. He had, of course.

I sat down next to David with a sigh and waited for the explosion. 'BOOM!'

The deep blast reverberated into the ground. Turning back, I could see a great cloud of smoke rising into the air. It signified the end of a long and crazy night, a mission that I would never forget.

Now all that was left to do, was wait. Sitting in a defensive circle trying to stay awake, we chatted about what a long day it had been and recounted a few of the hairier moments during the night.

At 13:00, three NH90's came to pick us up. It wasn't until we were all safely inside and the birds were in the air flying back to Gao, that we could truly relax. I was so tired I fell asleep straight away in the most uncomfortable of positions, dreaming of the mess hall and my bed back in Gao.

Azabara was reported in French news. We were scrolling through internet articles on our phones in the bar one evening, and it was surreal to see a reportage on the mission we had participated in the week prior.

''A force of over twenty Jihadists have been neutralised by French commando groups on Tuesday.'' Sipp was reading aloud as the rest of Spartan 30 sat around the picnic benches in the bar, sipping on beers and grinning at one another.

'Look, it doesn't even say the GCM! Three military personnel were wounded in action when a helicopter crash landed. All are in a stable condition and expected to recover.'

The day before, Little Max and the two Gazelle pilots had embarked on a plane back to France as soon as it became clear their injuries were no longer life threatening. We had visited Max in Gao's infirmary. He had seemed quite happy and well, but he had told us his near-death experience had put things into perspective for him. He was equal parts glad to be going home to appreciate his good fortune, and remorseful that he had to leave us for the rest of the opex.

"The mission began when the -" Sipp's jaw dropped in disbelief as he read the next part of the article.

'What?' Big Max pressed him, leaning over curiously and trying to see the article for himself.

"When the Groupment Commando Parachutists were called into action at 22:00."

There was a collective groan of disgust from around the table and shouts of 'no fucking way!' and 'are they serious?' We attracted more than a few curious glances from around the bar.

'How the hell did they get that wrong?' I moaned in disbelief.

'I can't believe it. They're giving the GCP all the credit and they weren't even there! They were in bed the whole fucking time!' David added, flushing with anger.

'Right, that's it. I'm writing to these arseholes.' Joyce took out his phone to look up the name of the reporter.

Between the 'Groupement Commando Montagne' (my unit) and the 'Groupement Commando Parachutistes', there had long since been a rivalry. The GCP had been around considerably longer than ourselves, and as many of the Generals were from ex-parachute regiments, they were often favoured on the terrain for the missions. This time, however, we seemed to have been trusted with many of the more prestigious missions reserved for commando units and were proving our worth- and then some.

This message finally seemed to be getting through to the 'higher-ups' and we were given more responsibility on the terrain. The same message, however, was slow to reach the rest of the army and the press. For us, the 'rising stars,' were the less well known of the two units. Clearly, the reporter had either gotten the facts horribly wrong, or had been deliberately given the wrong facts by someone in the army. Either way, it was incredibly frustrating that all our efforts had ultimately seemed to favour our rivals.

The GCP often made it into the military press. In fact, during my last tour of Mali, there was a reporter living in Gao with the aim of writing a story about the elite units of the army. But not once were we approached. After having lived on the FOB for several weeks, one day in August, her article was finally published, and Ricky had found it online. He came to our tent to sit outside on the benches with David and I to show us.

'You're gonna love this.' He was shaking his head, half in amusement, half in exasperation. He began to read, and it became clear that the reporter had become somewhat infatuated with the GCP. The article would have any reader believe that sunlight shone from the arses of the parachutists, buttering them up with heavy flattery that was almost cringeworthy.

'The GCP have conducted many successful operations in Sahel (the Mali conflict) and continue to display a professionalism that is the embodiment of an elite unit of the French military. The GCP train regularly in Gao with both shooting and combat drills, honing their skills for dangerous operations, such as the recent 'Azabara' on which they were recently deployed. Their Hollywood-esque faces and their bodies sculpted by CrossFit and Brasilein Jujitsu gleam with sweat as-'.

'Please stop.' David put his head in his hands and half laughed, half moaned. He looked up at Ricky and said, 'which one do you think she was fucking?'

'Maybe all of them?' We laughed.

Despite the inaccurate news articles, the politics in Gao continued to favour us. Through June and July there were more missions and their orchestrators soon developed an effective battle plan that yielded good results. Whenever the drone picked up images of an enemy encampment, the Generals would coordinate a JBU strike with a commando force, namely us. The bombs would hit the encampment and minutes later, we would be on the ground, ready to clear up any stragglers that had survived.

We were deployed on one such mission in early August, scouring an enemy encampment after a bomb blast. By now, the rainy season was well underway. Recent rainfall had saturated the ground, creating bogs and ankle-deep lakes in the lower, forested areas of Mali.

It was night, and we were wading through thick mud and water, swatting away the thousands of mosquitos that had gathered there.

'Keep eyes on each other.' Seb was reminding us through the radio as we advanced through thick vegetation. With the help of the rainfall, long grass had sprung up all over the terrain.

'There's the crater just up ahead.'

Through the green and black of our night vision, we could see that the JBU strikes had been a direct hit this time. The insurgents must have been grouped together to sleep for there were body parts strewn all around the edges of the crater. Explosions tend to mangle the flesh in bizarre ways. I saw many examples of body parts, mainly arms and legs, detached from their torsos by the force of the blast. One man had been cut in two: his arms still twitching uselessly as if trying to reach the pool of entrails that spilled from his belly.

'Right, we're going to move past it. Apparently, the Bombs didn't get all of them.'

Pat wanted us to scour the area around the encampment, too. We set off once the camp itself had been cleared. The terrain was awful, marshy, hot, humid and full of insects. It slowed our progress and the infernal mosquitos picked at us incessantly. We went slowly, advancing as a single line through the forest.

Every now and again someone would curse as they stumbled over a branch or slapped away another mosquito. The temperature, even in the night, must have been in the high twenties. After a few hours of walking I found myself tapping into my water reserves.

'At this rate we'll march all the way back to Gao.' I whispered to David, glancing in his direction only to see that he had stopped, and was focused on something through the trees.

'There, what is that?' He said, pointing. The light was good for the night vision, as by now the first light from the sun was illuminating the sky just a little. But the vegetation was blocking my vision.

'I can't see shit.'

'There, look, by that tree. I think it's a man, in the clearing there.' David pressed the button to speak into his radio with his weak hand, the other holding his rifle up and toward the danger.

'Seb, I think I've got something here. Looks like one guy sat by a tree fifty metres ahead of me. He's got an AK in his lap.'

'Okay, don't take any unnecessary risks. If he's armed, you can shoot him.'

As we neared, I could see more clearly the figure sat by the tree. We coordinated with Alex and Serge to the right who would back us up if the man decided to fight. Creeping forward, we reached the last few trees before the clearing and I gave David's shoulder a squeeze to tell him I was ready. With a deep breath, we burst through into the open, our rifles pointed at the figure who looked up at us with an emotionless expression.

'Don't move! Put your hands above your head!' David roared, his muscles tense, finger pressing slightly on the trigger, ready to fire. The man was sitting cross legged quite calmly and began to slowly raise his bare hands above his head. I approached, and keeping my rifle pointed at his chest, I bent to pick up the AK from his lap, maintaining eye contact with him all the while.

He wore a beige robe and trousers with brown sandals and a head scarf. But the most remarkable thing about him was his face. Deep scars had marred the surface of the weather-beaten brown skin and had clearly not been correctly treated for they had, obviously, healed poorly. Two deep-set dark eyes looked coldly back up at me from beneath bushy eyebrows. I knew a fighter when I saw one.

Then, Serge and Alex were behind him. He was shoved forward onto his stomach on the sand as the pair conducted a search of his person, before binding his hands and blindfolding him. Seb called it in to Pat and the decision was made to return to the crater made by the JBU. Once there, we would wait for daybreak so we could begin the usual collection of evidence. Our prisoner was marched along with us.

We were grateful to be able to rest our feet for a while. David had wisely thought to bring a compact mosquito net for the two of us to shelter under, and a good thing, too, as the little buggers seemed to be out in the millions around the dirty floodwaters. We sat in a half sitting position leaning back on our packs with the net resting over our helmets and knees. Between the time it took for the sun to rise enough for us to clearly see what we were doing, the mosquitos had bitten me around the area where the net had been resting on my knees, through my combat trousers, thin padding included. My knees were covered in itchy red bites that lasted for days. Even the foul-smelling spray that I regularly doused my clothes in seemed to have little effect. I had never been so grateful to see the sun, even with the awful heat it brought with it; at least the mosquitos would bother us no more.

Spartan 20 had the wonderful job of piecing together the human jigsaw puzzle, as the other two Spartan groups made a defensive cordon in which they could work. I could see Djo picking up a leg or an arm, trying to figure out which torso it belonged to before snapping a picture on a digital camera. By now, we had all long since grown used to seeing severed limbs and bodies ravaged by explosions and bullets. It was just part of the job.

The work was carried out quickly. DNA was taken with pictures, and the small arms were bagged and taken, while everything else of use was systematically destroyed. I gulped at my last bottle of water, finishing it and crushing it up. All the walking in the night had made us sweat; I had consumed over seven litres in almost as many hours.

The helicopters arrived for us while it was still early in the morning, and we climbed aboard with our prisoner strapped into a seat opposite Alex. Impassive as ever, he sat calmly without so much as a sound. Back in Gao, we passed him on to the interrogation team who led him swiftly away to the 'Chateau', where all prisoners were kept. Thinking I had seen the last of our prisoner, I clapped David on the back as we walked back down the airstrip toward the tents, wondering aloud if they were still serving breakfast in the canteen.

Around a week later, however, Seb relayed to us the result of the interrogation of our scarred prisoner. He had claimed that he had been a captive of the group of insurgents killed by the JBU strike - just a simple farmer who refused to help the terrorists who, in their wrath, had abducted him. When asked why he had been found with a rifle, he had answered that he had taken it from the encampment so that none of his captors could use it against us. This made us all laugh. Most likely he had gone for a shit at the perfect moment, luckily avoiding being blown to pieces.

Seb, however, did not laugh. Grimly, he went on to say that because the man was not in the DNA database that recorded all known terrorists, he was to be set free the next day, and it would be us who would do it. That earned a few noises of disgust from around the table. I am certain there was more to it than that, that there were politics involved and certain details that I will never be privy to. Either way, it was galling to be handed back the prisoner the following evening. Nevertheless, David and I blindfolded him once more.

As the aircrew made the pre-flight preparations, I said to David, 'you should probably have shot him the moment you saw the AK. Who knows what he'll go and do now. One thing is for certain, he's no farmer.'

'Hm.' David grunted, deep in thought. 'Maybe I should have.'

Forty minutes later the NH90 was touching down outside a village somewhere and we were frogmarching our captive out of range of the helicopter. We covered our faces, took off his blindfold and cut away his restraints. He blinked, his scarred face unreadable as ever. David dropped him a small water bottle and a snack as was standard procedure. Without further ado, we marched back to the helicopter and jumped in, giving the gunner the thumbs up.

As we pulled away, I saw the figure on the ground get to his feet, shielding his eyes from the sand kicked up from the blades and collect his water bottle from the ground before heading off toward the village. I remember thinking, if it were the other way around and that one of us were captured, we would almost certainly have been beheaded by a balaclava clad Al Qaeda operative whilst being filmed by another - just another 'snuff film' to end up on the internet somewhere. I am sure the families of the innocents slaughtered in recent terrorist attacks would say we were too lenient.

Morally, it is very hard to know where to stand. On the one hand, these were the same terrorist organisations that had orchestrated horrific attacks, the only provocation for which seemed to be because their beliefs were not shared by their victims. They had committed genocide and were responsible for the deaths of countless innocent men, women and children. On the other hand, the likelihood was that most of the insurgents we faced were simple men after a better life. This is the nature of war, it is unfair. In any case, I had a job to do, and to do it I had to leave my emotions at the door.

Sometime during the last quarter of the Opex, we received disconcerting news that the command was once again changing over. New Generals were taking over to relieve the old ones and it was unlikely that things would continue as well as they had. My fears were soon realised as the number of missions seemed to decrease sharply, and we seemed to be spending a lot more time in Gao. The new command was apparently afraid to risk French lives and seemed to prefer to keep us confined within the walls of the FOB. Pat was the most frustrated of all of us. He already had numerous successful missions under his belt from the last few months and saw no reason why the rhythm should stop. Unfortunately for us, Pat was just a Capitaine, and did not dictate the mode of action for the French forces deployed in Mali.

He was able to get us out for some shooting practice, however. Subsequently, we all amused ourselves shooting the H&K's, Minimi's, MAG58's and grenade launchers at sandy berms a few kilometres outside Gao, letting off some steam with some familiar shooting drills.

A few weeks went by with nothing notable at all happening. We went on with our regular routine of training, working out, eating and sleeping and were getting worryingly good at Mario Cart. We were bored - keen to get out and do something.

Pat, after weeks of moaning to his superiors about the lack of action, finally beat them down and managed to get us a patrol mission with the pickups. Even though last year had proved to be only marginally successful with anything that involved patrolling in the pickups, this year we had Pat, and it would seem that luck was on our side. It would only be for a total of five days, but it gave us something to prepare for. And besides, there had been less rain this year than the last.

In what turned out to be our last significant deployment of the Opex, all the boys from the Spartan groups would be deployed in two or three vehicles per group. Along with the command vehicles, there were a total of eleven pickups.

We left Gao on a clear sunny morning. I sat with my legs dangling over the side with Big Max beside me as we debated which of the air crew girls was the prettiest. The convoy rolled over the potholes of the FOB before exiting into the vastness of the desert. Under the direction of Pat, the convoy moved to reconnoitre several points of interest, locations insurgents were suspected to have camped recently, in the hopes we might stumble upon them. We had the transmission interceptors again: a couple of guys on one of the command vehicles with a bunch of electronic equipment and computers.

We camped in one of the Malian army bases near Mont Hombori, a unique mountain a couple of hundred kilometres south west of Gao. It was perhaps the most visually stunning part of the entire country. The enormous pillars of stone seemed to burst from the hills, vertical and bare. They dominated the landscape around them and could be seen for the best part of a hundred kilometres in any direction. The gigantic stone formations served as a marker the next day and we could see how far we'd come by glancing back toward them.

Before we'd left, the Malian soldiers had confirmed Pat's intel and we made our way to the forest in which the insurgents were last known to have hidden. It was in the early morning of the second day when we had first encountered the enemy.

The vehicles of Spartan 30 had been at the rear of the convoy, trundling along behind the others between scrawny trees and bushes, passing the odd goat or cow belonging to a shepherd from a nearby settlement. I was daydreaming about M and the time we had together, imagining her soft red lips caressing my cheek, the warmth of her breath on my neck, the roundness of her firm breas-

Gunfire.

'Contact! Contact!' Basto was shouting from above me on the MAG58, pointing to the head of the column of vehicles. Big Max and I craned our necks in an effort to see round the side of the pickup, but all we could see were the other Spartan groups racing off towards something.

'Hold on!' Alexi shouted into the radio. I gripped the side of the pickup tight as he accelerated in an attempt to keep up with the others.

'What's going on? I can't see anything!' I heard David shout from the other side of the pickup.

'Us neither!'

Sebs' voice explained calmly and quickly through the radio that two insurgents on a motorbike had shot at the lead pick-up, before zooming away into a denser part of the forest which they knew would be impossible for the pickups to traverse.

Already, we could see the other teams dismounting ahead, and soon Seb was in our ear again.

'Okay, Pat wants us to continue through the forest on foot. Two guys will stay with the vehicles here.'

I looked ahead to where the guns were pointing. The forest was dense; small, low trees and bushes made impenetrable patches here and there, but there seemed to be several pathways through made by animals - pathways large enough for a motorbike, but not a truck. Within a minute, all three groups were deployed in a line and began to hack their way through the undergrowth. If they were hiding, we would find them.

We took the left flank. I had to keep David in sight, but the vegetation was thick and it threatened to obscure my binome from view. With my free hand, I bashed away branches and stepped over roots. The progress was slow and made slower still by the fact that we knew there were armed insurgents nearby. There was no movement without half of our guns pointed toward the danger at any one time.

After what could not have been more than ten minutes later, there was another exchange of gunfire to our right. The silence was broken with the chatter of a minimi shooting 7.62mm rounds accompanied with rifle fire, which ceased after twenty seconds or so.

'Two insurgents down.' Seb said from somewhere. 'Clear the forest and we should be able to see where in a minute.'

Sure enough, the forest began to thin out a little, and David and I soon found ourselves breaking through the treeline. The guys from Spartan 10 had clearly found the insurgents as they had tried to escape on the other side of the forest. A motorbike lay on the ground and, several metres away, in addition to the driver and passenger - two thin, dark skinned corpses, with blood still flowing from the bullet wounds into the sand.

From there, we cleared the bodies and looked onward in the direction they had been travelling. The terrain opened here to the undulating sands of the Sahara once more, as a storm was fast approaching on the horizon. A village lay a couple of hundred metres away, the building made from mud and thatch.

'Look there!' Someone shouted and pointed at something in the distance. 'That big tree, do you see the guys under it?

Pat took a pair of binoculars to look. 'Yeah, that's got to be the rest of them.' He said after a moment.

'We surprised the bastards once. I doubt they'll let us do it again. They're so far away now. They knew we couldn't reach them in time, we're too slow.'

Pat turned to Seb and the other two Chef de Groupes. 'Right, we'll search this village. Have the pickups drive around this forest and find that track there.' He indicated towards other motorbike tracks that led in the direction of the tree on the horizon.

'Destroy the bike.'

David set about puncturing the tyres and set the bike alight by using a rag to ignite the fuel in the tank. Soon, we were heading towards the village, with the bike burning behind us, and left the bodies to rot in the sun.

The grey clouds were rapidly approaching now. Clearly there hadn't been much recent rainfall in the area for some time as a wall of sand formed ahead - only possible when the ground was dry - and we knew it would soon be upon us. Several bare footed little boys raced over the earth to their waiting mothers who ushered them inside the houses, casting anxious glances in our direction.

'We need to search all of these buildings!' Pat was shouting. 'Seb, take Spartan 10 and cover those huts over there!'

Seb began issuing orders and we formed the usual line to advance toward the first buildings. It was a small settlement, and very poor. No more than twenty buildings made from straw, sticks and tarpaulin stood on a clear sandy area. We approached the first, two pairs to a hut.

'Remember,' Seb said in our ears, 'there could be hostiles hiding in any of those buildings. And keep eyes up ahead, too. It's possible that they might use the storm to attack.'

The storm was so close. Wind picking up, it began to blow at our clothes. All the other guys were anticipating it and wrapped their faces and bare skin, attempting to seal the area around their goggles with thin scarves or buffs. I looked up after having protected myself as best I could and saw the sand racing towards me. And then it was upon us. The wind howled and buffeted us. Sand flew in every direction, instantly reducing visibility to no more than fifty metres. I squinted, despite my goggles sand was still getting in my eyes from somewhere. I gritted my teeth only to feel sand crunch between them. Looking around, Seb was waving us on, and we passed to the next building.

We drew back the flaps or basic wooden doors to find women and children huddling in the corners, but found nothing untoward. In the centre of the village stood the largest hut, a round construction with a conical roof. Some of the boys from Spartan 20 entered and a moment later one stuck his head out and gestured for Pat and the Doc. The line was halted, and we waited as the wind blew a gale around us to see what was going on.

'The Doc's giving birth.' Seb shouted over the radio. What? I must have heard wrong and turned to David whose brow was furrowed in confusion under his goggles. Apparently, we were not the only ones because Santo asked Seb to repeat himself.

'We are going to wait because the Doc is helping someone give birth.'

David might have been chuckling next to me, but it was hard to tell because the wind drowned out all but the loudest sounds. So we waited, peering through the sand that blew thick in the air. The Doc re-emerged fifteen minutes later taking off a pair of latex gloves, having just helped deliver a baby to a woman in the village. I shook my head. The timing couldn't have been worse!

'Mission success!' Seb shouted. The Doc gave us the thumbs up and we were able to continue. Hut to hut. By the time we had cleared the village, the storm had all but passed. We had found nothing to indicate that the villagers were hiding our enemies and no one else had decided to give birth. Indeed, now that we were able to have a conversation, Pat called the translator up who spoke to the chief of the village. We saw him indicating a direction and using strong hand gestures. When Seb gave us the translation through the radio, I learned that the Chief vehemently denied that he was working with the extremists and had even told us where to look for them. If I were him, I'd probably tell whichever group of heavily armed men passing through my village that I was on their side too.

The sharpshooters were peering through their scopes in the last known direction of the enemy, but saw nothing. They had gone for now. We linked up with the pickups once more to climb aboard. Alexi rolled down the window and laughed at us. 'You're all a bit sandy!'

'I hope you're enjoying the air conditioning in there, you bastard!' Big Max retorted, hauling his enormous frame onto the pickup with his minimi and attempted to dust himself off with a gloved hand.

We were away again, attempting to follow the tracks of at least two other motorbikes that we could see in the sand. Pat was like a hound that had tasted blood. And now that he had bitten, he wanted the whole kill and pushed us onward for the rest of the day. Unfortunately, the trail went cold by the early afternoon and he reluctantly let us set up camp early for the night.

The next day we took up the hunt once more. This time we used the transmission interceptors to try to pick up an enemy frequency that we could triangulate. It was a particularly hot morning, and the only respite was the breeze created by the forward motion of the Toyotas as they plodded along. The heat of the day only got worse and the air was still, a clear sign of a storm to come. Pat had us stop for an hour at 13:00 to eat, but I wished he hadn't. There were no trees in the area - no shelter from the sun. Big Max and I sat with our backs against the wheel of the pickup, trying to move and breathe as little as possible. Of all the time I had spent in the desert, that day was the hottest I had ever known. There was not so much as a puff of wind, the air moved not a bit and the sun was relentless. It was an inescapable furnace.

I sat on the sand that was so hot it burned and breathed little shallow breaths. Sweat poured down my forehead and into my eyes, but I didn't want to wipe it away because I felt like that little movement alone would cause me to overheat. I took a sip from my bottle and the water was as hot as tea. There was no escaping this sauna.

I remember saying to Big Max, 'If they attack us now, we're fucked.' I meant it too. The thought of running around and shooting in an environment like that was enough to make me nauseous. All he managed in reply was a 'yeah' a few seconds later.

Luck was on our side. We were not attacked and Pat, to our relief, had us climb back on to the Toyotas and we were driving once more, the air brushing our skin again.

After a day that had been altogether uneventful, we were setting up camp in a wooded area, hidden by trees, when there was news from Gao. Pat immediately told us to load up the trucks once more and we did so in confusion, not knowing what was going on. We saw Seb jogging back from Pat's pickup after a quick meeting and we all crowded round him as he explained.

'There is a large enemy force heading straight towards us. Around twenty pickups and twice as many motorbikes, eighty men at least. We're going to set up a defensive position here and hope they don't attack.'

There was a tense silence for a moment. Eighty men. That was a lot of guns and the likelihood was that they knew exactly where we were - they were always watching. We did not have the element of surprise, so the best we could do was dig in. If they did decide to attack, we would lose men for sure, terrorist pickups were often equipped with the DSHK's that fired a 12.7mm round. Twenty of those firing at once would cut down all the trees we sheltered behind in a matter of seconds and would tear our unarmoured pickups to pieces.

'What about air support?' Sipp piped up.

'There won't be any.' Seb pointed upwards. 'It's too dangerous to fly with the storm.'

There was silence as it sunk in that we would be alone, our reassuring Tigres would not be circling in the sky today.

Seb looked down at his watch. 'It's 18:00; I want double guard shifts until further notice.'

The formation we had created was that of a loose circle, some one hundred metres in diameter, the pickups facing outward with a guard on each gun and another below next to it. The trees were thick and blocked our view which meant at least we couldn't be seen, even if they knew we were here.

At 19:00, the sun had set and the wind had begun to blow. The storm would soon be upon us in earnest. There was more intel from Gao sourced from a drone that was in the air. The enemy force had split and was now flanking our position around a kilometre away. The transmission interceptors were picking up regular radio chatter, which our translator was relaying to Pat. They knew we were here and were waiting for the signal from their commander to attack.

I sat on guard on a little fold out stool, my H&K in my lap and a loaded grenade launcher at my feet, peering into the undergrowth and ready to shoot anything that moved. I brushed the safety with my index finger. If I'm honest, there was a part of me that wanted them to attack. I had come to enjoy a good scrap. But there was another part of me that was afraid; if they attacked, there was a very good chance that I would not survive. I began to think of all the things I still wanted to do with my life, I was only twenty-three. I wanted to see South America, visit the pyramids in Egypt, find a girl…

I had to shake myself out of it. It wouldn't do any of us any good if my mind wasn't in the game. That's why the waiting was worse - once you're in the fight your training and instincts kick in and you know what you have to do. But waiting, you think too much.

The situation was dire, and as the first fat droplets of rain began to fall from the night sky, I knew we were in for a long night. We were heavily outnumbered and surrounded.

Everyone was on full alert with half of us on guard at any one time, there were two hours to rest between shifts. None of us slept. The rain fell constantly, soaking our gear and we refrained from setting up a tarpaulin in case we needed to make a quick getaway. Even if it were dry, I would not have slept. My body seemed to be constantly tense, waiting for that first shot to echo out into the night and for hell to break loose. By midnight, I was already rubbing the sleep from my eyes and Joyce was passing around a strong coffee to keep us awake.

We waited and waited; time seemed to pass excruciatingly slowly. I was on shift again, staring through my night vision at the trees and bushes ahead of our pickup. By 02:00, the storm had abated a little, but it was still drizzling. No one spoke, or if they did it was only briefly and in whispers. I listened for the smallest sound, the crunch of a twig underfoot or the rustling of leaves. There was nothing. After what felt like an age, I was relieved from guard duty again, and joined David at the back of the pickup.

'Do we know what's going on?'

'They're trying to decide whether or not to attack us apparently.' David rubbed his eyes with a gloved thumb and forefinger.

'Have you slept?'

'Not a bit.' He replied. 'Should have got a fucking office job.' He muttered with a slight grin.

I snorted. 'Don't be silly, you wouldn't last a day!'

I lay down on the wet ground, keeping all my gear on my person, including my helmet and rifle. The fatigue was catching up with me and I drifted off into a fitful sleep for a while. I was woken by the sound of someone rustling in the undergrowth. My sleepy mind believing for a moment it was an attacker that had somehow breached our defences and I reached for my rifle. But it was only Basto taking a piss and I lay back down breathing hard, my heart hammering. I didn't even bother to try to sleep after that and distracted myself by eating a few biscuits from my ration pack.

Finally, the rain had stopped. An hour later, Pat was telling us the drone had images of the enemy's activity, or lack of it. They still had not moved and were apparently still deciding whether to attack us, unsure if we were French or Malian. They must have known that a French force would be better trained and well equipped - not so much of an easy picking.

At 04:45, the first tiny rays from the sun that was still far below the horizon could be seen. I willed the dawn to come, as if the daylight would save us from danger. Of course, it took as much time as it had every other morning and our enemy had not yet left.

We waited some more, the atmosphere in our camp silent and tense. Then, after what seemed like an age at around 05:30, as the sun was high enough for us to see clearly, Pat had intercepted more messages. Pat ran over to deliver the message himself.

'They're pulling away!' He told us. 'They've realised we're French and decided they would lose too many men with an attack. We'll stay for thirty minutes longer to be sure they've gone for good before we leave the forest.' I breathed a sigh of relief as Pat jogged away to tell the next pickup.

Sipp clapped me on the back and said, 'So, how did you sleep?' I laughed. Ten minutes later, Seb announced on the radio that the skies had cleared enough for the Tigres to fly. They had set off a few minutes ago to join us.

'Great timing.' Big Max slow clapped, sarcastically.

When we finally heard the beating blades of the Tigres and spotted two of the machines circling above us, we knew we were safe. Pat ordered us out of the forest and back onto the open plains of the desert.

'What a night.' David said beside me on the pickup.

'Longest night ever.' I said.

I was quite pleased with the anti-climactic ending to it, however, and knew that luck had been on our side that night. We were able to leave the forest safely, our enemies long gone, and began the return journey back to Gao. It was over.

With two weeks left before we rotated out of Gao and back to France, the general atmosphere was relaxed. We had not had a mission since the patrol with the pickups and now it looked increasingly as if the opex was over; in a week's time the first of our colleagues would arrive in Gao to relive us. Planning for an end-of-tour party was already underway. There was even a Puma helicopter engineer who was a DJ in his spare time and would get some music sorted out. Since I had just about watched all the films on my laptop, I spent more time in the bar with a beer in hand. But switched to soft drinks for the second round, as we were still technically on duty.

Others were not so disciplined, however. Some of the infantry guys from our rotation were already causing a ruckus, holding a few parties in a bar on the other side of the FOB that were sure to have driven the military police crazy.

The night before the first of us were to ship out, we shared our own party with all the French air crews, pilots, engineers and logistics teams for the helicopters whom we'd worked so closely with the last four months. The Colonel of the camp made a speech congratulating us on a particularly superb mission. Then, as some of the guys already had their rifles and gear packed away ready to be loaded onto cargo planes the next day and were now officially off duty, the beers were broken out and alcohol was consumed in copious amounts. The picnic benches in the bar were cleared which soon became a nightclub and the DJ worked his magic. An hour later everyone was dancing, working off the stress of the last few months and letting loose. Even the Colonel was spotted boogying on one of the tables, whilst at least sixty of us cheered him on. The afterparty lasted until the early hours of the morning, when we were forced to accept that the night was over.

The next morning, we bid goodbye to the first of our commando brothers who would fly to Niamey, and then to Crete, for their three days of R&R. Hungover, Spartan 10 shook hands with all of us before heading to the airstrip for the last time that year, and we told them we would see them back in France.

Later the same day, I was greeted by a few familiar faces that had just arrived. I found Lee, Oskari and Chef Jouk getting off the JGB that had dropped them off in front of their tents and shook hands with them all, with a smile on my face. It was good to see them after so long - Lee, jovial and cracking jokes as always, stocky little Oskari and the ever-calm Jouk. They asked me how it had been and I told them it was the best opex anyone could remember doing, assuring them they'd have a similarly good one.

Later in the week came more familiar face. My old Chef De Group, Matt and with him Dub from the 27 BCA greeted and we embraced gleefully, clapping each other on the back as we caught up. We all drank heavily together that night since we too were off duty now. Our mission was successfully concluded once we finished loading the equipment and boxes. When we got the plane back to Europe, I looked out of the window thinking what a mission it had been. During our mission we had captured or neutralised the best part of a hundred hostiles and destroyed countless enemy vehicles and weapons. It was good work, but whether it was worthwhile or not, who can say. I would certainly like to believe so.

# CHAPTER 16

I stood facing the code d'honneur that was displayed on an entire wall of the administrative office's second floor corridor. It was here that many of the officers worked, including the Chef De Corps, whom I was due to see in a few minutes time. I was wearing my formal dress uniform along with my Kepi Blanc. I was finally being sanctioned for my crime of leaving the country without permission back in 2016.

I was looking around at the pictures of the previous Chef De Corps - the old commanders of the regiment - when footsteps sounded behind me on the grey linoleum floors. A middle-aged female Capitaine came marching around the corner and I caught her eye. I knew who she was. She was the wife of a Commandant that also worked in 2REG, transferred from the regulars so she could work on the same base as her husband. Her husband, I knew, was an arsehole. And she proved to be a perfect match for him.

'Face the code d'honneur! All Legionnaires being punished must stand at attention facing the code d'honneur!' Her shrill voice echoed off the walls as she marched past.

I held her gaze for a moment longer than I ought before turning back to the wall. That was galling for a number of reasons. First, what right had she to talk about the code d'honneur? That was unique to the Legion. Not only had she been transferred over from a regular's base, but she was an officer too. What did she know about the struggles of a Legionnaire? I could just feel her judging me without even knowing what I had done. She probably assumed I was just another wayward Legionnaire. But my 'heinous crime' was going home to see my family. She had no clue what it was like to serve a foreign military, amongst a people that are not your own. Risk your life to defend the values of a culture that is not your own. My skin was still bronzed from the hot African sun, under which I had been sweating, fighting and suffering for four months while she had been sat on her arse in an office doing paperwork, eating three square meals a day, and sleeping eight hours each night. What right did she have to judge me?

She disappeared around the corner and I blew air from my cheeks in frustration. The army was one long humbling experience it seemed. Perhaps I thought too highly of myself after all. I sighed. In any case, I would soon serve a prison sentence that would surely remind me of my lowly position in the French Foreign Legion.

My name was called by a secretary and I was told to enter the wood panelled door of the Chef De Corps office. Knocking and asking for permission to enter, I opened the door and went inside. I moved straight for the regimental flag, which held the achievements of 2REG sewn into the fabric, and saluted it first as instructed. Failure to do so would result in a further ten days imprisonment.

Then, I turned to the Colonel himself. I presented myself in the formal fashion and waited for him to tell me I could stand at ease. He did and I stood with my hands behind my back and my feet shoulder width.

'So, Dobson, do you know why you're here?'

'Yes, Colonel.'

'Do you know why we must be strict with our rules?'

'Yes, Colonel.'

'Do you think we ought to make an exception just for you?'

'No, Colonel.'

Yes Colonel. No Colonel. Yes Colonel. It went on like that for a few minutes, I gave him all the answers he wanted and kept them as brief as possible. In the end, due to our exemplary work during my last deployment, my sentence was reduced to ten days. When I closed the door of his office behind him, I thought I had got off rather lightly.

It was late November when I finally made the journey from my cosy room to the front gate where the little jail house was located. I had a single bag with me with some fatigues, sports gear and some extra layers of warm clothing. It was cold here now, and there was already a fresh blanket of snow covering the ground. When a Sergeant showed me to one of the cells that lined the small courtyard of the jail, there was a caged roof to prevent us from scaling the walls and escape.

The other six or so inmates were wearing their yellow vests that marked them as such, and I gave them a nod. Almost as soon as I had come in, the military police burst through the door behind me and into the courtyard, led by the lieutenant of the PLE (Patrouille Éntrangère). The Lieutenant, I would come to learn, was a real ball breaker.

'Search all the cells!' He ordered his two Caporal Chefs, who got to work rummaging through the belongings of the inmates. The Lieutenant addressed the rest of us.

'I hear some of you have been smoking! It is prohibited and anyone caught hiding contraband will earn more time in here!'

He glared at us, pointing at the cells around us. One of the Caporal Chefs pulled my bag from my shoulder and began to dump its contents on the concrete floor. The Lieutenant bent down to pick up one of the two books I had brought. Mobile phones and any other electronic devices were of course prohibited.

'You're only allowed one book!' He tutted in satisfied triumph. 'Only here for five minutes and you're already breaking the rules. You'd do well to obey -' He read my name tag. 'Dobson. Clearly you're here because you already have trouble toeing the line. Now, go with the others and clear away the snow from the front entrance!'

'Yes, Lieutenant.'

I got to know the rest of the guys sharing the jail with me and knew a couple of them already. There was Nickola - the Serbian kickboxing champion who had pummelled me the last Camerone boxing match. Reti - a Hungarian recently back from French Guyanne. Lastly, Volkov - the enormous Latvian who was also from the Compagnie D'Appui.

I would also meet the crazy Adjutant Chef in charge of all prisoners, an older Frenchman who had never been on deployment due to some obscure injury, but maintained all the vigour of a young Legionnaire. Unfortunately for us, he liked running.

Now, just inside the entrance of 2REG there is a little shepherd's hut made from dry stone slabs. There is a little sign next to it saying something along the lines of, 'this hut was made from the sweat of and toil of Legionnaires. May its existence be a reminder to all of the merits of discipline.' Or something of the sort.

Every morning, the Adjutant Chef would take all the prisoners running around the mountains surrounding the regiment. At the foot of the first hill, he would have each prisoner collect a large stone, which he would then carry up and down the twenty-kilometre (a half-marathon) course. We'd then circle back to the gates of 2REG, and deposit his payload by the shepherd's hut to become a part of the sculpture.

The hut was made up of thousands of these large stones. The Adjutant Chef was immensely proud of his 'work' and would hold a little ceremony after each completed run during which he would have us all stand at attention while everyone among us had placed their rock. Five years ago, I sustained a foot injury during my first trip in Africa. Now, it was no surprise that the old break began to play up after wading through ankle deep snow, up and down rocky paths for hours on end.

Once this was out of the way, however, the rest of the day was pleasant enough. The Adjutant Chef gave us jobs to do around the regiment, usually involving chopping up fallen trees around the road that encircled the base. The base itself was huge, and we were largely left to our own devices to complete the task with no one in sight to reprimand us for taking a break every now and again. We loaded chopped logs into a tractor, as our breath steamed in the cool air. But at least the work kept us warm enough. I chatted with Nickola and the others and found myself having a pleasant time - being outside, doing some good work to clear up the regiment and enjoying the company of a couple of good guys.

We would eat in the canteen three times a day, each of us giving our desserts to Volkov. Our Capitaine had given him jail time for being too overweight. After dinner, the only job we had to was sweep the roads near the gate; a task that the Adjutant Chef liked us to save for later. He perfectly timed our task with when the bus took the Sous-Officiers home to the village would pass by, allowing them all to see us hard at work. In the evening, I would close myself in my little cell - which had its own radiator and was quite cosy. I would read the history book my friend Christian lent me by candlelight, as there was no electricity in the jail.

We had to avoid the Lieutenant of the PLE every now and again. But all in all, I did not have an entirely disagreeable stay in military prison. Nevertheless, I gladly took my leave on the 20th of November because there was something else to look forward to: the GCM tests.

During my absence, the other guys in the section had been organising the tests. Ricky, David, Fich, Djo and Katch were all there to oversee it, and welcomed me back the day before they were due to start. There were a good number of candidates this year, a little over thirty, and some I knew. Ross, my compatriot and good friend from the UK, Christian, the capable American, who was also a close friend and finally, Janne - the Fin who was in 2REP and had recovered from an injury sustained during a botched parachute jump.

I had given them as much advice as I could before their tests, but all that was left for me to do was watch. When the thirty of them were lined up early Monday morning, before our new Lieutenant, I reminded myself how nice it was to be on this side. To be one of the instructors and not a wide eyed, anxious looking candidate.

It was interesting to watch them run the first tests. And to see which ones made the cut and which did not. Unfortunately, my friend Christian failed the rope climbing test because of the shoulder injury. I could see the hurt on his face as he, and a couple of others, rang the bell in defeat.

A couple of days later, the candidates were whittled down to around twenty. We had them navigate to a local reservoir during the night because the next few trials were located there. By evening, we instructors had already made camp by a large reservoir, enjoying a couple beers with stew cooking. David was laughing at some joke Djo had made. Ricky was discussing which candidates were strongest with the Lieutenant. And Fich and I talked about what we would put in the Sketch Noel for the Christmas celebrations. It was great, being around my brothers. I felt relaxed and content, like I finally had a place in the Legion that I had earned. It was like - no, it was - a family. These were all guys I knew I could count on, good men that were a pleasure to know. Regrettably, my contentedness would only last until the morning.

We woke at 06:00, having directed the recruits to their camping zone in some trees nearby as they had trickled in during the wee hours. The air was cold as I woke and I crawled from my sleeping bag, stretching before heading out into the dawn to take a piss. The other guys were already awake. David and Fich were giggling together because not all the candidates had shown up last night. They wondered how lost they were, imagining them still marching around the countryside, unable to make sense of their maps.

I had been helping myself to a bunch of croissants that someone had bought for our breakfast when Ricky came into the tent with his phone against his ear to collect his jacket. A look of agony that I had never seen before settled on his face. The others noticed it too and silence fell. Ricky left once more, apparently listening intently to whoever was speaking on the other end of the line, without so much as glancing at the rest of us.

We exchanged a look. Ricky was not at all an emotional man, so whatever it was that had made him look as hurt as he had must have been grave indeed.

'What's going on?' Djo asked. There was silence.

David eventually said what we were all thinking, but wishing it was not. 'Could be news from Mali.'

We said nothing. If that were true, it would be someone we knew for Ricky to look like that. Was one of our friends injured? Or even killed? I had plenty over there: Lee, Oskari, Jouk, Matt, Dub and others. We left the tent to see Ricky pacing back and forth along the dam of the reservoir, still talking on the phone.

'Shit. Looks bad.' Djo said, watching Ricky rub at his eyes. A quiet tension seemed to build amongst us. Our minds imagined what could have happened, who might be dead or wounded. No one said a word in the minutes that ticked by until finally, Ricky finished on the phone and waved us over. We walked out to meet him on the concrete dam. The sound of the water passing through the overflow gate and trickling down the other side, broke the silence of the still morning.

We approached, with trepidation, to see that Ricky's eyes were bloodshot. He seemed to struggle to meet our gaze for a moment, taking a long shaky breath before looking up and addressing all of us.

'There has been an incident in Mali.' He spoke slowly, his voice wavering. 'Some of our guys have fallen.'

'Some,' he had said, meaning more than one. He let it sink in for a moment. The rest of us stared at him open mouthed for a few seconds before I asked, 'how many?'

Ricky looked at me and swallowed. 'Thirteen.'

I must have heard wrong. 'Thirteen?' He nodded. No. Thirteen was far too many, it couldn't be true.

'Jesus.' was all David said.

'D-do we know who?' Fich asked.

'No, only that six of them were GCM. The rest were air crew. Two helicopters went down. I need to make a call. I'll let you know as soon as I do.'

I remember as Ricky left us once more, Djo and I sat down on a nearby log, staring into space. David leaned against the low wall of the dam and Fich stood where Ricky had left us, frozen in shock. Thirteen French soldiers. Six of our GCM brothers were dead. It was so many. We sat for a long time saying nothing, processing the horrible news. Six of our brothers. They were our friends, men we had fought beside, trained with, shared memories together. And now they were gone.

We forgot all about the candidates camping down the slope. An hour later, Ricky gathered us to read the dreaded list. He cleared his throat and read aloud from his phone.

'ADC Julien Carrette, CNE Benjamin Gireud, BCH Romain Salles de Saint Paul, CNE Clement Frisonroche, CNE Nicolas Megard, CNE Romain Chomel de Jarnieu, LTN Pierre Bockel, LTN Alex Morisse, MCH Jeremy Leusie, MDL Alexandre Protin, MDL Antoine Serre, MDL Valentin Duval, SCH Andrei Jouk.'

Fich groaned and David cursed. Chef Jouk was dead. I had seen him a couple of months previously and had wished him luck for his opex. So, too, were Alex Protin and Jeremy Leusie - two solid guys I had done my commando training with. It was hard to believe that they were all gone. I sat back down again as Ricky went on.

'A Tigre and a Puma helicopter collided; we don't know how. But there was combat on the ground wherever it was they had been trying to land. It could have been for a hundred reasons; we just don't know.'

'And the others, they're okay? Is anyone else wounded?'

'No one else is wounded.'

I nodded. So Oskari and Lee were okay. But thirteen… It was the biggest loss of life in a single event that the French army had experienced since the 80s. When I finally managed to get in touch with Oskari a day later, he told me the only reason he hadn't been on the helicopter with Jouk was because there hadn't been enough space for him. The Puma were slightly smaller than the more modern NH90's and his Chef De Groupe had ordered him to stay behind, unknowingly saving his life. He also told me that it had been him and the other groups deployed to recover the bodies of their fallen comrades. The horror of such a task is near unimaginable. Having to collect what was left of your closest friends into plastic bags is enough to break a man. I cannot, for the life of me, understand why the French army did not use a different unit.

Jouk had left behind four children and a wife living in Saint Christol, who were still unaware of the accident. As Ricky was the head of the GCM in 2REG, he would go and break the news. I remember thinking I would rather be back in combat, being shot at by insurgents than be the one to tell Jouk's widowed wife. We finished the tests half-heartedly that week. A day later, David and I were sent to Saint Christol to collect the unwanted belongings of our late Legionnaire brother from his wife. She invited us into their home, teary eyed, and showed us to a metal chest full of military gear she hoped we would take and find useful. She certainly had no use for it anymore.

David and I awkwardly took it back to regiment and left it in the GCM hangar. Even though it was ours to use now, it somehow did not feel right going through the dead man's belongings, and I didn't touch a thing.

The deaths had hit the GCM hard. Six of our number had fallen and all had been well loved. Better men than most, they deserved a good send off and that, at least, we could give them. The official ceremony was held in the impressive courtyard of Les Invalides military hospital in Paris. The coffins were marched out and I was a part of the delegation sent to represent the Legion on the parade ground. The President, Macron, was present too and gave an appropriate speech. He bestowed upon the dead, the Legion D'Honneur, France's highest military honour.

Thousands attended. We remembered our friends in the cold winter air as their coffins were marched past us, covered with the red, white and blue flag of France. The onlookers stood solemnly until the last of the coffins had been paraded out of the courtyard. We followed suit, marching along in a column formation behind.

I had the chance to speak to my fellow commandos after the ceremony. It was clear that the deaths of our comrades had struck as crushing a blow within the other regiments as it had in our own. As to what exactly happened in the crash itself, I am still unsure. I know only that the helicopters collided. One of the helicopters could have taken an unlucky burst of gunfire, like Little Max during our last deployment. There could have been an engine malfunction. Or, perhaps, one of the pilots made a mistake and there had been a miscommunication. If the latter was true, there seemed no point investigating it now. The thirteen had all paid with their lives and an inquiry would not bring them back.

Our friends, the men who gave their lives for the French army, will never be forgotten.

In regiment, the atmosphere in the section was sombre for weeks after. It was an inescapable loss that weighed heavily on all of us. Once, I opened up the shared computer and saw that Jouk's name was still on the register. No one had thought to take it off yet. It was marked, 'on opex.' I sighed and wondered if things would ever go back to the way they were.

But time heals all wounds, and some normality returned to the section in the following months. In the last weeks of December, the GCM organised an exercise with the Italian special forces on the mountains bordering France and Italy. David, Fich, the Lieutenant and I sat on a hillside watching an 'enemy' compound far below through a high-powered lens. Not much of anything happened, save for a few comings and goings throughout the day that we were sure to photograph. We were given a bit of amusement when the Gendarme (French police) showed up. Apparently called by a civilian passing the compound who saw men clad in balaclavas holding AK's guarding the entrance.

Even from our high position on the mountainside we could hear the Gendarme shouting far below. The two "armed terrorists" were ordered to drop their weapons and get on the ground, which they did so immediately. The exercise's organiser had to run up to the gate and explain that they were military personnel on an exercise. The confusion had David and I in fits of laughter. The two guys guarding the gate had clearly shit themselves at the sight of the Gendarme pointing real firearms at them.

Christmas passed and I was allowed to return home to my family for what would be the last time before I was back for good. I even managed to get back in time on Christmas day, before the turkey had gone completely cold. And then it was the New Year. I realised I had less than six months left before I was a free man. Where had the time gone? It seemed like just the other day that I was walking under the stone archway at Fort De Nogent, the duty sergeant going through my bag, finding the book about the hunchback lawyer and frowning at me.

I was happy to volunteer for as many training courses as possible to keep myself busy. Between January and March, I did some more extensive training on treating battlefield wounds and fighting close quarter battle (CQB) in buildings. And then there were the new recruits to train - Ross, Janne, and a couple of Sergeants I had known from my time in the 2ème Compagnie, among them. I found myself giving lessons in the classroom on GCM protocol and procedures, passing on all the knowledge I had learned during my time in the section. For the most part, I was left to my own devices. Everyone knew I would be leaving in a matter of months and let me get on with my paperwork.

I had just finished my last course, photography, before March came around. I used up the last of my leave to go skiing with my cousin in the Alps. There had been word of a new, and worryingly infectious, disease all over the news that was spreading from country to country. It was called Coronavirus. And already the first mentions of a 'lockdown' were being debated within French government. The day I arrived on the slopes, the lifts were all shut down. Only several days later and they were evicting all tourists from the valley.

At least my cousin J and I got in a few good days of 'ski randonee'-skis with skins on the bottom that allowed you to walk up the slope as well as ski down. I got back to the regiment just in time for everything to shut down and for France to be officially put on a nationwide lockdown that was to last for several months. With these new and disruptive rules in place, the Legion was now offering three-month contracts to anyone due to leave in the near future, such as myself, so that they could wait out the lockdown in their respective regiments.

In hindsight, seeing how things had gone, it would not have been an awful idea. But to me, at the time, the thought of staying for another three months doing nothing was abhorrent. I had promised myself that I would leave after five years and not a day more. I had sacrificed my golden years to the Legion and it was time for me to live a little. It wasn't that I hated what I did, on the contrary. I was in the best section in the French Foreign Legion and loved the guys I worked with, but I was restless. It was time for me to move on. I didn't care that there was a deadly virus infecting half the nation, I was leaving one way or another and no one had the right to stop me. Even Ricky's promise of another opex the following January could not change my mind.

The lockdown in 2REG was not awful. The base was enormous and there was plenty of room to run and cycle within it. And we had a gym in the section. As for company, there was no better bunch. Lee and Oskari had returned from their nightmarish tour of Mali. Ross and Janne had their rooms next to ours and we often passed the evenings sitting in the corridor of our barracks, playing music and drinking beer.

It was somewhere around this time, around April, that I was lying in bed when it finally sank in that I was leaving in only a month!

I started having a little panic attack. My heart hammered in my chest and I began to sweat into the sheets. Oh shit, oh shit, I thought. In one month I'm leaving. What the fuck am I going to do?

The Legion had been all I had known since I was eighteen years old. It had made up nearly a quarter of my life! What the hell was I going to do in the civilian world? I still did not know what I wanted. Would I have to get a normal job and a mortgage on a house? Would I do the same boring routine day in, day out for the next fifty years? And how the fuck does one even do tax returns? I had to take a few deep breaths to calm down and remind myself that I had survived ordeals much more frightening than the civilian world. Whatever happened, it would be alright, I would do just fine. I was a commando in the French Foreign Legion for fuck's sake!

In early May, a couple of weeks before my departure for Aubagne, the boys of the GCM section held a party for me in the hanger. There was beer and snacks arrayed around tables someone had put out and all my closest friends had come to see me off. It still felt a little unreal, as if it were a party for someone else and not for me.

The Lieutenant said some wonderful things about me that seemed to be heart felt, that I was a fine example to the new guys, which was incredibly touching. They applauded and called for me to give a speech. I obliged them. I told them all that it was the honour of my life to have served beside them and that I had learned so much in the two and a half years I spent in the GCM section. It probably wasn't a great speech, but I meant every word of it. And they applauded it all the same. The lieutenant then awarded me with a steel sculpture of the CGM insignia crafted by the regimental blacksmith and the star of the GCM, marking me as a fully qualified commando.

Then, we drank. I shared a beer with everyone and along with Janne, Ross, Christian, Steinrod, Oskari, Lee and some others, drank until the warm May evening began to darken. A Caporal Chef shouted at us for making too much noise.

I had said my goodbyes to all the guys I knew on the regiment over last several days. On the day of my departure, I shook hands with Ricky and David. Two solid guys that I had been through the shit with and who would always have my respect. I hoped I had earned theirs along the way.

'Good luck, Dobson.' Ricky said with a smile, gripping my hand. ' Just remember, if ever you want to come back there'll be a place for you!'

'Ha! It won't come to that Chef!'

I promised to come back and visit sometime too, but not knowing when that would be. Ross had helped me bring my bags down from my room. Already having moved his things in, he preferred it to his old one. David and Ricky bid me goodbye and left me standing before the compagnie in my civilian clothes with all my bags. I watched them walk away, feeling melancholy at the loss of two good friends from my immediate life.

Then, another familiar face appeared. Romaric drove up to the building in his little Peugeot. The Serb I had served with in the second compagnie was finishing at the same time as myself and it seemed fitting that we would complete the passing out process together. He grinned as he hopped out of the driver's seat and shook my hand.

'Hey, Dobson! You ready to become a civilian or what?'

I laughed. 'You bet your arse I am mate!'

He helped me load my things into his already packed car and we squeezed into the front. From the open window Ross, who had been standing by put his arm through and slapped me on the shoulder.

'See you soon!'

'You will!' I assured him. With that, Romaric and I were driving towards the front gate of 2ème Regiment Étranger De Genie for the last time, passing the inmates at the entrance wearing their yellow vests and sweeping up pine needles half-heartedly. I smiled, and took a last glance back at the neat bushes of the place d'Arme and the words 'Honneur et Fidelite' boldly written on the side of the administrative building, before the guard had swung open the front gate to allow us through. We left behind the place that had been our home for the last five years.

At Aubagne, Romaric and I met a couple of others we had endured basic training with who had left for different regiments, only to be reunited after five years at the very end. We caught up a little while we waited outside various offices to receive signatures on our paperwork. It was the end of May and hot enough to make me sweat, but it had nothing on Mali; here it was pleasant. Romaric and I amused ourselves comparing the canteen of Aubagne to that of 2REG. Ultimately, we agreed that Aubagne was far better and made the most of the last of our free meals before a civilian life.

At the end of the week, we had our last formal ceremony with the Chef De Corps of Aubagne, who would congratulate all those passing out during the final week of May. He gave us a speech in which he mentioned, more than once, that we were always welcome to come back at any time should civilian life not be for us. He also said the words, 'once a Legionnaire, always a Legionnaire.' Regardless of what we went on to do next, we would always be Legionnaires. And that meant we had the reputation of the Legion to uphold, even long after we leave. That part was fitting. I vowed to do my best not to shame the organisation, not for the Legion itself, but for the men I cared for that called it home still.

Once finished, we all entered the Legion's museum for the second time in our careers and descended into the crypt. The wooden hand of Capitaine Danjou lay on a felt cushion in a glass box, the names of hundreds of Legionnaires carved into the stone walls around it. We stood in silence for a minute to remember the ranks of our fallen brethren, men who had risked all to come to France to fight for a foreign nation and who had paid the ultimate price in search for a better life.

After the ceremony, we were free to leave Aubagne and the Legion for good, and most of the other guys rushed off to get trains. My flight was the next day from Paris, so I was in no hurry. Romaric was driving all the way back to Serbia, so we had plenty of time to pack our things and head down to the front gate.

I was now free to leave. It seemed so strange. My life would now be void of sergeants shouting at me and cleaning the toilets at the whistle of 'corvee compagnie'. There would be no more marching up to the canteen whilst singing the compagnie chant. No more Camerone or Christmas with the Legion. No more missions or training courses, it would all come to an end. All the regular routine and structure that I had come to accept as a part of life for so long, gone. The day that I had been dreaming of for five years had finally arrived and I had never imagined myself to be so anxious about it.

Romaric and I made our way down to the car park in our civilian clothes and laden with bags. We passed the Caporal Chef sitting in the guard post. He gave us a nod, knowing we were leaving. I stopped just before the gate, took a deep breath and walked through. We deposited our bags next to Romaric's car and turned to stand side by side, looking back at the 1ère Regiment Étranger.

So that was it, I was out. I thought about everything that had happened: coming through the arch of Fort De Nogent, waiting day after day to be processed, being sent on to Aubagne and then to Castelnaudary where I did my basic training, choosing infantry but being sent to 2REG, marching in the Alps, my deployment to Mali, the GCM tests and then Mali twice more. I had met so many incredible characters, many of them good. Some of them dreadful and some who were downright bizarre.

There had been good times, and many more bad ones. I had suffered and even considered desertion. The Legion had tested me in every way and I was so used to being out of my comfort zone now, I felt as though I were ready for anything. I still do.

I thought about how the twenty-three-year-old man was completely different to the eighteen-year-old boy that had begun this journey five years ago. For better or worse, it had changed me forever. Now, I was more confident - capable and tough. But there were other side effects, too. I had come from a world that could be ultra-violent. I had fought, killed and seen plenty of men die. I knew myself now and what I was capable of, such as the aggression that could well up at the drop of a hat.

I might still be trying to figure out who I am, but the Legion had at least shown me what I am. I am a fighter, and I know that knowledge will open doors for me in the future. They will open or I will kick them down! Surely after these five years I can do anything I set my mind to. I'm sure I sound like an arrogant prick, and perhaps I am, but it is hard for me not to realise the depth of change that developed in my character over the course of my journey. I am changed forever, for better or worse.

When I look back and remember all the hardships, all the times the Legion fucked me over and how many of my superiors treated me and others like dog shit - the pain, the hunger, the cold and the heat - I ask myself was it worth it? What would my advice be to eighteen-year-old me as he stood before the archway of Fort De Nogent? Would I do it all over again?

And the answer is easy. Yes, I would do it again in a heartbeat. Forgetting all other reasons except for the men I would meet, and the bonds of friendship I would form. For that alone it was all worth it. Nowhere but the Legion will you find as many men like Romaric, Bailey, Steinrod, Fuchs, De Wolf, Savelli, Cabello, Botch, Istvan, Del Campo, Frank, Bax, Mark, Christian, Ross, Liska, Oskari, Lee, Janne, Djo, Ricky, David, Matt, Dub, Will, Val and all the others whom I am honoured to call my friends.

Sure, there were a lot of arseholes that I didn't get along with too, perhaps even the majority were. But even with just a few friends like I had at your side, it didn't matter. You could go through any adversity together and still laugh about it along the way. As I have said before, there is no greater bond formed than that between men who have suffered together. That is brotherhood: having each other's backs. As I stood at the gates of Aubagne, I felt all too plainly what I was leaving behind and I missed it already.

Somehow, re-signing for another few years did not seem too bad when I thought about it now, as long as I would have my mates with me. I looked at the words 'LEGIO PATRIA NOSTRA' emblazoned across the museum at the far end of the place d'arme and thought about everything they represented. I had learned so much and seen more, but now I felt that it was time to move on.

I clapped Romaric on the shoulder and said, 'Fuck it! Let's go get a drink!' And with that, we turned our backs on the French Foreign Legion and climbed into his car to drive away.

Five years had passed... five long years. Now, it was time to look forward. For there was a world out there to explore, new places I have yet to see and new people I have yet to meet.

Onwards then, to the next adventure!

# AFTERWORD

Since I wrote this book the GCM and my old comrades have completed several other tours of duty in Mali, not all of which have gone smoothly.

There was a firefight in which 'Big Kevin' and 'Nono' were shot, taking several rounds in the legs each when a terrorist opened fire on them from a bush only several yards away. Each has made a full recovery.

'Little Max' as I called him, has been killed in another firefight. They too were ambushed, and Max was shot in the neck. His real name was Maxime Blasco and he was a phenomenal soldier and a good man.

This is war.

As for myself, I'm doing just fine.

Printed in Great Britain
by Amazon

84765077R00210